Issues in Financial Development

ISSUES IN FINANCIAL DEVELOPMENT

Edited By
Prof. K. Sham Bhat
Head
Department of Economics
Pondicherry University
Pondicherry (India)

SERIALS PUBLICATIONS
New Delhi

First Published–2004

ISBN: 81-86771-50-6

Published by

Head Office : **SERIALS PUBLICATIONS**
4, B.S.S. Hall, Khyber Pass Market,
Civil Lines, Delhi–110054 (India)
Phone: 23245225
Fax: 91-11-23272135
e-mail: serials@satyam.net.in

Branch Office : *4830/24, Prahlad Street, Ansari Road,*
Darya Ganj, New Delhi-110002 (India)

Printed at :

PRINTED IN INDIA

Preface

Finance is an engine of economic growth and its importance is increasing day by day. Since, economic reforms has been formulated, its role further strengthened. Unless, it is managed properly, it may create havoc in the society. Hence, it is essential to know what are the issues in the area of finance in recent times? On this background, the present book consists of sixteen articles and addresses some of the issues in the area of monetary economics, international finance and government finance.

Mrs. Jayanthi K Anand exhaustively reviewed various literature in the area of finance and raised some of the issues as: (i) What types of causal nexus between financial development and economic growth exist? Besides, the paper examined the impact of financial deregulation, liberalisation, innovation, diversification and reforms on the relationship between financial development and economic growth; (ii) How far methodological differences will influences the results of nexus between financial development and economic growth; (iii) How far the present measurement of financial development can be used for research and what are its limitation. In this context, it is also essential to know what are the alternative scenario of measurement of financial development which is superior than earlier measurement; and (iv) what type of impact of financial innovation, technology and reforms exists on financial development and economic growth?

Christopher Gan and Patricia McGraw examined the impact of financial scandals on corporate governance in the corporate sector. The analysis revealed that there is a need for improved transparency and financial reporting on the part of the corporate sectors. Besides, executives should learn that trust, integrity and accountability do matter and are crucial to capitalism. Further, one of the major issue is how far corporate scandals will kill the political support for free markets and enhance the scope for government regulation?

Theodore Mariolis examined the Sraffian approach of accumulation and interest rate in a post-Keynesian model. Keynesian multi-sectoral model reveals a rise in the real wage rate per unit of utilised capital stock has ambiguous effects on the growth rate and degree of capacity utilisation and finally tends to increase output-capital ratio. This is due to the fact that the capital-capacity ratio reacts in an unpredictable way to changes in the distribution of income, technology, interest rates and fiscal policy.

Justin Paul and Kranti Gada elucidated the impact of deregulation of interest rate on the different segment of the society. He argued that lowering the interest rate is one of the factors to stimulate industrial growth. Much depends upon other factors like demand-supply situation, competitiveness of products global slowdown etc. However, there is a need for empirical verification about this argument in different sectors of the economy before arriving at definite conclusions. Further, investigations should be carried out in such a way that how far reduction of interest rate had a socio-economic impact on the savers whose major source of income is only interest earned from their deposit?

Thilak Ranaweera attempted to identify the long-run demand for money function for Sri Lanka. The analysis revealed high income elasticity of M2 which is a reflection of greater portfolio choices made available especially after economic liberalisation of 1977. The analysis is also observed that inflation and exchange rate depreciation is the most significant determinants of demand for money in Sri Lanka.

Arun Kumar Giri attempted to re-evaluate the performance of the money demand specifications in the context of identifying the suitable determinants. The analysis revealed that the income elasticity of demand for money is more than unity and it suggests that there is a economies of scale in holding money in India. Besides, inflation, real stock prices and exchange rate are the significant determinants of demand for money. Interest rate is not having significant influence on the demand for money. Hence, the monetary authorities should proceed on complete deregulation of interest rate. However, the analysis of the paper leads to raise the issue such that, is it not necessary to relook the entire analysis in the framework of socio-economic environment such as banking habits, black money circulation, corporation, election year etc. in addition to the factors mentioned in the analysis.

Kishore G Kulkarni and Meenakshi Rishi examined the emerging challenges of Banking industry of India in the framework of globalisation. The analysis concluded that banking industry in India faces the difficulty of extensive regulations, overstaffing, and trade union. Further, one of the important issue of this paper is that how far banking sector will reassess their performance under the globalisation and design an agenda for second generation reforms?

Amanulla S tested the hypothesis that monetary variable has any power in explaining the stock variability in India. The analysis supports that the stock return has 'contemporaneous relationship' with money supply and hence, the monetary portfolio model as well as efficient market model are accepted in Indian context.

Puja Padhi reviewed the issues pertaining to stock market volatility and stock returns in the India. The analysis revealed that trading hours are more volatile than non-trading hours in India. Besides, there is a positive relationship between ex ante volatility and expected risk premium.

Aravanan S examined the issues pertaining to Non-Voting shares in Indian context. The precautions suggested by the author in improving the Non-Voting Shares are: (i) It should carry higher rate of dividend or offered at a discount, (ii) Non-Voting Shares should be issued only by strong performance and growth oriented companies, (iii) If the companies failed to declare dividend in two consecutive years, than the Non-Voting share should be converted into voting share, and (iv) The listing requirements as per Section 73 of the Companies Act should be made applicable to the issue of NVS.

Dinakar N Nayak reviewed various theories explaining 'why', 'when' and 'where' international investment occurs? The analysis reveals that most of the theories were developed in an imperfect market set-up to explain investment from developed countries. Inspite of the differences in these theories, there is one unanimity that a firm moves abroad to reap the benefit of some advantaged in terms of location, firm specific or international marketisation. However, there is a need for relooking these theories from an angle of factors such as labour disputes and weak currency of host country.

Rajendran R reviewed the structural and non-structural model pertaining to exchange rate. The analysis concluded that the structural model cannot be ignored at the cost of time-series models though the latter are gaining more attention in the literature.

Justin Paul and Rushab Desai raised an issue that should nations invoice in Euro or in Dollars? The authors are under the opinion that the exporters should invoice in dollar than in Euro. This doesn't mean that Euro will fail, instead it will quite difficult job for Euro to overtake dollar as the world currency.

Vasudeva Murthy N.V. examined crowding in and crowding out effect relating to government investment, real gross domestic product on private investment. The analysis reveals that government consumption expenditure exerts a negative impact on private investment. Thus, the study calls for on the part of the government to concentrate in increasing investment in the area of infrastructure services, transportation, construction of paved roads connecting the presently inaccessible rural areas, electricity generation, facilitating telephone and the Internet diffusion instead of unproductive expenditure.

Sham Bhat, et. al. investigated the causal nexus between States Fiscal deficit and Macro-economic variables. The analysis reveals an independent relationship between the two. This is mainly due to: (i) the deficits incurred by the states are mainly due to increase in expenditure which is politically and bureaucratically motivated than growth oriented, (ii) the size or quantity of the most of the macro-economic variables is decided by the center alone and not by the states, and (iii) Most of the state government in India is not in a position to implement economic reforms due to political reasons.

Aravana S opined in the process of evaluation of a dividend tax that dividend distribution tax is a better system as it avoids double taxation and hence, the calls from an action from the part of Finance Minister to be consistent in retaining dividend distribution tax for favorable long term implication.

List of Contributors

Amanulla S., Reader, Department of Management, Pondicherry University, Pondicherry–14.

Aravana S., Selection Grade Lecturer, Department of Commerce, Pondicherry University, Pondicherry–14.

Arun Kumar Giri., Faculty of Economics and Finance Group, Birla Institute of Technology and Science, Pilani–333031.

Christopher Gan., Commerce Division, Lincoin University, Canterbury, New Zealand.

Dinakar N. Nayak., Reader, Department of Business Economics, Faculty of Commerce, M.S. University Baroda. Vadodara–390002.

Jayanthi Anand K., Reserve Bank of India, Mumbai Office, Mumbai.

Justin Paul., Assistant Professor, Narsee Manjee Institute of Management Studies, J.V.P.D. Scheme, Vile Parle West, Mumbai–400056.

Kishore G. Kulkarni., Professor, Metropolitan State College of Denver, CO. 80217-3362, USA.

Kranti Gada., Narsee Manjee Institute of Management Studies, J.V.P.D. Scheme, Vile Parle West, Mumbai–400056.

Meenakshi Rishi., Associate Professor, College of Business Administration, Ohio Northern University, Ads, OH 45810, USA.

Pratricia McGraw., Commerce Division, Lincoin University, Canterbury, New Zealand.

Prachitha, J., Research Scholar, Institute of Socio-Economic Change, Bangalore.

Puja Padhi., Research Scholar, Department of Economics, Central University of Hyderabad, Hyderabad–500046.

Rajendran R., Senior Lecturer in Economics, Postgraduate and Research Department of Economics, Government Arts College, Kumbakonam.

Rushab Desai., Management Trainee, GE India.

Sham Bhat. K., Professor and Head, Department of Economics, Pondicherry University, Pondicherry–14.

Thilak Ranaweera., Development Data Group, World Bank.

Throdone Mariotis., Professor, Department of Public Administration, Panteon University, Athens, Grece.

Tripura Sundari., Research Scholar, Department of Economics, Pondicherry University, Pondicherry–14.

Vasudeva Murthy N.V. Professor, College of Business Administration, Creighton University, 2500 California Plaza, Omaha.

Contents

1

Interlinklages Between Financial Development and Economic Growth: Theory and Experience

K. Jayanthi Anand*

Introduction

Rapid advancements in theoretical and empirical techniques combined with revisits in growth theories over the last decade have generated renowned interest in financial aspect of development both in academic and policy-oriented research. Historically, economists trace the origin of the literature to Bagehot (1873) and Schumpeter (1912). Most important contributions came from Gurley and Shaw (1955, 1956, 1957, 1960), Goldsmith (1954, 1955, 1957, 1958), McKinnon and Shaw (1973), Greewood and Jovanovic (1990), Romer (1990), Bencivenga and Smith (1991), Roubini and Sala-i-Martin (1992), King and Levine (1993). Some of the recent work includes King and Levine (1993a, 1993b), Levine (1998), Rousseau and Wachtel (1998), Odedokun (1996, 1998) and Rajan and Zingales (1998a, b). Following excellent surveys by Gertler (1988), Pagano (1993), Hermes (1994), and Levine (1997) theoretically and empirically, the entire literature can be classified into four major groups. The first one relates to financial intermediation, which can be traced

* Reserve Bank of India, Mumbai office, Mumbai. The views expressed in this paper are personal. Email: Jayanthikanand@rbi.org.in.

to Goldsmith (1969) and Gurley and Shaw (1955, 1957, and 1960). The second relates to financial repression and liberalisation (Mc Kinnon and Shaw, 1973). Third relates to endogenous growth literature [Greenwood and Jovanovic (1990), Romer (1990), Bencivenga and Smith (1991), Roubini and Sala-i-Martin (1992), King and Levine (1993)]. The fourth is the financial reforms, which is the outcome of innovations, deregulation, diversification, instability, and policy [Tobin and Brainard, (1963), Spellman (1976), Mathieson (1979), Fama (1980), Horngren (1985), Gelb (1989)] all of which have been well documented and researched. Theoretically, there is a broad consensus that financial development promotes economic growth. Several empirical works have substantiated these theoretical relationships while a few have shown contrary results leading to controversies. Nevertheless, there are several gaps in the extant literature both on the theoretical as well as empirical front.

In this context, this article provides a chronologically analytical survey of some of the major themes and studies in the literature in terms of models, channels of transmission, methodology, choice of variables, results and country experiences. The paper is organized as follows: Section 1 reviews theoretical developments. Section 2 is devoted to developments in empirical research including country specific and cross-country experiences. Section 3 discusses the issues. Lastly, Section 4 deals with concluding observations.

Section I: Theoretical Developments

Economists since Bagehot (1873) and Schumpeter (1936) to the recent economists like, King and Levine (1993a, 1993b), Levine (1998), Rousseau and Wachtel (1998), Rajan and Zingales (1998a, b), and Okedokun (1998) unanimously agree on the linkages between the financial and real sectors of the economy while there have been differences in their approaches. However, these linkages have been questioned lately with the improvements in both theoretical and empirical works.

Economists also classify theoretical developments into two broad categories: (1) the structuralists and (2) the repressionists. The structuralists [Goldsmith (1969); Gurley and Shaw (1955); Patrick (1966); Thornton, 1996; Demetriades and Luintel, 1996; Berthelemy and Varoudakis (1998)] allege that economic growth can be enhanced through increase in savings in the form of financial assets thereby increase capital formation. Thus, factors such as financial deepening (i.e. depth and size of aggregate financial assets relative to GDP) and the composition of the aggregate financial variables are important for economic growth. A recent expansion of the "financial deepening" phenomena incorporates stock market as a measure of financial development (Levine and Zervos 1998). The financial repressionists, led by, McKinnon (1973) and Shaw (1973) argue that financial liberalization in the form of an appropriate rate of return on real cash balances is a vehicle of promoting economic growth. The essential tenet of this hypothesis is that a low or negative real interest rate will discourage saving. This will reduce the availability of loanable funds for investment, which in turn, will lower the rate of economic growth. Thus, the "McKinnon-Shaw" model posits that a more liberalized financial system will induce an increase in saving and investment and therefore, promote economic growth. Subsequent extension of this view was found in the studies by Galbis (1977); Mathieson (1980); Fry (1988) and Roubini and Sala-i-Martin (1992). However, the structuralists and the repressionists unanimously agree that the efficient utilization of resources promotes economic growth.

Most of the recent theoretical models are the product of the endogenous growth theory. The basic AK-model, shows that the financial sector development influences economic growth by, (i) reducing transaction costs increase availability of savings for productive investments (Greenwood and Jovanovic, 1990), (ii) enhancing the productivity of investments (Bencivenga and Smith, 1991) and (iii) movements in the saving rate (Pagano, 1993). The endogenous growth theories have further strengthened the role of financial intermediaries in the economic growth process demonstrated by diverse activities. One of the key propositions is that the financial repression is detrimental to growth (Roubini and Sala-i-Martin, 1992 and King and Levine, 1993b).

On the contrary, there are others who claim that finance does not lead but follows economic growth (Robinson, 1952). Chandavarkar (1992) also points out that the financial aspects have been neglected in the mainstream of development economics. Finance is viewed as "handmaiden to enterprise by responding to the demand for particular types of financial services generated by economic development: (Luintel and Khan, 1999). Another view maintains the two-way relationship between finance and growth. The two-way relationship is: economic development promotes financial system, which in turn enhances growth (Greenwood and Jovanovic, 1990), Blackburn and Hung (1996).

Nevertheless, post financial crisis experienced in the several parts of the globe have rekindled interest on financial aspects such as stability, reforms (including legal reforms), developing early warning systems and prompt corrective measures, monitoring and supervision of the financial system, to cite a few. There is a booming literature on a variety of related subjects and it was considered to be a useful exercise to classify them thematically for simplicity and review as follows:

(a) Early Contributions

Early contributions on the interlinkages between financial development and economic growth can be traced back to Bagehot (1873) and Schumpeter (1912) who emphasised the important role of the banking system in supplying the necessary funds for growth. Bagehot (1873) argued that the financial system was an important medium to transfer funds. As Bagehot (1873, pp. 3-4) observes: *"At this moment, in colonies and all rude economies, there is no large sum of transferable money; there is no fund from which you can borrow, and out of which you can make immense works."* According to Schumpeter, the financial funds required by an entrepreneur are the essential component of the production process and one *"can only become an enterpreneur by previously becoming a debtor.... He is the typical debtor in capitalist society"* (Schumpeter, 1912).

Bagehot recognized the crucial role of financial intermediaries in enhancing efficiency of investments for the rapid industrialization of England in the early nineteenth century: *"In England, however,... capital runs as surely and instantly where it is most wanted, and where there is most to be made of it"* [1873]. For Schumpeter financial intermediaries promote growth through innovative projects as he puts it, *"The banker... stands between those who wish to form new combinations and the possessors of productive means...He makes possible the carrying out of new combinations, authorizes people, in the name of society as it were, to form them."* [1911].

Bagehot viewed that the interlinkages between financial development and economic growth is brought by investments in inventions. As he states, *"We have entirely lost the idea that any undertaking likely to pay, and seen to be likely, can perish for want of money; yet no idea was more familiar to our ancestors, or is more common in most countries. A citizen of London in Queen Elizabeth's time... would have thought that it was no use inventing railways (if he could have understood what a railway meant), for you would have not been able to collect the capital with which to make them"*. Schumpeter views that a sound financial system would encourage technological innovations through discovery and choice provide financial assistance to entrepreneurs who would profitably execute the productive processes. He states, *"the relation... etween ... Credit creation by banks and innovation... is fundamental to the understanding of the capitalist engine"* (1939, 111). Hicks (1969) also concurred that for the industrial english revolution, the financial innovation had played a paramount role.

The early contributions by the depression era economists such as, Keynes and Fisher in a sense viewed that economic growth is hampered by lack of developed financial system. The financial system had little impact on economic development and in certain cases was harmful for the distribution of income and capital, i.e., savings may be induced in the financial sector rather than being used as productive investment capital in the real sector. Financial restructuring may result in a wider choice of savings options. Keynes although recognized the importance of financial considerations in his theory of output determination, however, through his liquidity preference theory, showed that money was more important than credit. Fisher (1933) argued that poor performance of the financial markets leads to bankruptcies, which further aggravates the economic downturn. The deflation would redistribute wealth from debtors to creditors leading to further fall in output and further deflation (his famous debt-deflation theory). Subsequently, Schumpeter (1934) indirectly analysed the relationship between financial development and economic growth by suggesting a positive relationship between monopoly power and size on the level of inventive activities. This implied that there exists a positive relationship between incentive to innovate by financial intermediaries and market structure and economic growth. Hicks (1937) emphasized the relationship between financial markets and economic activity originating from the Keynesian liquidity preference theory (Keynes, 1936).

Prebsch (1950) emphasized on structural factors that even shaped the markets particularly associated with underdeveloped countries. According to Robinson (1952), finance mainly sub-served the industry and responded passively to other factors that caused the differences in the cross-country growth. Thus, viewed that financial development followed economic growth. Nurkse (1953) recognized that capital formation is one of the essential determinants of economic growth and aptly states that, *"Capital is a necessary but not a sufficient condition of progress"*. The stagnation theory of Hansen (1953) attributed cyclical instability to lack of profitable investment opportunities regardless of the rate of interest. Lewis (1954 a, b) recognizing the need of external finance for underdeveloped countries, which have embarked on a programme of economic development, states that, *"They usually have to begin with and concentrate on the development of locally available natural resources as an initial condition for lifting local levels of living and purchasing power, for obtaining foreign exchange with which to purchase capital equipment and for setting in motion the development process."*

Kuznets (1955) included human capital in his definition of capital, which according to him, "contribute(s) to economic growth by increasing the efficiency of a complex productive system". Goldsmith (1954, 1958) was the first to recognise the role of financial intermediaries in the growth process. Expanding his theory, Gurley and Shaw (1955, 1956) considered financial capacity as an important financial factor determining aggregate demand. They viewed that financial intermediaries could enhance borrower's financial capacity in the savings and investment process. In constrast, Modigliani-Miller (1958) proposition holds that real economic decisions are independent of financial structure. Several notable developments in theory especially by Gurley and Shaw (1955) and Patrick (1966), Goldsmith (1969), McKinnon (1973) and Shaw (1973) have further provided new dimensions. However, the issue of causality between financial development and economic growth remained theoretically controversial although the early contributions recognised their interlikages.

(b) Financial Intermediation

In the economic sense, financial intermediaries mobilise savings from the surplus sector, which augments real balances and transfers them to the deficit sector, which offers primary debt instruments in exchange. Thus, financial intermediaries play a crucial role of intermediation in the growth process by transferring financial resources from the net savers to net borrowers and thus influence investment and thereby economic growth. The importance of financial intermediaries (or financial institutions) and their role of intermediation in the economic growth process were first emphasized by Goldsmith (1954, 1958, 1969) who offered a definition of the role of financial institutions. It was later developed by economists such as, Gurley and Shaw (1955, 1957 and 1960), Radcliff (1959), and Patrick (1966) which was later extended by others under different economic models. They stressed the positive effect of the financial market development on economic growth. Specifically, they asserted that government quantitative restrictions on the banking system restrain the volume and the productivity of investments, and impede the process of economic growth. As a consequence, they recommend the liberalization of the financial system to increase the volume and the productivity of investments.

(i) Goldsmith Theory

Goldsmith (1954, 1955, 1958, 1969) was one of the foremost to recognise the role of financial intermediaries in the institutionalisation of savings. Since the growth process is financed either through domestic funds or foreign funds or both, the sources and uses of funds and their method of financing throw light on the factors determining the demand for funds. In this context, the role of financial intermediaries in mobilizing savings and channelling them to various sectors become crucial. Recognising this, Goldsmith analysed the volume of assets of various financial intermediaries, trends in their types and distribution, in relation to long-run economic growth.

According to Goldsmith, the development of financial intermediaries and the trend of their share in national asset and wealth particularly are important from the economist's point of view. It indicates the extent and character of financial interrelations, which in turn helps to determine how capital expenditures are financed and how existing assets are shifted among owners. These together are important in directing the flow of savings into investment and also their size, which in turn stimulates economic growth. Goldsmith (1958) illustrates that despite the growth of all financial intermediaries in the first half of the twentieth century, the claims of non-bank financial intermediaries increased relative to the claims of demand deposits of commercial banks thereby diminishing their importance among all financial intermediaries. This implied that with the relative decline in the share of commercial banks, the ability of the central banks to control economic activity weakens and it called for a direct control of the non-bank intermediaries.

Goldsmith (1969) found that the nature of financial structure in less developed countries as compared with developed ones is such that a small proportion of primary securities to Gross National Product and aggregate saving is issued by individual economic unit, which is acquired through financial intermediaries. Besides, the central bank accounts for about two-thirds of all claims on financial intermediaries, which are held by the public. This implies that there is greater dependence on self-finance and thereby hardly any direct contact between the primary borrower and the ultimate lender. He demonstrated that as real income and wealth increase both in terms of aggregate and per capita levels, the size and complexity of the financial super structure also grows. Economic growth was associated with expanding size and increasing complexity of financial structure. He concludes that financial structure in the economy *"accelerates economic growth and improve economic performance to the extent that it facilitates the migration of funds to the best user, that is, to the place in the economic system where the funds will yield the highest social return"* (Goldsmith, 1969).

(ii) Gurley and Shaw View

Motivated by Goldsmith's work, Gurley and Shaw (1955, 1956, 1960), contend that the process of financial development parallels real economic growth. They emphasized the reciprocal relationship between real and financial development and state that, *"Development involves finance as well as goods"*. (1955). The real growth process involves external finance in which surplus spending unit transfers their saving to deficit units in the form of bonds through financial intermediaries. There are only commercial banks in the system and in this process "diversification demand for money" is created with increased holding of bonds by the surplus spending units, since money is highly liquid. According to Gurley and Shaw an appropriate adjustment in supply of money is required to ease the interest rates. They stress the importance of financial intermediation in the economic growth process due to the relative importance of non-banks *vis-à-vis* the commercial banks. In their financial theory of growth, they argue that accumulation of debt and growth of non-monetary Intermediaries is a more useful instrument as compared with short-period liquidity theory for analysis of economic development. They view that the financial part should be integrated with real development.

The liabilities of non-banks termed as 'indirect financial assets' are a better substitute for meeting the diversified demand for money. Although these are less liquid as compared with money, nevertheless they offer the same degree of security, interest yield and other services. In their words. *"The necessary growth in the money supply may be high or low, positive or negative, depending on the growth of income, the share of spending that is externally financed (especially by long-term securities), the growth in demand by spending units for direct relative to indirect financial assets, and on the development of financial intermediaries whose indirect debt issues are competitive with money"* (1955).

The pioneering work of Gurley and Shaw (1960) points out that 'the principal function of financial intermediaries is to purchase primary securities from ultimate borrowers and to issue indirect debt for the portfolios of ultimate lenders.' Financial intermediaries have an important function in providing a market mechanism for the transference of claims on real resources from savers in the surplus sectors to the more efficient investors in the deficit sectors. The more perfect the financial market, the more nearly is the optimum allocation of investment. The channel of transmission is through the credit supply via financial intermediaries. Thus, according to Gurley and Shaw, an efficient financial intermediary transforms the process of 'internal finance' into 'external finance' with the debt-asset system as the main technique of savings mobilisation.

Since Gurley and Shaw's main focus is on analysing the relationship between real and financial growth in their 'Theory of Finance', the validity of their interpretation of long-run trends in the structure of financial institutions rests upon the classifying financial assets into direct and indirect securities. Direct or primary securities are defined to include debts other than that of financial intermediaries. Indirect securities or debt is defined as including obligations of all "Financial Intermediaries" including banks, and thus includes demand deposits. The accumulation of direct or primary securities accompanies real financial growth and since the principal function of monetary and non-monetary financial intermediaries is to purchase direct debt from the issuer of indirect debt to non-financial spending units, the concepts of direct and indirect debt is useful.

According to Gurley and Shaw, financial transactions and financial instruments have two distinct types of effects on economic behaviour corresponding to flow and stock relationships. The first is the 'Intermediation Effect', which is on account of properties of the financial assets, which tangible assets does not possess. Indirect exchange through the intermediation of financial instruments is technically a more efficient means of want satisfaction than direct exchange. Intermediation of money, which is generally accepted as a means of payment, permits purchase and sale of commodities decomposed into two acts, which are special in time. Consequently, the use of money eliminates the difficulties experienced in exchange in a barter system.

In addition, financial instruments play a fundamental role in production, integration and ownership of wealth, and in the creation of economic activity. These stock implications of financial assets, termed as 'Asset Transmutation Effect', follow likewise, from observation that financial goods possess characteristics, which is absent in tangible goods. Thus, the indirect ownership of real wealth through the holding of financial assets is a technically more efficient means of want satisfaction as compared with the direct ownership of tangible assets.

Recognising the importance of the structure of financial system, Gurley and Shaw (1960) state that, "The design and performance of a financial system may stimulate saving and investment in efficient uses or it may retard saving and divert it to inefficient uses." According to these economists, in a rudimentary economy, while there are several financial restraints on economic growth, "An immature financial system is in itself an obstacle to economic progress". In such an economy, money is the only available financial asset and Government is the only financial institution. Money is totally 'Outside' money; i.e., the net claim by the private sectors on an "outside" sector namely, the Government. The demand for real money balances occurs because money has an implicit marginal deposit rate that exceeds marginal returns to consumption and investment. Monetary impact is not neutral and the financial system is not congenial to rapid growth in real output, due to lack of different types of financial assets and markets to stimulate savings to allocate for investments.

When money enters a complex financial structure, they contend that a new theory of money emerges wherein the role played by financial intermediaries are important. In a financial structure with highly developed non-bank financial intermediaries (NBFIs), 'inside' money, i.e., based on private internal debt and counter-balanced by business primary debt, arises. Contrary to a rudimentary economy, any change in the price level gets translated into wealth transfer between the two private sectors, one gaining and the other losing by equal amounts and thus money will not be neutral. In support of their argument, they bring in the concept of 'overall liquidity' where different assets differ in their liquidity characteristic. In their theory of finance, they argue that the combination of 'inside' and 'outside' money implies that changes in the quantity of money will not simply produce a movement up or down in general price level but will also produce changes in relative prices and the money neutrality is not valid.

Gurley and Shaw distinguish between financial savings and real savings. The former can be transformed into investments while the latter cannot be transformed. They contend that there exists some relationship between financial development and economic growth. They illustrate the crucial role of capital stock, accumulated through investments in economic growth, which can be stimulated through financial intermediaries whose main function is to channelise savings into productive investment. In an economy without financial intermediaries, investment depends upon own resources, which may not equal the actual investment requirements, particularly which are very critical for the development process. Thus, higher the intermediation level in the financial sector, higher is the saving mobilised and higher would be investments, which in turn will increase the level of economic growth.

(iii) The Radcliff View

A Committee was appointed by the British Chancellor on May 3, 1957 in England under the chairmanship of Lord Radcliff, commonly referred to as the Radcliff committee, to "inquire into the working of the monetary and credit systems, and to make recommendations" in order to contain inflation. The committee submitted its report on July 30, 1959. According to the Committee, the linkage between financial sector and real sector is only indirect in terms of the relationship between money supply and economic activity. The Committee started from the premise that the important variable determining level of employment and the rate of change in price level is the aggregate demand. The committee considered a wider structure of liquidity and money supply although not an "unimportant quantity" formed as a part of this wider liquidity structure. In this context, the Committee observes, *"Though we do not regard the supply of money as an important quantity, we view it only as a part of wider structure of liquidity in the economy. It is the whole liquidity position that is relevant to spending decisions, and our interest in the supply of money is due to its significance in the whole liquidity structure. A decision to spend depends not simply on whether the would be spender has cash or 'money in the bank', although the maximum liquidity is obviously the most favourable springboard."*

Thus, the Radcliff Committee, on the contrary, emphasized the store value function of money that recognised its multifarious forms. The major argument is that differences in the rates of return on money substitutes would result in a shift in the asset preference against holding money in a liquid form. However, money is only a part of the overall liquidity that influences economic activity. The direct linkage is embodied in the famous Fisherian classical quantity theory of money, viz.,

$$MV=PT$$

Where, M= money supply, P= price, V= velocity and T= trade.

The Committee disagreed with the direct linkage as an explanation for the relationship between money and economic activity on the following ground: (i) A tight relationship between money supply as defined by the

Classical theory and level of economic activity measured by national income could not be discovered. (ii) In a highly developed financial system with money financial intermediaries, grave theoretical difficulties were posed in identifying or labeling some quantity as "The Supply of Money". (iii) The Committee considered velocity of money as a numerical constant devoid of any behavioural content. It was a variable whose value changed with the change in the definition of money. Therefore, it rejected the direct linkage since under a system of highly developed financial intermediaries providing substitutes for narrowly defined money; the velocity of circulation was thought to be indeterminate. The linkage was seen through the concept of liquidity used by the Committee and it states, "... *spending is not limited by the amount of money in existence; but it is related to the amount of money people think they can get hold of, whether by receipts of income (for instance, from sales), by disposal of capital assets or by borrowing.*"

Thus, according to the Committee, if there were a reduction in liquidity, the expenditure would reduce to the extent they exceed current income and vice versa. Contrarywise, according to the Committee, "*A fall in rates, on the other hand, strengthens balance sheets and encourages lenders to seek new business.*" (1959). In sum the Committee states that, "*Thus a tendency to increasing liquidity is a natural consequence of the development of the financial system*".

(iv) Patrick's 'Demand Following' and 'Supply leading' hypothesis

Patrick (1966), taking the cue from Goldsmith's analysis, further expanded the Gurley and Shaw thesis and stated that, "*the causal nature of this relationship between financial development and economic growth has not been fully explored either theoretically or empirically*". Moving away from the neo-classical state equilibrium analysis, to a highly developed financial system, consisting of financial intermediaries, leads to a 'demand following' phenomena (Patrick, 1960). Under this, in response to the demand from real economy, there is the creation of modern financial institutions, their financial assets and liabilities, and related financial services. The evolutionary development of the financial system is a continuous result of the pervasive, widespread process of economic development. The financial system is influenced by economic environment, institutional framework and also by individual motivations, attitudes, tastes and preferences. The demand for financial services is a function of growth of real output, commercialisation, monetisation of agriculture and other traditional subsistence sectors. The faster the growth in real national income, the greater will be the demand for external funds by enterprises. Financial intermediation plays a vital role, as internal funds generated are not sufficient for firms to finance expansion. Thus, finance is passive and permissive to growth process. Contrarywise, the "Supply Leading" phenomena refers to the creation of financial institutions and the supply of their financial assets, liabilities, and related financial services taking place, prior to their demand especially in the modern growth inducing sectors. 'Supply Leading' approach performs two important functions, viz., (i) transfer of resources from traditional (non-growth) sectors to modern sectors, and (ii) promotes and stimulates an entrepreneurial response in these sectors. According to Patrick, in actual practice, there is an interaction of 'supply leading' and 'demand following' phenomena. Prior to sustained modern growth 'Supply Leading' could induce real growth through innovative investments by financial means. With real growth, the 'supply leading' gradually becomes passive and the 'demand following' financial response becomes predominant.

According to Patrick, in the linkage between financial growth and economic development, one of the most important relationships is the stock of financial assets and liabilities to the real capital stock, apart from their optimal composition, rate of growth, their efficient allocation and utilization. Thus, the financial system influences the capital stock in three different ways. First, financial intermediaries through intermediation among various types of asset holders can encourage more efficient allocation of a given amount of tangible wealth. Second, by intermediating between savers and investors, they can bring in allocative efficiency in new investments, i.e., additions to capital stock from lesser to more productive uses. Third, by providing increased incentives to save, invest and work, they can induce an increase in the rate of capital.

While recognising the important role played by financial intermediaries and also the differences in the distribution of saving and investment in both developed and underdeveloped countries, Patrick views that with the perfection of financial markets, near optimum allocation of investment is possible and the financial system accommodates economic growth. On the contrary, if the financial system is underdeveloped or inefficient, the growth is restricted.

(c) McKinnon's Complementarity Hypothesis

McKinnon (1973) explains the relationship between financial development and growth through a model based on 'outside money" and analyses the impact of real interest rate on saving deposits, investment and growth through the Complementarity hypothesis. The Complementarity is illustrated in the money demand function.

$$(M/P)^D = L(Y, I/Y, \{d-P^e\})$$

Where, M is the money stock (which includes savings and time deposits, demand deposits and currency less M2), P is the comprehensive price index of goods in terms of money, Y is the real Gross National Product, I/Y is the ratio of gross investment to Gross National Product, and $(d-P^e)$ is the real deposit rate of interest (d being the weighted average of nominal deposit rate of all classes of deposits and P^e is the expected future inflation rate and both are compounded). The complementarity is stated to work both ways, as McKinnon (1973) puts it, *"The conditions of money supply have a first order impact on decisions to save and invest"*, it can also be expressed as an investment function as,

$$(I/Y)=f\ (r,\ \{d-P^e\})$$

Where, r is the average return to physical capital and the complementarity between money and physical capital arises in the partial derivatives as follows:

$$\eth\ (M/P)/\ \eth\ (I/Y)=>0;$$

$$\eth\ (I/Y)/\ \eth\ (d-P^e)=>0.$$

The complementarity hypothesis is based on the assumption that all the economic units are circumscribed to self-finance. It is also assumed that investment expenditures are lumpier than consumption expenditures, implying that aggregate demand for money will be greater with larger proportion of investment to total expenditures. According to McKinnon, economic units must accumulate money balances prior to investment in the case of underdeveloped countries. Therefore, there exists a complementarity relationship between real money balances and investment in physical resources. With the constraints of self-financing, domestic savings equals domestic investments. "Thus, domestic savings have a positive relationship with demand for real money balances.

(d) Shaw's Debt-Intermediation View

Shaw's Debt-intermediation view holds that larger the money stock in relation to economic activity, greater is the financial intermediation between savers and investors through the banking system. The expanded financial/ intermediation arising from financial liberalisation (higher real institutional interest rates) and financial development increases the incentives to save and invest besides raising the average efficiency of investment. In his framework, financial intermediation raises real return to savers, reduces real costs to investors, reduces risk through diversification/real economies of scale in lending, increases operational efficiency and lowers information costs to savers and investors through specialisation and division of labour. Financial intermediation is repressed and sub-optimal when interest rates are fixed administratively below equilibrium levels. The debt-intermediation of Shaw (1973) produces a demand function as follows:

$$M/Y=f\ (Y/P,\ v,\ \{d-P^e\})$$

Where, Y/P is the real income, v is the vector of opportunity costs in real terms of holding money and P^e is the expected inflation rate.

(e) Financial Deepening Hypothesis

According to Shaw's financial deepening hypothesis, financial liberalisation tends to raise ratios of private domestic savings to income. With real growth of financial institutions, there are many investors having access to borrowing. There arises incentives for saving with many players and borrowings become cheaper. The planning horizon of the savers shifts to distant future. Current consumption is reduced on account of expected increase in income. Savings also tend to rise in the Government sector. With financial deepening, savings from the foreign sector respond to financial liberalisation. There is inflow of capital and easy access to foreign capital markets, which remove distortions in relative prices. Liberalisation permits the financial process of mobilising and allocating savings to displace inflation and foreign aid. Liberalisation enables superior allocation of savings through widening and diversifying financial markets wherein investment opportunities compete for savings flow. The savers are offered a wider menu of portfolio choice. The market is broadened in terms of scale, maturity and risk. Information is available more cheaply. Local capital markets are integrated and new avenues for pooling savings and specialising in investments are possible. Prices are used to discriminate between investment opportunities. In this context, Shaw states that, *"Financial depth seems to be an important pre-requisite for competitive and innovative disposition of savings flows."* Thus, financial liberalisation and allied policies bring in equal distribution of income. It reduces monopoly rents arising out of import and other licences to few importers and bank borrowers. It contributes to the stability of growth in output and employment.

According to Shaw (1973), with the development of the financial system, alternate financial assets other than money becomes available as repositories of financial savings to be eventually used for investment in productive resources. The savings and investments could take place through accumulation of non-money assets. Thus, in contrast to McKinnon's hypothesis, cash balances are not required to be accumulated prior to investment and hence, there is no complementarity. The negative relationship between money demand and saving imply substitution of money to other non-monetary financial assets as the major repository of saving. Such a relationship implies some level of financial development leading to the emergence of alternate financial assets other than money and would not be consistent with self-financing condition. Financial intermediation is restricted due to financial repression and investors resort to informal credit market. Therefore, financial liberalization would lead to better integration of formal and informal credit markets, which will result in efficient transfer of funds between savers and investors. Economies of scale will result in reducing cost of financial intermediation, information costs and lowering risks due to diversification.

Shaw (1973) underscores the developmental role of finance by distinguishing between nominal finance and real finance. With financial repression, nominal values in general rise at some buoyant rate and if deflated by any index of prices, their rise is less rapid. The nominal finance takes a high growth path while the real finance takes the lower one. Therefore, the finance in the real sense is partly shallow due to inflation. On the other hand, there are several indicators of financial deepening such as stocks. With financial liberalisation and removal of distortions in financial prices, liquidity increases. There is less intervention. The financial assets grow in relation to income or in proportion to tangible wealth and their range of quality also widens. Maturities are lengthened and there is more entry of debtors in the financial markets. Diversification of financial assets takes place that facilitates borrowers to adjust their debt structures and lenders their portfolios by relatively small margins. Financial flows indicate financial deepening and it eases the strain on taxation and moderates demand for foreign savings as reserves' capital flight and savings are diverted from investments in fixed capital and velocity of money diminishes. Deepening increases the real size of the monetary system and generates profitable avenues for other institutions. Specialisation in financial functions and institutions takes place wherein the domestic institutions benefit as compared with foreign markets and curb markets. Deepening also implies that interest rates reflect opportunities for substitution of investment for current consumption and disinclination of consumers to wait. Real interest rates are high and interest rate differentials tend to diminish, removes leases in relative prices.

Moore (1986) argues that in the development process, financial accumulation simultaneously provides credit to finance real asset accumulation. Savings ratio and its growth rate measure the equilibrium long run ratio of financial asset to Gross Domestic Product. It is viewed that inflation necessarily entails capital losses on all existing financial asset holdings. Unless monetary savings comes in to offset such inflation induced capital losses, inflation will reduce the degree of financial deepening despite high savings ratio particularly in developing countries such as Korea. He further adds that the financial assets are denominated in fixed money units while nominal values of the real capital stock and real income are in effect indexed to inflation rate. Thus, a higher inflation rate would reduce the equilibrium level of financial assets to Gross Domestic Product generated by any given savings and real growth rate and also reduce the degree of financial deepening measured by ratio of money to income (M2/Gross National Product). This further reduces the volume of credit and the ability to finance capital formation. Thus, inflation has a negative effect on the growth rate of the economy.

(f) Savings and Investment Process

Tobin (1965), in his two-asset portfolio model considers role of monetary factors in determining the degree of capital intensity of an economy. For the purpose, monetary debt of the government is considered as one alternative store of value to show how sufficient saving could be channelled to make warranted rate of growth of capital equal to the natural rate. In the non-monetary neo classical growth models, saving takes the form of real investment. The yield on capital investment becomes zero or even lesser when the saving and investment augments capital stock at a faster rate than the growth rate in supplies of other factors. This may result in people to discontinue saving or consume capital. This response of saving to the interest rate helps in setting an upper limit to capital deepening and a lower limit to the rate of return on capital. Increased consumption automatically replaces investment. Tobin observes that the equilibrium degree of capital intensity and the corresponding equilibrium marginal productivity of capital and the rate of interest are determined by "productivity and thrift". In other words, through technology and saving behaviour, he addresses the rationale behind the community wishing to save when rates of return are too unattractive. According to Tobin this could be rationalised only if there are stores of value apart from capital, with whose rate of return the marginal productivity of capital must compete. In this regard, he considers monetary debt of Government as one alternative store of value and demonstrates how enough savings could be channelled in order to make the warranted rate of growth equal to natural rate. The portfolio behaviour, monetary factors, savings behaviour and technology determine equilibrium capital intensity and interest rates. In the portfolio behaviour, it is assumed that the holding of different assets depends upon their respective yields. The yield differentials occur due to two factors, viz., risk avoidance and function of money as a means of payment. Portfolio diversification takes place on account of changes in technology, labour force, saving behaviour, yield expectations or portfolio choices. It is also assumed that capital deepening in production requires monetary deepening in portfolios through the government. Capital intensity cannot increase beyond the equilibrium, where shares of money and capital in total wealth are constant so that their yields remain constant. The equilibrium depends on the fiscal policy that maintains the balance through deficit spending that keeps the balance between money and capital. However, according to Tobin, with portfolio imbalance, the Pigou effect and Wicksell effect are at war with each other and the balance is restored by factors such as, savings behaviour, money supply and technology which determine equilibrium capital intensity and interest rates in the long run.

Goldsmith (1969) emphasized the vital role of financial intermediation by banks and non-banks in the saving and investment process. Intermediation enables efficient allocation of resources through increasing real deposit rates to a level that improves quality of investment. Galbis (1977) suggests real interest rates could influence the average efficiency of investments. He provides a theoretical approach in the context of less developed countries and demonstrates that real interest rates are growth promoting even if total real savings is interest insensitive as they bring about an improvement in the quality of capital stock. Given the fragmented structure of the developing economies with wide disparities in rates of return to physical investments and existence of indivisibilities of physical capital, Galbis illustrates that improvements in the process of financial intermediation, brought about through higher equilibrium real, interest rates which shifts investments from, traditional low yielding to modern technological sectors would result in dramatic acceleration of overall rate of economic growth. Later Galbis (1979) argued that there exists complementarity between public and private investments when the latter provides social overhead capital that facilitates private investments.

Giovannini (1983) argues that the existing studies do not easily detect the real interest elasticity of savings and in the 'seventies they generally yielded insignificant interest rate parameters. Therefore he questioned the view that interest elasticity of savings is significantly positive and it is easy to detect it in developing countries. Abebe (1990) offers a theoretical account of savings and investment process and examines its applicability in Africa. He states that the level of saving and investment are the determinants of economic growth. The other factors influencing productivity include shortage of materials, unutilized industrial capacity and low availability of manpower. In this context, financial intermediation process is of paramount importance as it helps the development process in three ways, viz., (i) It increases the volume and rate of savings and ensures that a rise in marginal savings is expressed in financial form; (ii) It creates a wide variety of financial claims differentiated by liquidity, maturity, divisibility and safety; and (iii) It ensures most efficient transfer of funds to real capital formation. However, in many ways financial intermediaries may not lead to greater efficiency of investment allocation in the less developed countries due to credit from the unorganised sector finance expenditure, which does not accelerate economic growth and some is used for financing long-term investment. Second, the savings are transferred to commercial banks, which lend only to credit worthy borrowers at low risk.

Corsepius (1990) adopts a portfolio model based on demand theory and asserts that financial sector can play an important role in the mobilisation of domestic resources and assures their efficient use in the case of Peruvian economy. Selective reform induces changes in the level and structure of financial savings. Due to differences in maturities and reserve requirements, growth of various financial assets does not contribute the same kind of expansion in loanable funds. On the contrary, Stern (1991) views that while the financial markets are helpful at the initial stage of economic development, they are not essential for growth. De Gregorio (1992) examines the effect of financial market developments on savings rate in the context of borrowing constraints and human capital. Under a 3-year overlapping generations model in an endogenous growth framework, he argues that by reducing capital accumulation, borrowing constraints have negative effects on growth. It is assumed that education is free and the small open economy is endowed with one unit of non-leisure time in each of the first two periods. The individuals need resources for acquiring education and hence face borrowing constraints. The opportunity cost will induce individuals to reduce time devoted to education and increase time for work. The focus is on the trade-off between working and studying. Growth is sustained by accumulation of physical capital and human capital and the borrowing constraint affect growth by changing the composition of capital.

Morisset (1993) argues that financial flows through increases in real interest rate does not necessarily involve a positive effect on private investment unless, (a) bank deposits are close substitutes to unproductive assets such as, cash, gold and foreign assets rather than to capital goods; (b) the financial sector assures an efficient allocation of domestic credits and the flow of private sector is not absorbed by the need in the public sector. It is viewed that the McKinnon (1973)-Shaw (1973) hypothesis suggests that higher real interest rates would raise savings and increase the volume of domestic credits extended by the financial system thereby the equilibrium of investment. The external experts from the World Bank to International monetary Fund (IMF) have regularly advised to establish high real interest rates in less developing countries (less developed countries) and the rationale behind this is derived from the presence of liquidity constraints on private investment decisions. Morisset opposes the McKinnon-Shaw hypothesis through a simple model of investment behaviour. Focussing on the quality of investment he argues that the positive effect of high real interest on domestic credit market would be offset by the negative effect of a portfolio shift from capital goods and public bonds into monetary assets. He also demonstrates that the crowding out of private sector funds and financial liberalisation increasing demand for domestic credit by public sector is not a consequence of a change in government's behaviour but due to a shift in the portfolio of private agents. The portfolio model consists of real domestic money, real domestic assets and real foreign assets. The expected rate of inflation enters to represent portfolio shifts towards capital goods and government bonds (indexed assets) as the expected return on money falls. The expected rate of return on foreign assets is defined as the sum of foreign real interest rate and the expected rate of depreciation of the local currency. For introducing liquidity constraints on portfolio decisions, variations in bank credit to private sector and foreign capital inflows have been added. The positive link between money demand and real investment is introduced through the real budget constraint of the financial system. The banking system accumulates reserves, extends credit to government, private sector and issues liabilities besides integrating the central bank and commercial banks. Therefore, changes in real reserves and the real net profit of the banking system are included.

According to Pagano (1993), during the process of transforming savings to investment, financial intermediaries perform a key function of absorbing liquidity through spread between lending and borrowing rates for banks, commission, and fees for securities brokers and dealers. This absorption of liquidity is limited by taxation, reserve requirements and other restrictive and regulatory trading practices, which influences the proportion of savings deviated to investments and also the social marginal productivity of capital. Another major function of financial intermediation is their ability to allocate funds to projects having the highest marginal product of capital. The marginal productivity of capital is increased by, (i) collecting information and (ii) inducing individuals to invest in risky projects by offering risk-sharing avenues. According to Jappelli and Pagano (1994), much less attention has been devoted to the effect of liquidity constraints on aggregate saving rate. Using an overlapping—generation model, they illustrate empirically that liquidity constraints on households (i) raise the saving rate, (ii) strengthen the effect of growth or saving, (iii) increase the growth rate if productivity growth is endogenous, and (iv) may increase welfare. Exogenous and endogenous growth models are adopted. In the exogenous growth model liquidity constraints increase aggregate saving besides strengthening effect of growth on saving. In the endogenous growth model the liquidity constraints induce higher saving rate and also translate into faster growth.

Berthelemy and Varoudakis (1996) test the presence of a poverty trap linked to the development of the banking sector. In their theoretical model, banking sector and financial sector are interchangeably used. In their model multiple steady state equilibria exist due to a reciprocal externality between the banking and real sector. Real sector growth causes financial market expansion, thereby increasing banking competition and efficiency. The banking sector development raises the net yield on savings and enhances the capital accumulation and growth.

(g) Financial Repression

"Financial Repression" models are associated with McKinnon and Shaw (1973), Kapur (1976), Galbis (1977), Mathieson (1980) and Fry (1980a) and they all concurred with the view that financial repression has a detrimental effect on economic growth. In their model, money demand is a function of the real deposit rate of interest (d), which is assumed to be fixed. Higher expected inflation (P^e) reduces the demand for money in real terms. It is argued that with the contraction in the banking system's liabilities in real terms, their assets also decline. The portfolio of the households shifts in favour of unproductive inflation hedges against deposits when they carry a low real interest rates on deposits. Consequently, the supply of bank loans for investment purposes contract and rate of accumulation of productive capital slows down and thereby reduces the rate of economic growth.

McKinnon (1973) describes the phenomenon of "financial repression" thus: *"Bank credit remains a financial appendage of certain enclaves: exclusively licensed import activities, specialises large scale mineral exports, highly protected manufacturing, large international corporations, and various government agencies, such as coffee marketing boards or publicly controlled utilities. Even ordinary government deficits on current account frequently preempt the limited lending resources of deposit banks. Financing of the rest of the economy must be met from the meager resources of money lenders, pawn-brokers, and cooperatives."* McKinnon (1973) and Shaw (1973), emphasizing the critical importance of financial deepening for less developed countries, view that the third world economies suffer from 'financial repression' or 'shallow finance'. "Financial Repression or Shallow finance" is characterised by slow growth or even atrophy of financial assets and financial structure. Most often referred to as the "McKinnon-Shaw" hypothesis in the literature, the basic tenet of this hypothesis is that a low or negative real interest rate will discourage saving thereby reduce the availability of loanable funds for investment which in turn, will lower the rate of economic growth. Thus, advocates that a more liberalized financial system will induce an increase in saving and investment and therefore, promote economic growth. They content that an appropriate rate of return on real cash balances is a vehicle of promoting economic growth.

In 1973, McKinnon and Shaw wrote their seminal work on the impact of financial liberalisation. They argued that an economy that holds the interest rate below the market clearing value will generate less than optimal savings, thereby detracting from the pool available for investment. A smaller proportion of savings will be channelled through the formal financial system, presumably resulting in a less efficient allocation of investment. In addition, the low interest rate will make low yielding projects profitable and given a degree of randomness in banks lending decisions, there will be many low yielding investments that will serve to reduce the average rate of return on investment.

Roubini and Sala-i-Martin (1995) define financial repression "as the set of policies, laws, regulations, taxes, distortions, qualitative and quantitative restrictions, and controls imposed by governments, which do not allow financial intermediaries to operate at their full technological potential". Thus, "Financial Repression" is characterised by low rates of return in real terms and under-pricing scarce Capital by banks. A vicious cycle of low returns results in savers reducing their holdings much below the actual requirements and bank credit is also equally reduced thereby resulting in low ratios of money supply to Gross National Product which is a feature of developing countries. An increase in bank lending is a necessary condition for enlarging the real size of monetary system and for alleviating financial repression. Besides, the excessive control and regulation on the market by keeping interest rates below the market rates, which enabled reduction in the cost of servicing government debt. The level of development of financial markets is exogenously determined by legislation and government regulation, and this is termed as 'degree of financial repression'.

According to Jao (1976), financial repression is a consequence of inappropriate policies, which imposed ceilings on nominal interest rates, existence of fixed exchange rates, which overvalue the domestic currency, and inhibits the expansion of the fiscal base. These policies penalise savings, suppress market signals relating to capital scarcities and encourage lop-sided development of capital-intensive industries, which exacerbate unemployment. He also viewed that demand for savers and interest rate is positively related while the relation between loans and interest rates are negatively related. Under such conditions, the ceillings imposed on the interest rates are detrimental to economic growth and indicate the presence of financial repression. This leads to deterioration in the quality of investments. Kapur (1976) assumes the existence of unused fixed capital and therefore working capital acts as a constraint on output. Bank credit is used to finance all net working capital investment. Bank credit and money stock are linked through loans and high-powered money held by public and banks. He shows that economic growth is positively affected by monetary growth, output/capital ratio, ratio of loans to money, and the ratio of utilized fixed capital to total utilized capital. Galbis (1977) showed that financial repression not only worsens income distribution but also maintains economic dualism.

Mathieson (1980) assumes the full utilization of fixed capital and a fixed proportion of all investments are financed by bank loans. The rate of capital accumulation by firms is determined by fixed real return. Growth is related with nominal loan rate, expected inflation and output/capital ratio. It also has a direct positive relationship with real return on investment. The supply of loans is determined by the demand for deposits and the required reserve ratio as long as high-powered money is not backed by loans. It is assumed that Government fixes the deposit and loan rates. He illustrates that financial liberalization can make financial intermediaries, which hold a portfolio of loans yielding a low pre-reform return insolvent. Fry (1980a) examining the cost of financial repression in developing countries finds that saving is affected positively by real deposit rate of interest and real money demand. Credit availability is an important determinant of not only new investment but also capacity utilisation of the entire capital stock. Therefore, the growth rate is positively affected by real deposit rate of interest through (1) volume of saving and investment and (2) capital stock utilisation measured by capital/output ratio.

There also exists the curb market (informal credit market) where borrowers and lenders freely transact at uncontrolled interest rates. Buffie (1984) has developed a portfolio model of a financially repressed structuralist, where the curb market plays a crucial role as the marginal supplier of loanable funds. Financial liberalization may fail in the short-run. The demand for savers and interest rate are positively related while the relations between loans and interest rates is negatively related. Under these conditions, ceilings imposed on the interest rates are detrimental to economic growth and indicate the existence of financial repression. It leads to deterioration in the quality of investments and therefore affects economic growth.

The architects of financial repression model assume that in a developing economy only commercial banks, which dominate the financial system, intermediate between savers and investors. These economies are heavily taxed as inflation is considered as tax, which acts as a source of revenue to the government. According to Fry (1993), inflation tax on an average yielded a revenue equal to 2.8 per cent of Gross National Product in 1984 representing over 17 per cent of government's current revenue in a sample of 26 countries. Further high reserve requirements are imposed on the banking system along with high ratio of domestic credit to government to aggregate domestic credit. Interest rate ceilings are prescribed on deposits and loans. An estimate by Giovannini and Martha de Melo (1993) reveals that the tax revenue from repression works out to 1.8 per cent of Gross Domestic Product for 22 developing countries during 1972-1987. The link between financial development and economic growth is assumed to be positive. Real interest rates serve as a proxy to measure the degree of financial repression and are positively related to economic growth.

Prior to the 'seventies, Roubini and Sala-i-Martin (1995) point that many economists advocated financial repressionist policies on the following grounds:

(i) Control and Regulation of the banking system was necessary for the control of money supply by the central banks.

(ii) The need to impose anti-usury laws by the government led to the government intervention in the free play of the market.

Financial repression distorts the growth process through various channels. According to Goldsmith (1969), it affects through the efficiency of capital while Mckinnon and Shaw (1973) view that it affects efficient allocation of savings for investment through its effects on post-tax return on savings and investments. It is viewed that the McKinnon (1973)-Shaw (1973) hypothesis suggests that higher real interest rates would raise savings and increase the volume of domestic credits extended by the financial system, thereby the equilibrium of investment. According to Roubini and Sala-i-Martin (1995), financial repression affects growth directly by affecting the productivity of investment, by reducing the overall level of saving and investment and by increasing the intermediation costs of savings to investments. Fry (1997) illustrates that financial repression as a technique for reducing government's borrowing costs has also adverse effects on economic growth. Therefore, economists such as, McKinnon-Shaw (1973) strongly advocated financial liberalization policies particularly in the developing economies.

(h) Financial Liberalisation

According to the financial liberalisation school, full liberalisation of financial markets in developing countries would contribute positively to economic growth through increased interest rates. Initially savings would increase thereby increasing the investments, interest rates, and quality of investments would also improve, as low yielding investment projects will be replaced by high-yielding projects. Besides, McKinnon (1973) also "stressed the need for financial liberalisation in less developed countries in context of a model which incorporates specific elements of the financial sector of those countries." In the McKinnon model, the demand for cash balances is positively related to income, real interest rates and average rate of return in capital. Shaw (1973) too views that increase in real interest rates raises holdings of savings in the banks. He stressed the efficiency gains in the intermediation process with increase in individual's wealth with banks. Shaw (1973) strongly believed that financial liberalisation would have a positive outcome on the process of financial intermediation, which would then contribute to higher investment and growth (debt-intermediation view). He viewed that institutionalisation of savings may contribute to lowering the costs of lending to investors due to efficient operations of specialised financial institutions. Both McKinnon and Shaw contend that an increase in the amount and efficiency of investment in the outcome of financial liberalisation.

Financial liberalisation and deepening is characterised by interest and exchange rates reflecting relative scarcities; higher savings; efficient discrimination between alternative investments; replacement of capital-intensive process and technology by labour intensive process, provided that the elasticity of substitution between labour and capital is high; positive employment generation; and distribution effects favouring labour. All these contribute to higher growth and more equitable distribution of income.

Kapur (1992) observes that the neo-structuralist critique on the McKinnon Shaw financial liberalisation hypothesis primarily emerges from the distinction between formal financial intermediaries and informal ones in terms of reserve requirements. Besides, the economic functions of these reserves in terms of liquidity enhancement and seignorage creation have been ignored. According to Kapur, incorporation of the former function shows that financial liberalisation is welfare increasing. Although holding of reserves by banks (formal intermediaries) are mainly to enable them to meet immediate cash demands, it nevertheless allows banks to offer a liquidity facility to their depositors. The same is not possible in the case of informal intermediaries. The demand for liquidity stems from the need to meet unforeseen contingencies. Therefore, the asset holder at any given period deposits his wealth in the formal and informal sectors. The deposits in the informal sector gives the deposit a higher return than the formal sector as the latter holds non-interest bearing reserves and it is subject to administratively imposed interest rate ceiling. The former would not permit premature withdrawals of deposits. Kapur emphasizes that the formal and informal financial markets have complementary roles to perform in a fully liberalised financial system. Asset holders would prefer to hold deposits with formal and informal intermediaries as the former offers liquidity and the latter offers high returns.

Williamson and Mahar (1998) have recently constructed an index of financial liberalisation which takes into account six factors in financial liberalisation, viz., elimination of credit controls; deregulation of interest rates; free entry into the banking sector or more generally, the financial-services industry; bank autonomy; private ownership of banks; and liberalisation of international capital flows. Accordingly, they classified 34 countries during the period 1973-96 as repressed economies, partly repressed economies, liberalised economies and largely liberalised economies.

Bandiera *et al.* (1998) provide a more advanced methodology in constructing indices of financial liberalization by using the principal components method. Their index includes variables relating to: domestic financial liberalisation, such as, interest rates, pro-competition measures, reserve requirements, directed credit variables; banks' ownership and prudential regulation dummies; securities markets; and international financial liberalisation such as, degree of liberalisation for capital movements and exchange rates.

(i) Information Asymmetry

In the recent literature concerning theory of financial intermediation, one of the aspects that have gained prominence is the existence of asymmetries in information as between lenders and borrowers. The efficient functioning of the financial system is hampered by the presence of asymmetric information. This leads to two major problems viz., adverse selection and moral hazard. The former occurs before the transaction takes place and borrowers with bad potential credit risks seek out loans. Consequently borrowers who are likely to produce adverse results may be selected. The latter occurs after the transaction takes place and the lender is subject to moral hazards in the sense the borrower has the incentive to perform activities that may not be morally good. This occurs when the borrower has incentives to invest in highly risky projects. When he fails, the lender has to bear the loss. Banks due to their relative advantage over the other financial intermediaries are able to reduce adverse selection and moral hazard.

Stiglitz and Weiss (1981) point out that the essential problem of financial intermediation is how to cope with incomplete and asymmetric information. The availability of information involves fixed and variable costs. Diamond and Dybvig (1983) in a seminal paper consider financial intermediaries, like banks, to create liquidity by providing risk-sharing arrangements to insure against random consumption needs of depositors. The intermediary contracts prevent production in efficiencies. Diamond (1984, 1991) argues that financial intermediaries, such as banks, reduce information costs and incentive problems by monitoring the borrowers. The assets side of the intermediaries is dealt by Diamond (1984), Campbell and Kracaw (1980). The liabilities side of intermediaries was investigated by Diamond and Dybvig (1983), and Gorton and Pennacchi (1990).

Financial intermediaries, like banks, arise due to delegated monitoring (Diamond, 1984). The cost of monitoring the intermediary on the 'delegation cost' gets arbitrarily reduced with diversification by intermediaries across borrowers. This is possible as the optimal contract between lenders and the financial intermediary is again a (deposit) contract on which default is unlikely due to diversification. He analyses the determinants of delegation costs and develops a model wherein financial intermediary has a net cost advantage relative to direct lending and borrowing. Key element to the Net cost advantage is the diversification within the financial intermediary.

Ramakrishnan and Thakor (1984) develop a model, which provides a rationale for the emergence of financial intermediaries, viz., their ability to reduce information production costs. Their model cast in a financial market framework, points out that intermediaries improve welfare if informational asymmetries are present and the information provided to rectify these asymmetries is potentially unreliable. Romer (1985) points out that reserve requirements, inside money, financial intermediation and real interest rate ceilings etc., have little or no place in any macro model or general equilibrium micro model while these features of financial markets are central to the interactions of monetary and real forces. The differences between banks and other non-bank financial intermediaries are clearly stated. While banks are required to hold a fraction of deposits as reserves, non-banks have no such requirements. As financial intermediaries are competitive and intermediation is costless; for non-banks it implies that interest rate offered in deposits equals the rate charged on loans.

Williamson (1986) provides a link between equilibrium credit rationing and financial intermediation in a model with asymmetrically informed lenders and borrowers, costly monitoring and investment project indivisibilities. The intermediation dominates borrowing and lending between individuals. Financial intermediaries arise endogenously and are characterised by issue of securities having payoff features differing from what they hold; writing debt contracts with borrowers; hold diversified portfolios and processing information. Boyd and Prescott (1986) establish that financial intermediaries are part of an efficient arrangement needed to support investment opportunities of agents, which are private information. The financial intermediaries emerge endogenously and act as coalitions of agents and function as borrowing and lending agents, provide information on investment and also issue claims. Similar to Diamond (1984) and Williamson (1986) all agents are risk neutral.

Haubrich (1989), in an information-based banking model using Diamond's (1984) delegated monitoring model, is concerned with the consequences of entering relationships for bank structure and policy and allows repeated lending between the intermediary and borrower. This contract permits a financial intermediary, such as banks, to produce information and enforce compliance more easily than direct monitoring of the borrower's institution. Haubrich's model is an improvement on single-period general equilibrium banking models of Diamond and Dybvig (1983), Diamond (1984), Bernanke and Gertler (1987) and Haubrich and King (1989). The major conclusions that emanate are: (i) banks may have asymmetric structure with respect to long-term arrangements and specifically have enduring relationships with borrowers; (ii) intermediation is valuable and long term contracts are not sufficient for placing commercial papers; (iii) enduring relationships between banks and borrowers need not preclude loan participations; and lastly, (iv) the model suggests that long-term relationships will make a difference in any banking problem involving time.

Gorton and Pennacchi (1990), in contrast to Diamond and Dybvig (1983), do not rule out trading in stock market, but view that the presence of insiders in the market motivates the formation of intermediary. Besides, in their model the intermediaries explicitly will issue debt and equity and serve as a medium that split cash flows of their asset portfolios. Thus, intermediaries create a new liquid security and they can attract insiders to become equity holders. This debt, which is safer than the underlying assets, can also be used by uninformed agents for transaction purposes.

Sussman (1993) focuses on 'Gross markup' or the conventional cost of financial intermediation of the banking system. With a view to link finance and development, a special model of a monopolistically competitive banking system is adopted. It is assumed that banks are endogenously created in the system. A constant returns to scale technology in monitoring is also assumed so that as the banking system becomes perfectly competitive growth is balanced. As per their model, with increases in capital stock the market for financial intermediation grow and there is a rise in number of banks. Each bank becomes more specialised and hence efficient and the industry becomes more competitive. Consequently, cost of intermediation falls and the markup decreases. Adopting the theory of contracts with post asymmetry of information, it is implied that standard debt contract is more efficient if monitoring is costly. While Sussman recognises that his model has omitted regulation factor from the analysis, David Begg comments that, "A highly regulated banking system is unlikely to be a banking system in which free entry occurs. Regulation may well play a key role in financial development and the causation may run in both directions. By neglecting such regulatory issues, Sussman's model risks omitting one of the key aspects of the analysis". Rafael Repullo points out that there is no empirical evidence for the negative relationship between the intermediation markup and the capital stock. However, he views that the main contribution of Sussman is the model of imperfect competition wherein banks' market power is derived from informational advantages.

(j) Endogenous Growth Theories

With a rapid expansion in theoretical literature in the recent years on endogenous growth, relationship between financial development and economic growth has received new focus. This has been attributed to the writings of Romer (1986), Boyd and Prescott (1987) and Lucas (1988). Lucas (1988) contends that financial development naturally follows economic growth. These economists recognised the crucial importance of determinants of long-run economic growth relative to bussiness cycles or counter cyclical effects of monetary and fiscal policies. The key determinants, such as technological progress, which was exogenous in the neo-classical growth models, were now considered as endogenous and hence their models came to be called the endogenous growth models. It is assumed that the creation of knowledge is a side product of investment. If investment, measured by physical capital, is increased, production is efficient. The growth can be continuous as the return on investment in a variety of capital goods including human capital; does not diminish when economies grow.

According to Pagano (1993), the techniques of endogenous growth models have shown that, *"there can be self sustaining growth without exogenous technical progress and that the growth rate can be related to preferences, technology, income distribution and institutional arrangements."* He adds that it is possible to show both level and growth effects of financial intermediation.

According to Pagano (1993), there are three ways in which financial development can affect economic growth in an endogenous framework. These include,

(i) Absorption of resources by financial intermediaries in the process of transforming saving into investments by which savings are greater than investments. With financial development, lower is the absorption of resources and higher is the growth.

(ii) If savings channeled through financial intermediaries are efficiently allocated by choosing appropriate technology, higher productivity of capital results in higher growth.

(iii) By altering the saving rate which involves risk sharing.

Several models under the endogenous growth framework have dealt with specific issues concerning the relationship between financial development and economic growth. Prominent among them are informational advantage and allocation of financial resources to projects with highest yields and savers gain confidence in the ability of the financial intermediaries and thereby park an increasing proportion of their savings with intermediaries Greenwood and Jovanovic (1990). Economic growth is promoted via capital stock (Bencivenga and Smith, 1991) and investments in less liquid projects through portfolio diversification and reduction of liquidity risks (Levine, 1991; Saint-Paul, 1992), allocation of credit and efficiency of financial intermediaries in acquiring knowledge about the quality of individual projects thereby funding innovative products and productive processes that induce economic growth (King and Levine, 1992, 1993a, b, c), (De La Fuente and Marin, 1994), increasing productive investment through liquidity-risk management and effects of transaction costs on technology (Bencivenga and Smith, 1991, 1995), repressionist government policies hurt growth (Roubini and Sala-i-Martin, 1992, 1995); identifying multiple equilibria (Saint-Paul, 1992) for threshold effects (Berthelemy and Varoudakis, 1995). The Greenwood and Smith (1997) use two models with endogenous growth formation and examine the way banks and stock markets allocate funds to the highest value user(s).

Greenwood and Jovanovic (1990) show that financial intermediation promotes growth as it permits a higher return on capital. The growth in turn enables implementation of costly financial structures. Using a single model they address the two issues of: (i) link between economic growth and distribution of income; and (ii) the connection between financial structure and economic development. They show that growth provides the impetus for a developed financial structure and this in turn leads to higher growth due to efficient investments. In the early stages of development, due to the presence of large unorganised exchanges, growth is slow. With rise in the income levels, financial structure expands and growth becomes rapid resulting in widening income inequality. In a matured stage of development, fully developed financial structure enables stable income distribution and a relatively higher growth rate.

Levine (1991) stresses the importance of stock markets in orienting investments in less liquid projects. The consumer's liquidity risk is reduced through portfolio diversification. Saint-Paul (1992) also follows the same line of thought as Levine (1991) but in his model productivity is increased through specialization and division of labour. He studies the interaction between financial markets and technological choice. Financial markets permit the use of risky technology and the capital markets spread risk through diversification. The technological choice affects the viability of the financial market. Intermediaries choose less productive and specialised technologies. Consequently, multiple equilibria arise. This accounts for the persistence of differences in growth rates between countries. This, however, increases the risk from sectoral demand shocks. The sharing of risk efficiently raises productivity and growth.

Roubini and Sala-i-Martin (1992) recognise that financial intermediation is an important component of aggregate production function. They also link financial market policies to economic growth performance. They point out that the financial repressionist policies used by governments to finance budget deficits are detrimental to growth. They argue that given that the financial intermediation is an important component of aggregate production function, repressive policies of the government hurt growth more if the marginal product of capital of a financially developed economy is larger than that of a less financially developed economy. Further, Roubini and Sala-i-Martin (1995) argue that financial repression would lead to higher tax evasion, high inflation and low growth.

Bencivenga and Smith (1991) develop an endogenous growth model. With the introduction of intermediaries, composition of savings shifts in favour of capital accumulation, which in turn, promotes growth. It is also viewed that intermediaries generally reduce socially unnecessary capital liquidation, which tends to promote growth. They present a general equilibrium model in which behaviour of competitive intermediaries (banks) affects resource allocations in such a manner that have implications for real rates of growth and it provides partial characterisation when economies with competitive intermediaries grows faster than economies lacking such institutions. Financial intermediaries naturally may tend to alter composition of savings in such a manner, which is favourable capital accumulation. As a corollary, if the composition of savings affects real growth rates, then intermediaries will tend to promote growth. They argue that intermediation allows reduction of fraction of savings in the form of unproductive liquid assets and also prevents misallocation of invested capital due to liquidity needs. Using a 3-period-level-overlapping Generation Model, they assume that all agents including banks have access to 'liquid investment' which is not directly productive and an 'illiquid investment', which yields productive capital. Young workers own capital and the young agents make the savings decisions. Incentive exists for banks to form and provide "liquidity" to deposits through holding of liquid resources against predictable withdrawal of demand. As compared with the absence of banks which Bencivenga as Smith term as "financial autarky", the banks would reduce holding of reserves and thereby reduce liquidation of productive capital. Higher equilibrium growth rates could be observed in economies with an active intermediary sector. Their model is based on the following several important assumptions: (1) The level of development of financial markets is exogenously determined by legislation and government regulation to measure the 'degree of financial repression'; (2) Banks constitute the entire organised financial markets in underdeveloped economies; (3) The long gestation period between investment expenditures and receipts of profits from capital is assumed; (4) With the absence of banks, most part of the investment is self-financed which needs to be self insured for random liquidity needs as it could result in excessive investment in unproductive liquid assets. Therefore, it is viewed that absence of an intermediary sector results in composition of savings, which is unfavourable to capital accumulation; (5) Following 4, the most important role of banks as promoting growth is through providing liquidity and thereby improving savings-composition; (6) Lastly, it is viewed that economies with well developed financial system grow faster than those lacking such system.

Based on the above assumptions, they present a model where the agents face a trivial savings decision and compare equilibrium growth rates in economies with and without financial intermediaries. They stress that as the savings decision is trivial, intermediaries need not increase savings rates in order to lead to higher growth. At the same time, they also demonstrate that intermediation can result in higher equilibrium growth rates without increasing saving rates. Bencivenga and Smith point out the lags in the outcome of capital investments and view that lack of immediate effect arising out of financial liberalisation should not be construed as absence of liberalisation effect on increased growth rates, contrary to the empirically motivated criticisms of McKinnon (1973), Shaw (1973) and Diaz-Alejandro (1985). According to Bencivenga and Smith, it is independent of whether liberalisation is anticipated or not since the returns to capital is technologically fixed and is not affected by financial liberalisation. However, in the model presented by them, the effects of financial liberalisations are heavily dependent on the specification of technology. Another aspect that is dealt with is a situation, when development of intermediation tends to promote growth, a relatively small fraction would be invested in capital accumulation under financial autarky. Secondly, contrary to the general view (Diaz-Alejandro, 1985) that presence of developed banking systems necessarily enables higher savings rates as compared with other economies, they demonstrate that intermediation can result in high equilibrium growth rates although it may not necessarily raise savings.

In another study, Bencivenga and Smith (1995) analyse the effect of transaction costs in financial markets on the technologies used and the equilibrium growth rate as implied by Hicks (1969). Under a two-period overlapping endogenous growth model, they argue that the use of long-gestation capital production technologies require ownership of capital-in-process be transferred in a sequence of owners in the secondary capital markets. The liquidity in the financial markets is measured by their transaction costs. Liquid markets are associated with low transaction costs and illiquid ones with high transaction costs. Following Hicks, they illustrate how transaction costs affect equilibrium choice of production technologies and the equilibrium rate of growth. For the purpose, they consider an economy with unique non-trivial constant equilibrium rate of growth, wherein the equilibrium interest rate exceeds endogenous growth rate. In a comparative dynamic consequence of a reduction in the transaction costs in secondary costs in secondary capital markets, they show that the reduction in the transaction costs always favours reliance on the longer gestation capital production function (which is transaction intensive) technologies. While the lower transaction costs necessarily raise the equilibrium rate of return on savings, an increase in the technical efficiency of capital resale markets could lead to either an increase or reduction in the long-run equilibrium rate of growth. The equilibrium rate of growth depends upon five factors, viz., (i) capital production technology, (ii) its productivity, net of transaction costs, (iii) the savings rate, (iv) the composition of savings, and (v) the ratio of labour's share to the Capital's share in output. The employment of long gestation capital production technologies requires the support of financial markets. The transaction costs, therefore, influence technological choice. They suggest that the lowering transaction costs would enable the use of the long gestation technologies and raise the real return on savings but do not necessarily result in higher real growth. This is because the liquidity of the financial markets alters the composition of savings, which favours holding of financial assets (claims in existing capital-in-progress) at the cost of initiation of new capital investment. If this effect were large, improvements in the liquidity of financial markets would reduce growth and vice versa.

King and Levine (1992, 1993 a, b, c) link financial indicators to growth through two channels, viz., (i) share of Gross Domestic Product allocated to investments and (ii) the efficiency in resource utilization. They also provide theoretical exposition that links financial intermediation and economic growth. They view that the influence of financial intermediaries on the level of economic development and the rate of economic growth depends upon many factors, such as capital accumulation process, investment in general human capital (Lucas 1988), investments that enable production of variety of products (Romer, 1990), and investments in firm specific human capital (Prescott and Boyd, 1987). They explore questions regarding how important are financial markets for an economic system that fosters growth, development and international trade. It is argued that the *traditional view* considers financial markets simply as the handmaiden of industry but the *new view* (Romer, 1986 and Lucas, 1988) otherwise suggests that financial markets play a central role in determining a country's pattern of trade and growth. Their 'new view' suggests the presence of important connections between financial intermediation and productivity since all growth models, new and old, shows that productivity has an important effect in economic activity. The new growth models, in particular, lay emphasis on investments in physical capital accumulation, general human capital accumulation and other intangible productivity-enhancing capital goods, which all influence economic growth.

King and Levine (1993b) construct a Schumpeterian model of financial intermediation under endogenous growth framework, where financial systems evaluate prospective entrepreneurs, mobilize savings to finance productivity enhancing activities. At the centre of their theory is the entrepreneur who innovates i.e., invention of new product or modification of an existing one or adopting technology produced elsewhere or adopting technology or producing a product using different methods. The entrepreneurs are heterogeneous. Productivity enhancing investment involves construction of intangible capital goods. The returns on these are quasi rents determined by, (i) market size, (ii) rates of innovation of competitors, and (iii) taxation and public regulation. The financial intermediaries are endogenous as part of market mechanisms for screening entrepreneurs financing intangible, productivity enhancing investment by credit worthy entrepreneurs. Ceteris paribus, countries with superior financial system allocate savings more efficiently to more efficient and productive projects than countries with less efficient financial system. Efficient resource allocation translates into increased productivity and growth though physical capital accumulation, improvements in intangible capital and human capital. They conclude that like Schumpeter, central to the economic growth process is the nexus of finance and innovation.

Berthelemy and Varoudakis (1995) illustrate a case of multiple endogenous growth equilibria that is characterised by low or high real growth in accordance with the level of development of the financial sector. This results in threshold effect in economic growth and their omission would lead to specification errors in econometric estimation of growth equations.

(k) Impact on Policy

The traditional theoretical approach to monetary policy emphasized the medium of exchange function of money where there is no substitute for money. The concept of money did not go beyond coins, currency and demand deposits. Therefore, monetary policy was limited to the control of money supply, which also meant control of liquidity. Hence, a direct linkage between money and economic activity was postulated in the classical quantity theory, while the indirect linkage through interest rates was provided by the Keynesian approach.

The impact of the emerging financial intermediaries on the linkages between monetary policy and economic growth has attracted widespread attention in the literature right from Roosa (1951), Birnbaum (1958), Thorn (1958), The Radcliff Committee (1959), Gurley and Shaw (1960), Gustav (1960), Patinkin (1961), Joseph Aschheim (1963), Tobin and Brainard (1963), Brunner and Meltzer (1963), Wijnbergen (1983) to Morgan (1992).

Roosa (1951) through his "availability doctrine" brought out the scope for central bank control of non bank financial intermediaries. The central theme of Roosa's doctrine was that a huge volume of Government debt held by financial institutions would increase the scope and power of open market operations which would exercise an influence on economic activity to a greater degree than those arising from the banking system. Roosa conjectured that a small variation in the interest rate would greatly affect the supply of loanable funds, which in turn would significantly affect aggregate demand even if the demand for credit by borrowers were highly inelastic. Thus, it is implied that monetary policy impacts through influencing availability of credit.

Roosa points out that the emergence of the open market operations, as a major instrument of monetary policy, is the outcome of the shift from a purely defensive to dynamic central bank responsibility, which is marked by the passage of the Banking Act. Further, he points out that open market operations stems from the combined use of defensive and dynamic responsibilities of the central bank. The defensive policy on the other hand, in Roosa's words, was one of "keeping close watch on the absorption of reserves by other factors and then taking action day by day, to offset only enough of the reserve absorption to prevent the creation of even tighter conditions in the money market than the policy of the Federal Open Market Committee intended".

Birnbaum (1958) analyses the question whether the growth of non-bank financial intermediaries has narrowed the scope for effective monetary control. It is illustrated that the control of the monetary authorities have been more effective on the banking system; while the "uncontrolled" financial intermediaries have been a factor increasing the effectiveness of open market operations reflected in terms of increased average maturity of Government debt and holdings of large portfolio of long-term Government securities.

On the contrary, Thorn (1958) stressed the threat to the effectiveness of monetary policy arising out of the ability of non-bank financial intermediaries to expand credit in the short run which are outside the direct control of the central bank.

The Radcliff committee (1959) viewed that varying the amount of liquidity could be achieved by altering the interest rate structure. During monetary contraction, while the ability to lend declines, the borrower's desire to borrow remains unaltered. Liquidity is reduced with rising interest rates as it tends to reduce the capital value of assets held by individuals and financial institutions.

When money enters a complex financial structure, Gurley and Shaw (1960) contend that a new theory of money emerges within the financial structure and they develop the theme that financial intermediaries are important and their liabilities has certain implications on the analysis for monetary theory and policy. Here monetary policy becomes more effective when besides controlling the quantity of money it also takes into account the activities of the non-bank financial intermediaries. They stress that all types of financial institutions create loanable funds and therefore upheld that monetary authority's regulatory powers could be extended to non-banking financial intermediaries also, thereby making monetary policy to be wider in scope. They bring into their analysis the overall liquidity of the monetary and financial structure and differing liquidity characteristics of different assets, which were excluded by Patinkin. They argue that even within a strict neo-classical framework, monetary policy may not be neutral on real variables where there exists a combination of inside and outside money. In their theory of finance, they argue that the combination of inside and outside money implies that changes in the quantity of money will not simply produce a movement up or down in general price level but will also produce changes in relative prices and the neutrality of money vanishes.

Gustav (1960) argues that with the development of the financial system, there emerges a cashless mode of payments. The credit process itself creates "Money in account or deposit money" which also reflects the purchasing power of the individuals and this form of money has a qualitative relationship rather than quantitative relationship with the overall economic activity. He views that the effects on price level is not caused by income but by expenditure and only that part of income, which is actually used for purchases, forms part of the aggregate demand and this according to Gustav has nothing to do with the theory of money. Therefore, he provides a wider concept of financial assets, which includes all tangible and intangible assets, that links general business conditions with monetary conditions and terms it as "Liquidity Theory of Money". This definition of "liquidity" not only includes assets of banking institutions but, cash, bank accounts and credit facilities as well. Gustav implicitly states that financial development leads to increased general business activities and economic growth. Thus he views that the causal relationship between money and real economic activities or price level cannot fully be explained either through monetary theory or the Keynesian Income-Expenditure theory. He contends that overall liquidity or total financial assets comprising a wide range of tangible and intangible assets links the real economic activity with the monetary conditions.

Patinkin (1961) has shown that the existence of financial intermediaries does not in principle impair the efficacy of open-market policy. However, he views that it only affects the conditions under which the monetary authorities operate in the bond market with the assumption that the behaviour and functions of financial intermediaries are fully known. Nevertheless their existence may impair the efficacy of monetary policy mainly because it introduces an uncertain link between the actions of monetary authorities and their effects on the economy especially when there are lagged effects.

Aschhiem (1963) focusses on the question whether the widely accepted, conventional operating goals of monetary policy are necessary or desirable for future enhancement of their effectiveness given that financial institutions are adaptive as reflected in their diversification and proliferation. Brunner and Meltzer (1963) contend that while the influence of evolving financial institutions on the mechanism linking monetary policy with the pace of economic activity had attracted widespread attention, a systematic set of hypothesis describing financial markets and their interaction with the markets for real assets and output have not been provided. They provide a broad outline of a theoretical framework, which appears to explicate the role of financial intermediaries in the monetary processes. Tobin and Brainard (1963) address the questions such as, whether existence of uncontrolled financial intermediaries vitiates monetary control and the consequences of subjecting these intermediaries to reserve requirements or to interest rate ceilings. They mainly conclude that the presence of uncontrolled banks does not imply that monetary control through the supply of currency has no effect on the economy. Besides, the presence of non-bank intermediaries does not mean that monetary control through commercial banks is ineffective. These issues are theoretically considered under a general equilibrium model in financial and capital market and aim to trace the effects of monetary controls and of structural changes.

Winjbergen (1983) presents a theoretical macro-model having an in built financial system typical of the less developed countries, characterised by absence of security markets and existence of curb markets. In this context he analyses the credit policy and the transmission channel of monetary policy into the supply side of the economy through the cost of working capital. In these economies it is assumed that domestic credit is an effective instrument to control the net foreign exchange assets. Besides, it also assumes a high speed of adjustment in asset markets. According to Wijnbergen, this fails to capture the effect of credit policies on real growth and inflation. In order to analyse the long-run aspects, there is a need to construct an open growth model. Therefore, his model highlights the substantial difference between the speed of adjustment in the goods and asset markets. It is viewed that commercial bank credit is used almost exclusively for business loans to finance working capital requirements. Consequently, there is a direct transmission mechanism between domestic credit and production, which gives a strong stag-flationary bias to credit policy. He states that under such conditions tight credit policy would initially increase inflation and thereby result in a slow down in production but improve current account. Therefore, crucial expenditure adjustment is made via reduction in investment, which leads to the question of long-run consequences on long-run capital stock. He concludes that in the short-run, there is a direct credit supply side link though the financing of working capital which leads to: under estimation of inflation and overestimation of real growth and current account improvement. To capture the long-run consequences, accumulation over time along with price dynamics are introduced so as to analyse the steady state features of the model.

Morgan (1992) examines the 'credit view' and 'money view' of monetary policy. He argues that despite easy monetary policies pursued by the Federal Reserve Bank and the resultant fall in the short-term market interest rates have not generated any marked increase in economic activity, which the money view holds. While pleading for the credit view approach, the author contends that the force of monetary policy partly depends upon the willingness of banks to lend. If banks are shy of lending, economic activity would stagnate and the transmission channel for monetary policy would be through changes in bank loans.

(l) Financial Innovation

Schumpeter (1934) was the earliest to recognise the importance of innovation in the economic growth process. According to him, innovation is the 'fundamental impulse that sets and keeps the capitalist engine in motion" and the competitive innovative activity matters most in the market. Under capitalism, the process of "creative destruction" continuously destroys the old economic structure and creates a new one. Following him, the literature distinguishes between three stages of change, viz., invention, innovation and diffusion. Invention refers to formation of new ideas and its subsequent feasibility of implementation. Innovation is associated with commercialisation of an invention. Diffusion relates to the adoption of innovation over time by various users in the society.

Schumpeter distinguishes between five types of innovation. These include,

(i) Introduction of new product or service or an improvement in the quality of an existing product or service;

(*ii*) introduction of new method of production;

(*iii*) development of new market;

(*iv*) exploitation of new source of supply, and

(*v*) reorganisation of methods of operation.

Innovations can also be classified into, viz., circumventive and transcendental. The former relates to free market response by those who would like to circumvent consequences of regulatory and monetary controls. The latter is associated with all types of innovations that are unrelated with regulations, such as, emergence of Certificates of Deposits (CDs) and other money market instruments. Silber's (1983) constraint induced hypothesis considers internal and external ones. It is argued that the financial innovations in terms of new instruments or practices takes place to reduce the financial constraints on firms. Internal constraints take the form of balance sheet constraints such as, target growth rates, liquidity that influence utility optimisation problem. The external constraints take the form of Government regulations and market restrictions. A firm in normal conditions maximises its objective function subject to existing constraints.

Silber (1983) argues that innovations refine the financial system by, improving the ability to bear risk; reducing the transaction costs; and circumventing outmoded regulations. There are two processes of technological innovations, viz., technology-push and demand-pull hypothesis. The former assumes that the firm's research staff's initiates the innovative process. It is later commercialised by the marketing staff. The latter associated with Schmookler (1966) emphasizes the role of demand factors in inducing innovations. Under this, the marketing and the production staff identify the potential innovation and the research staffs study the feasibility of it. The former model of the incentive to innovate under different market structures was developed by Arrow (1962). The incentive to innovate is measured by the potential profit to be earned under competitive and monopolistic market conditions. These two market conditions are compared with socially optimal conditions.

Spellman (1976) adopted a one-sector model under long-run growth equilibrium. He finds that macroeconomic impact of financial innovation results in upward shift in the stock of demand for wealth, due to increased asset liquidity. It also reduces the dispersions in real yield on account of improved investment allocations.

Backus, Brainard, Smith and Tobin (1980), have developed a model of financial and non-financial economic behaviour under a flow of funds accounting framework to trace the asset accumulation process and economic activity and estimate for the United States. They consider institutional innovations, government policies, structural changes, demographic and technology to simulate short-term and long-term consequences. Their theoretical model consists of, (a) four sectors, viz., households, financial intermediaries, businesses and government; (b) five assets, viz., high-powered money, bank deposits, government bonds, business equity and business loans; and (c) one commodity. The four sectors are the columns and the five assets are the rows in the flow of funds accounting framework. A sixth row is introduced which is the negative sum of the first five and over these six rows, each column sums to zero. The sixth row or the IS equation implies that the sum of Household Saving, Business Investment, and Government Deficit equals zero. In the Household sector, the savings function include vector of real yields on the five assets including expectations of capital gain or loss, predetermined asset holding, factors determining net receipts and their expectations. The income account is given in the bottom rows. It is assumed that the business sector retains the entire real Gross National product for investment on replacement and net Investment, and sells Consumption and Government deficit to other sectors. The real earnings (RK-1), net of depreciation are distributed in dividends (RE per equity share) and in loan interest and NW/P is paid to household sector for labour. Income payment from Government bonds is the coupon while yield rb relevant for portfolio and savings decision depends on the expectations of bond prices and commodity prices as

$$P_B / P(1+r_b) = b + P_{b+1} / P_{+1} = b + P_{B+1} / P(1+\Pi_{+1})$$

Thus, if P_b is expected to remain unchanged, it will equal,

$$\frac{b}{rb\Pi_{+1} + \Pi_{+1}r_B} = \frac{b}{rb\Pi_{+1} + \Pi_{+1}r_B} \qquad (1)$$

They state that their model will address questions, such as whether effects of government budgets and debt crowd out or crowd in private capital formation, and what are the effects of regulations and innovations on financial intermediation. It is viewed that imperfect substitutability of bonds and capital implies that increases in the quantity of government debt may decrease the required rate of return on capital. Therefore there may be crowding in rather than crowding out. The effects of such changes could be inferred by simulation of the financial block through 'open market operations'.

Chamley and Honohan (1993) focus on the differences between various forms of repression and suggest that summarising their impacts on financial intermediation requires two measures, viz., intermediation cost wedge and the allowed loan interest spread over the cost of funds. Besides seignorage, other impositions on the financial system such as reserve requirements on banks and interest rate ceilings on bank lending are important particularly in developing countries. He adopts a simple competitive model of banking sector behaviour to illustrate the different impacts of reserve requirements and loan interest ceilings, so as to bring in the active role of banks in intermediating deposit funds into risky bank credit. The main role of banks is to select good loan projects. Under competitive equilibrium conditions, competition between banks would ensure that the rate of interest on deposits is lower than that of the marginal cost of funds by exactly the cost of holding required serves (the intermediation cost wedge). The banks also decide on the volume of lending and on the real resources devoted to monitoring and screening. It would ensure that the marginal return on lending equals the marginal cost of funds. The effect of policy instruments on bank behaviour depends upon whether the asset is risk free or not.

Melnick and Yashiv (1996) develop a theoretical model to capture the macro economic effects of financial innovation in Israel. By 'Financial Innovation', they "refer to the introduction of new, liquid assets that partially replace traditional money in agents' portfolio; technological progress in banking services that reduces the costs of transactions and changes in the regulatory environment that facilitate transaction". They argue that innovation affects the transaction costs of the consumers and thereby induces a portfolio shift. This affects the resources of financial intermediaries and hence their lending rate. The change in the interest rate further changes the long-term level of capital and thereby production and consumption.

(m) Regulation

Regulation is been viewed as the force behind financial innovation. Many have studied the relationship between the two and the most notable is that of Kane (1981). The regulatory dialectic view of financial innovation illustrates financial change as a consequence of continuing struggle between opposing economic (regulatees) and political (regulators). His main argument is that the burden of bank regulation increases the incentives to do things in a different way. Since, banks may adopt innovations, which may not be technologically beneficial but enables certain elements and concepts obsolete. Therefore, regulation reduces the innovation lags, which arise before an innovation is commercialised and runs parallel to regulation lags. Innovation lags are shorter than re-regulation lags as there is no profit incentives associated with the latter. Circumvention of regulation takes place through product substitution. Kane (1981) also demonstrates that financial innovations could be traced to some regulatory restrictions. According to Van Horne (1985), technological advances have been a major cause for innovation processes. He stressed that in the early 'seventies, regulatory changes induced financial innovations, while it was deregulation in the late 'seventies and 'eighties.

Regulation has been favoured in economic theory in terms of 'public interest'. The 'public interest' approach views that regulation is desirable for the consumers under conditions of monopoly and producer as well, for facilitating creation of mechanisms necessary for trade, and to correct market failure. Economists also recognise that costs of regulation involves moral hazards, compliance costs (extra costs imposed on private sector agents), dynamic costs (regulation as a barrier to change) and entry and exit costs. Thus, regulation is not an easy remedy and many factors, such as its format; appropriateness, objectives, implementation and its consequences need to be considered.

The importance of regulation has been dealt with by, Fama (1980, 1983), Horngren (1985), and Steinherr and Huveneers (1994). They view that in some of the developing economies, the regulatory measures are generally selective and are limited only to the banking financial intermediaries. The existence of other financial intermediaries, which are outside the central bank's control, sometime offset the direct effects of regulation.

Fama (1980) shows that the uniqueness of banks was the outcome of regulation and not due to the inherent financial intermediation process. Fama (1983) demonstrated that as currency and deposits are not perfect substitutes, under a simplified financial system, control of supply of currency is sufficient to control the price level. However, it is viewed that in the currency supply approach, price level control does not imply control of financial intermediation. In a subsequent paper in 1985, he presented evidence for the uniqueness of banks as a financial intermediary in terms of reserve requirements. Horngren (1985) investigates the effects of regulatory instruments within a framework of unregulated intermediaries and bank management under a financial general equilibrium model. In sum, he highlights that the existence of non-bank intermediaries and the ability of banks to circumvent regulations by active liability management are the two impediments in the use of bank regulations as instruments of monetary policy.

Ruminating on the performance of differently regulated financial institutions, Steinherr and Huveneers (1994) explore the question why regulatory approaches differ. They point out that the experiences in many countries show that the central role of financial intermediation in resource allocation has been brought under higher degree of controls than other sectors thereby reducing the role and scope of market forces, although this is justified in the early stage of the development process. However, they suggest that when major imperfections characterise financial markets, risk assessment becomes complicated due to uncertainty, insufficient information, excessive volatility in markets, markets incomplete and systematic risk not efficiently hedgeable; at this stage, financial intermediation by intermediaries becomes more important than by markets.

(n) Financial Fragility

In the literature a financial fragile situation is defined by Bernanke and Gertler (1990), as when the "potential borrowers (those with the greatest access to productive investments projects or with the greatest entrepreneurial skills) have low wealth relative to the sizes of their projects." This situation arises during the early stages of development in a prolonged recession or after a Fisherian debt-deflation situation, which leads to high agency costs and hence the poor performance of the investment sector and the economy.

Later, Mishkin (1996) defines a financial crisis: "A financial crisis is a nonlinear disruption to financial markets in which adverse selection and moral hazard problems become much worse, so that financial markets are unable to efficiently channel funds to those who have the most productive investment opportunities." According to Mishkin (1996), there are several factors that cause financial crisis which in turn adversely affect economic activity. These include,

(i) Increases in interest rates which lead to credit rationing and to adverse selection problem;

(ii) Increases in uncertainty in the financial markets due to failure of a prominent financial or nonfinancial institution, recession, political instability and stock market crash;

(iii) Asset market effects on balance sheets, for instance, deterioration of balance sheet worsens and results in adverse selection and moral hazard problems; and

(iv) Bank panics.

Tobin (1982) states that in the macroeconomic theory and policy, "financial and capital markets are at their best highly imperfect coordinators of saving and investment" which cannot be remedied by rational expectations. "This failure of coordination is a fundamental source of macroeconomic instability and the opportunity for macroeconomic policies for stabilization". He therefore, suggests asset disaggregation as essential for analysing financing of capital accumulation of Government deficits, money and debt management policies, international capital movements, foreign exchange markets and financial intermediation.

Bernanke and Gertler (1990), in their theoretical two-period general equilibrium model of investment finance, argue that financial instability or financial fragility occurs when entrepreneurs, want to undertake investment projects with low net worth. The heavy reliance on external finance that this implies causes the agency costs of investment to be high. High agency costs leads to inefficient investment. Thus, financial stability is an important goal of policy. More important is the relationship between financial stability and economic performance. In sum they illustrate that both quantity of investment spending and its expected returns will be sensitive to "credit worthiness of borrowers as reflected in their net worth positions".

Davis (1992) addresses the issue of predictive power of UK domestic bond market spreads in relation to indicators of financial fragility. In his theory of the determination of credit quality spreads, it is assumed that the spread between the yield on a private debt issue and a risk-free public bond in the domestic market depends on six factors, viz., (i) default risk, (ii) call risk (bonds may be liquidated early which is inconvenient for the lender), (iii) tax exemption status, (iv) term or period maturity, (v) screening costs and (vi) market liquidity. The most important is the default risk although any observed changes arise due to all the above factors. In order to cover the extra risk, the lender would desire a higher expected return as compensation. The market assessment of a default risk is the difference between the yield on a private and public bonds of similar maturity, callability and tax features. The overall default risk on the bonds varies according to the risk position of the borrower and the economy. The risk perception declines in the event of bailouts by central bank or government. Davis (1992) also observes that the traditional theory classifies default risk further into risk associated with the balance sheets, business risks and the state of the economic cycles. He states that all these risks together influence the probability of default by the bond issuer and are reflected in the yield spreads of private over government. He also considers factors such as quantity rationing of credit, market segmentation and market imperfections. Thus spreads may be a useful predictor of financial fragility.

Calomiris (1995) addresses the issue of how financial institutions, contracting firms and Government financial policies affect the degree of macroeconomic volatility. These relationships are referred to in the literature as 'Financial Fragility'. Defining the sources of financial "shocks" and those arising due to other shocks captures the volatility of the economic activity on account of the financial system. Financial shocks are those disturbances originating from financial markets, which affect real economic activity. The other shocks arise due to the method in which financial contracts, markets and intermediaries serve to aggregate shocks originating elsewhere. In the recent years, macroeconomic theorists and financial economists view that financial relationships are more than epiphenominal when output variance is more with financial arrangements acting as source and propagators of shocks. Financial propagation takes place in the form of cash-flow constraints, balance sheet constraints/leverage constraints, external supply of funds constraints (limitations on bank credit) and financial regulations that magnify business cycles. The economic activity is more volatile in response to variation in exogenous disturbances as a result of these related factors. Financial shocks can be as important as financial propagators in contributing macroeconomic fragility. Distinction between financial shocks and propagators is unclear. He also states that financial shocks can be as important as financial propagators in contributing macroeconomic fragility.

Distinction between financial shocks and propagators is however unclear. Thus, one literature focuses on the benefits of government intervention to stabilize financial markets. This calls for financial safety net, like deposit insurance, support by the central banks, regulation and deregulation of banks. The government intervention could offset negative externalities to produce greater systemic stability. Financial fragility can be overcome by government interventions, but it can have a destabilizing effect on the economy. The government policy should, therefore, take into account the destabilizing consequences in the areas of bank regulation, taxation, credit subsidisation, monetary control and the lender of the last resort. Financial fragility arises due to informational asymmetry and systemic risks, which cannot be avoided in a dynamic capitalistic economy.

Minsky (1995) argues that although financial factors find no place in the modern economic theory in the determination of the course of the economy, modern capitalist economies use Treasury or Central bank to prevent and contain financial instability. Instability arises due to increase in fragility and with complexity in the financial structure. Financial fragility is characteristic of an economy wherein the funds available to meet payment commitments on liabilities are determined by income flows (gross profits of firms and wages for households); although the income flows are determined by investment and consumption spending. The investment and consumption are financed by internal funds and borrowings. The financial system possesses two attributes, viz., robustness and resilience and fragility negates these attributes. The change in the importance of Government changes the fragility/resilience relations in the capitalist financial structures.

(o) *Financial Supervision*

Post financial crisis in Asia, recent research on financial sector stability and growth have emphasised the key role of effective financial regulation and supervision policy. Country specific and cross-country studies have confirmed the significant impact of prudential regulation policy on the stability and performance of the former financial sector [Brownbridge and Kirkpatrick, 2000; Williamson and Mahar (1998); Demirguc-Kunt and Detragiache (1998); Barth, Caprio and Levine, (2000)]. In developing countries, the bank based system prevail and major reforms took place during the mid 'eighties and early 'nineties. The US model of regulation and supervision has been adopted by most of them. The Prudential reforms followed were broadly similar, although the scope of the reforms differed between countries. The Basle Committee's Core Principles for Effective Banking Supervision, drawn up in 1997, was the basic framework that involves a set of detailed prudential regulations (e.g. minimum requirements for capital to risk assets, restrictions on banks' asset portfolios including restrictions on large loan exposures and insider lending, auditing requirements (CAMELS) etc.). Supervision entails on-site inspections and off-site monitoring of banks based around the CAMEL principles Supervisors aim to inspect banks at regular intervals and banks are required to submit regular financial reports to the supervisors.

The Basle Committee's new norms on capital adequacy based on three pillars (viz., minimum capital standards, supervisory review and market discipline) of 1999 were revised in 2001 and the country-wise comments have been made public. The G-7 countries established the financial stability forum to exchange information and extend cooperation among various agencies and institutions associated with financial stability. In order to strengthen the financial system, the forum established international codes and standards in April 2001 and also a task force to implement them.

Several LDCs experienced weaknesses in the implementation of prudential reforms. According to

Brownbridge and Kirkpatrick, (2000), there are three main sources of weakness. First, some of the important prudential restrictions were not included while provisions that are not strict or precise in banking legislations were included. Second, lack the requisite personnel to carry out effective supervision in some regulatory authorities. Third, lack of able or willing supervisors to rigorously enforce the prudential regulations. Several proposals and approaches have been made for the effectiveness of prudential regulations in developing countries (Caprio and Honohan, 1999; Honohan and Stiglitz, 1999; Brownbridge and Kirkpatrick, 2000). With the continuing fragmentation of financial markets in developing countries reflected in the growth of the microfinance sector, the microfinance institutions have expanded. This has in turn necessitated putting them into a regulatory framework.

Section 2: Empirical Research

The recent cointegration techniques with emphasis on estimation and identification of long run economic relationships between variables have made it suitable to apply to endogenous growth models in the empirical studies. Empirically, focus has been to assess the causal relationship between financial and real growth and identify new indicators of financial development. It is viewed that the new empirical research has gained prominence due to progress in theory and availability of historical data (Gertler, 1988). Early empirical contributions of Patrick (1966), Goldsmith (1969), McKinnon (1973) and Shaw (1973) asset that financial intermediation is an important determinant of real growth rate. Greenwood and Jovanovic (1989) on the other hand emphasize alternative channels by which intermediaries affect growth rates.

The empirical studies reviewed in this section are classified into cross-country studies and country-specific in a chronological order. The studies differ in terms of techniques/models and variables used.

(i) Cross-country Studies

Goldsmith (1969) was the foremost to study causal relationship between financial and real sectors using a time series analysis for 35 developed and developing countries from 1860 to 1960. He used Financial Ratios for the purpose of analysis. He identified the ratio of total financial assets to National wealth as an important indictor of financial development. Goldsmith illustrated a strong and positive relationship between ratio of financial institutions' assets to Gross National Product and the output per capita. He showed that the periods of rapid economic growth tend to be associated with above average rates of financial development. He found that as real income and wealth increase both in terms of aggregate and per capita levels, the size and complexity of the financial super structure also grows.

Importance of various financial institutions in terms of total assets of financial institutions or total financial assets was recognised by McKinnon in his complimentarity hypothesis. Shaw (1973) illustrates that the experience of countries such as Uruguay, Ghana, Iran and Thailand during 1963-68 show divergence between nominal and real financial growth. When finance is shallow in relation to national income or non-financial wealth, it bears a low, often low negative real rates of return. The holders of financial assets are not rewarded for real growth in their portfolios but are penalised.

Jao (1976) tests the hypothesis that economic growth is best measured by per capita real income and it is positively related to financial deepening as represented by rate of per capita real balances and the degree of intermediation. He finds a positive and significant relationship between them. The variables used include, per head of M1 (sum of demand deposits and currency with public) and M2 (sum of M1 plus time of saving deposits), M3 (sum of M2 plus deposit liabilities of non bank financial intermediaries) and per capita real income. The 34 countries including less developed countries and developing countries were also split according to the per capita nominal income after allowing for inflation and currency depreciation. In order to find the reciprocal relationship between economic growth and financial deepening, Spearman's rank correlation coefficients were worked out. It was found that the rank correlation between average proportionate growth of real per capita Gross Domestic Product is negatively correlated with M1/Y and positively with M2/Y although not very high. The real money balances-M1 and M2 and ratio of M1/Y and M2/Y were positively correlated. According to his study, the results strongly confirm that real balances as a factor input, contribute significantly to productivity and output growth due to their role in facilitating transactions and resource allocations reducing search and information costs, and providing exchange and specialization. It is also inferred that the results support the argument that inflationary finance, as long as it reduces real balances and discouraged the willingness to hold them, is detrimental to economic development in the long run. The relationship between output growth and intermediation was found to be tenuous. Of the 13 regression equations, 9 intermediation coefficients had the expected signs but only 3 were statistically significant. M3/Y performed better and it implied that intermediation should appropriately be measured by widening scope of monetary liabilities. Regarding intermediation effect, the empirical evidence supports the view that narrowly defined money is a poor indicator of financial development and economic growth is associated with accumulation of financial assets from the point of view of wealth holders.

Fry (1978) empirically tests the McKinnon and Shaw's model of finance in economic development and their alternate theories on how financial conditions affect saving and economic growth. The results of pooled time series analysis for seven less developed Asian countries support the view that financial conditions do influence saving and growth. However, Shaw's transmission mechanism is proved to be correct for 10 Asian less developed countries in the empirical tests and rejects McKinnon's complementary hypotheses. He finds a negative coefficient of the saving ratio, which is inconsistent with the complementary hypothesis. There is substitution between money and other financial assets as indicated by the negative coefficient of (d-P^e). He finds a positive effect of real rate of interest on domestic saving and economic growth. Thus, McKinnon and Shaw's stress on importance on financial conditions in the development process is fully justified. He points out that the Asian countries used in his analysis have achieved stages of development beyond those held by the complementarity assumptions. There exist institutional and non-institutional modern financial systems. Deliberate intervention has resulted in differentiation of assets.

Fry (1980a) presents a quantitative estimate of cost of financial repression in developing countries and concludes that in the estimates of savings and growth functions, the cost of financial repression appears to be around half a percentage point in economic growth foregone for every one percentage point by which real deposit rate of interest is set below the market equilibrium rate. He finds evidence for real credit availability mechanism from pooled time series, cross-country analysis of interdependency of Saving, Investment and growth in 61 developing countries. The investment function consists of the ratio of domestic credit to Gross National Product, ratio of Currency to income. Signs of coefficient agree with apriori expectations in the saving function. It includes variables such as, per capita income, share of mining sector in Gross National Product, purchasing power of exports and the lagged saving rate which all raise the national saving rate, while foreign saving rate and predictability of inflation reduce it. The saving function indicates that investment will adjust through the real credit availability mechanism to national and foreign saving.

Adopting the approach by Fry (1978, 1980b) and for the same set of countries but for a different sample period, Giovannini (1983) estimates the effect of real rate of interest on savings. For the dependent variables he uses aggregate domestic savings (households, corporate and government). The explanatory variables include, real income growth, level of per capita real income in logarithms, nominal interest rate less the realized future rate of inflation, foreign savings relative to income, lagged dependent variables and a set of dummy variables. He assumes rational expectations, wherein the difference between the realized (ex post at time t) and ex ante real interest rates has zero mean and is uncorrelated with variables known at time t-1. He finds that coefficient of real interest rates is negative and insignificant for 6 countries in the instrumental variables regressions. The coefficient of per capita income and foreign savings are not significant. It implies that only increases in transitory income raise savings level and savings and investments determine the trade balance deficit. This is in contrast with the work on savings in the less developing countries where foreign savings substitutes domestic savings; while the former itself being is a determinant of domestic savings.

Goldsmith (1983) used Financial Interrelations Ratio (FIR) for India to explore the relationship between financial development and economic growth. He concludes that the financial and economic development takes place together and the financial structure has a significant impact on the economic infrastructure by accelerating the growth of real Gross National Product and wealth.

Jung (1986) explores international evidence for 56 countries on the causal relationship between financial development and economic growth and also its temporal behaviour by using Granger tests. Two alternative proxies for financial development are used, viz., currency ratio, defined as the ratio of currency to narrow money (M1), and the sum of currency and demand deposit. The latter is used to study the complexity of the financial structure. He assumes that a decrease in currency ratio is accompanied by real growth initially, as there is diversification of financial assets and liabilities and more transactions take place through non-currency. The second measure is the ratio of broad money (M2) to nominal Gross National Product or Gross Domestic Product, which is regarded as a monetisation variable. It is viewed that increased specialization in the use of productive factors would generate a rising stream of income and stock of real and financial assets. The monetisation variable is designed to reveal the real size of the financial sector of a growing economy. The increase in the ratio would reflect the faster development of the financial sector and vice versa. Of the 56 countries chosen, 19 were developed industrialized countries and each had at least 15 annual observations. Four regressions were run for each country-two for currency ratio and two for monetisation and income with a maximum lag of 2 years. The results suggest a moderate support for supply leading phenomena for the less developing countries when currency ratio was used. The causality running from financial development to economic growth was found to be both unidirectional and frequently observed than the reverse. This was particularly observed when the currency ratio was used as a proxy thereby validating Patrick's (1966) views on the importance of financial development in the less developing countries. In the case of developed countries, the reverse causal direction was observed, regardless of the pattern of causality used. The use of monetisation variable for developed and less developed countries yielded similar results in terms of the causality pattern. Mixed results were obtained on the Patrick's hypothesis in the case of temporal causality patterns.

Gupta (1987) examines the role of financial factors as determinants of savings in developing countries. For the purpose, using real interest rate and financial intermediation and pooled-time series data, he estimates a model of savings for Asia, Latin America and the total sample as well for the period 1967 to 1976 for 22 countries. The variables used were Gross national Savings, Gross National Product, Financial Intermediation Ratio, Consumer Price Index, and 12-month time deposits of commercial banks. He found that there are sufficient differences in the effects of variables to caution against pooling of data. He found overwhelming support to permanent income hypothesis in its weak form in both these regions thereby stressing the importance of income growth as a determinant of saving. He finds no support for the financial repressionist of Structuralist hypothesis in Latin America. However, he found some support for these in Africa. For both the regions, nominal interest rate had a positive sign thereby supporting the financial repressionist view that removal of interest rate ceilings will be conducive for increasing savings in the developing countries.

Dornbusch and Reynaso (1989), test the impact of increased real interest rates represented by real deposit rates on the efficiency of investment measured by incremental capital output ratio. The ratio of quasi money to Gross Domestic Product is used as a financial deepening variable. A sample of 41 cross section countries using averages for the period 1965-85 is considered. In order to discern the growth effects on investment and inflation, the variables used include, per capita growth rate, level of per capita income in 1965, average change in capital-labour ratio and an inflation dummy. They find that high inflation interferes with growth. They conclude that the empirical support for growth effects of a liberalised financial system is episodic.

There is a large volume of literature on the interest elasticity of savings and investment using a large cross section of countries particularly in the mid eighties. However, the evidence is not firm and is also contradictory. Reynoso (1989) found that savings increase rapidly as real interest rates move from sharply negative to just below zero. However this effect tapers off with the interest rates becoming positive and negative, as real rates become highly positive. Using 23 developing countries, for the period 1975-87 Gelb (1989) found a positive though weak relationship between aggregate investment and interest rates. Gelb (1989) also found that most of the positive association between real interest rates and growth stem from the efficiency effect rather than the level of investment. He finds a positive though weak relationship between aggregate investment and interest rates.

Gelb (1989) in his sample of 34 developing countries for the period 1974 to 1985 used real interest rates and monetary aggregates as an indicator of financial development. He found that one group of countries showed a positive real deposit rates of interest, the second showed a moderately negative deposit rates of interest and the third group experienced strong negative deposit rates. This was despite the fact that deposit rates were administratively fixed. He found strong and positive relationship between economic growth and real deposit rate of interest. Greene and Vilenueva (1991) found a negative and significant effect of real interest rates on investment. Demetriades and Devereux (1992) with a sample of 63 developing countries and a data spanning from 1961 to 1990, find that the effect of higher interest rates is stronger on the cost of capital than the effect on enhanced supply of investible funds. Thus a higher interest rates went on to diminish investment.

Fry (1978, 1980 and 1995) in his several studies found that across a sample of 14 Asian developing countries saving rate was positively influenced by increases in real interest rates. Giovannini (1983, 1985) pointed out that the Fry's findings were not robust to the changes in time or region.

Later Fry (1995) himself agreed that the effect was small and diminished in the more recent years mostly in Asia.

Laumas (1990) examines the role of financial liberalization in a developing economy in the context of decline in the barter sector. The data on monetised sector for India is used from the period 1954-55 to 1974-75. The money demand function comprises interest rate on time deposit with a maturity structure of 12 months as a proxy for weighted average, expected rate of inflation represented by rate of change in Gross National Product deflator lagged by one period, Investment to Income ratio to reflect demand for money for investment finance and time deposits. Laumas found complementarity between money and capital in estimating demand for money function; and complementarity between money and capital in estimating investment function. The two stage least square estimation procedure is used on corrected first order auto correlation of time series data. The exogenous variables include real rate of return, real interest rates, ratio of government investment to income, real monetised income. He provides evidence for the efficacy of financial liberalization as a method for increasing capital formation in India. For the investment function, Laumas used the ratio of sum of profits before tax, depreciation provisions and other provisions to Gross Fixed Assets as a proxy for real rate of interest. For measuring inflation, he used Gross National Product deflator. He finds that the demand for real time deposits is positively related to real monetised income.

Feldman and Gang (1990) explore the link between financial development and the low relative prices of services in less developed countries (less developed countries). They use a three-sector model with non-traded goods to trace the causal relationship between financial policies and structure of relative prices and also study the effect of financial repression on relative prices of non-traded goods. The variables used include, per capita Gross Domestic Product (as it raises the relative demand for services), M2 (as government policies affect money supply), ratio of M2 to Gross Domestic Product (as financial repression reduce the loanable fund from the domestic sources), and M2/Gross Domestic Product (as it measures the income velocity of money). Using a simple Ordinary Least Square regression (log and log-linear), they find, negative correlation between income velocity and relative price of non-traded goods, which is strong and significant. To find the robustness, Two Stage Least Square method was adopted. The additional variables include, price level, real government spending per capita and real per capita money supply. They find support for their hypothesis that financial repression depresses the relative price of non-traded goods.

Gavin and Hausmann (1990) view that the banking crisis originates in a credit boom which permits almost any borrower to service debt by borrowing from alternate source. This robs the lender from the information required by him to distinguish between sound and risky borrowers. In a macroeconomic crisis, continued debt servicing becomes difficult and several borrowers default on their loans.

St. Hill (1992) analyses the implications of various stages of banking for economic development and explores empirical evidence to suggest policy guidelines. In his empirical analysis, similar to that of Jung's (1986), a contingency table approach is used. The currency ratio, monetisation ratio and relative size of manufacturing sector are used. The services sector in less developed countries is largely a subsistence type sector where monetary transactions are relatively unimportant. Therefore, he uses manufacturing output in Gross Domestic Product as a proxy for size of the monetised sector. High currency ratio indicates dominance of Supply leading phenomena and a low ratio implied the dominance of the Demand following phenomena. A low monetary ratio implied Supply leading and a high ratio Demand following. He used Granger Causality test and his empirical analysis supports a supply-leading pattern among less developed countries at a relatively low level of financial development.

Li and Skully (1992) compare financial performance of two groups of Asian economies, viz., Newly Industrialized Economies of Hong Kong, Taiwan, Singapore and Korea, and less developed, Association of South East Asian member economies of Thailand, Indonesia, Malaysia and Philippines. They focus on how financial variables such as savings, capital and money affect economic development. According to them there are two frameworks of analysis in the development financial literature, viz., (i) two-gap analysis, (ii) Financial repression-McKinnon and Shaw (1973). The former pointed the inadequacy of foreign exchange and domestic savings as two important constraints in capital accumulation. The investment, saving gap tends to be the initial constraint and replaced by trade gap. The latter emphasized the problem of 'shallow' finance and recommended a policy of financial liberalization and quality of investment. They use the Ordinary Least Square method and initially estimate for the period 1953-54 to 1976-77 and extend it for the period 1976-77 to 1988-89. They cover different measures of monetary aggregates, viz., M1, M2 and M^* (includes deposits in development banks and postal saving banks) savings rate, foreign resource use and ratio of money stock to capital formation. Their results support the two-gap hypothesis that an economy to be less reliant on external borrowings the marginal savings rate must rise over time. This is valid for Newly Industrialised Economies and three Association of South East Asian economies. With regard to marginal rate of foreign resource use the Newly Industrialised Economies perform better as compared with the poor performance of the Association of South East Asian economies, which is explained by the financial sectors' institutional structure. As regards money stock to capital formation ratio, it showed a negative relationship with M1 and M2 for the entire period in four Newly Industrialised Economies and four Association of South East Asian economies. It implies that the economy is 'shallow', and the monetary variable has a weak influence on investment growth. The process of financial liberalization differed from economy to economy. It showed that financial performance of some Association of South East Asian countries was less than satisfactory as compared with Newly Industrialised Economies. For the former, despite increase in marginal savings rate, foreign capital inflows did not result in income generation and improvement in investment. Newly Industrialised Economies did better where the foreign capital inflows as the past helped investment to expand in such a way that capital could be generated to remove foreign exchange constraint.

Saint Paul (1992) shows that financial markets affect technological choice. In the absence of financial markets, risk-averse individuals may prefer flexibility in technology rather than high productivity. With the presence of financial markets, there is the advantage of holding a diversified portfolio, which insures against negative demand shocks and it enables choice of productive technology.

Roubini and Sala-i-Martin (1992) recognise that financial intermediation is an important component of aggregate production function and emphasize the role of government policy while analysing the relationship between financial intermediation and growth. They find that the financial repressionist policies have negatives effects on economic growth. They conclude that there exists a systemic inverse relationship between growth and several measures of financial repression measured by real interest rates, distortions in financial markets, (bank reserves to M1 and inflation rates), and a negative relationship between growth and inflation rate. Further, their empirical analysis revealed that negative relationship exists between initial level of income and growth; human capital positively affects growth; Non-productive consumption and political instability are harmful to growth; distortion in the price of investment goods are negatively related to growth; and financial repression leads to negative real interest rates, high required reserve ratios and choice of a high inflation tax.

Ghani (1992) used a cross-country sample of 50 developing countries and obtained significant positive coefficients for human capital measured by number of years of schooling and financial development as measured by ratio of total assets of the financial system to Gross Domestic Product in 1965. However, he obtained negative coefficient while using per capita real Gross Domestic Product during the period 1965-1989.

De Gregorio and Guidotti (1992) examine empirical relationship between long-run growth and degree of financial development in the case of middle and low-income countries for a sample of 98 countries during 1960-85. Financial development is represented by ratio of bank credit to private sector to Gross Domestic Product. It is found that this indicator is significantly and positively related in the growth equation on a large cross-country sample but is negatively related while using panel data for 12 Latin American countries for the period 1950-85. The correlation was not significant during the 1950s and 1960s but was strongly negative in the 1970s and 1980s. Their major finding is that the main channel of transmission from financial development to growth is the efficiency of investment rather than its volume.

De Gregorio (1992) provides empirical evidence on the effects of borrowing constraints on human capital accumulation for two sample countries. The first one is of OECD countries and the other pertains to developing countries. He found that countries with borrowing constraints had lower human capital accumulation. Borrowing constraints had negative effects on secondary school enrolment ratios. Evidence also showed that tightening the borrowing constraints lowered growth. After controlling for human capital accumulation it was found that borrowing constraints were negatively correlated with growth.

King and Levine (1992) state the importance of allocating credit instead of merely using proxies for the overall size of the financial system as commonly used in the past studies. In their study four categories of financial indicators are used, viz., traditional measures of the size of formal financial system; relative importance of different financial institutions; relationship between growth and the distribution of assets by the financial system; and lastly interest rates measures to identify financially repressed economies and to quantify distortions. The size of the financial system is measured in terms of ratio of M1 to Gross Domestic Product; ratio of liquid liabilities; ratio of quasi-liquid liabilities and ratio of claims on the private sector by the Central Bank and deposit Money banks to Gross Domestic Product. Liquid-liabilities are defined as M1 plus interest bearing liabilities of the banking system plus demand and interest bearing liabilities of non-bank financial intermediaries. Quasi-liquid liabilities equal Liquid liabilities less M1. The relative importance of commercial banks and central banks is measured by ratio of central bank domestic assets to Gross Domestic Product; ratio of Deposit Money Banks Domestic Assets to Gross Domestic Product; and ratio of Deposit Money Banks Domestic Assets to Deposit Money Bank plus Central Bank Domestic Assets. The assets distribution is measured by the ratio of claims on the Non-Financial Private Sector by the Central banks and Deposit money Banks to total domestic credit as these represent broad indicators of the importance of asset distribution. In order to measure empirical relationship between interest rates and growth, a repressed interest rates variable is used which equals 1 if expost real interest rates average less than –5.0 during 1974 and 0 otherwise. The difference between the lending rate and the deposit rate is also used as another measure. King and Levine (1992) use three different methods to study the relationship between financial indictors and growth. Cross-country regressions with data averaged over the 1960-89 periods are used to gauge the robustness of the partial correlation between growth and the financial measures. Lastly, pooled cross-country time series regression with data averaged over 5 year intervals during the 1960-89 period is used to examine the partial correlations between growth and the financial indicators and the channel through which this relation runs. To measure the channels to growth, first growth is decomposed into investment share component and efficiency of investment component. Then their correlations with average and initial financial size indicators are examined. As per their major findings, many financial indicators are significantly correlated with growth. The partial correlation between growth and other financial measures remain statistically significant after controlling for initial conditions, dummy variables for countries in Sub-Saharan Africa and Latin America, and measures of monetary, fiscal and trade performance. Empirical relationship between growth and measures of asset distribution remain significant even when the regressions simultaneously include measures of overall financial size. The financial performance indicators are highly correlated with each other. Lastly, the channels through which growth and financial indicators are correlated, the cross-country regressions suggest that financial system indicators tend to be robustly correlated with growth only because they are highly correlated with the ratio of national investment to Gross Domestic Product while the pooled cross-country time series analysis suggests that they are linked through both investment and efficiency channels.

King and Levine in their empirical analysis have examined the relationship between financial Intermediaries and economic growth across a wide range of countries. The indicator of real economic activity is represented by Gross

Domestic Product Per Capita and the financial indicators is represented by M1/Gross Domestic Product, Liquid Liabilities to Gross Domestic Product, Central bank Domestic Credit, Deposit Money Bank Domestic Credit, Gross Claims on private sector to Gross Domestic Product and Claims on non-financial sector to total domestic Credit. In another article, King and Levine (1993a) present cross-country evidence on Schumpeter's view that financial system can promote economic growth covering 80 countries during 1960-1989. Based on their empirical findings the authors conclude that financial sector reform can importantly promote economic growth by improving the effectiveness of public policies.

Atje and Jovanovic (1993) address the question whether financial development measured by stock market development affects the level and/or growth rate of economic activity. Their results show that it has substantial effect on both. The growth effect of financial intermediation is classified into permanent and transitory. In the Greenwood-Jovanovic (1990) model, the financial intermediation is endogenous with no diminishing returns. To the reproducible factor, a permanent exogenous improvement in the financial structure would cause a permanent increase in the rate of growth. Atje and Jovanovic argue that if the returns to the reproducible factor diminish, better in intermediation could lead only to level effects. Therefore, they try to capture both growth and level effects for 94 countries. The variables used include, Gross Domestic Product per adult in 1985, growth rate of working age population between 1960-1985, investment as percentage of Gross Domestic Product averaged for period 19960-1985; percentage of working population in secondary school averaged for the period 1960-1985 the value traded in stock markets as a percentage of Gross Domestic Product averaged over the period 1980-85; growth rate of per capita Gross Domestic Product over the period 1980-1985; claims on the private sector by the monetary authority and deposit money banks as a percentage of Gross Domestic Product. The results show that in the growth effects, the credit extended to private and government banks to Gross Domestic Product has no effect on raising the return on investment. On the other hand, the ratio of annual value of all stock market trades to Gross Domestic Product affects growth strongly and positively. In the level effects, they find that the intermediations share in income tends to rise with the level of development both over time and across countries.

Hassan, Samad, Islam (1993), in their empirical study of McKinnon Complementarity and Shaw's financial deepening hypotheses in the case of Five South Asian Countries, find evidence for the Complementarity hypothesis in the less developed countries particularly with repressed financial markets. They use two-stage least square and Ordinary least square method to estimate the money demand function and the savings function. In their money demand function, per capita broad money deflated by Gross Domestic Product deflator expressed in natural logarithms is used as a proxy for money demand. The independent variables include ratio of Gross Domestic Savings to nominal Gross Domestic Product, real per capita Gross Domestic Product expressed in natural logarithms, actual inflation, and proxy for money demand lagged by one year. The variables in the savings function include proxy for money demand, real per capita Gross Domestic Product expressed in natural logarithms, growth rate of real per capita Gross Domestic Product and ratio of foreign savings to nominal Gross Domestic Product. Their regression results show a positive relationship between money demand and domestic savings. Pooled regression results further confirmed the existence of complementarity feature in the money demand function.

Jappelli and Pagano (1994) argue that real interest rates cannot serve as the channel of transmission but are a poor indicator of financial intermediation and generally of financial development. Under an over-lapping generations model where individuals live for three periods, they illustrate that liquidity constraints on households raise saving rate, strengthen the effect of growth on savings, increase growth rate if productivity growth is endogenous and lastly may increase welfare. Assuming the Hicks neutral technical progress, relate total factor productivity as an increasing function of time. Their result suggests that financial deregulation in the 1980's have contributed to the decline in national saving and growth rates in OECD countries. They test the effect of growth on saving with liquidity constraints and use national savings as percentage of Net national Product (NNP) and maximum loan to value Ratio. While presenting an endogenous and exogenous growth models, it is illustrated that in the latter, liquidity constrains raise aggregate savings and strengthen the effect of growth on raising and in the former, the higher saving rate induced by liquidity constraints too translates into faster growth. It is also suggested that the test of significance of loan to value ratio coefficient is a test of endogenous growth and imperfect capital mobility. While a zero coefficient of the loan to value ratio may indicate either that growth does not depend upon liquidity constraints or that there is free capital flows across national borders, a positive coefficient is consistent with endogenous growth and imperfect capital mobility. In contrast to the findings of Roubini and Sala-i-Martin (1991), where proxies for financial market distortions are negatively correlated with growth, Jappelli and Pagano find that financial development tends to promote growth rather than inhibiting growth and complements the view that financial repression in the business loans market reduced productive investment and growth.

Gregorio and Guidotti (1995) argue that in cases of prolonged or deep recessions associated with financial crises using data averages over long periods may be contaminated by cycle effects. They show that while in cross-sectional regressions involving a worldwide sample of countries financial intermediation is positively linked with growth, in panel regressions only for Latin American countries the relationship is negative. They view that their results for Latin America may reflect the lasting impact of the frequent financial crises, which the region had suffered. However, they do not offer direct evidence to show that financial crises distort the relationship between financial intermediation and growth.

Johnston and Pazarbasioglu (1995) dealt with the role of financial reforms to promote growth. They find that financial reforms have structural effects and the financial variables and reforms are important determinants of growth. However, the impact of reforms depended on whether the country experienced financial crisis and the quality of reforms. Pill and Pradhan (1995) used broad money, narrow money, bank credit and real interest rates as indicators of financial development and for growth use per capita Gross Domestic Product as a proxy. Ahmed and Ansari (1995) explored the applicability of "McKinnon-Shaw" hypothesis for Bangladesh and found weak support for their hypothesis. They chose price variables to proxy financial factors for growth.

Demetriades and Hussein (1996), found little evidence for financial sector development to lead economic growth. They found that causality patterns varied across countries. On the other hand, Wachtel (1995) found that financial sector development Granger causes economic growth.

Berthelemy and Varoudakis (1996) test the existence of multiple steady states associated with financial and educational development. In their empirical analysis for 95 countries during the period 1961 to 1985, the financial sector indicator is measured by ratio of Money plus quasi money to Gross Domestic Product. They use secondary school enrolment rate as a proxy for initial stock of human capital.

The degree of openness is measured by ratio of imports plus exports to Gross Domestic Product as international trade would promote growth and reap benefits arising out of specialisation. It would also reflect policy-induced distortions, natural distortions arising from size and geographical location (transportation costs). The control variables for steady states growth are government consumption expenditure as percentage to Gross Domestic Product, and indicator of political instability and expect a negative relationship. The results obtained with Ordinary Least Square method show that all the estimated coefficients had the expected sign and were significant except Government expenditure. The negative coefficient of initial level of per capita Gross Domestic Product indicated existence of global convergence across national economies. It showed strong influence of money supply on growth rate. It showed a positive influence of openness on long run growth. According to them, the conjunction of the financial sector's positive influence in capital efficiency and real sectors external effect on the financial sector via the volume of savings sets a cumulative process, which is a potential source of poverty traps.

Thornton (1996) applied Granger-causality tests on 22 Asian, Latin American and Carribean developing countries. He finds that financial deepening does not make much difference to economic growth. In the case of 8 countries, no lead-lag relationship was detected and in 6 countries economic growth led to financial deepening. Financial deepening is measured by ratio of total bank deposits to nominal Gross Domestic Product and real output is measured by real Gross Domestic Product in 1985 prices. He finds that in 8 of the 22 countries deepening and growth appeared to be contemporaneously determined. In 5 countries financial deepening promoted economic growth at 5 per cent level of significance and in 2 countries at 10 per cent. In these cases there was no evidence for unidirectional causality from financial deepening to economic growth, while in the case of Mexico the same was negatively observed. Unidirectional causality from economic growth to financial deepening in the case of 4 countries at 5 per cent level of significance and for 2 countries at 10 per cent was observed. Feedback effects between financial deepening and economic growth was observed in the case of 2 countries.

Demirigüc-Kunt and Detragiache (1997), in a study covering the period from 1980 to 1994, use a number of variables to determine the probability of banking crisis. These relate to: real interest rate, share of credit to private sector and growth in credit and all three variables are positively and significantly related to the probability of occurrence of a banking crisis. Besides, the interest rate, credit to private sector, and growth in credit are influenced by factors other than financial liberalisation. Demirguc-Kunt and Detragiache (1998) also investigated empirically on a panel of fifty-three countries during the period 1980-95 and showed that a banking crisis was more likely in a liberalized financial system, particularly when the institutional support was weak.

Honohan (1997) alleges that the causes of banking crises span a wide spectrum. He divides banking crises into three syndromes: (i) Macroeconomic epidemics; (ii) Microeconomic deficiencies and (iii) Endemic crises in a government protected system. Categories (ii) and (iii) describe the underdeveloped and government managed financial system typically found in a financially repressed economy. Honohan attributes change of regime, which altered the nature, scale, frequency and correlation pattern of shocks to the economic and financial system for increasing the riskiness of traditional behaviour, or introducing new and inexperienced players. Citing the cases of developing countries, Honohan defines the types of regime changes as financial repression, financial liberalisation, structural transformation, political developments, privatisation, and technological innovation and globalisation in finance. Of these, financial liberalisation, structural transformation, privatisation and technological innovation and globalisation often result from financial reforms.

Arestis and Demetriades (1997), find that the relationship between the level of development of a country's financial system and its economic growth performance is not necessarily robust. The health of a country's financial system, its institutional structure, notably the respective roles of banks and the stock market, all can have an important impact on growth, which is not always explicit. They find weak correlations between the development of the banking system and the level of economic growth when the financial system suffers from ill health. In countries that have experienced financial crises, such as Chile and Spain, the banking system development tends to lag behind the economic growth. In case of Germany and Japan, where the banking system development has been without problems, the banking system stimulates growth in other sectors of the economy. According to them, since 1980, over 100 developing countries have suffered some kind of serious banking crisis, which has left many banks insolvent and lead to a loss of depositors' confidence. As a result, substantial direct costs of these crises tend to fall on taxpayers. In Kuwait the cost amounts to as high as 50% of its GDP, followed by Chile with 30% and Venezuela with more than 20%. Several other countries, like Mexico, the Czech Republic and Hungary, are still going through such crises at costs that are more than 10% of their GDP. In Germany, Arestis and Demetriades find that the development of the banking system is directly linked to economic growth and that the direction of causality runs from the former to the latter. The development of the stock market is also correlated with economic growth but the link is a less direct one: stock market development helps to explain the development of the banking system. However, stock market volatility has a negative effect on German output: In the US, banking system and the stock market appear to be competing forces in that development of one seems to come at the expense of the other. Second, while both banking system and stock market developments are positively correlated with US output in the long run, causality runs from output to the financial system and not *vice versa*.

Arestis and Demetriades (1999, p. 447) stressed that the lack of experience by banks, borrowers and prudential supervisors in a context of financial liberalization (albeit not complete) was surely a main factor explaining the subsequent crises. In general, financial liberalization meant international markets displaced domestic markets. Long-term productive investment never materialized either. Instead short-term speculation activities flourished whereby firms adopted risky financial strategies, causing banking crises and economic collapse. Arestis and Demetriades (1999) stated that theoretical models predict that financial liberalisation can promote economic development, by increasing saving, investment, and the productivity of capital, which depends on the assumptions of perfect information and perfect competition.

Arestis and Demetriades present new evidence on the role of financial repression (government controls on the banking system, notably interest rates) in South Korean economic growth. Contrary to the convention that controls are detrimental to the development of the banking system, they find that imposition of such controls enhanced the Korean banking system's development and they speculate that this result may reflect its cartel nature. Under such a situation, financial liberalisation (freeing interest rates and other financial prices from government control) could have a negative impact on banking system development and growth.

Levine and Zervos (1998) found that stock market liquidity and banking development, for 47 countries during

1976-1993, had a positive effect on economic growth, capital accumulation and productivity, despite controlling for important factors such as, fiscal policy, openness to trade, education and political stability. Singh and Weisse (1998) recently examined stock market development and capital flows for less developed countries. Slightly digressing, La Porta et al. (1997, 1998, 1999), Levine (1998, 1999) and Barth Caprio and Levine (2000) show that it is institutional factors that are key to financial structure changes and in particular the legal systems. Levine (1998), examined the relationship between the legal system, banking development and its impact on long run rates of growth, capital stock and productivity growth while Jayaratne and Strahan (1996) found that real per capita GDP rose significantly when intrastate banking restrictions were relaxed via improvements in the *quality* of bank lending. They stressed that states did not deregulate their banks to accommodate future growth opportunities, as only weak evidence was found for increased bank lending after banking branch reform while no evidence was found for increase in the rate of investment post reform thereby implying causality from financial development to growth.

Kwan, Wu and Zhang (1998) show, by employing exogeneity tests for several high performing Asian countries, that financial deepening has had a positive impact on output growth. Rajan and Zingales (1998*a*) stress that the initial level of financial development could be a leading indicator instead of a causal factor, if financial markets increase their lending in anticipation of faster growth. They stressed that financial development reduces the costs of external finance to firms and promotes their growth. Assume that different industries have their own efficient demand for external finance (investment minus internal cash flow) and that the distribution of the need for external finance by industry is very comparable across countries. In this setting, an industry with more demand for external finance should grow faster in countries with more developed financial markets. They used the US as a benchmark country with relatively frictionless financial markets, and found that industries more dependent on external finance grow faster in countries with more developed banks (as measured by PRIVY) or stock markets (stock market capitalisation).

Rousseau and Wachtel (1998) studied data from 5 OECD countries at the time of rapid industrialization during 1871 to 1929 and found strong evidence of one-way causality from finance to growth. However, some economists are unconvinced about the ability of cross-country regressions to explain the direction of causality. Rousseau and Wachtel hold that often components, even pre-determined, measuring financial sector development, remain correlated with the contemporaneous measures. Besides, GDP growth rates tend to be serially correlated and therefore cross-country analysis do not remove all uncertainty of direction of causality. Rousseau and Wachtel (2000) show how inflation affects the finance-growth nexus. They contend that uncertainty in the information about investment projects becomes more predominant in an inflationary environment thereby makes financial intermediation more difficult. High inflation could result in repressing financial intermediation by eroding the usefulness of money assets. According to them, financial deepening no longer increase economic growth if inflation exceeds the 15 to 25% range.

Williamson and Mahar (1998) have recently constructed an index of financial liberalisation based on which they classify 34 developed and developing countries during the period 1973-96 as repressed economies, partly repressed economies, liberalised economies and largely liberalised economies. They show that almost all the 34 countries experienced some form of systematic financial crisis since the early 1980s and July 1997 and many suffered new and severe crisis later that year. The authors view that ill-timed and inappropriately sequenced financial liberalization has been an important contributory factor to the boom and crash in emerging economies.

Bandiera and Others (2000) based on a multidimensional process of financial liberalization in eight countries over a 25 years period, find that liberalising reforms aimed at financial development do not reliably increase aggregate saving. However, the signs to show that the overall liberalization, and particularly factors relaxing liquidity constraints, could be related to a fall in saving. Even a lower overall rate of saving could promote rapid growth when there is an improvement in efficiency in the allocation of investable funds.

Reinhart and Kaminsky (1996) using cross-country probit estimations detect causality between banking crises, balance of payment crises, and financial liberalisation. Their findings show that, although banking crises tend to precipitate balance of payments crises, the reverse is not always true. Importantly, they find that financial sector liberalisation is positively and significantly related to subsequent banking crisis. Kaminsky and Reinhart (1999) found that in their sample of twenty-six, there were banking crises in eighteen countries that had liberalized the financial sector in the last five years.

Mavrotas (1999) discusses the measurement of financial liberalisation so as to test the relationship between financial sector development and savings mobilisation empirically. He critically assesses relationship between financial sector development and savings mobilisation by formal as well as informal institutions of developing countries and in particular the effect of social security reforms on savings. He looks at the nexus between financial sector development and savings mobilisation, as well as the importance of financial sector development in the process of financial liberalisation.

Rajan *et al.*, (1997) present a model for inefficient cross-subsidies that however aims to correct biased incentives for divisional managers to choose investments that directly enhance their power instead of other positive spillover to other divisions. Using a panel of US diversified firms during the 1979-1993 period they find that capital misallocation of this type is likely to be more pronounced in firms with very different investment opportunities across divisions. Rajan and Zingales (1998*b*) emphasised the free cash flow problems in Asian countries. They contrast a relationship-based system with respect to legal infrastructure and relative capital abundance. In Asian countries, where the quality of legally infrastructure is relatively low, they view that relation-based system is has been dominating. Rajan and Zingales (1999) underscore the role of political interference in markets during war in Civil law countries. They hold that Civil Law with the centralisation of legal system is more vulnerable to political pressures as compared with Common Law with the decentralisation of legal system. Rajan and Zingales (1998*a*) find that the development of domestic financial markets and institutions increases the growth of industries, like Computers or Pharmaceuticals, which need long-term external finance.

Rajan and Zingales (2000) explain the broad patterns of financial development in developed countries over the twentieth century. They find that indicators of financial development do not seem monotonic over time. In particular, they find that by most measures, countries were more financially developed in 1913 than in 1980 and that a major reversal took place between 1913 and 1950. Outlining a simple theory of the political economy of financial development they find that the forces opposing financial development will be weaker when a country is open to international trade and capital flows both in the case of cross-section and over time. According to them, in periods of free capital movement worldwide, a country's level of financial development is directly related to its openness to trade. When there are low frequency movements of financial development over time appear to be correlated with the degree of mobility of capital worldwide.

Khan and Senhadji (2000) provide new empirical evidence on the relationship between financial development and economic growth for a large cross section of countries using banking and security market indicators of financial depth. Their results indicate a positive relationship of financial development on economic growth. Their analysis reveals that financial development is an important determinant of cross-country differences in growth and some indicators are insignificant when growth equations are estimates with panels. This is attributed to nonlinear relationship between financial depth indicators and growth, the former in certain countries varies slowly while the latter is volatile, and lastly, the financial indicators in some countries may not precisely capture the changing structure of financial markets. It is viewed that while financial development may explain growth, changes in financial structure are related to changes in growth and if the indicators do not capture these changes, then they may not explain the time variation in growth.

Levine, Loayza, and Beck (2000) address the issue of joint endogeneity of financial development by using instrumental variables in their growth regressions. To capture financial depth, they use the countries' legal origin as the "external" instrument in their cross-sectional regressions. In their pooled (cross-country and time-series) regressions, they use lagged observations of all explanatory variables as "internal" instruments. The data panels consist of about 74 countries covering the period during 1960-95. They use with non-overlapping five-year averages to smooth out transitory or business-cycle fluctuations. Levine et al. find robust evidence for financial development and depth leading to improved growth performance.

Beck, Levine, and Loayza, (2000) empirically assesses the impact of banks on productivity growth, capital accumulation, private saving rates, and overall growth. The causal impact of financial development on growth and its sources were examined using a cross-country sample with data averaged over the period 1960-95 and the legal origin of countries as instruments to assess the long-run impact of the exogenous component of financial development on economic growth and its sources and controlling for the country-specific effect and the possible endogeneity of the regressors. They find a significantly positive causal impact of financial development on real per capita growth and productivity per capita growth. The results are robust to the use of different estimation procedures, conditioning information sets, and indicators of financial development. The results are more ambiguous in the case of regressions with physical capital per capita growth and saving although there tends be a positive link between banking sector development and both physical capital accumulation and private saving rates, the results are sensitive to alterations in estimation techniques and measures of banking sector development. Their results support the view that better functioning banks improve resource allocation and accelerate total factor productivity growth with positive repercussions for long-run economic growth.

Michael Leahy, Schich, Gert Wehinger, Pelgrin and Thorgeirsson (2001) examine the role of financial systems in OECD countries. They provide evidence to suggest that financial system characteristics are linked to growth patterns in OECD countries. They use simple bi-variate relationships and find significant relationships between financial development growth over and above the links via investment indicating impacts via overall economic efficiency. Their results show some tentative links between investor protections, and particularly their enforcement, to innovation in OECD countries. Evidence show that financial development is related to economic growth through its relationship with fixed investment and through other channels. The results appear to be strongest for stock market capitalisation, although the contribution of private credit issued by deposit money banks is also significant. These financial development variables are also shown to have positive links to the indicators of financial framework conditions.

Tuuli Koivu 1 (2002) analysed the link between banking sector development and economic growth in a panel of 25 transition countries during the period 1993-2000. The interest rate spread and the amount of non-performing loans were found to be negatively and significantly correlated with economic growth. The results are economically significant as the economic development can be considerably intensified if the financial sector efficiency is improved. The amount of bank credit allocated to private sector, is negatively associated with economic growth in transition countries. This is contrary to earlier results probably due to numerous banking crises in the transition economies during the study period. Overall, the results indicate that financial sector development can accelerate economic growth by raising the share of savings channelled to investments or by improving the productivity of investments or by affecting saving rate.

Loayza and Ranciere (2002) attempt to reconcile the contradictions on the effects of financial intermediation on economic activity. One finds a positive effect of financial depth as measured by, for instance, private domestic credit and liquid liabilities (e.g., Levine, Loayza, and Beck 2000). The other finds that monetary aggregates, such as domestic credit, are among the best predictors of crises and their related economic downturns (e.g., Kaminski and Reinhart 1999). Working with a panel of cross-country and time-series observations, they find a positive long-run relationship between financial intermediation and output growth co-existing with a mostly, negative short-run relationship. They illustrate that the growth enhancing effects of financial depth are weaker in countries that experienced crises. They distinguish between transitory and trend effects of domestic credit aggregates on economic growth. They find that a positive long-run relationship between financial intermediation and output growth co-exists with a mostly negative short-run relationship.

Koeva (2003) provide new empirical evidence on the impact of financial liberalisation on the performance of Indian commercial banks during 1991-92 to 2000-01. More specifically, behaviour and determinants of bank intermediation costs and profitability during the liberation period is studied. The results show that ownership type has a significant effect on performance indicators. It has noticed that the increase in competition was related to lower intermediation costs and profitability of Indian banks.

Favara (2003) re-examines empirical relationship between financial development and growth based on 85 cross-section and panel data from 1960 to 1998. Cross-sectional evidence show a positive and significant relationship and reinforce findings of King and Levine (1993a). However, in reverse causality the contribution of financial development in growth is found to be negligible. Panel data based on General method of moments (GMM) estimator results show that financial development is not significantly related to economic growth. More specifically, it shows that exogenous component of financial development does not spur economic growth. The linkage is non-linear. If a dynamic specification and slope heterogeneity is taken across countries, the estimated effect of financial development in growth is often negative. It is viewed that measurement errors, business-cycle effects and omitted variables may affect the validity of these findings and therefore future research is required for the convergence of theoretical models with more sophisticated proxies of financial depth. There is decline in the concentration of the

Indian banking sector, bank spreads and profitability. The main determinants of intermediation costs and profitability are operating costs, priority sector lending and non-performing loans, investments in Government securities and composition of deposits.

(ii) Country-specific Studies

Backus, Brainard, Smith and Tobin (1980), in their empirical model for United States estimate and simulate the general structure in a more disaggregated manner. In this study they explicitly use the subjective prior information on the estimation. They have used Theil-Goldberger mixed estimation technique to combine their beliefs with data. The simulation results illustrate the response of the system to the open market operations in the long-term securities and changes the reserve requirements on time deposits. Further, the effects of these on excess demand for unborrowed reserves dominate their differences in other markets. Debt management is active even though switching longs for short had a much smaller effect than switching either one for high-powered money. The risk of mortgage-banked bonds is captured in the increase in mortgage-assets and long liabilities of federal agencies. They find substantial differences in the quantitative response of the required rate on capital. The capital and bond are not perfectly substitutable for interest-paying financial assets. They argue that increases in the quantity of Government debt may decrease rather than increase the required rate of return on capital. Thus, there may be "crowding in" and not "crowding out". In their simulation model, the consequences of government deficits for supplies of government debt and crowding out will be reckoned automatically. The effect of changes in relative supplies can be inferred through simulation by open market operations.

Bernanke (1983) emphasized the non-monetary causes particularly bank crisis in the propagation of the Great

Depression. He states that, "the financial crisis of 1930-33 affected the macroeconomy by reducing the quantity of certain financial services, primarily credit intermediation". He contends that bank failures in the US reduced the money supply and simultaneously increased the cost of credit. Besides, bankruptcies among businesses resulted in reluctance to lending which inturn led to depression. The variables used for analysis were bank deposits and unanticipated money and prices. His empirical analysis showed that the deposits of banks and businesses that failed had statistically significant effect on industrial production despite accounting for lagged values of income, unanticipated money and unanticipated prices. The results showed that debt and bank failures had a significant impact on the economy and it also was closely associated with bank failures. Therefore, it was difficult to assess the true impact

De Melo and Tybout (1986) examine the effects of financial liberalisation on savings and investments with the transition of the Uruguayan economy from a tightly regulated financial system to a liberalised one. 'Financial Liberalisation' hypothesis as popularised by McKinnon and Shaw (1973) states that substantial improvements in growth are possible with financial market deregulation. At the micro level, interest rates ceiling in countries with high inflation may make the real cost of credit highly negative. Thus, excess demand for credit results in rationing of savings according to criteria such as firm size, rather than excepted returns. At the macro level, as the interest elasticity of private savings is positive, the removal of ceilings, raise private savings rates. With increased financial resources, liquidity constraints on investments are relaxed and thus capital formation is accelerated and in turn growth increases. It is found that Gross Domestic Product growth picked up during reform period. Private investment rose along with marginal efficiency of investment. However, foreign saving funded this rise, while private domestic savings declined. The savings behaviour exhibited a shift between the 'sixties and 'seventies. In the former period, savings rate was sensitive to foreign capital inflows while in the later period, real exchange rate played a dominant role. In particular, real appreciation discouraged savings. However, savings rate shifted upward with the implementation of financial liberalisation and reforms. With regard to investments, it was found that the standard accelerator effects were significant throughout the sample period (1962-1983) suggesting that the Uruguayan economy was not savings constrained despite the pressure of "financial repression" in the pre-reform period. Several shifts in the structure of private investment function was found due to first, the intercept term shifted upwards significantly after controlling for other factors during the reform period. Second, in the later years, the responsiveness of investment to interest rates and real exchange rates appeared to increase. It is viewed that these changes are consistent with the changes in the regulatory environment. The savings rate function include ratio of domestic savings to Gross Domestic Product, which is regressed on real income growth, lagged savings, foreign savings and some measure of real interest rate. Income growth is included to proxy deviations from 'permanent income', which theoretically should induce savings rate fluctuation. Lagged savings is used as the adjustment process that could spread over multiple periods and foreign savings is included as it may 'crowd out' domestic savings by permitting residents to consume more at any given rate of capital accumulation. Interest rate is used, as savings behaviour may be insensitive to real returns. For the investment function, ratio of private investment to Gross Domestic Product as a function of lagged real income growth, current and lagged real money growth, real interest rate, real exchange rate, a dummy for post reform period and lagged investment is used.

Odedokun (1989), studies the causality between M1, M2 and total credit and Gross Domestic Product, Price level industrial activities and imports using the quarterly data during the period 1970 to 1983 for Nigeria. Using Granger causality test he found causation from Gross Domestic Product to total credit of price level to M1; each from M1 and M2 to industrial production; reverse causation between Gross Domestic Product and M2; total credit and price level; M2 and price level; and import levels and each of M1, M2 and total credit. Their findings have important implications for model building as well as monetary and credit policies.

Corsepius (1990) in his portfolio model for Peru, based on demand theory, relates desired real wealth in financial sector to past wealth, permanent income, expected average nominal return on portfolio and expected rate of inflation. Quarterly data is used and stock adjustment process is adopted, as savers cannot fully realise desired level of wealth within the period. The financial assets considered are deposit certificates denominated in US Dollar, Money demand, savings and time deposits. He examines the effect of partial financial reform and finds that increases in nominal interest rates and introduction of deposit certificates mobilized additional savings. It also confirms the shifts in the structure of financial assets.

The non-monetary effect of financial crisis is dealt by Haubrich (1990). He used several regressions to assess the role of the banking system during the depression period in Canada in terms of cost of credit. His empirical analysis focussed on whether financial crisis emanating from banking system or debt market helps to explain depression after accounting for money and other factors. In the context of absence of bank failures in Canada, he used proxies for cost of credit, such as, branches measure to indicate availability of credit and other financial services and bank stock prices which measure the health and profitability of the banking sector. The other measures of money supply and production to control these important effects are also employed. Though reduced form equations, regressions in the levels and first differences are specified. Then Chow tests and vector autoregressions are applied to check the robustness, stationarity and structural biases of the results. The variables used include, industrial production, growth rates of money and prices, debt to Gross National Product ratio, spread between safe and risky bonds, branches and stock prices. He found that the domestic debt crisis had little effect on the economic growth as the depression was transmitted from abroad, in part from the US. The role of money was found to be ambiguous. The contraction in the banking system, whether measured by branches, stock prices or loan or commercial failures did not influence significantly the economy.

In the context of checking the ability of monetary policy to influence real economic activity in the US economy, Friedman (1990) examines the stability of the relationship between economic activity and financial variables that could exert influence on monetary policy through reduced form equations. The growth variables used include real Gross National Product, implicit price deflator and real high employment federal expenditures. The financial variables include, growth rates of M1 and M2; total domestic non-financial debt outstanding, nominal interest rates on commercial and corporate bonds; the difference between commercial paper rate and rate of Consumer Price Index; difference between corporate bond rate and one year average Consumer Price inflation; the change in each of these nominal and real interest rates; difference between corporate bond rate and commercial paper rate; difference between commercial paper rate and Treasury bill rate; and change in each of these spreads. The results show that the short term interest rate level and its changes are the only financial variables that show a statistically significant relationship to real economic activity for the two sample periods viz., 1960-75 and 1976-1988. In the first sample period, growth of credit, nominal and real long-term interest rates, the long-short rate spread and the default premium on commercial paper showed a significant relationship. The monetary base was weakly significant in the second sample period.

Habibullah (1991) argues that with the rapid growth and structural sophistication in the Malaysian financial system financial innovations have become frequent, which have implications on the public portfolio behaviour and monetary policy. He empirically determines the degree of substitution of the interest bearing financial assets for money in a developing economy. He uses the time services data for the period 1979 to 1985. The variables used are money, commercial bank saving and fixed deposits (1, 3, 6, 9 and 12 months) or proxies for interest bearing financial assets; non-convertible debentures at commercial banks, finance company's saving and fixed deposits (3, 6, 9 and 12 months), merchant bank's fixed deposits (1, 3, 6, 9 and 12 months) National Saving Bank's saving deposits and employee Provident Fund deposits; and the respective deposit rates. His empirical results showed that (used 2 stage least square, maximum likelihood estimates and substitution elasticities) merchant banks were the main competitors to other financial institutions. This has been due to a higher level of minimum deposits and higher rate of returns as compared with others. The finance companies have been the main competitors for commercial banks even prior to the liberalization of interest rate in 1978. The rate of interest offered were 1 to 2 per cent higher than commercial banks deposits of financial companies, commercial banks and employees' Provident Fund.

Sussman (1992) analyses the Israeli experience of financial liberalization in isolation and the use of dollar-indexed time deposits as a device of stabilisation. While stressing the role of fiscal factors in liberalization, only partially supports the McKinnon's ordering theory, which presupposes liberalization of the current account prior to that of capital account. According to Sussman the Government expenditures must follow a U-shaped path; fall after liberalization when aggregate demand is increased and vice versa. However, it is implied that fiscal balance prior to liberalization is not sufficient to eliminate its destabilising effects. He advocates a simple tax on financial intermediation, which could have resulted in more efficient allocation of capital. Until full liberalization takes place, there would also be wide differences between the borrowing and lending interest rates and local and foreign rates.

Davis (1992) in his econometric tests to assess the usefulness of spreads in UK, the indicator properties of spreads in predicting defaults, real Gross Domestic Product and industrial production are tested through simple time series models. The results show that the UK spreads behaved similar to those in the US during the 'sixties and 'seventies but changed somewhat in the 'eighties. During 1968-77 they find the spreads improve the predictive power of bankruptcies (both short and long run) and Gross Domestic Product. It also predicts a variety of leading variables associated with financial fragility. Spreads respond either negatively or not at all to higher issuance in corporate to public bond markets but respond to defaults in the long run for US only. During 1978-89, spreads were significantly positively related to Gross Domestic Product, insignificant in a dynamic equation for bankruptcies (negative in the long run) and rose in advance of high real interest rates and in anticipation of economic growth. Spreads respond positively to higher issuance in corporate bond markets and also respond to defaults in the long run to different variables or with opposite sign in all sub-periods in the UK. His major conclusion is that long-term yield spreads are not useful monetary indicators in relation to the then bond market and their increase and level may not foreshadow recession and defaults at the macroeconomic level so as to measure or predict. However, it may be wrong to disregard them entirely.

Most of the individual country studies on interest elasticity of savings show that the growth stems from increased efficiency in allocation of investment instead of a larger volume of investment. Fidel Jaramillo, Fabrio Schianterelli and Andrew Weiss (1992) for Ecuador, find that post financial liberalisation, there was an increase in the flow of credit to technologically more efficient firms after controlling for firms other characteristics. They also found it to be robust to changes in assumption about production function and estimation methods. As the larger Ecuadorian firms were more technologically efficient, the flow of credit moved from smaller to larger firms post liberalisation.

Post financial deregulation In Indonesia, credit was reallocated from manufacturing and agriculture to other sectors. Studies by John Harris, Fabrio Schianterelli and Miranda Siregar (1992) find that the more the firm is technologically efficient, the greater is the proportion of new credit received post liberalisation. While credit inclined to increase for small and large firms, it decreased for medium firms.

Atiyas (1992) shows for Korea that post liberalisation small firms could get more access to external finance. Credit flows migrated from light industrial manufacturing to services, utilities and construction. In the case of Mexico, Gelos (1997) offers econometric evidence to show that financial constraints were eased for small firms in manufacturing sector after financial liberalisation. Morisset (1993) finds that the effect of financial liberalisation on quality of investment was consistently positive, it had a weak effect on the quantity of investment. Although most evidence is for more efficient credit allocation, it is not unanimous. Gregorio and Guidotti (1992) find that credit to the private sector was negatively related to growth in the 1970s and 1980s. They attribute this negative correlation to inefficient lending by banks due to poor regulatory incentives.

Many economists also examined the impact of financial deregulation on financial deepening in depth Margaritis Dimitri, Dean Hyslop and David Rae (1994) for New Zealand, show that financial liberalisation is positively related to the growth of ratio of broad money to GDP. While post liberalisation in the developing countries like Argentina, Brazil, Thailand, Indonesia, Mexico, Malaysia etc., the ratio of M2 to GDP showed an increase, it showed a decline in Colombia, Venezuela, Philippines and Turkey.

The literature on correlation between financial liberalisation and savings is again contradictory. Chapple (1991) in New Zealand, finds fall in the household and corporate saving since liberalisation. Hussain (1996) shows that post liberalisation, in Egypt, financial savings increased on average by 6 per cent of GDP over the level with the absence of financial liberalisation. There is also a study by Lopez-Meija (1991), to provide evidence for consumption boom post financial liberalisation in the case of United Kingdom in the late 1980s which contradicts the McKinnon and Shaw hypothesis that financial liberalisation will lead to increased savings.

Morriset (1993) developed a model for Argentina to examine the short-run effect of a variety of shocks on private investments and other endogenous variables. He did a simulation exercise over the period 1961 to 1982 and found that the quality of investment is little responsive to movements in interest rates, despite the fact that Argentina was affected by various interest rate policies for the last 20 years. He found that the crowding out of private sector funds with financial liberalisation increasing demand for domestic credit by public sector does not result from a change in government's behaviour but from a shift in the portfolio of private agents.

In Barbados, according to Wood (1993), due to the reverse causation viz., economic growth stimulating financial sector development (termed as "demand following" phenomena), the real sector generates new and additional demand for financial services. This in turn leads to the establishment and promotion of financial institutions. He further argues that in the less developed countries such as Barbados, lack of financial institutions, itself manifest lack of demand for their services. He also opines that there is little quantitative evidence on the view that the direction of causality between financial development and economic growth changes over the course of development (Patrick, 1966), both for developed and developing countries. Wood uses a bivariate statistical framework for the purpose and adopts the Granger causality testing procedure based on ordinary least square estimates and the conventional Fisher-Snedecor F-Test of joint statistical significance. Financial development is measured by the ratio of M2 to Gross Domestic Product, which is also widely regarded as monetisation variable. The empirical analysis of Wood is presented in two segments. First, causal relationship between financial development and economic growth is investigated. Second, "supply—leading" and "demand following" hypothesis are studied. The results showed evidence of a supply-leading causality pattern emphasising the importance of financial development in the Barbadian economy. Besides, there is also considerable evidence of a demand following financial response. However, the results provide no support for Patrick's hypothesis that the direction of causality changes over the course of economic development.

Murinde and Eng (1994) empirically examine for Singapore two competing hypotheses regarding financial development and economic growth as stipulated in the seminal paper by Patrick (1966). These relate to "demand following" hypothesis postulating a positive causal relationship between economic growth to financial development and the "supply-leading" hypothesis postulating a positive causal relationship from financial development to economic growth. They view that financial restructuring strategies pursued in Singapore tantamounts to 'supply-leading finance'. Using a Bivariate Vector Autoregressive model, tests for stationarity, cointegration, exogeneity and Granger-causality largely supports the supply-leading hypothesis only when broad monetary aggregates and a monetisation variable are used as surrogates for financial development. The 1st model predicts that financial development affects growth while the second suggests that financial growth does not induce real growth. Another endogenous growth model of Bencivenga and Smith (1993) also shows indeterminate theoretical relationship between financial and real growth. They use a bi-variate autoregressive model to encapsulate the main predictions of economic theories over the last 3 decades. The proxy variables used to indicate financial development are (1) Financial Intermediation Ratio, (2) Monetary aggregates (M1, M2 and M3), (3) Currency ratios, (4) total domestic credit, (5) Monetisation variable (V3= M3/Gross National Product), (6) Total finance=M3+Bonds+Capital accounts (Gupta 1984), and (7) Real Gross Domestic Product.

Murinde and Eng first applied Engle and Granger's (1991) two-step Cointegration procedures prior to causality testing. They used Augmented Dickey Fuller test, to test non-stationarity of the data. The number of lags was determined by using Lagrange Multiplier test for serial correlation and 6 lags were found to be sufficient. When tested at all levels, unit root was found in all variables but variables were stationary in first difference form. As Augmented Dickey Fuller relies on parametric approach to deal with serial correlation and heterogeneity, which may reduce the power of the test, Philips and Perror test procedure were further applied and were found consistent with Augmented Dickey Fuller results. After computing Ordinary Least Square, cointegration test was done. The result showed that the variables were cointegrated and it was used as first differences for Granger-Causality testing. A maximum of 5 lags and a minimum of 2 lags were experimented and as the equations included lagged dependent variables, Durbin-Watson statistic could not be used. Following Pyndick aznd Rubinfield regression residuals were obtained and estimation was revised. The DW Statistic result showed that coefficient was statistically different from zero and it was corrected by using Cochrane-Orcutt iterative technique. In addition, following Pindyck and Rubinfield, Box-Pierce's Q-statistic was calculated for each of the residual series and calculated values turned out to be white noise. Their results showed evidence for strong support to 'supply leading' hypothesis when M1, V1, and V3 (monetisation variables, M1/Gross National Product, M3/Gross National Product) are used as proxies for financial development.

Hassan (1995) tested complementarity between money and capital in Bangladesh using a two-stage least squares technique and found evidence for McKinnon's hypothesis implying that the financial system had not achieved a stage of development wherein alternative non-monetary assets replace money as the principal repository of domestic savings.

Gunther, Lown and Robinson (1995) investigate the relationship between bank credit availability and economic activity. They adopt a vector auto regressive model and used quarterly data for the period 1976 to 1990 for the Texas economy. In order to examine the relationship between financial and real sectors, they employed banking variables to explain the fluctuations in economic activity. The banking variables include, bank loans outstanding, real commercial and industrial loans, loans to asset ratios of banks, real book-value equity capital of banks, equity to asset ratio. The measures of economic activity include, total non-agricultural employment, index of industrial production, and real personal income. As the US economy also impacts Texas economy, the macro variables of the US economy and oil prices are also included. The results showed that economic events had strong impact on the banking sector of the State. However, they do not find support for the hypothesis that banking sector served as a propagator of shocks arising in the oil sector. Measures of bank lending and bank capital provide some support for the hypothesis that weakness in the region" banking sector had a major impact on the regional economy.

Leigh (1996) views that a rapid expansion in theoretical literature on endogenous growth, relationship between financial development and Growth has received new focus. Besides, recent co-integration techniques with emphasis on estimation and identification of long run economic relationships between variables have made it suitable to apply to endogenous growth models. Drawing on the theoretical foundations of endogenous growth and endogenous financial models, Leigh employs the Vector Auto regression techniques to analyse the impact of financial development on economic growth in Singapore. He has found that financial development positively affects both transitional and long-term growth in Singapore. Leigh using co-integration techniques under endogenous growth model uses a supply-side framework for Singapore. The results are in line with the predictions of endogenous growth models. It is found that financial development positively affects both transitional and long run growth in Singapore.

Hataiseree and Phipps (1996) using a cointegration approach explores whether or not various money and credit aggregates have leading relationships with economic activity and whether money has a stable long run relationship with nominal income in Thailand. They adopt a multivariate model with additional variables such as, exports, revenue, government expenditure, besides variables such as nominal income (Gross Domestic Product), monetary aggregates (M1 or M2) and monetary base and interest rate. The results show that the levels of all the time series data are characterized by unit root, non-stationary processes. The results further implied that exports played an important role in explaining economic activity. The estimated co-efficient on government expenditure was statistically significant and had positive signs. While using the credit aggregates or monetary base it failed to reveal any cointegrating vectors. This has implications for the conduct of monetary policy.

Melnick and Yashiv (1996) in their empirical analysis for Israeli economy examine both the 'credit channel' and 'money channel' focuses on financial innovation. In the 'credit channel' of monetary transmission, the asset side of the balance sheet plays an important role. Banks reduce lending with the tightening by the central bank. Consequently, firms reduce their borrowing, as non-bank credit is more costly or unavailable. Firms cut investment spending, employment and thereby production. In the 'money channel' bank's liabilities are affected due to innovation on the portfolio of composition of consumers. This in turn affects bank's assets due to differential reserve requirements, which affects loan supply. Thus, there is a credit supply affect. They test their model by estimating a series of vector auto regressive models having four endogenous variables, viz., real activity variables provided by non-available consumption, State of economy index indicating business cycle, non-residential investment; deposit and lending real interest rates and finance ratio (M1/ M2, M2/ M3). To control monetary policy responses and inflationary developments, they include loan from central bank to banks and inflation rate. They find that the introduction of indexed deposits along with technological progress and regulatory change had contradictory effect on real activity as it reduced bank's resources for lending. The short-term deposits increased at the cost of demand deposits post 1982. Stabilisation in 1985 did not alter their roles and innovation had expansionary effect.

Caprio, Wilson and Sanders (1997) find that a rapid expansion of lending to consumers was a major factor for the collapse of banks in Mexico in 1994. A boom in lending for consumption was due to the pent up demand from past financial repression and also because of exporters being accustomed to other methods of financing during the years of nationalisation. The authors also cite inadequate supervision, lack of proper incentives and existence of broad deposit insurance have all reduced the need for bankers to diversify risks in newly liberalised environment.

Muhsin Kar and Eric J. Pentecost (2000), examine the causal relationship between financial development and economic growth in Turkey for the period 1963-1995. Granger causality tests are applied using the cointegration and vector error correction methodology (VECM) to five alternative proxies for financial development. The empirical results show that the direction of causality between financial development and economic growth is in sensitive to the choice of proxy used for financial development. Financial development as measured by the money to income ratio is used, the direction of causality runs from financial development to economic growth, but when the bank deposits, private credit and domestic credit ratios are used, growth is found to lead financial development. However, on the whole, for Turkey, growth seems to lead financial sector development.

Section 3: Issues in Finance and Growth

Even since the contributions of Goldsmith, Gurley and Shaw to the modern endogenous growth theories, the issues relating to financial development have multiplied. The World Bank Development Report (1989) addresses four major issues in the context of financial reform. First, it emphasizes the need for macroeconomic stability for economic growth without which premature opening of the capital markets could aggravate domestic instability through international capital flows. Second, financial liberalization is favoured, as rigid ceilings on interest rates have hampered growth in financial savings and efficiency of investment in developing countries. The liberalisation should be more broad-based across money and capital markets and non-banks. Third, it is against government intervention for credit allocation as it is an inefficient method of redistributing income and dealing with market imperfections. Fourth, in the design of the financial system, it calls for improvements in the legal and accounting systems, disclosure norms, prudential regulation and supervision.

The experiences of developed and developing countries raise the following issues (Park, 1994):

1. Whether financial control has been effective in mitigating adverse consequences of failure of financial markets?
2. Does finance matter in promoting economic growth or it matters only in certain cases?
3. Whether financial deregulation leads to financial instability and institutional failures?
4. What would be the role of financial system with a highly developed structure with banks and non-banks in allocation of credit? Countries differ regarding the degree of Government intervention. In some countries historically informal markets do play an important role.

On the above background, this section devotes its attention on the issues cited in the literature and are grouped and presented under the six categories as follows:

(i) Financial Structure

One of the issues that have been debated by economists for many decades is about the pros and cons of an ideal structure of the financial system. Should it be bank-based or market-based or financial services oriented or legal-based?

(ii) Financial Institutions

Patrick (1990) argued that for efficient functioning of a highly competitive market based financial system; there is a need for adequate institutional infrastructure. These include legal and regulatory system, existence of effective information system that minimises uncertainties and costs of financial intermediation, prudential regulations to ensure stability of financial system, protecting investors and supervision by Government.

Few economists have held that the financial systems of developed countries too comprise market and non-market institutions. It has been argued that private internal capital markets develop due to market imperfections and transaction costs. In developing countries, the traditional financial markets are featured by structural and policy induced distortions but the private internal capital markets may be inefficient due to their limited size. Lee and Haggard (1995) argue that in such an environment, it may be efficient for the Government to create its own internal capital market so as to improve effectiveness of credit allocation.

(iii) Financial Markets

A related issue is whether free-market system is better than a controlled market system (Levine, 1997). In a free competitive market, trading in financial instruments and commodities as well is constrained due to market imperfections such as, asymmetry in information and costly contracts. According to Stiglitz (1989) such problems are inherent in all financial markets and credit and equity are rationed even in financial markets that are free of Government intervention. According to Cho (1986) financial liberalisation could lead to inefficient allocation of credit in the absence of well-functioning equity markets. Stiglitz (1989) argues that even equity rationing could take place due to the problem of adverse selection. Equity markets may not be able to distinguish between good and bad issues with lack of good information. Thus, they may discount share prices of good issues.

(iv) Financial Policy

Another issues cited in the literatures is the role of Government intervention through financial policies in the financial system. While the financial repressionist school advocates state intervention, the financial liberalisation school advocates free market system (Lee and Haggard, 1995). The former leads to misallocation of resources due to three reasons. First, the Government bureaucrats lack information and incentives to allocate credit efficiently and the allocative decisions rest with them. Secondly, they are likely to be influenced by other factors such as distributive aspects rather than rates of return. Third, it would lead to the adoption of more capital-intensive techniques.

According to Lee and Haggard in practice, the economic success of Japan, Korea and Taiwan since early sixties contradicts traditional arguments against financial repression. On the other hand, the experiences of Southern countries, such as, Argentina, Chile and Uruguay suggest the failure of financial liberalisation due to lack of adequate regulation of financial markets by Government.

It also gave the awareness that even with optimal macroeconomic stability coupled with credible and efficient regulations, complete financial liberalisation may not given the desired results due to presence of the asymmetric and imperfect information in all the financial markets. Thus, under certain situations, State intervention could bring about proper credit allocation and efficient resource use thereby promoting rapid growth.

(v) Regulation Vs Liberalization

The services provided by the financial system are in the nature of public utility. It is important to distinguish between financial deregulation and liberalisation. Since public utility services are being provided, along with liberalisation to promote competitiveness, regulation in the form of prudential norms becomes necessary.

The emergence of information theory of finance has revolutionised the theoretical approach to the role of financial system as a whole. Under this, financial intermediaries mitigate the information asymmetries of open securities markets and direct investment by savers. Theoretical choice between banking markets and securities markets are more relevant to the highly developed financial markets.

(vi) Financial Fragility

The contradictory experience of financial liberalisation in developing and developed countries led to the issue of financial fragility.

Section 4: Concluding Observations

In sum, surveys of the existing literature are important as it gives rich insights on the issues and latest developments. This would help in examining the issues separately for individual countries as well as over a large cross section of countries by adopting customized techniques to suit the specific macroeconomic conditions and data availability ad gain from policy implications. Theoretically, prior to the 'fifties, the interlinkages between finance and growth was recognized. In the 'fifties, concentration was on identifying structural factors in this relationship. The 'sixties established theoretical relationships and recognized the role of financial intermediaries. In the 'seventies the focus was on issues relating to financial repression and liberalisation. In the eighties, importance was given to transmission channels. Since the 'nineties with the development of the endogenous growth theories, emphasis was on developing sophisticated models which could be empirically tested. Theoretically, there is a broad consensus that financial development promotes economic growth.

On the empirical front, some of the country-specific studies find that financial development positively affects economic growth while others did not find support to this argument. Empirical cross-country studies using large sample conclude that financial variables significantly impact growth and vice versa. Certain other studies have also given contrary results. However, empirical studies differed in terms of methodology and models, indicators used for financial development, and results. The studies related to causality, transmission channels, testing various indicators for financial development and growth, index of financial development etc. Methods adopted include, bivariate graphs, correlation, cross-country regressions, and pooled cross-country time series regression. Granger causality tests, bivariate vector autoregressive and multivariate analysis.

The models employed were, one-sector model under long-run growth equilibrium, portfolio models, model of investment behaviour, over-lapping generation model., endogenous growth model, monopolistic competitive spatial models, two-stage model.

The choice of variables include, Financial Ratios like, the ratio of total financial assets to National wealth, ratio of financial investment to total assets of financial Institutions or total financial assets, ratio of broad money to nominal Gross Domestic Product (GDP), real interest rates and monetary aggregates, ratio of total assets of the financial system to Gross Domestic Product, ratio of bank credit to private sector to Gross Domestic Product, domestic credit by public sector, ratio of M1 to GDP; ratio of liquid liabilities; ratio of quasi-liquid liabilities and ratio of claims on the private sector by the Central Bank and deposit Money with banks to GDP to measure size. The relative importance of commercial banks and central banks was measured by ratio of central bank domestic assets to GDP; ratio of Deposit Money Banks Domestic Assets to GDP; and ratio of Deposit Money Banks Domestic Assets to Deposit Money Bank plus

Central Bank Domestic Assets. The assets distribution was measured by the ratio of claims on the Non-Financial Private Sector by the Central banks and Deposit money Banks to total domestic credit. In order to measure empirical relationship between interest rates and growth, a repressed interest rates variable was used. The difference between the lending rate and the deposit rate, per capita Gross Domestic Product were also used as proxies.

As regards to empirical results, Patrick (1966) and Goldsmith (1969) postulated a positive bivariate relationship between financial interrelations ratio and economic growth. Gupta (1984) found support to 'Supply Leading Hypothesis' (SLH) in the case of 14 developing countries. Jung (1986) and St. Hill (1992) found a moderate support for 'SLH' and a close support for Demand Following Hypothesis (DFH) for developed nations. DeGregorio and Guidotti (1993) found that the ratio of bank credit to private sector to GDP is significantly and positively related in the growth equation on a large cross-country sample but is negatively related while using panel data for Latin America. The main channel of transmission from financial development to growth is the efficiency of investment rather than its volume. King and Levine (1993 a, b) find that many financial performance indicators are significantly correlated with growth. Empirical relationship between growth and measures of asset distribution remains significant even when the regressions simultaneously include measures of overall financial size. Later (1993c), they find that in the cross-country analysis, financial system indicators tend to be robustly correlated with growth only because they are highly correlated with the ratio of national investment to Gross Domestic Product, while in the pooled cross-country time series analysis they are linked through both investment and efficiency channels. Ghani (1992) obtained significant positive coefficients for human capital measured by number of years of schooling and financial development. However, he obtained negative coefficient while using per capita real Gross Domestic Product. Morriset (1993) found that the crowding out of private sector funds with financial liberalisation increasing demand for domestic credit by public sector does not result from a change in government's behaviour but from a shift in the portfolio of private agents. Pill and Pradhan (1995) find that financial deregulation affects financial variables changing their indicator properties and usefulness as intermediate targets. They also find that private sector credit aggregate is the preferred financial indicator during the period of ongoing financial liberalisation. Each indicator is affected differently depending upon the institutional background and the extent of deregulation. It is also found that in Asia where the financial liberalisation is strong, there is a weak evidence of preference to credit as a financial indicator. Contrary-wise, in Africa where financial liberalisation has failed to develop the financial system, the behaviour of financial indicators is erratic and there is no guide to economic activity.

Many empirical works have substantiated these theoretical relationships. Nevertheless, there are several gaps in the extent literature both on the theoretical as well as empirical front. More specifically, there is a growing debate on the causal linkage between financial development and economic growth. It is still a matter of doubt whether financial development leads or lags real sector or is a 'demand-following' or 'supply-leading' phenomena or whether the causation runs both ways and significant or whether the interest rates or savings rate or investment provides the transmission channel; whether financial deregulation, liberalistion, innovation, diversification and reforms is an unequivocal policy panacea. Secondly, the conclusions are divergent both in the cross-country and country-specific studies in terms of direction of causality, financial and growth indicators, models employed. As the growth paths are not similar over the long run, earlier models cannot be easily adopted in developing countries.

Thirdly, there are methodological differences that necessitate careful interpretation of the empirical results. Fourthly, it is necessary to consider various dimensions in respect of new determinants, variables, structural disturbances over the long periods that are absent in the earlier studies. As the financial development varies at different points in the growth path, a systematic testing on a country-specific basis over sufficiently long periods of time through the use of latest advanced techniques has become a necessary exercise in itself

For future research, one area could be the construction of a comprehensive Divisia type of index to capture full extent of financial intermediation which according to Chandavarkar (1992) even Goldsmith has not developed. Another area of promising research would be to study the impact of innovation in the financial sector on economic development. Providing evidence on this causal influence is crucial not only for academicians but also for policymakers who look for optimal solutions for taking decisions on reform. More recently the endogenous growth theories have emphasized the crucial role of economic policies particularly financial policies to enhance growth. Chandavarkar (1992) also observes that financial ratios do not figure even in the pioneering list of 'Great Ratios in Economics' of Klein or in the latest Simon's, "The Great and almost Great Magnitude in Economics" which include real risk-less rate of interest, rate of return on common stocks but leaves out significant ratios of monetisation and financial intermediation. Furthermore, although there have been few studies in the recent years on index of financial liberalization, developing an index of financial development and construction of a national balance sheet (Venkatachalam and Sharma, 1976) will help in a long way to understand the interlinkages. A study of the regulatory framework for strengthening the financial system has become very essential particularly in the context of technological advancements. Lastly, an analysis of the impact of financial innovation, technology and reforms is another area for future research. Research in these directions could provide some rich insights into our understanding of macroeconomics.

References

1. Abebe Adera (1990), *"Financial Repression and its Impact on Financial Development and Economic Growth in the African Least Developed Countries"*, Savings and Development, Volume XIV, Number 1 (pp. 55-85).

2. Arrow Kenneth (1962), *"The Economic Implications of Learning by Doing"*, Review of Economics and Statistics, June (pp. 155-173).

3. Ahmed, Syed-M and Ansari, Mohammed I (1995), "Financial Development in Bangladesh-A Test of the McKinnon-Shaw Model", *Canadian Journal of Development Studies*, 16 (2), pp. 291-302.

4. Arestis, Philip and Demetriades, Panicos. (1996). "Finance and Growth: Institutional Considerations and Causality", Department of Economics Working Papers, Keele University.

5. Arestis, Philip and Demetriades, Panicos. (1997). "Financial Development and Economic Growth: Assessing the Evidence", *The Economic Journal*, 107 (May): 783-799.

6. Arestis, P. and P. Demetriades, (1999), Financial liberalization: the experience of development countries. *Eastern Economic Journal*, 25 (4), pp. 441-457.

7. Aschhiem Joseph (1963), *"Financial Institutions and Monetary Policy: A Re-Examination of their Interrelationship-Financial Intermediaries and the Goals of Monetary Policy"*, American Economic Review, Volume 53, papers and proceedings of the 75th Meeting of the American Economic Association.

8. Atje Raymond and Jovanovic Boyan (1993), *"Stock Markets and Development"*, European Economic Review, Volume 37, (pp. 634-640).

9. Atiyas, Izak. (1992) Financial Reform and Investment Behaviour in Korea; Evidence from Panel data,. Development Economics Department, World Bank.

10. Backus David, Brainard William. C, Smith Gary and James Tobin (1980), *"A Model of US Financial and Non-Financial Economic Behaviour"*, Journal of Money, Credit and Banking, Volume 12, Number 2, May (pp. 259-293).

11. Bagehot, Walter (1873), *Lombard Street*. Homewood, IL: Irwin.

12. Bandiera, O., G. Caprio, P. Honohan and F. Schiantarelli (1998), "Does Financial Reform Raise or Reduce Savings?" mimeo, World Bank, September 1998.

13. Bandiera, Oriana, Gerard Caprio, Patrick Honohan, and Fabio Schiantarelli. (2000). "Does Financial Reform Raise or Reduce Saving?" *Review of Economics and Statistics* 82 (2): 239-63.

14. Beck Thorsten, Levine Ross, and Loayza Norman (2000), "Finance and the Sources of Growth" *Journal of Financial Economics*, 58 (1-2), 261-300.

15. Ben Bernanke (1983), *"Non-monetary Effects of the Financial Crisis in the Propagation of the Great Depression"*, American Economic Review, 73, (pp. 257-276).

16. Ben Bernanke and Mark Gertler (1987), *"Banking and Macroeconomic Equilibrium"* in New Approaches to Monetary Economics, Edited by W.A. Barnett and K. Singleton, Cambridge University Press, New York, (pp. 89-111).

17. Ben Bernanke and Mark Gertler (1989), *"Agency Costs, Net worth, and Business Fluctuations"*, American Economic Review, 79 (1) March, (pp. 14-31).

18. Ben Bernanke and Mark Gertler (1990), *"Financial Fragility and Economic Performance"*, Quarterly Journal of Economics, Volume CV, February, Issue 2 (pp. 87-114).

19. Bencivenga. V and B Smith (1991), *"Financial Intermediation and Endogenous Growth"*, Review of Economic Studies 58 (pp. 195-209).

20. Bencivenga. V and B Smith (1993), *"Some Consequences of Credit Rationing in an Endogenous Growth Model"*, Journal of Economic Dynamics and Control 17 (1-2), January-March (pp. 97-122).

21. Bencivenga Valerie R and Smith Bruce D (1995), *"Transaction Costs, Technological Choice, and Endogenous Growth"*, Journal of Economic Theory, 67, (pp. 153-177).

22. Berthelemy J.C and Varoudakis (1994), *"Thresholds in Financial Development and Economic Growth"*, in Supplement to the Manchester School Papers in Money, Macroeconomics and Finance-Proceedings of the Money, Macroeconomics and Finance Research Group, Blackwell Publishers (pp. 70-84).

23. Berthelemy J.C and Varoudakis A. (1996), *"Economic growth convergence clubs and the role of financial development"*, Oxford economic papers, Volume 48 (pp. 300-328).

24. Berthelemy, Jean-Claude and Varoudakis, Aristomene (1998), "Financial Development, Financial Reforms and Growth: A panel data approach", *Revue-Economique*, 49(1), pp. 195-206.

25. Birnbaum (1958), *"Growth of Financial Intermediaries and the Effectiveness of Monetary Policy"*, IMF Staff Papers, November.

26. Blackburn, K. and Hung, V.T.Y. (1998). A theory of growth, financial development trade, *Economica*, 65, 107-124.

27. Boyd and Prescott (1986), *"Financial Intermediary Coalitions"*, Journal of Economic Theory, 30, (pp. 211-232).

28. Brownbridge and C. Kirkpatrick (2000), 'Financial regulation in developing countries', Journal of Development Studies 37/1.

29. Barth, James, Gerard Caprio, and Ross Levine (2000), "Banking Systems around the Globe: Do Regulation and Ownership Affect Performance and Stability?" National Bureau of Economic Research.

30. Brunner and Meltzer (1963), *"The Place of Financial Institutions in the Transmission of Monetary Policy"*, American Economic Review, Volume 53, May (pp. 381),

31. Buffie Edward F. (1984), *"Financial Repression, The New Structuralist and Stabilization Policy in Semi Industrialized Economies"*, Journal of Development Economics, 14 (pp. 305-322).

32. Campbell. T and Kracaw (1980), *"Information Production, Market Signalling and Theory of Financial Intermediation"*, Journal of Literature, 35, (pp. 305-322).

33. Chamley and Hanohan (1993), *"Financial Repression and Banking Intermediation"*, Savings and Development, 17 (3) (pp. 301-308).

34. Chandavarkar Anand (1992), *"Of Finance and Development: Neglected and Unsettled Questions"*, World Development, Volume 20, No. 1 (pp. 133-142).

35. Calomiris Charles W. (1995), *"Financial Fragility: Issues and Policy Implications"*, Journal of Financial Services Research, 9, (pp. 241-257).

36. Caprio, Gerard, and Patrick Honohan. (1999). "Restoring Banking Stability: Beyond Supervised Capital Requirements." *Journal of Economic Perspectives* 13 (4): 43-64.

37. Caprio, P. Honohan, J. Stiglitz, (2001), 'Financial liberalization: how far, how fast?' Cambridge University Press.

38. Caprio, P. Honohan, J. Stiglitz, (2001), 'Finance for Growth. Policy Choices in a Volatile World', World Bank and Oxford University Press: Washington DC.

39. Chapple, Simon (1991). Financial Liberalisation in New Zealand, 1984-90. UNCTAD Discussion Papaer No. 35.

40. Corsepius Uwe (1990), *"The Structure of Financial Savings and Loanable Funds: Evidence from Peru"*, Savings and Development No. 1, xiv (pp. 89-100).

41. Davis. E.P. (1992), *"Credit Quality Spreads, Bond Market Efficiency and Financial Fragility"*, The Manchester School, Volume LX Supplement, June (pp.21-46).

42. Demetriades, Panicos O., and Michael P Devereux (1992). Investment and "Financial Repression: Theory and Evidence from 63 LDCs", Working Paper in Economics 92/16, Keele University December.

43. Demetriades. Panicos and Luintel, Kul B (1996), "Financial Development, Economic Growth and Banking Sector Controls: Evidence from India", *Economic Journal,* 106 (435), pp. 359-74.

44. Demirguc A. and G. Degatriache, (1998), The Determinants of Banking Crises in Developing and Developed Countries, International-Monetary-Fund-Staff-Papers; 45 (1), 81-109.

45. Demirguc A. and G. Degatriache, (2000), Banking Sector Fragility: A Multivariate Logit Approach, *World Bank Economic Review,* 14 (2), 287-307.

46. Demetriades, P. and Hussein, K. (1996), "Does Financial Development Cause Economic Growth" Time Series Evidence from 16 Countries", *Journal of Development Economics,* 51, 387-411.

47. De Gregorio Jose (1992), *"Economic Growth in Latin America"*, Journal of Development Economics, 39 (pp. 59-84).

48. De Gregorio Jose and Guidotti Pablo E. (1993), *"Financial Development and Economic Growth"*, Washington D.C., International Monetary Fund, July.

49. De Melo and Tybout (1986), *"The Effects of Financial Liberalisation on Savings and Investment in Uruguay"*, Economic Development and Cultural Change (pp. 561-587).

50. De Gregorio Jose and Guidotti Pablo. (1995), "Financial Development and Economic Growth", *World Development,* 23 (Mar.): 433-438.

51. De La Fuente, Angel and Marin, Jose Marias (1994), "Innovation, Bank Monitoring and Endogenous Financial Development", Universitat Pompeu Fabra Working Paper, No. 59.

52. Diamond Douglas. W and Dybvig Phillip H (1983), *"Bank Runs, Deposit Insurance and Liquidity"*, Journal of Political Economy, 91 (3), June (pp. 401-419).

53. Diamond Douglas. W (1984), *"Financial Intermediation and delegated monitoring"*, Review of Economics and Studies, 51 (pp. 393-414).

54. Diamond Douglas. W (1991), *"Diamond DW –1991; Monitoring and Regulation. The choice between Bank loans and privately placed Debt"*, Journal of Political Economy 99, (pp. 689-721).

55. Diaz Alejandro (1985), *"Goobye Financial Repression, Hello Financial Crash"*, Journal of Development Economics, 19 (1-2) September-October (pp. 1-24).

56. Dornbusch R and A Reynoso (1989), *"Financial Factors in Economic Development"*, American Economic Review, 79 (2), May (pp. 204-209.

57. Fama Eugene F (1980), *"Banking in the Theory of Finance"*, Journal of Monetary Economics, January.

58. Fama Eugene F (1983), *"Financial Intermediation and Price Level Control"*, Journal of Monetary Economics, July.

59. Favara Giovanni (2003), "An empirical Reassessment of the relationship between Finance and Growth", IMFWP 103/123, June.

60. Fidel Jaramillo, Fabio Schiantarelli, and Andrew Weiss (1992), "The Effect of Financial Liberalisation on the Allocation of Credit: Evidence from a Panel of Ecuadorian Firms", World Bank Working Paper No. 1092.

61. Fisher Irving (1933), *"The Debt Deflation Theory of Great Depressions"* Econometrica, Volume 1 (pp. 337-357).

62. Feldman David H and Gang Ira N (1990), *"Financial Development and the Price of Services"*, Economic Development and Cultural Change (pp. 341-352).

63. Friedman (1990), *"Changing Effects of Monetary Policy on Real Economic Activity"*, in Monetary Policy Issues in the 1990s, A Symposium Sponsored by the Federal Reserve bank of Kansa City.

64. Fry Maxwell J (1978), *"Money and Capital or Financial Deepening in Economic Development?"*, Journal of Money, Credit and Banking, Vol. 10, No. 4, November (465-475).

65. Fry Maxwell J (1980a), *"Saving, Investment, Growth and the Cost of Financial Repression"*, World Development, Vol. 8, (317-327).

66. Fry (1980b), *"Money, Interest, Inflation and Growth in Turkey"*, Journal of Monetary Economics, Vol. 6, No. 4, October (pp. 535-545).

67. Fry Maxwell J (1988), *"Money, Interest and banking in Economic Development"*, The John Hopkins University press, Baltimore and London.

68. Fry Maxwell J (1993), *"The Fiscal Abuse of Central Banks"*, Washington D.C., IMF Working Paper, 93/58, July.

69. Fry, M.J. (1995), *Money, Interest and Banking in Economic Development*, 2nd ed. Baltimore: Johns Hopkins University Press.

70. Fry Maxwell J (1997), *"Financial Repression in Emancipating the banking System and Developing Markets for Government Debt"*, Routledge, New York.

71. Galbis, (1977), *"Financial Intermediation and Economic Growth in less developed countries: A Theoretical Approach"*, The Journal of Development Studies, 4 (160-180).

72. Galbis, (1979), *"Money, Investment and Growth in Latin America: 1961-73"*, Economic Development and Cultural Change, 27, April (pp. 423-443).

73. Gavin, Michael and Ricardo Hausmann (1997). The roots of banking Crisis: The Macroeconomic Context. In Ricardo Hausmannand Liliana Rojas-Suarez eds., *Banking Crisis in Latin America*, IMF

74. Gelb, Alan H (1989), *"Financial Policies, Growth and Efficiency"*, Washington D.C., World Bank, Country Economics Department, PPR Working Paper, WPS 202, June.

75. Gelos, Gaston (1997). How did Financial Liberalisation in Mexico Affect Investment? Evidence from Manufacturing Sector, Department of Economics University.

76. Gertler Mark (1988), *"Financial Structure and Aggregate Economic Activity: An overview"*, Journal of Money Credit and Banking, Volume 20, No. 3 (August, part 2).

77. Ghani Ejaz (1992), *"How Financial Markets Affects Long run Growth: A Cross-country Study"*, Washington D.C., WB, Country operations, PR Working Paper, WPS 843, January.

78. Giovannini Alberto (1983), *"The Interest Elasticity of Savings in Developing Countries: The existing Evidence"*, World Development, Volume 11, No. 7, (pp. 601-607).

79. Giovannini, A. (1985), "Saving and Real Interest Rates in LDCs", Journal of Development Economics, Vol. 8, August.

80. Giovanini Alberto and Martha de Melo (1993), *"Government Revenue from Financial Repression"*, American Economic Review, 83 (4), September (pp. 953-963).

81. Goldsmith, W. Raymond (1954), *"The Share of Financial Intermediaries in national Wealth and national Asset, 1900-1949"*, National Bureau of Economic Research, Occasional Paper No. 42, New York.

82. Goldsmith, W. Raymond (1955), *"A Study of Saving in the United States"*, Princeton. N.J., Princeton University Press.

83. Goldsmith, W. Raymond (1957), *"Summary of Flow of Funds Accounts Annual Estimates, 1950-55"*, Federal Reserve Bulletin, April.

84. Goldsmith. W. Raymond (1958), *"Financial Intermediaries in the American Economy Since 1900"*, Princeton University Press.

85. Goldsmith R (1969), *"Financial structure and Development"*, Yale University Press, Princeton NJ.

86. Goldsmith (1983), *"The Financial Development of India: 1860-1977"* New Haven: Yale University Press.

87. Gorton Gary and Pennachhi George (1990), *"Financial Intermediaries and Liquidity Creation"*, The Journal of Finance, Volume XLV, Number 1, March (pp. 49-71).

88. Greenwood Jeremy and Bcyan Jovanovic (1990), *"Financial Development, Growth and the Distribution of Income"*, Journal of Political economy, 98, (5, l, October) (1076-1107).

89. Greenwood, J. and Smith, B.D. (1997). Financial markets in development, and the development of financial markets. *Journal of Economic Dynamics and Control*, 21, 145-181.

90. Greene, Joshua, and Delano Villanueva (1991). Private Investment in Developing Countries: An Empirical Analysis., *IMF Staff Papers* 38 (March 1991) pp 33-58.

91. Gunther W. Jeffery, Lown S Cara and Robinson J Kenneth (1995), *"Bank Credit and Economic Activity: Evidence from Texas Banking Decline"*, Journal of Financial Services Research, Volume 9 (pp. 31-48).

92. Gupta Kanhaya L. (1984), *"Financial Liberalisation and Economic Growth: Some Simulation Results"*, Journal of Economic Development, 9(2), December (pp. 25-43).

93. Gupta Kanhaya L. (1987), *"Aggregate Savings, Financial Intermediaries and Interest Rate"*, Review of Economics and Statistics, 69(2) (pp. 303-311).

94. Gurley J.G and E.S.Shaw (1955), *"Financial Aspects of Economic Development"*, The American Economic Review, Volume XLV, No. 4, September, (515-538).

95. Gurley J.G and Shaw E.S. (1956), *"Financial Intermediaries and the Saving-investment process"*, Journal of Finance, Volume 11, No. 2, May, (pp. 257-76).

96. Gurley J.G and E.S.Shaw (1957), *"The Growth of Debt and Money in The United States, 1800-1950: A Suggested interpretation"*, Review of Economics and Statistics, (250-262).

97. Gurley J.G and E.S.Shaw (1960), *"Money in a Theory of Finance"*, Washington D.C., Brookings Institution.

98. Gustav Schmolders (1960), *"The liquidity Theory of Money"*, Kyklos, Volume 13, (pp. 346-358).

99. Habibullah Muzaffar Shah (1991), *"Money and its Substitutes in a Developing Economy: Empirical Evidence from Malaysia"*, Indian Economic Journal, July-September (pp. 60-86).

100. Hansen (1953), *"A Guide to Keynes"*, McGraw Hill, New York.

101. Hassan Kabir M, Samad Abdul, Islam Faridul (1993), *"A Reexamination of McKinnon-Shaw Hypotheses: Evidence from Five South Asian Countries"*, The Bangladesh Development Studies, Volume XXI, Number 4, December.

102. Hassan Kabir M (1995), *"Testing complementarity between money and capital in Bangladesh"*, The Bangladesh Development Studies.

103. Hataiseree Rungsun and Phipps Anthony (1996) *"The relationship between Money and Income in Thailand: some Evidence for the 1980s using a cointegration Approach"*, Savings and Development, Number 4, Volume XX (pp. 389-405).

104. Haubrich Joseph. G. (1989), *"Financial Intermediation Delegated Monitoring and Long-term Relationship"*, Journal of Banking and Finance, March, Vol, 13, No. 1 (pp. 9-20).

105. Haubrich Joseph. G. and King (1989), *"Banking and Insurance"*, Journal of Monetary Economics.

106. Haubrich Joseph. G. (1990), *"Non-Monetary Effects of Financial Crisis: Lessons from the Great Depression in Canada"*, Journal of Monetary Economics, 25 (pp. 223-252).

107. Hicks, J.R (1937), *"Mr. Keynes and the Classics: A suggested Interpretation"*, Econometrica, 5, April (pp. 147-59).

108. Hicks, J.R (1969), *"Capital Essays in Monetary Theory"*, Chapter 9, Claredon Press, (pp. 155-173).

109. Hermes Niels (1994), *"Financial Development and Economic Growth: A Survey of Literature"*, International Journal of Development Banking, Vol. 12, No. 1, January.

110. Horgren Lars (1985), *"Regulatory Monetary Policy and Uncontrolled Financial Intermediaries"*, Journal of Money Credit and Banking, Vol. 17, No. 2 (May).

111. Honohan, Patrick (1997), Banking System failures in Developing and Transitional Countries: Diagnosis and Prediction,. BIS Working paper No. 39, Basle, Bank for International Settlements.

112. Honohan, P and J. Stiglitz (1999), "Robust Financial Restraint", mimeo, World Bank, Washington DC

113. Honohan, P. (1999), "The Evolution of Interest Rates across Countries: Statistical Evidence", mimeo, World Bank, Washington DC.

114. Hussain, M. Nureldin (1996). Financial Liberalisation, Currency Substitution and Investment: The case of Egypt. African Development Bank Research Papers No. 24, Addis Ababa, African Development Bank.

115. Jayaratne Jith and Philip E. Strahan (1996), "The finance-growth nexus: Evidence from bank branch deregulation", *Quarterly Journal of Economics*, CXI, pp. 639-671.

116. Jao Y C, (1976), *"Financial Deepening and Economic Growth: A Cross Section Analysis"*, Malayan Economic Review, Volume 21, Number 1 (pp. 47-58).

117. Jappelli, Tullio and Marco Pagano (1994), *"Saving, Growth, and Liquidity Constraints"*, Quarterly Journal of Economics, 109 (1), February (pp. 83-109).

118. John Harris, R. Fabio Schiantarelli, and Miranda G Siregar (1992). The Effect of Financial Liberalisation on Firm. S Capital Structure and Investment Decision: Evidence for a Panel of Indonesian Manufacturing Establishments 1981-88. World Bank Working Paper No. 997.

119. Johnston Barry R and Pazarbasioglu Ceyla (1995), *"Linkages between Financial variables, Financial Sector Reform and Economic Growth and Efficiency"*, IMF Working Paper, WP/95/103, October.

120. Jung Woo S. (1986), *"Financial Development and Economic Growth: International Evidence"*, Economic Development and Cultural Change, 34(2), January (pp. 333-346).

121. Kaminsky,. G. and C. Reinhart, 1999, The twin crises: the causes of banking and balanceof-payments problems. *American Economic Review*, 89, pp. 473-500.

122. Kaminsky, G., S. Lizondo, and C. M. Reinhart, 1998, Leading indicators of currency crisis. *IMF Staff Papers*, 45(1), pp. 1-48.

123. Kane (1981), *"Accelerating Inflation and Technological Innovation, and the Decreasing Effectiveness of Banking Regulation"*, Journal of Finance, 36, (pp. 355-367).

124. Kapur Basant K (1976), *"Alternative Stabilization Policies for less developed economies"*, Journal of Political Economy, 84(4) (pp. 777-795).

125. Kapur (1992), *"Formal and Informal Financial Markets and the Neo-structuralist Critique of the Financial Liberalization Strategy in Less Developed Countries"*, Journal of Development Economics, 38 (pp. 63-67).

126. Koeva Petya (2003), "The performance of Indian Banks during Financial Liberalisation", IMF WP/03/150 July.

127. Keynes Maynard John (1936), *"The General Theory of Employment, Interest and Money"*, London, Macmillan.

128. Khan S. Moshin and Senhadji Abdelhak S (2000), "Financial Development and Economic Growth: An Overview", IMF Working Paper, WP/00/209 December.

129. King Robert G and Ross Levine (1992), *"Financial Indicators and Growth in a Cross Section of Countries"*, Policy Research Working-Paper No. 819, World Bank, January.

130. King Robert G and Ross Levine (1993a), *"Finance and Growth: Schumpeter Might be Right"*, Quarterly Journal of Economics, 108(3), August (pp. 717-737).

131. King Robert G and Ross Levine (1993b), *"Financial, Entrepreneurship, and Growth: Theory and Evidence"*, Journal of Monetary Economics, 32(3), December (pp. 513-542).

132. King Robert G and Ross Levine (1993c), *"Financial intermediation and Economic Development"*, Chapter 6 in Capital Markets and Financial Intermediation, Ed.-Colin Mayer and Xavier Vives, Centre for Economic Policy Research, Cambridge University Press.

133. Kuznets Simon (1955), *"Economic Growth and Income Inequality"*, American Economic Review., 45, March (pp. 1-8).

134. Kuznets Simon (1961), *"Capital in the American Economy"*, Princeton University Press.

135. Kwan, Andy C., Wu, Yangru and Zhang, Junxi (1998), "An Exogeneity Analysis of Financial Deepening and Economic Growth: Evidence from Hong Kong, South Korea and Taiwan",

Journal of International Trade and Economic Development, 7(3), pp. 339-54.

136. La Porta, R., F. Lopez-De-Silanes, A. Shleifer And R.W. Vishny (1997) "Legal determinants of external finance", *Journal of Finance* 52 (3), pp. 1131-1150.

137. La Porta, R., F. Lopez-De-Silanes, A. Shleifer And R.W. Vishny (1998) "Law and finance", *Journal of Political Economy* 106 (6), pp. 1113-1155.

138. La Porta, R., F. Lopez-De-Silanes, A. Shleifer And R.W. Vishny (1999) "The quality of government", *Journal of Law, Economics, and Organization* 15 (1), pp. 222-279.

139. Laumas Prem S (1990), *"Financial Liberalization and Economic Development"*, Economic Development and Cultural Change, Volume 38(2), (pp. 377-390).

140. Lee Chung H and Haggard Stephen (1995), *"Issues in Finance and Development"*, Oxford Economic Bulletin.

141. Leigh Lamin (1996), *"Financial Development and Economic Growth: An Econometric Analysis for Singapore"*, IMF Working Paper, February.

142. Levine Ross (1991), *"Stock Markets, Growth and Tax Policy"*, Journal of Finance, 46, (pp. 1445-65).

143. Levine, R. And S. Zervos (1996), "Stock market development and long-run growth", *World Bank Policy Research Working Paper*, No. 1582, March.

144. Levine, R. (1997), "Financial development and economic growth: views and agendas", *Journal of Economic Literature*, Vol. XXXV, June, pp. 688-726.

145. Levine, Ross (1998), "The Legal Environment, Banks, and the Long-Run Economic Growth", *Journal of Money Credit and Banking*, 30(3), pp. 596-613.

146. Levine, R and S. Zervos (1998), "Stock markets, banks and economic growth", *American Economic Review*, 88 (3), June, 537-58.

147. Levine, R. (1999), "Law, finance and economic growth", *Journal of Financial Intermediation*, 8(1-2), January-April, pp. 8-35.

148. Levine, R. (2000), "Bank-based or market-based financial systems: which is better?" Finance Department, Carlson School of Management, University of Minnesota, *mimeo*, January.

149. Levine R., N. Loayza, and T. Beck, 2000, "Financial Intermediation and Growth: Causality and Causes," *Journal of Monetary Economics*, 46(1), 31-77.

150. Lewis. W.A. (1954a), *"Economic Development with Unlimited Supplies of Labour"*, The Manchester School Vol. 22, (pp. 139-191).

151. Lewis. W.A. (1954b), *"The Theory of Economic Growth"*, Allen and Unwin.

152. Li Kui Wai and Skully Micheal (1992), *"Accumulation of Financial Resources in Asian Economies"*, Savings and Development, Volume XVI, Number 3 (pp. 225-241).

153. Loayza Norman and Romain Ranciere (2002), "Financial Development, Financial Fragility, And Growth", Working Paper, February, Central Bank of Chile.

154. Lopez-Meija, Alejandra (1991), "Excess Smoothness, Excess Sensitivity of Consumption and Financial Liberalisation: The UK Evidence", Department of Economics Paper No 239, University of London, Queen Mary and Westfield College.

155. Lucas Robert E (1988), *"On the Mechanics of Economic Development"*, Journal of Monetary Economics, 22 (1), July (pp. 3-42).

156. Luintel and Khan, (1999), "A quantitative reassessment of the finance-growth nexus: evidence from a multivariate VAR", *Journal of Development Economics*, Vol. 60, pp. 381-405.

157. Mathieson, Donald. J. (1979), *"Financial Reform and Capital Flows in a Developing Economy"*, International Monetary Fund Staff papers, 26(3), September (pp. 450-489).

158. Mathieson, Donald. J. (1980), *"Financial Reform and Stabilization Policy in a Development Economy"*, Journal of Development Economics, 7(3) (pp. 359-395).

159. Margaritis, Dimitri, Dean Hyslop and David Rae (1994). Financial Policy Reforms in New Zealand in Caprio, Atiyas and Hanson eds., *Financial Reform*, pp 140-183.

160. Mavrotas (1999), *"Financial Sector Development And Savings Mobilisation: An Assessment"*, School of Economic Studies, University of Manchester & Roger Kelly Institute for Development Policy and Management, University of Manchester, November.

161. McKinnon R.I (1973), *"Money and Capital in Economic Development"*, Washington D.C., Brookings Institution.

162. Melnick Rafi and Yashiv Evan (1996), *"The Macroeconomic Effects and Financial Innovations: The case of Israel"*, Chapter 8 in Financial Factors in Economic Stabilization and Growth, Edited by Mario

Blejer, Zvi Eckstein, Zvittercowitz and Leonardo Leiderman, Cambridge University Press.

163. Michael Leahy, Sebastian Schich, Gert Wehinger, Florian Pelgrin and Thorsteinn Thorgeirsson (2001)6, "Contributions Of Financial Systems To Growth In OECD Countries", OECD's Economic Department Working Papers No. 280.

164. Minsky (1995), *"Financial Factors in the Economics of Capitalism"*, Journal of Financial Research, 9, (pp 197-208).

165. Mishkin Fredrick S (1996), *"Asymmetric Information and Financial Crisis: A Historical Perspective"*, National Bureau of Economic Research.

166. Modigliani. F and Miller. M (1958), *"The Cost of Capital, Corporation Finance and the Theory of Investment"*, American Economic Review, June.

167. Moore Basil J. (1968), *"An Introduction to the Theory of Finance-Asset Holder Behaviour Under Uncertainity"*, Amerind Publishing Company (P) Limited.

168. Moore Basil J. (1986), *"Inflation and Financial Deepening"*, Journal of Development Economics, 20, (pp. 125-133).

169. Morisset Jacques (1993), *"Does Financial Liberalisation really improve private investment in developing countries?"*, Journal of Development? "Economics, 40 (pp. 133-150).

170. Morgan Donald P (1992), *"Are Bank Loans Force in Monetary Policy?"*, Federal Reserve Bank of Kansas City-Economic Review, Second Quarter (pp. 31-41).

171. Muhsin Kar and Eric J. Pentecost (2000), Financial Development and Economic Growth in Turkey: Further Evidence on the Causality Issue, Economic Research Paper No. 00/27, December.

172. Murinde Victor and Eng Fern S.H. (1994), *"Financial Development and Economic Growth in Singapore: Demand-Following or Supply-Leading"*, Applied Financial Economics, 1994, 4 (pp. 391-404).

173. Niehans J. (1980), *"A Theory of Money"*, John Hopkins University Press.

174. Nurkse. R. (1953), *"Problems of Capital Formation in Underdeveloped Countries"*, Basil Blackwell, Oxford.

175. Odedokun M.O. (1989), *"Causalities Between Financial Aggregates and Economic Activities in Nigeria: The Results from Granger's Test"*, Savings and Development, No. 1, volume xiii (pp. 101-111).

176. Odedokun, M.O. (1996). Alternative econometric approaches for analysing the role of the financial sector in economic growth:

time-series evidence from LDCs. *Journal of Development Economics,* 50, 119-146.

177. Odedokun, M.O (1998), "Financial Intermediaiton and Economic Growth in Developing *Journal of Economic Studies,* 25 (3), pp. 203-234.

178. Pagano (1993), *"Financial Markets and Growth: An Overview",* European Economic Review, 37 (pp. 613-622).

179. Park Yung Chul (1994), *"The Financial Development of Japan, Korea and Taiwan",* Edited by Patrick H.T.

180. Patinkin (1961), *"Financial Intermediaries and the Logical Structure of Monetary Theory"* in Studies in Monetary Economics, Harper International Edition.

181. Patrick Hugh. T. (1966), *"Financial Development and Economic Growth in Underdeveloped Countries",* Economic Development and Cultural Change, Vol. XIV, No. 2, January.

182. Patrick Hugh T (1990), *"The Financial Development of Taiwan, Korea and Japan: Framework for Consideration .of Issues"*— Paper presented at the Conference on Financial Development in Japan, Korea and Taiwan, Institute of Economics, Academia Sinica, Taipei, August 27-28.

183. Patrick Hugh T (1994), *"The Financial Development of Japan, Korea and Taiwan",* Edited.

184. Pill and Pradhan (1995), *"Financial Indicators and Financial Change in Asia and African Countries",* International Monetary Fund, Working Paper.

185. Prebisch. R. (1950), *"The Economic Development of Latin America and its Principal Problems",* UND, New York.

186. Ramakrishnan Ram T S, Anjan V Thakor (1984), *"Information Reliability and a theory of Financial Intermediation",* Review of Economic Studies, 1984, LI (pp. 415-432).

187. Rajan, R. and L. Zingales (1998*a*), "Financial dependence and growth", *The American Economics Review,* 88: pp. 559-586.

188. Rajan, R. and L. Zingales (1998*b*), "Which capitalism? Lessons from the East Asia crisis", *Journal of Applied Corporate Finance.*

189. Rajan, R. and L. Zingales (1999), "The politics of financial development", mimeo, University of Chicago.

190. Rajan, R. and L. Zingales (2000), "Financial systems, industrial structure and growth", paper prepared for the Symposium of the International Competitiveness of the Swedish Financial Industry organized by the Bank of Sweden Tercentenary Foundation.

191. Reinhart, Carmen, and Gariela Kaminsky (1996). The Twin Crisis: The Cause of Banking and Balance of Payments Problems., IMF Seminar Series No. 96/12.

192. *Report of the Committee on the Working of the Monetary System of the Exchequer,* (1959), (Radcliffe Committee).

193. Robinson Joan (1952), *"The Generalization of the General Theory"* in the Rate of Interest and Other Essays, London.

194. Romer Davi (1985), *"Financial Intermediation, Reserve Requirements and Inside Money-A General Equilibrium Analysis"*, Journal of Monetary Economics, 16 (pp. 175-194).

195. Romer Paul M (1986), *"Increasing Returns and Long run Growth"*, Journal of Political Economy, Volume 94, October (pp. 1002-1037).

196. Romer David (1990), *"Endogenous Technological Change"*, Journal of Political Economy, 98 (5, ii, October) (pp. S71-S102).

197. Roosa Robert V (1951), *"Interest Rates and the Central Bank"*, Money, Trade and Economic Growth: Essays in Honor of John H Williams, New York, Macmillan.

198. Roubini Nouriel and Sala-i-Martin Xavier (1991), *"Financial Development, the Trade Regime, and Economic Growth"*, Cambridge, National Bureau of Economic Research, Working Paper No. 3876, October.

199. Roubini Nouriel and Sala-i-Martin Xavier (1992), *"Financial Repression and Economic Growth"*, Journal of Development Economics, 39 (pp. 5-30).

200. Roubini Nouriel and Sala-i-Martin Xavier (1995), *"A Growth Model of Inflation, tax evasion, and Financial Repression"*, Journal of Monetary Economics, 35 (pp. 275-301).

201. Rousseau, P.L. & Wachtel, P. (1998). Financial intermediaiton and economic performance: historical evidence from five industrial countries. Journal of Money, Credit and Banking 30, 657-678.

202. Rousseau, P.L. & Wachtel, P. (2001). Inflation threshold and the finance-growth nexus. Forthcoming.

203. Saint Paul G (1992), *"Technological choice, Financial Markets and Economic Development"*, European Economic Review, 36 (pp. 763-781).

204. Schmookler Jacob (1966), *"Invention and Economic Growth"*, Cambridge, Harvard University Press.

205. Schumpeter, J.A. (1911), 'Theorie der wirtschaftlichen Entwicklung', Duncker & Humblot, München.

206. Schumpeter, Joseph A. (1912). *Theorie der Wirtschaftlichen Entwicklung (The Theory of Economic Development).* Leipzig: Dunker & Humblot, Translated by Redvers Opie, Cambridge, MA: Harvard University Press. 1934.

207. Schumpeter J.A (1934), *"The Theory of Economic Development"*, Harvard University Press.

208. Shaw E.S (1973), *"Financial deepening in Economic Development"*, Oxford University press, London.

209. Silber W.L (1983), *"The Process of Financial Innovation"*, American Economic Review, May (pp. 89-95).

210. Singh, Ajit and Weisse, Bruce A (1998), "Emerging Stock Markets, Portfolio Capital Flows and Long-Term Economic Growth: Micro and Macroeconomic Perspectives", *World Development*, 26(4), pp. 607-22.

211. Spellman Lewis J (1976), *"Economic Growth and Financial Intermediation"* in money and Finance in Economic Growth and Development: *Essays in Honour of Edward S. Shaw*. Ed., by McKinnon. R.I., New York: Marcel Dekker (11-22).

212. St. Hill, Rodney L. (1992), *"Stages of Banking and Economic Development"*, Saving and Development, 14(1) (pp. 5-20).

213. Steinherr. A and Ch. Huveneers (1994), *"On the performance of Differently regulated financial institutions: Some empirical evidence"*, Journal of Banking and Finance 18, January (pp. 271-306).

214. Stern Nicholas (1991), *"The Determinants of Growth"*, The Economic Journal, 101, January (pp. 122-133).

215. Stiglitz, Joseph E and Weiss (1981), *"Credit Rationing in Markets with Imperfect Information"*, American Eco0nomic Review, June, (pp. 393-410).

216. Stiglitz, Joseph E (1989), *"Markets, Market failures and Development"*, American Economic Review, 79(2) (PP197-203).

217. Sussman Oren (1992), *"Financial Liberalization: The Israeli experience"*, Oxford Economic Papers, Volume 44 (pp. 387-402).

218. Sussman Oren (1993), *"A Theory of Financial Development"* in Finance and Development: Issues and Experience, Ed. By Alberto Giovannini, Cambridge: CEPF, Cambridge University Press (pp. 29-57).

219. Thorn R (1958), *"Non-Banking Financial Intermediaries, Credit Expansion and Monetary Policy"*, IMF Staff Paper, November.

220. Thornton (1996), *"Financial Deepening and Economic Growth in Developing Economies"*, Applied Economic Letters, Volume 3, Number 4, April (pp. 243-246).

221. Tobin James and Brainard W.C. (1963), *"Financial Intermediaries and the Effectiveness of Monetary Controls"*, American Economic review, 53, May (pp. 383-400).

222. Tobin James (1965), *"Money and Economic Growth"*, Econometrica, October, Volume 33, Number 4, (pp. 671-684).

223. Tobin James and Brainard W.C. (1969), *"Pitfalls in Financial Model Building"*, American Economic Review 58, May.

224. Tobin James (1971), *"An Essays on the Principles of Debt Management"*, In Essays in Economics, Volume 1, Macroeconomics, New York, North-Holland Publishing Company.

225. Tobin James (1982), *"Money and Finance in the Macroeconomic Process"*, Journal of Money, Credit and Banking, Volume 14, Number 2, May (pp. 171-204).

226. Tobin James (1984), *"On the Efficiency of the Financial System"*, Lloyds Bank Review, 153, July (pp. 1-115).

227. Tuuli Koivu 1 (2002), "Does financial sector development affect economic growth in transition countries?", For presentation at the Nordic Conference in Development Economics, Bergen, Norway, April.

228. Van Horne J.C. (1985), *"Of Financial Innovation and Excesses"*, Journal of Finance, July (pp. 621-631).

229. Venkatachalam T.R and Sharma Y.S.R (1976), *"Structure and Trends in the National Balance Sheet for India"*, Journal of Income and Wealth, Volume 1 (pp. 95-136).

230. Wachtel, Paul and Rousseau, Peter (1995), "Financial Intermediation and Economic Growth: A Historical Comparison of the United States, United Kingdom, and Canada", In *Anglo-American Financial Systems: Institutions and Markets in the Twentieth Century*, edited by Michael D. Bordo and Richard Sylla, pp. 329-81, Burr Ridge, 11.: Business One Irwin.

231. Wachtel, Paul and Rousseau, Peter (1998), "Financial Intermediation and Economic Performance: Historical Evidence from Five Industrialized Countries", *Journal of Money Credit and Banking*, 30 (4), pp. 657-678.

232. Winjbergen Van Sweder (1983), *"Credit Policy, Inflation and Growth in a Financially Repressed Economy"*—Journal Development Economics, volume 13 (pp. 45-65).

233. Williamson (1986), *"Costly Monitoring, Financial Intermediation and Equilibrium Credit Rationing"*, Journal of Monetary Economics, 18 (pp. 159-179).

234. Williamson, J. and Mahar, M. (1998) *A Review of Financial Liberalisation,* South Asia Region: Internal Discussion Paper (IDP-171), The World Bank.;

235. Wood Anthony (1993), "Financial Development in Barbados, Savings and Development", No. 4, XVII, (pp. 379-390).

236. World Bank (1989), "World development Report 1989: Financial Systems and Development", New York, Oxford University Press.

2

The Crisis of Capitalism in the Financial Markets

Christopher Gan*
Patricia McGraw*

Introduction

A nation is more prosperous today the fewer obstacles it has placed in the path of laissez-faire capitalism. The characteristics of modern capitalism are mass production and consumption of goods by the masses and a continuous improvement in the average standard of living (von Mises, 1972). The free capitalist system makes those capitalists prosper who have succeeded in meeting the wants of the people in the best possible and cheapest way. However, markets are fragile and can be shattered easily.

Recent corporate fraud and scandals (see Appendix 1) have created unprecedented scepticism about the credibility of laissez-faire capitalism and investors have began to see past business success as nothing but a corporate hoax. There is no justification for this extraordinary crisis. For example, Enron, World Com, and other corporate accounting scandals shared a common dishonest culture-explosive growth supported by innovative structured finance (also known as

* Commerce Division, Lincoln University, Canterbury, New Zealand.

securitisation) that passed along credit risks to others without proper disclosure about the nature and amount of the obligations (Timmons, 2002). Executives manipulated the markets and misled the public and their employees about their company's debt and stock earning prospects. They put their self-interests above those of their clients and employees fuelling anti corporate sentiments. Billions in losses hit the portfolios of pension funds, insurance companies and mutual funds, the main buyers.

However, corporate scandals are nothing new. The Milken junk-bond insider trading schemes in the 1980s and the Prudential Securities limited partnership scandal in the early 1990s contaminated the honesty, ethics and integrity of the corporate culture (including the principles of laissez-faire capitalism). Why have business professionals failed to learn from the mistakes of the past? The industry has continuously resisted calls for corporate governance change, even in the face of repeated corporate corruption because of the "entrepreneurial culture". Unless the free-market economies strive to develop market ethics among business professionals, corporate scandals will be repeated many times. The emphasis should be on the business not individual achievements.

Just about everywhere, investors are advocating for more transparency in accounting and greater checks and balances between management and board of directors (Rossan et al., 2002). The Enron scandal is contagion. For example Air New Zealand collapses due to the collapses of Ansett Australia (a bad investment) while the collapse of Swissair had tainted the paradise world of Switzerland. New Zealand and Scandinavian corporate practices were under the microscope with several golden handshake deals. In Germany, a series of corporate collapses, most recently the explosion of the Kirch Media Empire is overhauling German corporate governance (Rossan et al., May 6, 2002). In Japan, the opaque relationships between banks and corporate firms are under pressure for reforms. The collapse of Daewoo in 1999 revealed the chairman had engaged in creative accounting by inflating the books of Daewoo by $30 billion. This led to major reform in Korean corporate codes requiring listed companies to fill at least half of the board seats with outside directors (Rossan et al., 2002).

The recent spate of corporate frauds, ethical lapses and outrageous CEO payouts conjure up Schumpeter's hostile view of capitalism. Schumpeter would argue that these types of relationships exploit capitalist values by irrational behaviour that leads to an attitude hostile to corporations, to big business in general and to the capitalist order (Bottomore, 1942). In other words, the capitalist process is capable of generating an atmosphere of hostility to its own social order as well as violating the implicit moral contract. The public feels disillusioned and disgusted with the market system. This only lends greater credence to the belief that laissez-faire capitalism is inherently corrupted. Credibility and trust is vital to a free-market system and widespread greed overwhelms the system.

As the market tries to comprehend the consequences of the Enron, WorldCom, and other corporate scandals, the list of suspected culprits is growing. This includes the Security and Exchange Commission criminal investigation of the Merrill Lynch-Enron private equity deals involving violation of accounting rules and fraudulent promotion of the stocks of companies. In addition, Citigroup and J.P Morgan Chase & Co. are also under scrutiny for their billion dollars deal with Enron. Whilst the failure of Enron took most of the blame, critics have shifted their argument to include the failure of free market capitalism, where financial market discipline is being eroded. They argue that the ease with which companies can unload risk to others has actually made the financial system more fragile and vulnerable to shocks. The Enron scandal became hazardous to the multibillion-dollar commercial paper market that companies use to raise short-term capital. Companies that are still in the market have to pay more to issue commercial paper (Miller et al., 2002). Schumpeter would argue that such behaviours invite aggression especially if there is opportunity to profit from them. The aggressors will work themselves up into a state hostility to capitalism, which is self-destructive (Bottomore, 1942). It is tempting to shift the blame to market forces in the wake of the recent corporate scandals. However, this runs the risk of ignoring the lessons that could be learned from such corporate transgressions.

The health of an economy depends on the financial market to raise and allocate capital. The financial market, in turn, is built on honesty, transparency and accountability (Spitzer and Rohatyn, 2002). However, the financial market also breeds self-interest leading to destructive capitalist characteristics because there are no countervailing forces to keep it in check (Arndt et al., 2002). The purpose of this paper is to examine the impact of recent corporate corruptions and scandals such as Enron and Worldcom on laissez-faire capitalism. The paper will examine whether market capitalism based on Adam Smith's philosophy of laissez-faire should be blamed and whether the corporate corruption and scandals are an urgent and unmistakable call for tighter financial discipline to increase institutional and government controls on both lenders and borrowers.

The Laissez-Faire Capitalism Spirit

Adam Smith's laissez-faire invisible hand theory and David Ricardo's Law have been well documented in almost all economic systems including the economies in transition from communism to a market economy. Both theories assume that free trade will increase economic wealth, efficiency, economies of scale and result in specialization. It is believed that allowing investments and lending the mobility to seek out rewarding opportunities is economically efficient.

According to Adam Smith's laissez-faire invisible hand theory, the common interest is best served by allowing market participants to pursue their own self-interest with minimal or no state intervention. The theory believes that markets tend towards equilibrium. The behaviour of both demanders and suppliers of goods are monitored via the price system. However, such self-correcting equilibrium behaviour is not applicable to the financial market, which are inherently unstable and risky. Equilibrium applies to markets with known quantities: financial markets deal with risk and uncertainty. Financial markets also deal with discounting the future, which is not only unpredictable but also indeterminate most of the time. Financial players are constantly attempting to predict the future which itself is conditioned upon present decisions. By contrast, equilibrium produces a determinate result.

Incentives matter to all participants in free market capitalism. Given their respective constraints, consumers maximize their utility while producers maximize profit. In the financial markets, investors maximize their net worth given the risk. However, the incentive structure in the financial markets is complicated by asymmetric information, panic, mania, speculation, and herd behaviour (Hu, 1998). Where asymmetric information may lead to an unsustainable expansion of credit as a result of an incomplete evaluation of credit risks' implications, a small shake of confidence may lead to panic and the withdrawal of funds from the affected markets.

The World Trade Organization preaches the laissez-faire, free market capitalist philosophy where every country should have a fully liberalized economic system, including a financial system, in which the state has only a minimal role. Deregulation is the basic building block of capitalism. It includes clarity, transparency, accountability, fairness and openness. However, there is the inherent danger that business professionals could abuse the "corporate freedom" in an undisciplined and costly manner. For example Enron operated in a culture where contractual rights were protected, where there was a system of recognition of rights, and where companies did have a set of rules and regulations that was understandable and enforceable. Why did Enron collapse? The free-market system depends on the flow of credible information-transparent and reliable reports prepared by executives and independent boards and certified by auditors who adhere to accounting professionalism and are free of conflict of interests. Investors should be allowed to assume risk in the financial markets. They should be free to buy the next stock available in the market. However, their investment decision should be based on the knowledge and information available as to how much risk to take (Mandel, 2002). Enron collapsed and took investors with them because information Enron provided was not credible, leading investors to make wrong assessment of risk.

Why do investors suddenly loathe capitalism? Why do they, while enjoying the fruits of capitalism, advocate for more state intervention? Proponents of free market capitalism argue that competition is inherently more efficient because government intervention is corrupted by politics. Competition and self-policing produce the best results while regulations retard growth. For example, consumers do not really care who sells them groceries or airline services. What is more important is that it is done at minimum cost (Morgan, 2003). However, competition and self-policing in the financial market did not produce the best results. Corporate executives manipulated the system, and self-policing became self-interest and self-aggrandizement. Executive capitalism replaced the laissez-faire capitalism spirit. Investors lost confidence in the credibility of the corporate leaders who were supposed to protect the interests of shareholders (Nussbaum, 2002).

Confidence in the markets is built up gradually but can be shattered without warning. The recent epidemic of corporate frauds beginning with Enron has shattered investors' trust and confidence in the free market system. Investors are now restructuring their investment portfolios and repricing stocks to reflect the real earnings of the firms. They become more and more disenchanted with equities, cashing them faster than leaves falling from the trees before the equities become lemons. Investors are selling shares of former highfliers who manipulated their accounting practices and are even questioning such blue chip stars as General Electric Company (Miller et al., 2002).

What is Corporate Fraud?

Fraud involves the use of dishonest or deceitful conduct in order to obtain some unjust advantage over others (Grayear and Smith, 2002). In the corporate world, fraud takes many forms. Therefore, it is very difficult to prevent. The most common forms of corporate fraud are asset misappropriation, corruption and fraudulent statements.

Corrupt executives siphoned hundreds of billions of dollars into their personal bank accounts. They seriously damaged the financial status of investors and broke investors confidence in the stock market. Much of the abuse has been driven by self-interest greed (Gallon 2002). Those greed include:

- the strong push for annual profit increases via creative accounting practices
- stock option incentives to corporate executives who can push up the price of their companies' stocks
- politicians looking for quick financial fixes (contributions) from the very corporations they are supposed to regulate
- exorbitant remunerations in the tens and hundreds of millions of dollars to corporate executives who don't warrant it and who don't need it
- insider trading

These improper economic drivers distort the free market system and divert human effort and ingenuity away from true production and economic growth in a country. The narrow parameters, enforced by greedy and unbiased third-party accounting firms, also thwart the achievement of long-term goals such as better corporate productivity, energy efficiency, worker and society benefits, and environmental protection (Gallon, 2002)

Massive fraud also ruin nations' economies. The President of Kenya and his family plundered the country's wealth, with all the money going to Swiss Bank Accounts. Mexico's vibrant economy was almost ruined by the nepotism of the previous President and his cronies before Vicente Fox took over, while Zimbabwe has been ruined by President Mugabe and his corrupt regimes (Gallon, 2002).

According to the Association of Certified Fraud Examiners, over 80% of occupational fraud involves asset misappropriation, with cash or its equivalent being targeted 90% of the time. On an average, the fraud scheme lasts about 18 months before it is detected. Of these corporate frauds that are investigated, more than half cost their victims at least $100,000, with nearly one in six causing losses of $1 million or more. Typically, frauds with larger amounts of losses are associated with mid to upper management (Ketchen, 2002).

Why Does Corporate Fraud Happen?

Corporate fraud happens due to a number of reasons. One reason why corporate fraud is on the raise is the significant change in the culture of the workforce (Ketchen, 2002). Nowadays, newly employed staff generally have little company loyalty. Therefore, fraud involving the companies'own employees is more likely to happen.

Besides that, the implementation of downsizing by a corporation also increases the likelihood of corporate fraud (Ketchen, 2002) because downsizing involves cutting out middle management and delegate more power to lower level managers and employees. This breaks down one of the fundamental rules of fraud prevention, that is segregation of duties. In this situation, it is common for asset misappropriation and corruption to happen. For example, the employee of a company might siphon off a small amount of cash, knowing that it will not be detected because companies usually do not worry about relatively small losses (Ketchen, 2002).

However, the occurrence of corporate fraud is not limited to small companies with limited resources for proper fraud prevention programmes. Corporate fraud also happens in many large stock exchange listed corporations involving senior management. In fact, the fraud schemes designed by senior management are usually significantly larger. The recent episodes of corporate fraud involving senior management take the form of fraudulent misstatement. The senior management of these corporations cooked the books to inflate revenues and earnings to boost the companies' share prices. The high share price and good credit rating given to these corporations have then misled the public into thinking that these companies were a good investment. This happened in Enron where the senior management used fraudulent accounting practices to achieve short-term stock price maximization in order to dump their stock options quickly.

Besides reporting inflated earnings in their accounts, some of these companies also have all sorts of corporate risks unrecorded in companies' account. As a result of this information asymmetry, investors are unable to make informed investment decisions. In addition, the independence of the auditors who reviews the accounts of these corporations is also questionable. Besides acting as the external auditors of corporations, many of these audit firms also provide internal auditing and consultancy services to the same corporations as another important source of revenue for the audit firm. As a result, auditors are under financial pressure not to report fraudulent misstatement by these companies.

Laissez-faire Capitalism and Corporate Frauds

Capitalism rewarded the companies that hit their earnings targets while often taking full advantage of flexible accounting rules. Their malfeasance and fraudulent practices continue to erode the trust and integrity so vital to a free-market system (Arndt et al., 2002). Capitalism also breeds self-interest leading to destructive corporate characteristics. Greed and self-interested behaviour overwhelmed the foundations of laissez-faire capitalism because there was no countervailing force to keep it in check (Arndt et al., 2002). Audit firms were supposed to counter check such practices but their focus was on lucrative consulting fees.

Capitalism is not self-regulating in today's volatile financial markets. Auditors are not saints and entrepreneurs and traders are governed by greed and self-interest. Brokers encouraged investors to purchase shares in companies to earn big commission fees without providing adequate information about the companies to the investors. Corruption of deregulation is ever present in every imperfect market. For example, Enron used its extensive political connections and influences to undermine the regulatory system itself-on trading, audits, and disclosure (Bernstein et al., 2002). This resembles guanxi capitalism of the Far East where politically connected businessmen are beneficiaries of opaque environment.

Schumpeter recognizes the fruits of the capitalistic system-raising the country's standard of living and level of output, but he also believes that the system is self-destructive (Bell, 1953). Capitalism is an evolutionary process, which in the end, must discriminate and decide what it is salvageable and what it will ignore. According to Schumpeter's business cycle theory, as economic boom continues in a country, disorders will begin to appear because dynamic forces tend to work against the fruits of the boom (Schumpeter, 1939; Bell, 1953). In his famous classical seminal thesis on Capitalism, Socialism, and Democracy (1942), Schumpeter argues that capitalism is non-stationary and will eventually fail because its very success will undermine the discipline and values that support it. This was evident during the 1930s Great Depression era and the recent corporate scandals when capitalism failed to live up to its standard. The Enron, WorldCom, and other corporate scandals reflect Schumpeter's view of capitalism as a "perennial gale of creative destruction" without market discipline (McEachern, 1991). The recent U.S. corporate scandals have pushed the free market system to the edge of an abyss that could set off a failure in other markets.

In hindsight, it was obscure insider corporate practices, diminished discipline in the financial system, and poor corporate governance that contributed significantly to the collapse of many corporate firms in the U.S. For example, off-balance sheet financial engineering became the ultimate method to boost earnings and stock prices and disciplined accounting practices were replaced by idiosyncratic measures. Slowly but surely, the financial truth of the company disappeared (Nussbaum 2002), enriching insiders and inflating Enron's earnings by almost $1 billion. Laissez-faire capitalism does not (and indeed cannot) address "the red-light activities of national finance" such as rigged-price fixing, questionable and sleazy practices by brokers, dealers, analysts, and other assorted market hustlers. These activities go against free-market principles. The free-market principles depend on the flow of credible information-transparent and reliable reports prepared by executives and independent boards certified by auditors who adhere to accounting professionalism free of conflict of interests.

Discipline in the corporate sector was sacrificed in the name of quick wealth and prosperity at the expense of investing public. This is incontrovertible proof that a corporate sector without discipline is a sector without control and an invitation for financial disaster. It has also highlighted certain institutional idiosyncrasies. Implicit stock options given to executives encouraged them to engage in personal greed (Mushkat, 1998).

Pay disparity between executives and workers threatens the credibility of market capitalism. For example, in the past decades workers' wages increased 36% while executive pay increased 340% mostly through stock options (Byrne et al., 2002). They were repriced or swapped when the price started to fall. But critics argued that stock option overload contributed to the accounting scandal at companies such as Enron and WorldCom Inc.

In the early 1990s, stock options were given to executives as pay for performance. They were supposed to motivate managers who would do whatever it took to boost productivity, profits and shareholder returns. However, executives abused the stock option privileges and resorted to questionable accounting practices and hasty acquisitions to pump up earnings and boost share prices. In addition, companies were not required to record stock options as expenses like cash bonuses and salaries. Thus companies had the incentive to offer "overdoses of options" in lieu of cash compensation causing serious dilution to outside shareholders. To make the market more credible, option expenses should be recorded against earnings, thus giving more accurate earnings numbers. Disciplining stock option compensation would reduce manouvering of stock prices through fraudulent practices by executives.

The market welcomed the equity culture of the' 90s that was characterized by high risk, high-growth of a deregulated financial system and opportunity to profit. However, the stream of indictments, investigations, financial failures, conflicts of interest and executive greed have led to a breach of the capitalist ethics of trust, integrity and accountability between the public and the business world in the equity market. The complexities of equity capitalism and the severe punishment it imposes on imprudent behaviour suggest that markets will continue to be volatile, that risk will not be completely removed, and that corporate corruption will continue to threaten in the future. This should come as a warning to market participants to behave in a disciplined manner. The investing public will participate only if corporate governance is reformed so that trust may be restored.

Market Discipline in the Capitalist System

Free market capitalism does not imply a system free of any form of government intervention. There is no single market operating in the absence of a vigorous, competent and public-minded government. Fundamentally, the whole system of capitalism depends on investors' confidence in the financial performance of their invested portfolio. Capitalism itself requires rules that govern everything from financial and intellectual property rights to constraints on opportunistic practices such as Enron's off-balance sheet financial engineering practices that undermined the efficiency and integrity of the market system (Kuttner, 2002). What is wrong with the free capitalist system is not the pursuit of wealth, but the inappropriate mechanisms and behaviours in pursuing the wealth.

Growth in capitalism without market discipline causes inefficient economic outcomes, impedes long-term domestic and foreign investment, and distorts sectoral priorities and technology choices (Gray and Kaufmann, 1998). For example, the collapse of Enron and Arthur Andersen had nothing to do with laissez-faire capitalism being evil. Enron and Andersen created their own downfall through a series of fraudulent accounting practices and disclosures. The Enron-Arthur Andersen scandal occurred in a system in which all of the emphasis was on after-the-fact enforcement. And if the rules are lax, it is because accountants and auditors haven't wanted them tightened (McNamme, 2001). Thus corruption and cronyism overrode institutional laws and regulations for personal self-interest and gain, giving rise to over-ambitious CEOs, not to mention the financiers who foolishly lent them the money in the first place (Engardio and Clifford, 1999). Reflecting on Schumpeter's theory of business cycles, these behaviours are self-perpetuating and dynamic within the system, and create wave-like behaviour that pulls the system towards disequilibrium and subsequent repercussions (Schumpter, 1939; Bell, 1953).

Lenin once proclaimed that accounting and control are the main ingredients necessary for the correct functioning of the market system (von Mises, 1972). In order to raise capital through investment in joint-stock companies, it is necessary to offer investors some protection against the unforeseen risk of bankruptcy, which does happen in the financial markets. Thus rules and laws were established to strengthen the accountability of companies to their shareholders (Shutt, 1998). In addition, it gave the rights to create companies where the liability of the shareholders was limited to the value of the total equity they had subscribed. The privilege of limited liability has never been seriously challenged and debated until the Enron-Arthur Andersen scandals.

The corporate scandals from Enron to Wall Street included auditors and even regulators and lawmakers who fell prey to greed and self-interest. Those who are supposed to provide crucial monitoring and balances in a system that favours unfettered capitalism, have in many cases been compromised (Byrne, et al., 2002). Auditors responsible for certifying the accuracy of corporate accounts traded their responsibilities and integrity for hefty audit fees and consulting work. They manipulated the audit system creating less-than-pristine certification of accounts for bigger consulting contracts. There is an immediate need for strengthening discipline in the corporate sector to monitor such practices and punish those who abuse the system. The legal system in the corporate sector must be well designed and enforceable to ensure that offenders will be punished severely (Lane, 1993).

The Enron-Arthur Andersen debacles and other corporate scandals have profoundly shattered the investing public's perception of financial market rewards (especially the equity markets), accounting practices and corporate governance and ethics. It sends tremors worldwide about the honesty and integrity of the corporate cultures and undermines the transparency on which efficient markets depend (Nussbaum, 2002). This conjures up Schumpeter's hostility towards market capitalism which he believed would break down under the weight of economic failures and the social institutions which protect it (Bottomore, 1942). However, Schumpeter failed to acknowledge that a capitalist system with market discipline and good governance could survive.

Laissez-faire Capitalism and Corporate Reform

What can the markets do to restore investors' confidence as Enron, WorldCom, Global Crossing, Kmart and a host of other companies are investigated for corporate scandal and corruption? How can companies, led by executives who are well paid, emphasise trust, integrity and accountability? Fundamentally, the whole system of capitalism depends on investor confidence in the financial market. There is great urgency for markets to strengthen corporate governance rules as the global capitalist system is in peril. Investors won't trust business again until real reforms are put into place. Auditors and business professionals need to work hard to restore the basic integrity of capitalism. This includes more disclosure of off-balance sheet financing, transparent accounting policies and reports, and management informing investors about their stocks' health. Investors want timely and value-added disclosure.

Industry regulators need to be more proactive in preventing corporate scandals or the scandals are mere 'rituals of outrage'-disgrace and a crackdown that produces little legislated reform.

Restructuring and improvement in corporate governance is essential in preventing corporate scandals. This involves a comprehensive and integrated approach linking fundamental changes within the relationships between the government, corporate firms and accounting institutions involved (Iskander et al., 1999). This should diminish "relation-based" audit practices while restoring confidence in the financial system with an effective new legal, regulatory, accounting, and institutional framework. In turn, this would lead to a competitive corporate and financial system that minimizes excessive risk-taking in a disciplined fashion; it would install equitable risk sharing and responsibility among corporate leaders. There is a definite and distinct change needed to make executives responsible and accountable for their actions. After the Enron-"Arthur Anderson debacles, executives of giant corporate firms simply cannot make a move without being seen, heard and judged.

Strong leadership and disciplined governance is imperative given the volatility and turbulence in today's equity markets. In addition, a system of effective and reliable laws and regulations is required to stipulate the contractual rights and responsibilities of market participants so as to encourage discipline and prudent behaviour. The corporate death sentence for a breach of corporate code and ethic to promote corporate accountability should help create a disciplined climate for monitoring risk-taking between creditors and borrowers in the equity market.

Changes are needed in the boardroom. Independent boards should be established to oversee the company's accounting practices and the audit partners should be rotated every 5 years to limit conflict of interest and fraudulent practices within the industry. Accountability should be a two-way street. It is inadequate that the board monitors management. Shareholders must also monitor the board. However, shareholders are seldom invited to meetings and thus do not know what goes on behind the closed doors of the boardroom. To ensure accountability, shareholders resolutions that pass by a majority of the shares must be made binding (Byrne et al, 2002) In addition, a ban on stock sales by directors for the duration of their terms would encourage them to blow the whistle on management when necessary.

There is an urgent need to revise and simplify the more than 100,000 plus pages of generally accepted accounting practices (GAAP) in line with the international accounting standards and principles. This includes improvement in the corporate merger disclosures common to international standard. This puts the burden on corporate clients to ensure that their accounting practices meet the standard (Borrus and McNamee, 2002).

It is important to ensure that to ban accounting firms from performing consulting services for audit clients, and to require companies to deduct the cost of stock options from earnings and to cap the amount of company stock in employee retirement plans (Borrus, et al., 2002). Shareholders should approve all stock option plans. Auditing should be more forensic to certify audited accounts instead of just meeting GAAP.

Stock options should be treated like other forms of compensation, expensing them against the company's earnings. This will provide transparency and accuracy in the company's financial statement to shareholders. Hidden liabilities in the so-called "special purpose entities" (SPEs) should be consolidated on the balance sheet of the company. It is the hundreds of SPEs created to hide potential losses and debts from the investing public, which caused the collapse of many big companies. In addition, companies should also disclose to shareholders what are included and excluded in calculating operating earnings. They must also provide details to show what they added and subtracted from GAAP net income to get to their pro formas (Arndt and Scherreik, Feb. 18. 2002).

Restoring investors' confidence in the equity market requires transparency so that investors can distinguish honest companies from dishonest one. Additionally, the equity culture is built on trust that markets reflect the real value of the underlying companies. Thus policymakers and regulators must define the toughest standards requiring companies to operate by them. There must be criminal sanctions against executives who abuse investors' trust by manipulating the companies' accounts and falsifying financial statements. White-collar criminals should be sent to jail to send the right signals to potential offenders.

Conclusions

The recent corporate scandals are helpful in overhauling the corporate governance practices in the corporate sector. The government and lawmakers have to ensure that the legislative mechanism contributes toward improved corporate governance in this post-corporate scandal era. This requires a cohesive and comprehensive strategy and cooperation from firms, financial institutions and governments. Investors are also putting pressure on companies to reveal more about their operations and financial health. For example, Amazon. Com Inc. shareholders are demanding management to disclose monthly figures for changes in sales in each of its major categories (Barrett, et al., 2002). Improved transparency and financial reporting on the part of corporations will result in less uncertainty. This new ethic of disclosure is positive for the market. Executives have to learn that trust, integrity and accountability do matter and are crucial to capitalism.

Instead of corporate ownership, in which the majority of the rewards were concentrated at the top of the managerial hierarchy, critics advocate "distributed capitalism", in which ownership focuses more on integrity, trustworthiness, accountability and responsibility to shareholders and the community at large (Byrne, 2002).

The spectacular rise and fall of Enron didn't serve to validate Schumpeter's classical theory of "creative destruction." The Enron collapse was one of creative accounting not creative destruction, in which several top executives got wealthy at the expense of outside shareholders. Capitalism has avoided devastating crises such as the 1997 Asian financial crises and will weather through the Enron-Arthur Andersen debacle and other corporate scandals because of the robustness in changes and adaptation in the market. (Byrne, 2002).

The recent corporate scandals have changes how companies disclose information to investors. They are responding to investors' demand for better disclosure in financial reporting and less margin for error. For example, IBM announced it would expand the information it provide investors such as the intellectual property income at the impact on earnings of the company's overfunded pension plan (Barrett et al., 2002). General Electric Co. promised to provide more details on how the company's individual units generate their earnings. Franchising giant Cendant Corp has put detailed information on its web site about its off-balance sheet entities. The market will continue to punish and penalise companies who ignore this demand for transparency (Barrett et al., 2002). Perhaps this new ethic of disclosure will generate more accurate stock valuations, less uncertainty and volatility in the markets and increase investors' confidence.

Proponents of laissez-faire capitalism fear that Enron and other corporate scandals will kill the political support for free markets and invoke more regulations. Over zealous regulations could punish law-abiding corporations. Corporate lobbyists argued that Enron's scandal was merely a business went wrong, not an impeachment of freer markets (Berstein et al., 2002; Kuttner, 2001). Their intense lobbying is to convince lawmakers that an over zealous ambition to regulate corporate behaviour could raise costs and perhaps muddle the stock market. Regulation can solve corporate corruption, but it also discourages innovation and takes away incentives for companies to be efficient. Regulators need to balance regulations with market openness to maximise economic growth and benefits.

It can be argued that government intervention is perceived as good and serves to protect the public interest. However, is there such thing as public interest? Investors will remain elusive and sceptical about laissez-faire capitalism if regulators do not punish the organisations and the executives and the professionals who enriched themselves at the expense of so many stakeholders. Corporate corruption and scandals are heady, intoxicating and stifling all at once but this does not imply the fall of capitalism. The market might be contaminated and trust may be shattered but if the management starts promoting the company instead of stock value, the integrity in the market can be restored. The message is not power or riches. It is, rather, the excellence in performance teamed with accountability and transparency in the corporate sector.

References

1. Arndt, Michael, Wendy Zellner and Mike McNamee. (2003) "Restoring Trust in Corporate America: Business Must Lead the Way to Real Reform." *BusinessWeek,* June 24, pp. 37-41.

2. Arndt, Michael and Susan Scherreik. (2002), "Five Ways to Avoid More Errons." *BusinessWeek,* February 18, pp. 36-37.

3. Barrett, Amy, Spencer E. Ante and Mike McNamee. (2002), "Slammed: Investors are Telling Companies that Creative Accounting Will No Longer Fly." *BusinessWeek,* March 4, pp. 34-35.

4. Bell, John Fred. (1953), *A History of Economic Thought*. The Ronald Press Company, New York.

5. Bernstein, Aaron, Brian Grow, Darnell Little, Stanley Holmes and Diane Brady. (2002), "Bracing for a Backlash." *BusinessWeek*, February 4, pp. 46-48.

6. Borrus, Amy, Mike McNamee and Paula Dwyer. (2002), "What Cleanup?" *BusinessWeek*, pp. 36-37.

7. Borrus, Amy and Mike McNamee. (2002), "The Overhaul Wall Street Really Needs." *BusinessWeek*, May 20, pp. 40.

8. Borrus, Amy, Mike McNamee, and Susan Zegel, (2002), "Corporate Probes: A Scorecard," *BusinessWeek*, June 10, pp. 40-41.

9. Bottomore, Tom. (1942), *Joseph A. Schumpeter: Capitalism, Socialism and Democracy*. New York: Harper and Rows, Publishers.

10. Byrne, John, Louis Lavelle, Nanette Byrnes and Marcia Vickers. (2002), "How to Fix Corporate Governance." *BusinessWeek*, May 6, pp. 45-52.

11. Byrne, John. (2002), "After Enron: The Ideal Corporation." *BusinessWeek*, August 26, pp. 40-43.

12. Engardio, Pete and Mark L. Clifford. (1999), "Where Asia went wrong." *BusinessWeek*, November 29, pp. 82-84.

13. Gallon, Gary. (2002), "Enron and Corruption in America." *The Gallon Environment Letter*, Vol. 6, No. 15, July 18.

14. Gray, Cheryl and Daniel Kaufmann. (1998), "Corruption and Development." *Finance and Development*, March, pp. 7-10.

15. Grayear, A and R. Smith (2002), Identifying and Responding to Corporate Fraud of the 21st Century, Australian Institute of Criminology, Sydney, March 20.

16. Hu, Fred. (1998), "The Myth of the Chinese Wall," *Far Eastern Economic Review*, Vol., 161, No. 44, October 28, pp. 30.

17. Iskander, Magdi, Gerald Meyerman, Dale F. Gray and Sean Hagan. (1999), "Corporate Restructuring and Governance in East Asia." *Finance and Development*, March, pp. 42-45.

18. Ketchen, R. Corporate Fraud: (2002), A Growth Industry Nobody Can Shut Down. Reorter Associate, May 27. Downloadable: http://www/treasurypoint.com/knowledge/articles/policy/pp_corp-fraud.asp

19. Kuttner, Robert. (2001), "The Lesson on Enron: Regulations Isn't a Dirty Word." *BusinessWeek*, December 24.

20. Kuttner, Robert. (2002), "Enron: A Powerful Blow to Market Fundamentalists." *BusinessWeek,* February 4, pp. 14.

21. Lane, Timothy D. (1993), "Can market Forces Discipline Government Borrowing?" *Finance and Development,* pp. 26-29.

22. McEachern, William A. (1991), *Economics: A Contemporary Introduction.* South-Western Publishing Company, Dallas.

23. McNamee, Mike (2001), "The Big Five Need to Factor in Investors." *BusinessWeek,* December 24, pp. 34.

24. Mandel, Michael. (2002), "A New Economy Needs a New Morality." *BusinessWeek,* February 25, 2002, pp. 56-57.

25. Miller, Rich, Heather Timmons, Andres Park and Charles Haddad. (2002), "A New Credit Crunch." *BusinessWeek,* February 18, pp. 32-33.

26. Morgan, Gareth. (2003), "Let Market Rule on Airline Services." *The Press,* Christchurch, New Zealand, April 26, pp. C2.

27. Mushkat, Miron. (1998), "What Really Caused Asia's Crisis?" *Times,* March 9, pp. 21.

28. Nussbaum, Bruce, (2002), "Why the World needs New Thinking." *BusinessWeek,* August 26, pp. 38-39.

29. Nussbaum, Bruce. (2002), "Can You Trust Anybody Anymore." *BusinessWeek,* January 28, pp. 39-40.

30. Rossant, John, Jack Ewing and Brian Bremmer. (2002), "The Corporate Cleanup Goes Global." *BusinessWeek,* May 6, pp. 54-55.

31. Schumpeter, Joseph A. (1939), *Business Cycles: A Theoretical, Historical, and Statistical Analysis of the Capitalist Process.* Volume II, New York: McGraw-Hill Book Company, Inc.

32. Shutt, Harry. (1998), *The Trouble with Capitalism: An Enquiry into the Causes of Global Economic Failure,* White Lotus, Bangkok.

33. Spitzer, Eliot and Felix Rohatyn. (2002), "How Corrupt is Wall Street? *BusinessWeek,* May 13, pp. 37-42.

34. Timmons, Heather. (2002), "Everybody Out of the Risk Pool?" *BusinessWeek,* September 2, pp. 52-53.

35. Von Mises, Ludwig. (1972), *The Anti-Capitalistic Mentality.* Libertarian Press, Inc., Sprint Mills, Pennsylvania.

Appendix 1: Corporate Fraud: A Summary

ACCOUNTING

Arthur Andersen

- Destruction of documents relating to its audits of Enron and allegations of shortcomings in its audits of Enron, Global Crossing, Qwest, and WorldCom. Criminal trial under way on obstruction of justice. Andersen denies wrongdoing.

Deloitte & Touche

- Deloitte' s audits of Adelphia Communications and its failure to tell Adelphia's audit committee that the founding Rigas family used company credit lines to buy Adelphia stock. Deloitte says it met professional standards.

Ernst & Young

- Marketing agreement to sell software with People Soft, an auditing client, may violate auditor independence rules. The SEC wants E&Y to give back People Soft audit fees paid between 1994-2000. E&Y.

Ernst & Young is fighting the charge. The SEC is also scrutinizing the firm's audits of companies such as Computer Associates and PNC Financial Services.

KPMG

- KPMG's failure to catch alleged revenue-inflating maneuvers by Xerox, an audit client. KPMG denies wrongdoing. Also, the accounting firm's $25 million investment in the AIM mutual fund, an audit client, alleged in violation of auditor independence rules. Without admitting fault, KPMG agreed to take steps to avoid future investments in audit clients.

Pricewaterhouse Coopers

- PwC's audits of MicroStrategy, which settled SEC charges of financial fraud in 2001 for overstating revenues without admitting fault, are still under investigation.

ENERGY

CMS Energy

- Round-trip trades with other energy wholesalers that allegedly overstated revenues by $1 billion in 2000 and $4.2 billion in 2001.

The Justice Dept., Commodity Futures Trading Commission, and the Federal Energy Regulatory Commission are also investigating.

Dynegy

- Round-trip trades that allegedly inflated revenues. Also, a natural gas transaction that allegedly made cash flow from operations appear larger than it was.

Enron

- Widespread alleged abuses of accounting and disclosure rules to inflate profits. Ongoing probes by the SEC and a Justice Dept. task force.

Halliburton

- Accounting policies that treated cost overruns on construction jobs as revenue, regardless of whether its customers agreed to pay part of the overbudget costs. Halliburton says it stands by its accounting.

Reliant Resources

- The energy trader's restatement of earnings for two quarters in 2001 after it determined that some derivative transactions accounted for as cash-flow hedges should have been valued at the market price.

SOFTWARE

Computer Associates

- Overstating revenues in 1998 that allegedly inflated its stock price just before and after the awarding of $1 billion in stock to three top managers. Ongoing SEC and Justice Dept. investigations.

Network Associates

- Alleged accounting inaccuracies that may have understated expenses or overstated revenues in 1998-2000.

TELECOM

Global Crossing

- Capacity swaps allegedly done with other carriers for the purpose of inflating revenues. Ongoing SEC and Justice Dept. investigations.

Lucent Technologies

- Booked $679 million in revenue from sales to its distributors before the distributors were able to actually sell the products.

Qwest Communications

- Capacity swaps with others carriers as well as equipment sales to customers in return for Internet services, both allegedly designed to inflate revenues.

Worldcom

- Accounting practices, including treatment of goodwill, and company loans totalling $408.2 million to former CEO Bernard Ebbers. WorldCome defends its accounting.

WALL STREET

Credit Suisse First Boston

- CSFB's allocation, as lead underwriter, of share of hot IPOs to customers in return for allegedly excessive commissions on other trades Similar practices alleged at J.P. Morgan Chase, Morgan Stanley Dean Witter, Goldman Sachs, and other investment banks under investigation. CSFB agreed to pay a $100 million fine to the National Association of Securities Dealers and to change how it allocates IPO shares, without admitting fault. The others are cooperating with the probe.

Hedge Funds

- Incidents of fraud, conflicts of interest at firms that manage both hedge funds and mutual funds. The SEC is considering the need for regulation.

Capital Markets

- Alleged illegal trades that iCapital, formerly Datek Securities, made for its own account through Nasdaq's small-order execution system from 1993-1998. Investigation settled after iCapital Markets agreed to pay a $6.3 million fine, without admitting fault.

Merrill Lynch

- Alleged conflicts of interest for research analysts who work alongside investment bankers. Merrill agreed to pay $100 million in a May 21 settlement with New York Attorney General Eliot

Spitzer without admitting wrongdoing. SEC probe is ongoing. Other brokers, including Morgan Stanley and Goldman Sachs, are also being investigated by the SEC, as well as by state officials.

OTHER INDUSTRIES

Adelphia Communications

- The cable-TV operator's alleged failure to adequately disclose $5.6 billion in loan guarantees to the family of founder John Rigas. SEC. Two grand jury investigations are ongoing.

Edison Schools

- For-profit operator of public schools didn't disclose that nearly half its revenues consisted of funds that school districts paid directly to teachers and vendors. Edison agreed to add a director of internal audit, without admitting fault.

Kmart

- Accounting for vendor discounts and other transactions that allegedly underreported 2001 losses by at least $1.7 billion. SEC probe is ongoing; FBI and Justice are also investigating.

PNC Financial Services

Both the SEC and Federal Reserve and investigating the Pittsburgh bank's accounting treatment of three companies it set up with insurer American International Group to hold corporate loans PNC wanted off its balance sheet.

Trump Hotels

- Allegedly misleading statements in a 1999 press release that suggested the company's positive results were due to operations rather than a one-time gain. Without admitting or denying guilt, Trump consented to an SEC cease-and-desist order.

Waste Management

Founder and five former top officials allegedly used fraudulent accounting to inflate profits by $1.7 billion between 1992 and 1997. The SEC filed suit in March 2002, charging the ex-execs with falsifying and misrepresenting the company's results. They deny the charges.

Xerox

Accelerated recognition of lease and servicing revenues in a scheme that allegedly inflated revenues by $3 billion from 1997-2000.

SEC settled with the copier maker in April 2002, imposing a record $10 million fine. Xerox agreed to restate earnings for 1997-2000 and form a panel of its outside directors to review accounting policies and practices without admitting guilt.

Source: Amy Borrus, Mike McNamee, and Susan Zegel, "Corporate Probes: A Scorecard," Business Week, June 10, 2002, pp. 40-41.

3

Distribution, Accumulation and Interest Rate in a Post-keynesian model: A Sraffian Note

Throdone Mariotis*

Introduction

As it is well known, one of the key findings of modern post- keynesian theory, which is connected with the works of Marx, Kalecki, Baran and Steindl, and which focuses its attention on investigating the interaction between the distribution and growth of income in the framework (chiefly) of one-good models, is the following: in economies with generalised excess capacity and market imperfections, a redistribution of income from capitalists to workers (who have a higher propensity to consume) *may* imply a rise in the level of consumption, in effective, demand, in the level of capacity utilisation, and by inducing firms to invest more, in the growth rate and the profit rate. This means, of course, that (in contrast with what holds in the framework of neoclassical, of neo-Recardian and of the 'Cambridge' (a la kaldor) growth theory, *in which it is assumed that capacity is fully utilised in the economy),* the relationship between the growth (profit) rate and the real wage rate is not necessarily inverse, and also that a 'bad income distribution' may be the

* Professor, Department of Public Administration, Panteon University, Athens, Greece.

cause of economic stagnation (see e.g. Dutt, 1984, 1987A, 1987B, Bhaduri and Marglin, 1990).

On the other hand, as is also well known, it has been shown by Sraffa, 1960, that in sytems of 'Production of Commodities by Means of Commodities', the traditional neoclassical propositions concerning the relationship between the distribution of income, commodity prices and technical conditions of production have no general validity (see also Kurz and Salvadori, 1995, Ch. 14). This means, of course, that a rise in the real wage rate does not necessarily imply the reduction of the prices of those commodities, the production of which is ' capital-intensive', and the rise in the capital-capacity ratio, the capital-labour ratio and consumption per unit of labour employed, and to be precise, it means that the effects of a rise in the real wage rate are neither known a *priori* nor independent of the initial level of the real wage rate.

In this paper, we shall show that Sraffa's aforementioned contribution retains its significance also in the framework of the simplest possible system of 'Production of Commodities by Means of Commodities' with undesired excess capacity: if it is assumed that the desired rate of accumulation of capitalists depends on the degree of capacity utilisation and the aggregate profit share (Bhaduri and Marglin, 1990, Kurz 1990A), then the aggregate capital-capacity ratio enters into the determination of the equilibrium between investment and savings, which (ratio) depends (in a particularly complex manner) on the distribution of income. Therefore, the effects of a redistribution of income on the level of consumption, on the degree of capacity utilisation and on the growth rate are neither known a priori nor independent of the initial state of equilibrium of the system.

Evidently, this result does not negate the aformentioned key finding of modern post-Keynesian theory, but on the contrary reinforces it from a theroretical viewpoint, for it shows that the interaction between the distribution and growth of income tax, in reality, forms, which are much more complex than those which may be manifested in the framework of a one-good model. On the other hand, however, it is a result which impels us to view with scepticism the redistribution of income (from capitalists to worker or vice versa) as a way of dealing with stagnation.

The paper is organised as follows. In Section 2 we construct and investigate a multisectoral model with generalised excess capacity. Because our sole aim is to determine the effects of the existence of produced means of production, the assumptions we introduce are extremely restrictive. Thus, the exposition is more in the nature of an exercise, rather than the formulation of a complete theoretical and analytical framework. Section 3 takes into consideration the existence of technological change, a rentier class and government fiscal activity. Finally, Section 4 concludes.

The Basic Model: Construction and Investigation

Consider a closed, capitalist economy wihtout government fiscal activity, in which there are n ($\geq$2) sectors of single production. Let the technology be representd by a positive, constant, row vector of labour input coefficients $\ell \equiv \lfloor \ell_j \rfloor$ and a semi-positive, constant and indecomposable, nxn matrix $A \equiv \lfloor a_{ij} \rfloor$, where a_{ij} denotes the quantity of capital good i that has to ve installed to produce one unit of output of sector j.

Also, we shall assume that the following hold:

A.1. There are no non-produced inputs.

A.2. Capital goods do not depreciate.

A.3. The economic system under considertion is subject (also) to the *principle of effective demnad*. Consequenlty, it is entirely possible for the levels of aggregate effective demnad to allow for the existence of equilibrium with excess capacity. We shall assume, however, that producers do not hire labour they do not need for production.

A.4. There are two classes in the economy: workers and capitalists. Workers, who are in unlimited supply, consume all their income and capitalists save a constant (and given from outside the system) fraction s (where $0 < s \leq 1$) of their income.

A.5. The composition of consumption of workers and capitalists is the same and it is given from outside the system.

A.6. As a result of the inter-sector perfect mobility of both labour and money capital, the nominal wage rate (w) and the profit rate (r) are both uniform as between the different sectors.

A.7. Wages are paid at the end of the production period.

A.8. The economy is growing at a uniform positive growth rate (g), that is, we limit ourselves to positions of *balanced* growth.[1]

On the basis of these assumptions, the model is formed by following system of equation:

$$P_j = \left[\sum_{i=1}^{n} P_i\left(K_{ij} / X_j\right)\right] r + w\ell_j, (j = 1,2,\ldots,n)$$

$$= \left[\sum_{i=1}^{n} P_i\left(K_{ij} / X^*_{ij}\right)\left(X^*_{ij} / X_j\right)\right] r + w\ell_j \Rightarrow$$

$$P_j = \left[\sum_{i=1}^{n} P_i a_{ij}\left(1 / u_{ij}\right)\right] r + w\ell_j, (j = 1,2,\ldots,n) \quad (1)$$

$$w = p(c\delta) \tag{2}$$

$$p\,\delta = 1 \tag{3}$$

$$X_i = \left[\sum_{j=1}^{n}\left(K_{ij} / X_j\right)X_j\right]g + c_T(\ell X)\delta_i, (i = 1,2,\ldots n)$$

$$= \left[\sum_{j=1}^{n}\left(K_{ij} / X^*_{ij}\right)X^*_{ij} / X_j\right]g + c_T(\ell X)\delta_i \Rightarrow$$

$$X_i = \left[\sum_{j=1}^{n}a_{ij}\left(1 / u_{ij}\right)X_j\right]g + c_T(\ell X)\delta_i \Rightarrow$$

$$x_i = \left[\sum_{j=1}^{n}a_{ij}\left(1 / u_{ij}\right)x_j\right]g + c_T\,\delta_i, (i = 1,2,\ldots,n) \tag{4}$$

$$\ell x \equiv 1 \tag{5}$$

$$r = g/s \tag{6}$$

where $P \equiv \lfloor P_j \rfloor$ is the row vector of commodity prices, K_{ij} denotes the stock of the capital good *i* in existence in sector j, X^*_{ij} the potential output of sector *j*, which corresponds to the stock of the capital good *i* in existence in sector $j\left(X_{ij} \equiv K_{ij} / a_{ij}\right), u_{ij}\left(\equiv X_j / X^*_{ij}\right)$ the degree of utilistion of the output capacity $X^*_j\left(0 < u_{ij} \leq 1\right), \delta \equiv [\delta_i]$ is a given semi-positive column vector, which represents the composition of consumption, *c* is a scalar, which represents the level of the real wage rate (because of equation (3), which is the arbitrarily chosen normalisation equation of commodity prices, *w* = *c* holds), $X \equiv [X_i](x \equiv [x_i])$ is the column vector of output (the column vector of output per unit of labour employed), and c_t is a scalar, which represents the level of total consumption per unit of labour employed. Finally, ceteris paribus, equation (6) results directly from assumptions **A.4** and **A.8**.

This model has 2n+4 independent equations and n^2 + 2n + 5 variables *(p, u_{ij}, r, w, c, x, g, c_T)*. For the sake of *simpliying* the discussion, we could assume, first, that within each sector there is a uniform degree of capacity utillsation, although the degrees of capacity utilisation can differ from one sector to another, and, second, following Bhaduri and Marglin, (1990), Kurz (1990A, pp. 219-221), that the *desired* rate of accumulation in each sector is an increasing function of the porfit share and the degree of capacity utilisation of that sector. In this case, the system would have only one degree of freedom, because systems (a) and (4) would take the following form

$$p = pA\hat{U}r + w\ell \qquad (1a)$$

$$x = A\hat{U}xg + c_T\delta \qquad (4a)$$

and furthermore the following equations would hold:

$$g_j = g_j\left(h_j, u_j\right), (j = 1,2,\ldots n) \qquad (7)$$

$$h_j \equiv \left(P_j - w\ell_j\right) / P_j = v_j\left(r / u_j\right), (j = 1,2,\ldots,n) \qquad (8)$$

where

$$v_j \equiv \left(\sum_{i=1}^{n} P_t a_{ij}\right) / P_j \qquad (9)$$

and

$$g_j \stackrel{!}{=} g, (j = 1,2,\ldots,n) \qquad (10)$$

where $\hat{U}$ is the diagonal matrix of the reciporcal of the sectoral degrees of capacity utilistion (u_j), equations (7) are the sectoral investment demand functions (given from outside the system), g_j is the desire rate of accumulation in sector j, and v_j is the capital-capacity ratio of sector j (a magnitude which depends on the relative prices of commodities, and consequently, on the profit rate and the sectoral degrees of capacity utilisation). Finally, equations (10) define the goods market equilibrium.2

However, in the following we shall assume that the following hold (simplifying the model to the greatest extent possible):

A.9. Both whithin each sector and between the sectors there is a *uniform* degree of capacity utilisation u (this is clearly an 'heroic assumption'). Consequently, systems (1) and (4) take the form

$$p = pA(1/u)r + w\ell \qquad \text{(1aa)}$$

$$x = A(1/u)xg + c_T\delta \qquad \text{(4aa)}$$

A.10. The inverstment function of the system has the following simple linear form

$$g = a_0 + a_1 u + a_2 h \qquad \text{(7a)}$$

where a_0, a_1, a_2 are positive constants (given from outside the system), and h is the aggregate profit share, that is

$$h \equiv (px - w\ell x)/px = v(1/u)r \qquad \text{(8a)}$$

where $v \equiv pAx/px$ is the capital-capacity ratio of the system, a magnitude which in the general case *depends both on prices and on the composition of output*.

The model based on assumptions **A.1-A.10** has $2n + 6$ independent equations and $2n + 7$ variables. In what follows, we shall assume that the level of the real wage c is given from outside the system, that is[3]

$$c = c \tag{11}$$

Despite the exceptionally restrictive nature of our assumptions, the model is in fact rather 'complex' (as far as its investigation is concerned). From equations (1aa), (2) and (3), we get the so-called' c - r - u frontier of the system (i.e., the locus of all combinations of the real wage rate, the profit rate and the degree of capacity utilisation compatible with the system of production under consideration; see Kurz, 1990A, p. 214, for a one-sector version of the present model)

$$c = 1/\ell B(u,r)\delta, \text{ for } 0 \leq r < (u/\lambda) \text{ and } 0 < c \leq (1/\ell\delta) \tag{12}$$

where $B(u,r) \equiv [I - A(r/u)]^{-1}$ is a function which is homogeneous of degree zero, I is the nxn identity matrix, λ is the Perron-Frobenius eigenvalue of A, u/λ $(1/\lambda)$ is the maximum feasible profit rate (the maximum profit rate), and $1/\ell\delta$ is the maximum of the level of the real wage rate.[4] From (12) we get

$$\partial c/\partial r < 0, \partial u > 0, dc/d(r/u) < 0 \tag{12a}$$

and

$$dr/du = r/u \tag{12b}$$

that is, for any given (feasible) level of the real wage rate, the profit rate is a striculy increasing linear function ofthe degree of capacity utilisation.

At the same time, from equations (4aa) and (5) we get the so-called 'c_T - g - u forntier'[5] of the system

$$c_T = 1/\ell B(u,g)\delta, \text{ for } 0 \leq g < (u/\lambda) \text{ and} 0 < c_T \leq (1/\ell\delta) \tag{13}$$

where $B(u,g) \equiv \left[I - A(g/u)\right]^{-1}$, and clearly, whatever holds for the 'c - r- u forntier also holds for this ' c_T - g -u frontier'.

Moreover, from equations (1aa), (2), (3) and (4aa), we get

$$v = \left[\ell B(u,r)AB(u,g)\delta\right] / \left[\ell B(u,r)B(u,g)\delta\right] \tag{14}$$

Finally, from equations (6), (7a), (8s) and (14), we get the following relationship between the profit rate and the degree of capacity utilisation:

$$rs = a_0 + a_1 u + a_2 \left\{\left[\ell B(u,r)AB(u,sr)\delta\right] / \left[\ell B(u,r)B(u,sr)\delta\right]\right\}(r/u) \tag{15}$$

where (consider Franke, 1999, pp. 46-9)

$$dh / d(r/u) > 0 \Rightarrow \left[dv(r/u) / vd(r/u)\right] > -1 \tag{15a}$$

Consequently, the equilibrium values of r and u are determined by equations(12) and (15). the complete analysis (static and comparative static) of this sub-system (and therefore also of the system as a whole) would be a rather simple matter if the capital-capacity ratio were a purely technological parameter, i.e. magnitude, which does not depend on the distribution and growth of income. In other words, the complexity of the present model is due, in the final analysis, to the fact that very few things can be said a priori about the behaviour of the magnitude $v = v(r/u)$ (apart from the fact that its elasticity with respect to r/u is greater than minus one.)

However, even if we ignore the aformentioned fundamental issue, we should note that the reaction of r (but not of u) to a variation in c is not unambigous, and this can be proven if, ceteris paribus, we assume that δ is the Perron-Frobenius eigenvector of matrix A, normalised in such a way that $\ell\delta = 1$. In this case, the system under consideration is a Standard system a la von Charasoff, 1910, Ch. 10 and

Sraffa, 1960, Ch. 4, and, as can easily be shown, the following hold:[6]

$$c = c = 1- \lambda(r/u)=1-h \tag{16}$$

where

$$(dr / du) = (1 - \bar{c}) / \lambda \tag{16a}$$

and

$$x= \delta, v = \lambda \tag{17}$$

while equation (15) takes the following form

$$rs=a_0+a_1u+a_2\hat{\lambda}\ (r/u) \Rightarrow$$
$$r=u\ (a_0+a_1u)/(us-a_2\lambda) \tag{18}$$

where

$$dr / du = \left[a_1su^2 - a_2\lambda(2a_1u + a_0)\right] / (us - a_2\lambda)^2$$
$$= \left[a_1s(u - u_1)(u - u_2)\right] / (us - a_2\lambda)^2 \Rightarrow$$
$$dr / du \gtrless 0 \Leftrightarrow u \gtrless u_1 \tag{18a}$$

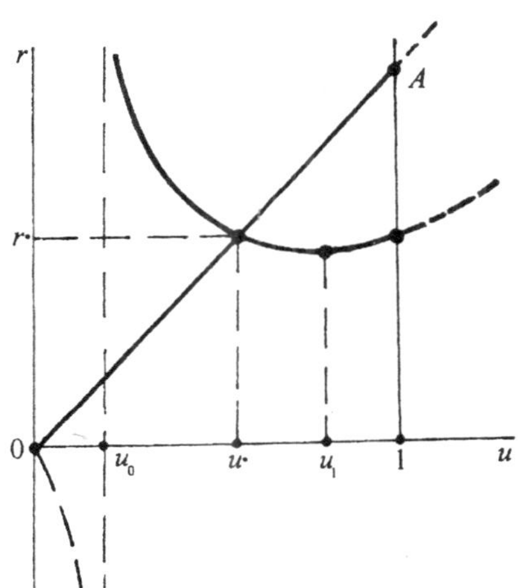

Figure 1

and u_1 (u_2) is the positive (negative) root of the derviative[7] dr/du. Therefore, the equilibrium for the model is shown in Figure 1, where straight line OA represents (16), the discontinuous curve represents (18), $u_0 \equiv a_2\lambda/s$, and we asume that $u_1 < 1$ holds (u_1 is a strictly increasing (decreasing) function of a_0, a_2 and λ (of a_1 and s)).

Finally, for the equilibrium values of u and r we get[8]

$$u^* = \lambda\left[a_0 + a_2(1-\bar{c})\right] / \left[s(1-\bar{c}) - \lambda a_1\right] \tag{19}$$

$$r^* = (1-\bar{c})\left[a_0 + a_2(1-\bar{c})\right] / \left[s(1-\bar{c}) - \lambda a_1\right] \tag{20}$$

where

$$(1-\bar{c}) \geq \left[\lambda(a_0 + a_1) / (s - \lambda a_0)\right] \tag{21}$$

$$(du^* / d\bar{c}) > 0, \left(dr^* / d\bar{c}\right) \underset{<}{\overset{\geq}{}} 0 \tag{22}$$

We conclude, therefore, that this Standard system is characterised by the coexistence of two (in the general case) different 'regimes' of steady-state equilibria (consider Figure 1, in which each increase in $\bar{c}$ implies a clockwise rotation of the line OA). In the framework of one of these 'regimes' $(:0 < \bar{c} < c_1$, where c_1 is that value of $\bar{c}$, which is determined by (19) and implies a value of the degree of capacity utilisation equal to u_1), each increase in the level of the real wage rate implies a reduction of the profit rate (and therefore also of the degree of capacity utilisation, while in the framework of the other 'regime' $c_1 < \bar{c} < c_m (< 1)$, where c_m is that value of $\bar{c}$, which is determined by (19) and implies a value of the degree of capacity utilisation equal to unity[9]), each increase in the level of the real wage rate implies a rise in the profit rate and in the degree of capacity utilisation.[10] [11]

Let us now return to the general case, i.e., the case in which the system is strictly multisectoral. From equations (6),

(7a), (8a) and (14), we get the following implicit function between r and u

$$r = u(a_0 + a_1 u)/(us - a_2 v\ (u, r) \tag{23}$$

where

$$(dr / du) = \{a_1 u^2 - a_2 r[v - u(\partial v / \partial u]\} / \{su^2 - a_2 u[v + r(\partial v / \partial r]\} \tag{25}$$

and

$$(\partial v / \partial u) = -(r / u)(\partial v / \partial r) \tag{25a}$$

Therefore, nothing rules out the existnece of a 'peculiar' relation between r and[12] u. In other owrds, in the transition from a (quasi-) one-sector system to a multisectoral system, the 'only' thing that changes in Figure 1 is the form of the curve which represents equation (23): Because (12b) holds, equation (12) continues to be represented by a straight line, the slope of which, however, is not equal to $(1-\bar{c})/v = (1-\bar{c})/\lambda$, but to $[1-(\bar{c}\ell\delta)]/v_w$, where $v_w \equiv (pA\delta / p\delta) = \bar{c}\ell B(u,r)A\delta$ is the capital-capacity ratio of the sub-system a la Sraffa, 1960, Appendix A, which produces the workers' consumption basket[13] δ. Also, because of (12a), each increase in $\bar{c}$ continues to imply a clockwise rotation of the said straight line.

Ceteris paribus, we conclude, therefore, that multisectoral systems are not characterised by the existence of multiple points of equilibrium[14], but first, by the complexity of the conditions which ensure the existence of an econmically meaningful and stable equilibrium (as well as the existence of a full cause unpredicatble changes in the profit rate and the degree of capacity utilisation, and, third, by *the co-existence and 'reswitching'* of three different 'regimes' of steady-state equilibria. So, apart from the two 'regimes' which we have already determined, the existence of an additional 'regime' is possible, in the framework of which each *rise* in the level of the real wage rate implies the *reduction* of the profit rate and of the degree of capacity utilisation15 (Figures 2a to 2e represent a four-sector model, the data of which are given in the Appendix. Specifically, Figure 2a expresses whatever figure 1 expresses, while Figures 2b, c, d, e represent, respectively, *v*, *h*, *u* and *r* as functions of *r/u* and, thus, indirectly as functions of *c*).

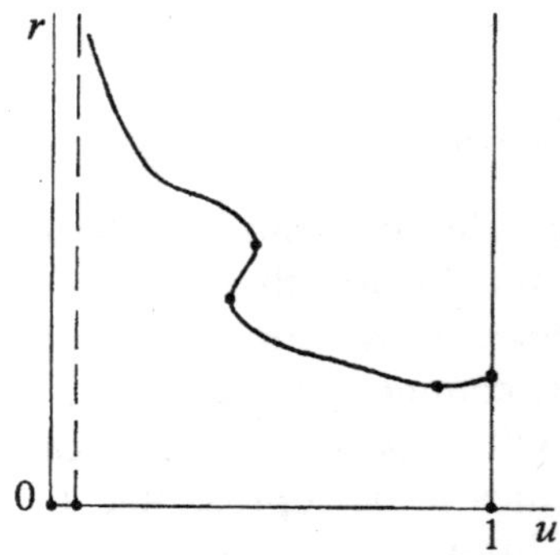

Figure 2a

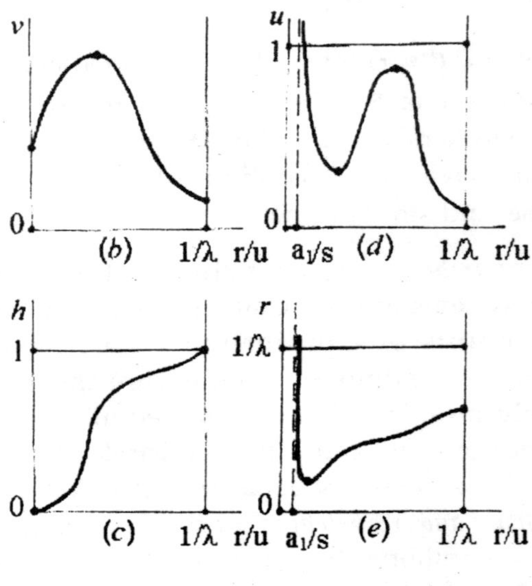

Figure 2b-e

We do not think it is possible to say which of the said features are the most significant. What is most important is that they stem from the fact that the capital-capacity ratio is not given prior to and independent of the determination of commodity prices, distribution and growth of income. In other words, that issue, which is fundamental (see Sraffa, 1960, 4 and 48) for investigating systems, which always stay (by construction) 'on the wage-profit frontier' (Dutt, 1987B, pp. 77-9), is also fundamental for systems, which can be 'inside the wage-profit frontier'[16] (Dutt, ibid.)

Extensions of the Basic Model

In what follows, we shall extend our Basic model, in order to investigate briefly (and on the basis of certain simplifying assumptions) the existence, first, of alternative methods of production, and the consequences of technological change (3.1), second, of a rentier class (3.2), and, lastly, third, or government fiscal activity (3.3).

Choice of Technique and Technological Change

Let us consider, for a moment, the one-good version of this model and let us assume the exstence of two alternative methods of production (*I,II*), which are defined by the following pairs of scalar quantities $[\alpha, \ell]$ (:I) and $[\alpha, \ell']$ (:II). In agreement with the signification and syntax of the model, we should consider that the comparison of the methods with respect to their profitablility presupposes as given the real wage rate and the degree of capacity utilisation, and specifically that method *II* is more profitable than (equally profitable to) method *I* if the following hold, respectively:

$$\Delta\alpha(\bar{r} / \bar{u}) + \bar{c}\Delta\ell < (=) 0 \tag{28}$$

where $\Delta\alpha \equiv \alpha' - \alpha$ and $\Delta\ell \equiv \ell' - \ell$. Because, given c and u, the profit rate which corresponds to *II* is greater than (equal to) the profit rate which corresponds to *I* if (28) holds.

Of course, in reality (with regard to both the model and the objective economic world) the choice and, subsequently, the use of one or the other production method implies, in the general case, the change in the initial degree of capacity utilisation (through the savings-investment mechanism), a change which can most certainly lead to the inversion of the initial (based on condition (28) ordering of the production methods (see also Kurz, 1990A, pp. 232-3). Therefore, even in the framework of a one-good system,the introduction of a 'new', more profitable, production method has ambiguous effects on the profit (growth) rate and on the degree of capacity utilisation. These effects, summarised in the following Table 1 [which is based on relations17 (18)-(20) and (28)], and on the assumption that method *II* constitutes the 'new', more profitable, method) on the one hand depends (also) on the initially ruling 'regime', and on the other imply (also) the shift of the system from one 'regime' to the other and/or the elimination of the 'regime of underconsumption' (see e.g. Figure 3, which is based of Figure 1 and corresponds to one of the sub-cases of the third row of Table 1; see also Kurz, 1990A, pp. 227-35, for a different diagrammatic representation, inthe framework of a more general one-good model *and for a given mark-up rate.*).

Table 1

	Overaccumulation		*Undercomsumption*	
$\alpha = \alpha'(\Rightarrow \ell' < \ell)$	$\Delta r > 0$	$\Delta u < 0$	$\Delta r \gtrless 0$	$\Delta u < 0$
$\alpha > \alpha'\left(\Rightarrow \ell' \gtrless \ell\right)$	$\Delta r \gtrless 0$	$\Delta u < 0$	$\Delta r \gtrless 0$	$\Delta u < 0$
$\alpha < \alpha'(\Rightarrow \ell' < \ell)$	$\Delta r > 0$	$\Delta r \gtrless 0$	$\Delta r > 0$	$\Delta u \gtrless 0$

Also, if the tow methods are equally profitable (in which case one method will be used, which constitutes a convex linear combination of the two methods), then the only thing that can be said is that the equilibrium values of the profit rate

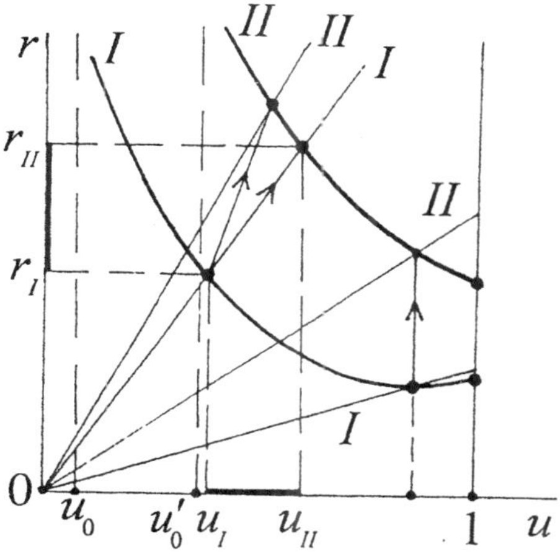

Figure 3

and the degree of capacity utilisation will be within an a priori determinated interval (see, for example, in Figure 3, where such a case is depicted and $r_I \leq r^* \leq r_{II}$ and $u_I \leq u^* \leq u_{II}$ hold). Finally, given all the above, it follows (also) that the rise in the wage rate has ambiguous effects on the equilibrium values of the profit (growth) rate and of the degree of capacity utilisation.[18]

Now, let us return to the case of a multisectoral system. If we assume that there are two alternative methods of production (*I,II*) of commodity k ($1 \leq k \leq n$), then, as can be shown (consider, for example, Kurz and Salvadori, 1995, Ch. 5, Mariolis, 2000, Appendix), condition (28) takes the following form

$$\bar{p}\Delta A(\bar{r} / \bar{u}) + \bar{c}\Delta\ell < (=) 0 \qquad (30)$$

and the following holds:

$$\ell' B'(\bar{u}, \bar{r}) < (=) \ell B(\bar{u}, \bar{r}) \qquad (30a)$$

where $\Delta A \equiv A' - A$ ($\Delta \ell \equiv \ell' - \ell$) is a matrix (vector) whose column k (the component k) is non-zero, while all the other columns (components)are zero. So, given that the introduction of a 'new' method of production presupposes the validity of condition (30) (and of (30a) and thus implies an unpredicted change in the capital-capacity ratio[19], it follows that it is not possible to predict the effects of introducing a new method of production on the equilibrium values of the profit (growth) rate and degree of capacity utilisation.[20]

Of course, the inability to predict the aforementioned effects does not indicate incompleteness within the economic theory of the capitalist mode of production, but rather expresses a fundamental feature of this mode of production, which can be stated as follows: the effects of certain rational choices of autonomous, independent producers are determined by forces, which act, in the final analysis, 'behind their back'.

Rentier Class

Ceteris paribus, we shall assume, following more or less the one-sector approach of Dutt, 1989, Hein, 1999, and Hein and Ochsen, 2001 (and despite their various defferences[21]),that, *first*, part of the investment is financed externally by loans from the rentiers' households, and, thus, that the total profits are split into income of the capitalists (who own the firms and save a constant and given fraction s, $0 < s \leq 1$, of their income) and rentiers' income, i.e., interest payments, *second*, the rentiers' households save a constant and given fraction s_R, $0<s_R < 1$, or their income, *third*, there is a *uniform* debt-capital ratio, which is denoted by ε ($0<\varepsilon<1$), *fourth*, the rate of inflation is equal to zero, *fifth*, the desired rate of accumultion of capitalists depends negatively on the interest payments per unit of nominal capital stock, that is, on the magnitude $i\varepsilon$ (where i is the interest on the firm' loans), and *sixth*, the composition of consumption is the same for all social classes. Consequently, the model is formed by the equations (1aa), (2), (3), (4aa), (5), (8a), while (6) and (7a) are replaced, respectively, by the following equations:

$$S = s(pKr - Z) + S_R Z \Rightarrow$$

$$rs - i\varepsilon(s - s_R) = g \tag{6a}$$

$$g = a_0 + a_1 u + a_2 h - a_3 i\varepsilon, \; g > 0 \text{ for } r > i \tag{7b}$$

where $K \equiv Ax(1/u)$, S is the nominal total savings per unit of labour employed, $Z \equiv iE$ is the firms' interest payments per unit of labour employed, E is the nominal stock of loans per unit of labour employed, $\varepsilon = E/pK$, and, a_3 is a given postive constant.

The short-run Keynesian equilibrium of the system is determined (given c, i, ε) by (6a) and (7b), while its stability requires the validity of the condition $(sh/v) > a_1$. We conclude, therefore, that if the capital-capacity ratio were independent of the growth of income, then the following would hold (see also Hein, 1999, pp. 15-17, where $s = 1$):

$$s - s_R - a_3 \, 0 \Rightarrow \partial r/\partial i > 0, \partial u/\partial i > 0, \partial g/\partial i \gtrless 0 \tag{31}$$

$$s - s_R - a_3 \leq 0 \Rightarrow \partial r/\partial i \leq 0, \; \partial u/\partial i \leq 0, \; \partial g/\partial i < 0 \tag{31a}$$

, while regarding the effects of a change in the wage rate, whatever held also in the framework of the Standard system of section 2 would, in the final analysis, hold (excluding the fact that it is possible for the so-called 'case of profit-led expansion' to appear). However, because the capital-capacity ratio depends on g/u and r/u and because g, r and i or are interrelated through (6a), it follows that in reality the effects of a change in i or c cannot be deduced from the relationships[22] (31), (31a) or, correspondingly, from (19), (20).

Finally, the long-run equilibrium of the system is defined as one inwhich the debt-capital ratio remains constant over time, that is

$$d\varepsilon/dt = (dE/dt)/pK = 0 \tag{32}$$

where

$$dE/dt = pK\,(g - sr) + Ei - E\,(dL/dt)\,(1/L) \Rightarrow$$
$$dE/dt = pK\,(g - sr) + E\,(i - g) \tag{32a}$$

and $(dL/dt)\,(1/L)(=g)$ is the growth rate of the labour employed ($L \equiv \ell X$). Consequently, the equilibrium value of ε is

$$\varepsilon^* = (sr - g)/(i - g) \tag{33}$$

and the system as a whole has two degrees of freedom, which can be eliminated through the exogenous determination of c and i.

From (33) and (6a) we get (the solution $g = sr$ is unacceptable)

$$g^* = (1 - s + s_R)i = \sigma i,\ \sigma \equiv 1 - s + s_R \tag{34}$$

Therefore, the equation of the present model, which corresponds to equation (23) of the Basic model, is

$$r = u\left[(1-\sigma)(a_0 + a_1 u - i\sigma) + a_3 i\sigma\right] / \left[a_3 su - (1-\sigma)a_2 v\right] \tag{35}$$

where

$$v = v\,(r/u,\ \sigma i/u) \tag{35a}$$

from which we conclude that the complete investigation of the effects of a change in the wage rate or interest rate will arrive at result which are much more ambiguous than the results already arrived at by the investigation of a one-sector model.

Government Fiscal Activity

Ceteris paribus, we shall assume, following the one-sector approach of You and Dutt, 1996, that, *first*, there are only two kinds of taxes, namely a tax on the capital income(:profits from current production plus interest income paid by the government) at a given rate t_c and a tax on the wage income at a given rate t_w second, the nominal interest rate (i) on the government debt is given from outside the system, third, the rate of inflation is equal to zero, and, fourth, the real government expenditures remain in a constant proportion to the capital stocks. Therefore, the model is formed by the equations (1aa), (2), (3), (5), (8a), while the equations (4aa), (6) and (7a) are replaced,respectively, by the following equations:[23]

$$x = Kg + G + c_T\delta,\ K \equiv Ax(1/u),\ G = \mu K \tag{4b}$$

$$S = pKr\left[t_c + s(1-t_c)\right] + wt_w - i\Theta(1-t_c) - pG \Rightarrow$$

$$r\left[t_c + s(1-t_c) - t_w\right] + (u/v)t_w - i\vartheta(1-s)(1-t_c) - \mu = g \tag{6b}$$

where

$$v = (r/u,\ (g+\mu)/u) \tag{6ba}$$

$$g = a_0 + a_1 u + a_2 h\ (1-t_c) \tag{7c}$$

where S is the nominal total savings per unit of labour employed, G is the vector of real goverment expenditures per unit of labour employed, μ is a given positive constant, Θ is the nominal stock of government debt per unit of labour employed, and $\vartheta \equiv \Theta/pK$ is the debt-capital ratio.

The short-run Keynesian equilibrium of the system is determined (given c,∂) by (6b) and (7c), while its stability requires the validity of the condition

$$(1/v)\left[hs(1-t_c) + ht_c + (1-h)t_w\right] > a_1 \tag{36}$$

We conclude, therefore, that *if* the capital-capacity ratio were independent of the growth of income, then the following would hold (see also You and Dutt, 1996, pp. 338-40 and 344-5):

$$t_c + S(1 - t_c) - t_w \gtrless 0 \Rightarrow$$

$$\partial r / \partial y \gtrless 0, \partial u / \partial y \gtrless 0, \partial g / \partial y \gtrless 0, \text{ where}^{24} y = \vartheta, \mu, i \qquad (37)$$

,while regarding the effects of a change in the wage rate, whatever held also in the framework of the Standard system of Section 2 would, in the final analysis, hold (excluding the fact that it is possible for the so-called 'case of profit-led expansion' to apper).However, because the capital-capacity ratio depends on r/u and $(g + \mu)/u$, and because g, r,i , μ and ∂ are interrelated through (6b), it follows that the aforementioned effects do not correspond to reality and that the effects which actually occur are shaped in a much more complex and indirect way.

Finally, the long-run equilibrium of the system is defined as one in which the debt-capital ratio remains constant over time, that is

$$d\vartheta/dt = (d\Theta/dt)/pK = 0 \qquad (38)$$

where

$$d\Theta / dt = pG - \left[t_w W + t_c\left(pKr + i\Theta\right)\right] + (i - g)\Theta \qquad (38a)$$

Consequently, the equilibrium value of the debt-capital ratio is

$$\vartheta^* = [\mu - r\ (t_c - t_w) - t_w(u/v)]/[g - i\ (1 - t_c)] \qquad (39)$$

and the system as a whole has one degree of freedom, which is eliminated through the exogenous determination of the wage rate. On the basis, therefore, of equations (12), (6b, ba), (7c), (39), we conclude that the complete investigation of the effects of a change in c or i or, finally, in the tax rates will arive at results, which are much more ambiguous than the results already arrived at by the investigation of a one-sector model.

Conclusion

In the framework of the *simplest* possible post-Keynesian

multisectoral model, a rise in the real wage rate (or, equivalently, a decrease in the aggregate profit share implies the reduction of profit per unit of utilised capital stock (r/u), has ambiguous effects on the growth (profit) rate and on the degree of capacity utilisation, and finally, tends to increase the output-capital ratio (u/v). If a rise in the real wage rate does not cause a rise inthe capital-capacity ratio, then the output-capital ratio necessarily increases (consider equation (19a)). However, because the decrease in the capital capacity utilisation, it follows that it is entirely possible that a rise in the real wage rate, which causes the reduction of the capital-capacity ratio, leads to the reduction of the degree of capacity utilisation and of the profit (growth) rate, and to the increase in the output-capital ratio and in the total nominal consumption per unit of nominal capital stock ($u(1\text{-}sh)/v$). Clearly, the said inverse movement between the degree of capacity utilisation and the output-capital ratio (which presupposes the - inconceivable in the context of traditional neoclassical theory-inverse movement between the real wage rate and the capital-capacity ratio), as well as that inverse movement caused by the simultaneous rise in the degree of capacity utilisation and in the capital-capacity ratio, is impossible in the context of a (quasi-)one-good world.

More generally speaking, the 'peculiar' behaviour of a multisectoral model is due to the fact that the capital-capacity ratio reacts in an unpredictable way to changes in the distribuation of income, in technology, in interest rates and in fiscal policy, which implies that the effects of these changes on the degree of capacity utilisation, on the growth rate and on the profit rate are unknown a priori. This basic conclusion does not lead, however, to agnosticism, but rather contributes to the development of the positive and critical economic theory of contemporary society, since it sheds further light on certain aspects of the way in which this society operates and reproduces itself. Finally, the aforesaid conclusion does not mean that the "different political ideologies regarding the managment of the capitalist economy" (Bhaduri and Marglin, 1990) are devoid of content from a purely abstract viewpoint, but that they are highly debatable from a theoretical and practical view point, to the extent that these ideologies are not in a position to know the results of their suggestions.

References

1. Abraham-Frois, G. (1991). *Dynamique economique*, Paris, Dalloz.

2. Bidard, C. (1991). *Prix, reproduction, rarete*, Paris, Dunod.

3. Bidard, C. (1997). *Pure joint Production, Cambridge Journal of Economics*, 21, 685-701.

4. Bidard, C. and Steedman, I. (1996). Monotonic Movement of Price Vectors, *Economic Issue*, 1,41-4.

5. Bhaduri, A. and Marglin, S (1990). Unemployment and the real wage: the economic basis for contesting political ideologies, *Cambridge Journal of Economics*, 14, 375-93.

6. Charasoff, G.v (1910). *Das System des Maxismus*, Berlin, H. Bondy.

7. Dumenil, G and Levy, D. (1995). A post-keynesian Long Term Equilibrium with Equalized Profit Rates? A Rejoinder to Amitava Dutt's Synthesis, *Review of Radical Political Economics*, 27, 135-41.

8. Dutt, A.K. (1984). Stagnation, Income Distribution and Monopoly Power, *Cambridge Journal of Economics*, 8, 25-40.

9. Dutt, A.K. (1987A). Competition, Monopoly Power and the Uniform Rate of Profit, *Review of Radical Political Economics*, 19, 55-72.

10. Dutt, A.K. (1987B). Alternative closures again: a comment on 'Growth, Distribution and inflation', *Cambridge Journal of Economics*, 11, 75-82.

11. Dutt, A.K. (1988). Convergence and Equilibrium in Two Sector Models of Growth, Distribution and Prices, *Journal of Economics*, 48, 135-58

12. Dutt, A.K. (1989). Accumulation, Distribuation and inflation in a Marxian/Post-Keynesian Model with a Rentier Class, Review of Radical Political Economics, 21, 18-26.

13. Dutt, A.K. (1994). Classical Competition and Post-Keynesian Monopoly Power: A Possible Synthesis, pp. 40-51 in Glick, M.A.

(e.d), *Competition, Technology and Money,* Aldershot, Edward Elgar.

14. Dutt, A.K (1995). Monopoly Power and Uniform Rates of Profit: A Reply to Glick-Campbell and Dumenil-Levy, *Review of Radical Political Economics*, 27, 142-53.

15. Dutt, A.K. (1997). Profit-Rate Equalization in the Kalecki-Steindl Model and the "Over-Determination" Problem, *The Manchester School*, 65, 433-51.

16. Dutt. A.K. and Amedeo E.J. (1990) (eds). *Keyne' Third* Alternative? *The Neo-Ricardians Keynesians and the Post Keynesians, Aldershot,* Edwar Elgar.

17. Franke, R. (1999). Technical Change and a Falling Wage Share if Profits are Maintained, *Metroeconomica*, 50, 35-53.

18. Garegnani, P. (1983). Two Routes to Effective Demand: Comment on Kregel, pp. 69-80 in Kregel, J.A. (ed.), *Distribution, Effective Demand and International Economic Relations,* London, MacMillan.

19. Glick, M. and Campbell, D. (1994). Post-Keynesian and Classical Theories of Competition, pp. 24-39 in Glick, M.A. (ed.), *Competition, Technology and Money,* Aldershot, Edward Elgar.

20. Harris, D.J. (1975). The Theory of Economic Growth: A Critique and Reformulation, *American Economic Review,* 65, 329-37.

21. Hein, E. (1999). Interest Rates, Income Shares and Investment in a Kaleckian Model, *Political Economy. Review of Political and Social Sciences,* Issue 5, 5-22.

22. Hein, E. and Ochsen, C. (2001). Regimes of Interest Rates, Income Shares, Savings and Investment: A Kaleckian Model and Empirical Estimations for some Advanced OECD-Economics, *Wirtschaftswissenschaftliche Diskussionbeiträge,* Universität Oldenburg.

23. Hosoda, E. (1990). The Relationship between per Capita Consumption and the Growth Rate: A Note, *Cambridge Journal of Economics,* 14, 331-8.

24. Kurz, H.D. (1990A). Technical Change, Growth and Distribution: A Steady - State Approach to 'Unsteady' Growth, pp. 211-39 in Kurz, H.D. *Capital, Distribution and Effective Demand. Studies in the "Classical" Approach to Economic Theory,* Cambridge, Polity Press.

25. Kurz, H.D. (1990B). Accumulation, Distribution and the 'Keynesian Hypothesis', pp. 396-412 in Bharadwaj, K. and

Schefold, B. (eds), *Essays on Piero Sraffa. Critical Perspectives on the Revival of Classical Theory*, London, Unwin Hyman.

26. Kurz, H.D. (1995). The Keynesian Project: Tom Asimakopoulos and "The Other Point of View", pp. 83-110 in Harcourt, G.C., Roncaglia, A. and Rowley, R. (eds), *Income and Employment in Theory and Practice: Essays in memory of Athanasios Asimakopoulos*, New York, St. Martin's Press.

27. Mariolis, T. (1999). The so-called Problem of Transforming Values into Prices, *Political Economy. Review of Political Economy and Social Sciences*, Issue 5, 45-58.

28. Mariolis, T. (2000). The Role of Non-Basic and Non-Reproductive Commodities in Neo-Ricardian Models, *The Indian Economic Journal*, 47, 30-41.

29. Mariolis, T. (2001). On V.K. Dmitriev's Contribution to the so-called. "Transformation Problem" and to the Profit Theory, *Political Economy. Rcview of Political Economy and Social Sciences*, Issue 9, 45-60.

30. Mariolis, T. (2000). On the Lack of Correspondence between Surplus Value and Profit, pp. 193-212 in Kalafatis, A., Livas, P. and Skountzos, T. (eds), *Essays in Honour of Professor Apostolos Lazaris*, Vol. I, Piraeus, University of Piraeus, Department of Economics (forthcoming).

31. Mariolis, T. (2003A). Controllability, Observability, Regularity, and the so-called Problem of Transforming Values into Prices of Production, *Asian-African Journal of Economics and Econometrics*, Issue 4 (fothcoming).

32. Mariolis, T. (2003B). A Sraffian Approach to the Stolper-Samuelson Theorem, *mimeo*, Panteion University, Athens.

Appendix

The technical coefficient, the composition of consumption, and the parameters of the four-sector model mentioned in the text are as follows:

$$A=\begin{bmatrix}5 & 2 & 1 & 2\\ 1 & 5 & 1 & 3\\ 2 & 2 & 4 & 2\\ 3 & 3 & 2 & 1\end{bmatrix}, \ell=[10,20,30,40], \delta=\begin{bmatrix}1/2\\ 1/6\\ 1/36\\ 1/8\end{bmatrix}$$

$$s = 0.99,\ a_0 = 10^{-6},\ a_2 = 5 \times 10^{-2}$$

Notes

1. Regarding the assumptions of the model, we should briefly note the following: Evidently, assumption **A1.** is in agreement with **A.8**. The introduction of depreciation into the discussion, as well as the existence of supplementary or 'overhead' labour (see **A.2** and **A.3.**) could be based on the approach already put forward by Sraffa, 1960, Ch. 10 Steindl, 1979, pp. 1-3, Rowthorn, 1981, pp. 3-5 and Kurz, 1990A, pp. 213-4. The existence of a rentier class (see **A.4.**) will later be incorporated in the model (see Section 3), in agreement with Dutt, 1989, Hein, and Ochsen, 2001. In addition, it would be possible, based for example on Kurz and Salvadori, 1995, pp. 475-80, to take into consideration workers' savings. If we were to assume that the composition of consumption of workers and capitalists depends on commodity prices and/or that it is different for workers and capitalists (see **A.5.**) then we would considerably complicate the investigation of the present model, for it would not always be possible to separate the quantity system of the economy from the corresponding price system (regarding this kind of complication, in the framework of a neo-Ricardian model, see Hododa, 1990, Bidard, 1991, Ch. 17 and Kurz and Salvadori, 1995, pp. 102-4, while regarding how these complications grow, in the case where the capital stock matrix is decomposable, when they are combined with the issue of choosing the standard of value, i.e., the numeraire, see Mariolis, 2000). So, generally speaking, all these assumptions are indeed restrictive, but they do not affect the main conclusion of this investigation. On the other hand, of course, assumption **A.6.** is in principle of a different nature, which moreover should be stressed (given **A.4** and **A.6**, it could be condiered that **A.8** is introduced solely for the sake of simplification, while **A.7** is more or less neutral in respect of the issues being investigated here). **A6**. implies, to a greater or lesser degree, that the commodity prices which are shaped in the framework of the economy under consideration correspond to so-called 'prices of (re-) production 'or 'long-period prices' (see e.g. Kurz and salvadori, 1995, Ch.1), i.e to the classical theory of competition and thus is (or could be or appears to be) in conflict with **A.3**. For the latter corresponds (more or, according to others, absolutely) to the post-Keynesian theory of competition and, more specifically, implies that firms set prices according to a mark-up over prime costs. In the following, we shall not delve into the theoretical substance of this issue, regarding which there is no general agreement in the literature (Harris, 1975, Garegnani, 1983, Dutt, 1987A, 1987B, 1988, 1994,1995, Dutt and Amadeo,

1990, Ch. 4-6, Kurz, 1990B, 1995, Glick and Campbell, 1994, Dumenil and Levy 1995), although we shall return to this issue when we deem it necessary, Specifically, we shall consider that the 'competitive conditions [are] close to free competition' (i.e., that commodity prices are determined on the basis of the uniform wage rate, the uniform profit rate and the sectoral degrees of capacity utilisation) and thus, we shall interpret 'the underutilisation of productive capacity as caused essentially by an insufficient effective demand' (Kurz, 1995, pp. 96-7).

2. Clearly, the introduction into the initial model (: (1) - (6)) of (8), of n^2 investment functions of the form $g_{ij} = g_{ij}(h_i, u_{ij})$, where g_{ij} is the desired rate of accumulation of capital good i in sector j, and, finally of n^2 equilibrium conditions $g_{ij} \overset{!}{=} g$, leads to the existence of only one degree of freedom.

3. In the framework of a one-sector model (see e.g. Dutt, 1987B, pp. 77-8, Kurz, 1990A, pp. 220-1), the exogenous determination of the real wage rate is entirely equivalent (and not only from a formal viewpoint) to the exogenous determination of profit share ant to the assumption that firms set prices according to a (given) mark-up over prime costs. For Clearly, the introduction of the equation

$$p = w\ell(1 + \overline{m}) \tag{11a}$$

Where $\overline{m}$ is the mark-up rate (a magnitude which supposedly depends primarily on industrial concentration and the class struggle), implies the unambiguous determination of w/p and of $h = m/(1 + m)$, and vice versa. However, the introduction of (11a) into his model is economically insignificant, in the sense that (11a) and (1aa) imply the validity of $\ell A(r/u)(1 + \overline{m}) = \ell\overline{m}$, i.e. that l is the Perron-Frobenius eigenvector of A (case of 'equal organic composition of capital'). Therefore, this model can close either by means of equation (11) or by means of the equation

$$p = w\ell\left\lfloor I + \hat{\overline{M}} \right\rfloor \tag{11b}$$

where $\hat{\overline{M}}$ is the diagonal matrix of the sectoral mark-up rates. Of course, none of these ways to close the system leads to the explicit determination of profit share, while the latter of the two ways, first leads to the explicit determination of the relative commodity prices, second, thus, it is specifically post-Keynesian, third, it is, clearly, inconsistent with equation (1aa), and thus, forth, as shown by Dutt, 1997, in the framework of an anti-critique of Park, 1995, it presupposes the replacement of (7) by an aggregate investment function of the form $g=g\ (h,\ u_1,\ u_2,.....,u_n)$. It should be noted, finally, that in Dutt, 1984, pp. 32-5, 1994, pp. 47-9, certain ways to close the system are outlined by correlating the unknown sectoral mark- up rates with the growth rate or with the respective degrees of capacity utilisation, while regrading the closure of a neo-Ricardian model by means of the exogenous determinaticn of the aggregate wage share, see Frnake, 1999. In the following, however, we shall no be dealing with these alternative possibilities.

4. In other words, there is a 'c - (r/u) trade-off: for $0 \leq c \leq (1/\ \ell\delta\ )$ there is one and only one value of r/u, where $0 \leq (r/u) \leq (1/\lambda)$, and u/r is the Perron-Frobenius eigenvalue of matrix $A\ [I - c\delta\ \ell\ ]^{-1}$

5. The existence of this 'frontier' is the consequence of **A.5** (see footnote 1).

6. From (16) it follows that the exogenous determination of the real wage rate is completely equivalent to the exogenous determination of the profit share, but not to the existence of a uniform mark-up rate. This happens, of course, because the Standard system under consideration is a quasi-one-good system, in the framework of which, however, commodity prices are not proportional to the labour input vector (see footnote 3).

7. Evidently, these roots always have a different sign, and $u_1 > (a_2\lambda)/s$ holds.

8. The independence of equilibrium values from the labour input vector is only apparent and it is due to the normalisation equation $\ell\,\delta = 1$. Also equilibrium (Keynesian) exists between investment and savings, it is stable and economically meaningful iff condition (21) holds.

9. Clearly, this is the maximum value of the level of the wage rate, which is indeed feasible. Also, as can easily be shown, the maximum-indeed feasible- value of the profit rate corresponds to the zero value of the wage rate.

10. Following Kurz, 1990A, pp. 222-4, the former case may be characterised as a 'regime of overaccumultion', while the latter a 'regime of underconsumption'.In agreement with Bhaduri and Marglin, 1990, both these cases may be characterised as 'wage-led expansion', precisely because they imply a rise in the degree of capacity utilisation. On the other hand, all attempts to identify

these cases as 'realisation crises', that is, on the basis of the traditional Marxian notions/magnitudes of value and surplus value, are unforunded, precisely because these notions have absolutely no economic significance,nor any relationship with prices and, correspondingly, profits (Steedman, 1977, Mariolis, 1999, 2002, 2003A).

11. It appears that very few things can be said a priori about the changes in commodity prices in the framework of these' regimes'. However, because (12a) holds, prices are functions of the variable *r/u*, and, thus, it is possible to follow the approaches suggested by Bidard and Steedman, 1996, and Mariolis, 2003B.

12. If matrix A is diagonalisable, then we can apply the following similarity transformation to the system$[A, \ \ell \delta]$

$$\tilde{A} = Q^{-1}AQ, \tilde{\ell} = \ell Q, \tilde{\delta} = Q^{-1}\delta \tag{26}$$

where Q is the modal matrix of A, that is a matrix, the columns of which are the right eigenvectors q_i of A normalised in such a way that $\ell q_i = 1$ (if ℓ is not orthogonal to q_i) and $\tilde{A}$ is the diagonal matrix of the eigenvalues of A. The capital-capacity ratio of the transformed system, evidently, is equal to that of the original system and is expressed as follows:

$$\tilde{v} = v = \left[\tilde{\ell} C(u,r)\tilde{A}C(u,g)\tilde{\delta}\right] / \left[\tilde{\ell} C(u,r)C(u,g)\tilde{\delta}\right] \tag{27}$$

where. $C(u,y) \equiv \left[I - \tilde{A}(u,y)\right]^{-1}$, $y = r, g$. Because of the fact that $\tilde{A}$ is a diagonal matrix, equation (27) is reduced to a form, which is exceptionally simpler (especially if we set $\boldsymbol{s} = 1$) than (14). Again, however, the reaction of v to changes in *r/u* cannot be predicted, precisely because the components of $\tilde{\delta}$ are not known a priori.

13. It should be noted that it is always (i.e., even when **A.5** does not hold) the sub-system, which produces the workers' consumption basket. Regarding the significance and role of the said sub-system within the framework of certain neo-Ricardian models (a la V.K. Dmitriev) and the so-called 'Fundamental Marxian Theorem', see Mariolis, 2001,2002.

14. Evidently, in order for there to exist multiple points of equilibrium, the function $v = v\ (r/u)$ would have to have been multiple-valued, which is not possible.

15. In agreement with what was said in footnote 10, this case can be described as 'Keynesian' (Kurz) or a case of 'profit-led expansion' (Bhaduri and Marlin). As can easily be shown, if $\ell\delta = 1$ the following hold (compare to equations (19) and (20)):

$$u^* = v\,[a_0\,(v_w/v) + a_2\,(1-\bar{c})]/[s(1-\bar{c}) - v_w a_1] \qquad (19a)$$

$$r^* = (1-\bar{c})[a_0 + a_2\,(v/v_w)\,(1-\bar{c})]/[s(1-\bar{c}) - v_w a_1] \qquad (20a)$$

We conclude, therefore, that in the framework of a multisectoral system the reaction of the degree of capacity utilisation and of the profit rate is determined by the reactions of v and v_w. More specifically, because $v_w/(1-\bar{c})$ ($=v_w/h_w$, where h_w is the profit share of the sub-system which produces, δ, and $sh_w > a_1\, v_w$ is the Keynesian stability condition) is a strictly increasing function of $\bar{c}$, it follows that u increases without fail if v does not decrease and that the necessary condition for the decrease in u is the decrease in v (exactly for this reason, in the framework of a (quasi-) one-good system, where $v=v_w$ is invariable, u does not decrease). It should be noted, lastly, that if it had been assumed ceteris paribus that the desired rate of accumulation depends positively only on the degree of capacity utilisation and the profit rate (if, that is, in the place of (7a) a linear investment function a la Steindl, 1952, Rowthorn, 1981, and Dutt, 1984, having the form $g = g\,(u, r)$ had been introduced into the model), then, first, the capital-capacity ratio would not have been involved in the determination of the equilibrium values of r and u (that is, in the place of the curve of Figure 2a a constant straight line with a positive slope would have appeared), and thus, second, the only 'regime' which would have existed would have been that of 'underconsumption'. This, of course, underlines the significance of Bhaduri and Marglin's critique, 1990, of the aforementioned investment function.

16. In the framework of system, which is characterised by the validity of (11b) (see footnote 3), the said issue continues to exist.

17. Consider what was said in footnote 8.

18. There is, of course, at (at least) one cases, which allows an unambiguous conclusion to be drawn. Let us assume that the technical possibilities of the system can be represented by alinearly homogeneous Cobb-Douglas function of the form:

$$1 = \alpha^{\gamma}\,\ell^{\,1-\gamma} \qquad (29)$$

From the first order conditions of cost-minimisaton and the normalisation eqaution $p = 1$ we get

$$r/u = \gamma/\alpha \ (\Rightarrow h \equiv \alpha\ (r/u) = \gamma) \quad (29a)$$

$$c = (1-\gamma)/\ \ell \quad (29b)$$

Thus, from equation (29)-(29b) and (18) (where $\lambda = \alpha$) we conclude that the rise in the wage rate implies a decrease in ℓ, and a rise in a, r, u.

19. Evidently, the capital-capacity ratio changes because the relative prices, production technique and composition of output change. However, while the first two changes are neceesarily limited by the validity of conditions (30) and (30a), the latter change is not subject a priori to any limitation.

20. It is not neccessary, of course, to dwel on the fact that the existence of the 'reswitching of techniques' phenomenon (see Sraffa, 1960, Ch. 12 and Kurz and Salvadori, 1995, Ch 5 and 14) further complicates the problem of prediction. It should also be noted that due to the possibility of the existence of a positive correlation between c and r, and the possibility of a decrease in r as the consequence of using a costminimising technique, the present system behaves as though it were a Sraffian joint production system(see Bidard, 1997). However, because these latter systems have particular significance in the theory of international trade (Mariolis, 2003C), it must be examined whether this also holds for the present system.

21. For a broader analytical framework, see e.g. Abraham-Frois, 1991, pp. 202-8.

22. Nevethele, the final conclusion of Hein, 1999, p.18 continues to hold; "... no generally valid statement about the onsequences a changing interest rate has for the equilibrium rates of capacity utilisation, accumulation and profit can be made.... assessing the effects of interest rate changes on capacity utilisation, accumulation and the profit rate requires some knowledge about the parameters in the accumulation and savings funciton[and about the date [A, ℓ δ] and the initial state of the economy-TM].. In other words, in a post-Keynesian framework we need a concrete historical analysis in order to judge the effects of monetary policy". For an empirical investigation, within the framework of a one-sector model. see Hein and Ochsen. 2001.

23. As noted by you and Dutt, 1996, p. 338:<<The rate of interest as a determinant of investment demand is ignored for now, given the assumption that it is fixed. In assuming that the interest rate is fixed, we are following a frequent practice in the post-Keynesian Literature which assumes that money supply is

edogenously deternmined by money demand at a given interest rate".

24. In the framework of subcase $y = i$, we ignore the fact that a rise in the interest rate can, first, have a "negative effect on investment spending due to the higher cost of finance", and, second, lead to higher commodity prices (You and Dutt, 1996, p. 345).

4

Lowering Interest Rates: Impact Analysis

Justin Paul*
Kranti Gada**

Introduction

Interest is the cost of funds from the borrowers point of view while it is the yield on capital from the lenders point of view. Interest rates in India are now at historic lows. The Reserve Bank of India's bank rate is down to 6.25 per cent. Banks are giving out loans below their prime-lending rate. Inflation (which has been below 4 per cent) is also at an all time low. Over the last five years a regime of low interest rates has set in for the Indian economy. Despite the implementation of reforms, structural rigidities remained in interest rate structure distorting the true market-determined rates. Rates had been kept artificially high by offering high-administered rates on small savings and provident fund. The gap between the short-term and long-term rates tended to remain high on account of this. The interest rates had been and continue to be very high relative to the rates prevailing in global markets.

* Assistant Professor, NMIMS, J.V.P.D. Scheme, Vile Parle West, Mumbai-400056 E-mail: justin@iitb.ac.in, justin@nmims.edu

** Narsee Monjee Institute of Management studies (NMIMS), J.V.P.D Scheme, Vile Parle West, Mumbai-400056 E-mail: kranti9@hotmail.com

Industrial growth is a pre-requisite for economic development. Every industry requires finance for the establishment, expansion and working capital management. Bank credit is considered as the most important source of industrial finance in India. The dependence on bank for finance could vary according to the size of the companies and to the availability of the credit at lower cost. The small-scale industrial units depend on banks for credit because they have virtually no access to the capital market.

Against the backdrop of slowing Indian economy, bank rate and administered rates on small savings have been cut. Added to this the Reserve Bank proclaimed the policy of pursuing lower interest rate regime. With the US economy signaling lower interest rates it appears as if the global economy is bracing lower rate regime as well. Globalization will ensure that India will not remain immune to this global phenomenon. Through this paper, we attempt to contemplate the following aspects of 'Lowering of Interest Rates' and study the impact. We put forward some concrete suggestions for the betterment of the economy and banking sector.

- The effect of Interest rates on money supply, aggregate demand, inflation, stock prices, Exchange rates etc.
- Lower interest rates and India Inc.
- Lower interest rates and the common man
- International scenario
- Sentiments of the common

Interest Rates and the Economy

Monetary policy aims to influence the overall level of monetary demand in the economy so that it grows broadly in line with the economy's ability to produce goods and services. This stops output rising too quickly or slowly. Interest rates are increased to moderate demand and inflation and they are reduced to stimulate demand. If rates are set too low, this may encourage the build-up of inflationary pressure; if they are set too high, demand will be lower than necessary to control inflation. How does this work?

The Bank Rate

Monetary policy operates by influencing the price of money, i.e. the cost of borrowing and the income form saving. The Reserve Bank of India sets the bank rate. This is an interest rate for the Reserve Bank's own market transaction with financial institutions-the rate at which the Reserve Bank will make short-term loans to banks and other financial institutions. This rate is known as the bank rate.

From the Bank rate to inflation

Changes in the Bank rate then affect the whole range of interest rates set by commercial banks, other financial institutions, etc. for their own savers and borrowers. It will influence interest rates charged for overdrafts and mortgages, as well as savings account. A change in the Bank rate will also tend to affect the price of financial assets such as bonds and shares, and the exchange rate. These changes in financial markets affect consumer and business demand and in turn output. Changes in demand and output then have an impact on the labour market-employment levels and wages costs-which in turn influence producer and consumer prices.

Bank Rate to Prime Lending Rate and Deposit Rates

As there is a positive correlation between cut in Bank rate and movement in interest rate, most banks make downward adjustment in their respective lending and deposit rates following slash in Bank rate. While cut in lending rate would bring down the interest income, it is only logical that most banks would try to compensate for the loss of income by bringing down the interest out-go through adjustment in deposit rates so as to neutralise the impact on their net interest income. To that extent, this would definitely reduce their cost of funds as also bring down the interest income.

The Effects on Demand - Spending and Saving Decisions

When interest rates are changed, demand can be affected in various ways. A change in the cost of borrowing affects spending decisions. Interest rates will affect the attractiveness of spending today relative to spending tomorrow. An increase in interest rates will make saving more attractive and borrowing less so. This will tend to reduce current spending, by both consumers and firms. That includes spending by consumers in the shops and spending by firms on new equipment, i.e investment. Conversely, a reduction in interest rates will tend to increase spending by consumers and firms.

Cashflow

A change in interest rates will affect consumers' and firms' cash flow. For savers, a rise in interest rates will increase the money received from interest-bearing bank and other deposit. But it will also mean higher interest payments for people and firms with loans-debtors-who are being charged variable interest rates (as opposed to fixed rates which do not change). These include many households with mortgages on their homes. These fluctuations in cash flow are likely to affect spending. Lower interest rates will have the opposite effects on savers and borrowers.

Asset Prices

A change in interest rates affects the value of certain assets, such as house and share prices. Higher interest rates increase the return on savings in banks and PPF. This might encourage savers to invest less of their money in alternatives, such as property and company shares. Any fall in demand for these assets is likely to reduce their prices. This reduces the wealth of individuals holding these assets, which, in turn, might influence their willingness to spend. Again, lower interest rates have the opposite effect; i.e. they tend to increase asset prices.

Stock Prices

As seen above, ordinarily, the significant fall in interest rates can be expected to reflect in higher stock prices. Long-term interest rates have declined more than 25 per cent in the last year and half. However, a commensurate increase in stock prices has failed to happen. Indeed, index values are virtually at levels seen in June 1999- since then, long-term interest rates have come down from around 12 per cent to close to 8 per cent now. A probable reason for this phenomenon is that given the uncertainty in the Indian as well as global markets, the investors prefer to stay liquid.

Exchange Rates

A particular influence on prices comes through the exchange rate. A rise in interest rates relative to those in other countries will tend to result in an increase in the amount of funds flowing into India, as investors are attracted

Table 1: Trend in Bank Rate

Date	*Change in Bank Rate*
April 2, 1998	Reduced from 10.5% to 10%
April 29, 1998	Reduced to 9%
March 1, 1999	Reduced to 8%
April 1, 2000	Reduced to 7%
July, 2000	Increased to 8%
March 1, 2001	Reduced to 7%
April 1, 2002	Reduced to 6.5%
October 26, 2002	Reduced to 6.25%

Source: Report on Trend and Progress of Banking in India, RBI, Dec 1999, Page 3 and RBI Announcements in 2000, 01 and 2002

to the higher rates of interest. This will tend to result in an appreciation of the exchange rate against other currencies. In practice, the exchange rate will be influenced both by expectations about future interest rates and any unexpected changes in interest rates. That is because if investors expect interest rates to rise, they may increase the amount they invest in a currency before interest rates actually rise. So there is never a simple relationship between changes in interest rates and exchange rates. Other things being equal, an increase in the value of the rupee will reduce the price of imports. In addition, a higher Rupee will tend to reduce the demand abroad for Indian goods and services.

Table 2: Interest Rate Cut-Small Saving Schemes

Scheme	*2002*	*2001*	*2000*
PPF	9.0%	9.5%	11.0%
NSS	9.0%	9.0%	10.5%
NSC	9.0%	9.5%	11.0%
Post Office Savings	3.5%	3.5%	4.5%
Post Office Time Deposit	7.25%	7.5%	8 (1 year)
	7.5%	8	9 (2 year)
	9.0%	9	10.5 (5 year)

Source: Union Budget Document 2002 and 2001, Ministry of Finance, Govt. of India.

Table 3: Trends in Prime Lending Rates(PLR) of Commercial Banks

Year	*Interest rates (%)*
1999-2000	12 to 12.5%
2000-2001	11 to 12%
2001-2002	11 to 12%

Source: RBI Bulletin Sep., 2002

Impact of Lower Interest Rates in India Inc

India's current real interest rates are one of the highest in the world. They result in inflating the cost of production making the industry less competitive in the world market. The economic survey (2001) has clearly stated that India is going through a phase of slowdown. All three sectors viz. Agriculture, industrial and services sectors are showing signs of slower growth. The reduction in interest rate will have a twofold effect:

(a) It will bring down the interest burden of the corporates.

(b) It will help to reduce cost of capital.

The reduction in cost of capital will stimulate industrial growth and investment.

It will also enable the small and medium industries to compete with cheap imported products that have been flooding the Indian markets post globalisation.

The Feel Good Factor

Cut in interest rate at this stage is a step in the right direction. This is more so in view of the fact that the economy, in general, was expecting a boost in the form of policy support. Immediate fall out of this step would be two-fold: one it's a definitive step towards a low-cost economy, and the other, which is more important, is that it creates a "feel good" atmosphere when the economy is going through "slowdown". Obviously, lower interest rate regime will facilitate the economy traversing a high-growth trajectory. Hence, the positive activism in the industry will certainly enthuse the financial markets in a big. The cut in interest rates has certainly had a positive impact on market sentiment.

Real Effects

- If we look at the current scenario, the blue chip

corporates have already delinked themselves from the PLR as they havebeen accessing the funds through other routes like bonds and Non Convertible Debentures (NCDs) at a sub PLR rate. Reduction in deposit rates and limited safe investment options have enabled corporate houses to raise cheap capital through Company deposit and NCDs.

- Already the corporate sector has saved over 1,200 crore in interest costs during the first quarter of the current financial year.[2]

Why Interest Rate Cuts have not been so Effective?

- The average cost of borrowing for the corporate sector has remained at around 11 per cent. The fall in interest rates has been accompanied by deterioration in the industrial climate, and the risks involved in lending to companies have therefore increased. The tightening of prudential and capital adequacy norms in the banking sector has added to the bank's caution. And since the Reserve Bank has stipulated a maximum spread above the prime lending rate the banks do not want to lower their PLR. At the same time, they can lend at sub-PLR to blue-chips companies.

- The structure of corporate borrowing does not give much leeway to borrow entire amounts at around prime lending rates. Bank borrowings are limited in utility in the sense that they are used for working capital requirements. Growth in money supply between 17 per cent to 18 per cent has led to sharp deposit growth in the banking system in recent times.With poor credit offtake, banks and institutions have made large investments in government securities leading to a bull run in the g-sec market and interest rates touching new lows every fortnight. Thus the lower interest rates are probably not reaching the Industries.

Bottom Line

- Recent monetary measures augur well in the current economic situation where the country's foreign exchange reserve are at peak levels and the inflation rate is at a reasonably low level. A further rate-cut will give impetus to economic growth and exports. The imminent bank interest rate cuts, including reduction in export credit finance, will make exports more competitive and bring down inflation and cost of production.
- A rough estimate, based on the aggregate borrowing by 1,100 companies in 2001-02 pegged at around Rs. 1,89,000 crore, is that the corporate sector can easily save around Rs. 3,800 crore annually if interest costs come down by another 200 basis points[3].
- With the latest slash in Bank Rate, Indian interest rates have become truly competitive and a further rate cut would definitely enhance their competitiveness. But it would be grossly fallacious to consider that interest rate as the only trigger to set right all the adverse trends on the economic front. No doubt, interest rate cut can have salubrious effect on the industrial activity and, to that extent, facilitate perking up the economy. But certainly this is neither the end nor the ultimete objective. The policy makers must address to the other critical aspects. Serious attempts need to be made to find out ways and means to improve the general level of productivity and efficiency. Equally important is to contain and gradually bring down the fiscal deficit and observe fiscal prudence in whichever way it is feasible.

Lower Interest Rates and the Common Man

Over the last couple of years, the investors have come more confused about where to put their money because of the following reasons.

- Most people who have played the equity market recently have lost money;
- Invesments in growth funds have not paid returns, and on the contrary, in some case, the principal amount has been eroded;
- Returns on tax free relief bonds have been cut and investments have been capped at Rs. 2 lakh;
- Bank deposit rates have come down anywhere between 3 and 4 percentage points;
- Return on PPF, NSC, NSS, post office savings etc have been cut;
- Once trustworthy institutions like UTI have shaken public trust;

The rate at which capital would have grown over the last one year can be seen from the table 4:

Table 4: Comparison of Investment Returns on Different instrument

Instrument	*Worth of Rs. 1 Lakh invested one year back*
Gold	Rs. 1,16,085
Stock Market	Rs. 98, 200
Equity fund	Rs. 1,15,860
Debt fund	Rs. 1,17,690
Balanced fund	Rs. 1,11,160
Fixed deposit	Rs. 1,09,000
Real estate	Rs. 1,00,000
Single premium insurance plan	Rs. 1,08,000
Relief bond	Rs. 1,08,000
Public provident fund	Rs. 1,09,000

Source: Saving and Hard times - Business Standard, Sept 7th, 2002.

There is no question that individuals are feeling the pinch. The worst hit are the senior-citizens who have retired and depend heavily on pension and interest incomes. Assured return schemes are an achronism. High fixed returns to investors cannot be promised when the yield on investment is not fixed. What makes it worse for the common man is;

- India has no social security support
- Life expectancy is increasing.
- Medical costs are rising.
- Career spans are shortening.
- Inflation could erode savings.

High rates of return are not sustainable and savers find themselves face to face with this new reality. If they want high returns, they will have to tap the equity market. But the chance are that one may burn fingers there. If the investor doesn't want to take risk, he will have to stay put in a bank deposit or a post office instrument and earn little after paying tax. Risk-averse savers may have even worse days ahead. With no signs of an economic revival in sight, the interest rates could fall further.

(a) Real interest rates are high

A study[5] claims that the conservative investor is actually better off today. If we compare the real interest rates

Table 5: Nominal and Real Interest Rates

	Nominal Interest Rates		*Real Interest Rates*	
Instrument	*1993*	*2002*	*1993*	*2002*
PPF	12%	9%	3.1%	4%
RBI bonds	9%	8%	0.1%	3%
5-yr bank FD	13%	8.5%	4.1%	3.5%

Source: Business World, Sep., 23, 2002

that existed prior to interest rates cuts we get a clearer picture of what this really means. The nominal interest rate on investment has to be adjusted for inflation to get the real returns. The calculations are based on the CPI (Consumer price index) and not on the WPI (wholesale price index).

(b) Lower interest rates mean cheaper loans for the common man too

Lower borrowing rates for banks also mean that the lending rates for loans (housing loans, car loans, consumer loans, etc) have also come down. Today we see a trend where banks are eager to give out loans to enable the common man to spend. The cost of a home loan is just about 8.5%, which is probably an all time low. Getting a loan was never so easy; in fact one can actually get an interest-free loan. We are already seeing a sharp increase in banks' retail lending portfolio (credit card receivables, car loans, home loans, etc,) and this trend is here to stay, as in the developed economies. Lower interest rates will only accentuate this trend and indeed help the flagging economy by creating demand for goods and services.

International Scenario

With increasing integration of the Indian economy into the global arena, one would expect a convergence of the real interest rates. Nominal interest rates, would however, continue to be a function of the domestic inflation and GDP growth. For example if one expects inflation to stabilize at 6 per cent levels, factoring in the global real interest rates of 2 to 2.25 per cent, ordinarily, one could predict a nominal rate of 8 to 8.50 per cent in the long run. However, this is contingent upon a full integration of the Indian economy with the global economy, including in terms of (no control on) capital flows. If this does not happen, Indian interest rates will continue to be "administered" by the Government, and assuming fiscal prudence, one can assume a steady decline in the interest rates over time.

A lower interest rate regime globally strengthens the assumption that domestic interest rates are bound to head southwards. In the post-reform phase, India is no longer insulted from global economic trends. In most of the developed countries current trends are obviously towards lower interest rates in order to reverse the economic downturn Slowdown in domestic economy has also been partly impacted by the global economic slowdown. It is, therefore, eminently difficult for the Indian economy to remain outside the global economic cycle. Since integration with the global economy is more a compulsion than a choice, interest rates (both nominal and real) are expected to move downwards in alignment with the global trends in this respect.

The sharp economic slowdown in the US is a major cause of concern having it's own impact on the world output growth. At the backdrop of this, the recent reduction in the benchmark interest rate will certainly result in much warranted short-term demand stimulus. The reduced cost of borrowing will definitely boost the credit off take from industry putting economy into a higher growth trajectory. The US is expected to reduce the interest rats further to boost its economy. The cut in the US interest rate could thus create lower interest rate environment internationally which could also lead to further softening of India's interest rates.

Sentiments of the Common Man

We know that to a great extent, sentiments drive the economy. The actual effect of any policy measure depends on how people perceive it and react to it. Hence, we conducted a sentiment survey to get a deeper understanding on how the people react to the cut in interest rates and to know whether they have switched over their investment preference from bank deposit and small saving schemes to other investment avenues like equity. The survey seeks to answer the following questions. a) If the investor is aware of the interest rate cuts (b) To what extent he has changed investment patterns (c) Difference in savings behaviour amongst differently employed people (d) Investment patterns of different professionals (employees, self-employed, business men). The survey result are given below:

Classification by Occupation

The Service Class (Fixed Income-low Income)

- 50 percent of this class invested 5 to 15 per cent of their incomes
- 25 per cent of this class invests less than 5 per cnet of their income. This is because they have a very small disposable income
- Most of them invest only in safe instrument which offer assured returns like Bank Fixed Deposit, PPF, Govt. bonds etc.
- 91.6 per cent of them are aware of the reduction in intrest rates.
- But only 8.3 per cent have been shown sensitivity to this reduction by changing their investment patterns.
- 6.6 per cent of them don't believe that they will be able to get cheaper loans. This is probably because they are a low earning group and cannot give security.
- 33.3 per cent of this class actually favours a further cut in interest rates.

Self-employed/professionals

- 33.3 per cent of this class invest 5 to 15 per cent of their incomes.
- 41.6 per cent of them invest 15 to 25 per cent of their income.
- Most of them save in safe instrument like PPF, LIC

policies & Bank Savings. However, 25 per cent of them invest in equities and mutual funds also.

- 91.6 per cent of them are aware of the cut in interest rates.
- 41.6 per cent of them have shifted their saving patterns in view of interest rate cuts.
- Over 90 per cent of this class believes that interest rate cuts will enable them to get cheaper loans.
- 16.6 per cent of them favour a further cut in interest rates.

Business Class

- Only 22.2 per cent of them invest regularly.
- 55 per cent of this class invests in equity. Bank savings are popular. Jewellery and Real estate are also used as investment tools.
- 100 per cent of them are aware of ongoing interest rate cuts.
- 33.3 per cent have shifted their investments.
- 70 per cent of them do believe that interest rate cuts will enable them to borrow at a cheaper rate.
- Over 40 per cent favour a further cut in interest rates.

Summary and Suggestions

In the last few years interest rates have been deregulated. After the deregulation, interest rates initially moved up. However in recent times, interest rates have begun to come down mainly because of ample liquidity prevalent in the system. The integration of the domestic economy with global economies also had a positive impact on interest rates. When global interest rates witnessed a downward movement, a similar declining trend was also observed in Indian interest rates especially over the last year. Upto last year couple of rigidities existed in the interest rate structure, which have since been rationalized in the current year's budget. In calender year 2001 and 2002, interest rates across all small savings instruments like PPF, Post office monthly income schemes, RBI relief bonds have been reduced

- It is evident that India Inc (including the small, medium and large sectors) will benefit from interest rate cuts. They strongly favour a further lowering of interest rates. At the same time one thing to remember is that the reduction in interest rate is only one of the factors to stimulate the industrial growth. Much depends upon other factors like demand-supply situation, competitiveness of Products, global slowdown, etc.
- On the other hand the investors feel distressed by lowering of interest rates and strongly oppose it. To a certain extent they are justified too. The scenario in India is not comparable to that in the developed countries. The poor banking structure, inability of banks to adjust to interest rate-cuts and disburse loans speedily, the absence of investor-friendly stock-exchanges, absence of healthy and reliable investment options are among other factors which put a question mark to the justification of lower interest rates.
- However, globalisation compels India to adjust its interest rates to those existing internationally. Sooner or later the interest rates especially the actual lending rates to the industry will have to be brought in line with global levels.

The Indian scenario and conditions are not comparable to world standards. We lack the maturity of financial markets and strong infrastructure. This is the reason why India should not blindly follow International practices of lowering interest rates. The following points should be considered in depth before interest rates are lowered further:

Lowering PLR

If observed carefully, in the last few years the bank rate and the interest rates on small savings as well as deposit have come down. In relation to this the PLR has remained steady (high) over the last 2 to 3 years. This means that the borrowing rates for Industry still remain high. Barring a few blue-chip companies, most others still borrow at high rates. Thus, instead of further cutting the blank rate and interest rates on savings, PLR should be brought down.

Strengthening the Banking Structure

The banking structure of India should be made stronger. This will help in making the measures to control credit and money supply more effective. It will enable wider disbursement of cheaper loans and only them will the benefits of lower interest rates will actually be felt. Also a stronger banking structure will make it possible for the banks to borrow from a wider population at a lower rate.

A 'Senior citizen's fund' or a ' Pension fund' should be set up

The worst hit by lower interest rates are senior citizens, who have no means of earning and depended on interest income. Some sort of security should be provided to them. It can be in the form of a fund which is only for senior citizens and yields an interest rate of 9 to 10 per cent p.a. A cap of maximum amount that can be invested in this fund can be set to avoid misuse.

Notes

1. Economic Survey 2001-2002.
2. India Inc's borrowing cost sticky'-Business Standard, Oct 7th, 2002.

3. Business Standard, October 7, 2002
4. 'Saving and hard times'-Business Standard, Sept 7th, 2002.
5. *'The great rate trick'* by Navjit Gill, Published in Business World, Sep 23, 2002.

5

Long-run Demand for Money in a Developing Country: The Case of Sri Lanka During 1950-2000

Thilak Ranaweera*

Introduction

The recent Asian crisis has once again shifted considerable attention on financial policy in developing countries and has led to a re-examination (and a revision) of the standard policy prescriptions recommended by the Bretton Woods institutions. An important element in this process is the issue concerning the nature and extent of financial liberalization in a given country. Some economists have argued that the existence of substantial unregulated financial markets needs to be taken into account in the formulation of monetary policy in a given context. This study attempts to shed some light on this issue by studying the long-run behaviour of the demand for money in one developing country, i.e. Sri Lanka.

Recent changes in the Sri Lanka financial system pose challenges for the conduct of monetary policy. With the landmark liberalisation process initiatet in 1978, a number of changes have taken place in the financial system of the country. The central bank has moved away from administratively set credit controls and interest rates to open

* Development Data Group, The World Bank.

market operations (See, Central Bank Annual Report, 2000) New financial products and procedures have complicated the interpretation of monetary aggregates and the focus has shifted from controlling money supply to "inflation" targetting and exchange rate management. The characteristics of assets that were traditionally included in monetary aggregates have also undergone changes requiring re-consideration of the concept of "money". Sri Lanka's differential taxation of financial products has further complicated the evaluation and movement of monetary aggregates. While these changes in the financial sector have altered constraints on portfolio choices and the pricing of assets, trade and goods market liberalization have altered the incentives for precautionary savings. Thus, understanding how these changes have altered the demand for money and the relationship among money, prices, and output is a critical element of macroeconomic policy that has a direct bearing on macroeconomic policy in Sri Lanka.

Taking advantage of new time series data available from the Central Bank of Sri Lanka (CBSL 2001), this study attempts to uncover any stable money demand relationships during the period 1950-2000, especially in light of recent changes in the financial system. The constancy of the estimated money demand function is a central issue in many countries [Adam (1999)] and in the IMF approach to economic stabilization [Mussa and Savastano (1999)]. A stable demand for money is a key element both for economic policy and forecasting. A non-stable money demand function leaves unresolved the question whether the observed predictive failure arises from parameter shifts or whether it is simply a consequence of model misspecification.

While the demand for money is one of the most widely researched topics in the world, in the past, there had not been many studies that focused on the demand for money in Sri Lanka. Some of the earlier studies include Ranaweera (1971),

Colombage (1978), Dheerasinghe (1988), Perera (1988), and Weliwita and Ekanayake (1998). These studies invariably covered a limited period due to data availability at the time of the investigation. However, due to the publication of the Central bank of a new data set covering 50 years since independence, it is possible to analyze the demand for money for Sri Lanka during the last half a century.

The current study starts with a brief historical perspective. In section 2, the theoretical aspects of money demand are considered. Section 3 is devoted to the exploration of the time series properties of the variables used in the study and section 4 presents the empirical results. Section 5 contains some concluding remarks.

A Brief Historical Perspective

In Sri Lanka, the immediate years after independence (i.e., the period 1948-59) were characterized by a relatively liberalized economic regime with relatively low investment (14.7 per cent of GDP) and domestic savings (11.7 per cent of GDP) and annual average growth around 3.4 per cent per annum during the period 1951-60. As in the colonial period, the plantation sector continued to dominate the modern sector of the economy. The government played a key role in formulating and implementing social and economic policies, but such interventions started to increase only towards the latter part of 1950.

In 1948, at the time of gaining independence, Sri Lanka's financial sector was "dualistic" in nature with organized and unorganized sectors existing side by side. The country had a relatively underdeveloped money market consisting of a few banks and other financial institutions and a limited number of financial market instruments. There were 9 foreign and 2 domestic commercial banks operating in the country in 1948 and the money supply was managed by a Currency Board (Karunatilaka, 1973). In that framework, the amount of currency issued was directly linked to the amount of foreign currency reserves. The Currency Board was discontinued and the Central bank of Sri Lanka was established in 1950 to regulate the monetary and banking system of the country. In the early 1950s, during the so-called "Korean" boom years, commercial banks were highly liquid and as such Central Bank's interest rate policy did not affect their operations. However, in the post-boom period, commercial banks resorted to depending on borrowing from the Central bank and its interest rate policy gained prominence. The organized sector consisting of banking and other financial institutions was focused on the plantation and urban mercantile sectors and was thus very limited in scope. The major activity in the money market was restricted to purchase and sale of bills of exchange. The unorganized sector consisting of money lenders, pawn-brokers, traders, and boutique keepers was more widespread, and was the source of funds to the rural farmers ad the urban workers.

The years of the controlled regime, 1960-77 was characterized by imposition of controls at the outset, partial relaxations in brief periods, and re-introduction of various forms of controls towards the latter part of the period.

During 1961-68, in the face of adverse external conditions, the government resorted to restrictions on external trade and payments. In addition, subsidies, extensive price controls and administered pricing policies (especially relating to public sector corporations) greatly increased the financial burden of the government. To cope with the growing demand for social expenditures, the government had greater recourse to borrowing from the Central bank, whose credit to government averaged well over 16 per cent of GDP. Thus, there was a major increase in reserve money and therefore money supply, brought about by the need to sustain effective demand through social expenditures (Karuntatilaka, 1973).

Prior to 1966, Sri Lanka maintained a fixed exchange rate system. Low commodity prices, mounting import costs, and a devaluation of the pound Sterling led to a devaluation of the Sri Lanka rupee by 20 per cent in November 1967. In 1968, a dual exchange rate system called the Foreign Exchange Entitlement Certificate Scheme (FEECS) was introduced with a view to discourage "non-essential" imports and encourage export diversification. In 1972, the rupee was linked to Sterling following the collapse of the Bretton Woods fixed exchange rate system. However, the rupee was re-linked to the US dollar in 1976.

The period 1969-70 was marked by some degree of relation of trade and payments restrictions in force at the time. Some imports were permitted under Open General Licenses (OGL) and Foreign Exchange Entitlement Certificate (FEEC) schemes. Through the FEEC scheme, which was essentially a dual exchange rate system, the government intervened to control exports and imports in line with its overall growth and distribution objectives. The FEEC scheme operated through the issue of FEECs for pre-specified exports upon surrender of export receipts. FEECs needed to be surrendered for imports of goods other than those which could be imported at the official exchange rate.

In spite of the operation of the FEEC system, there was no basic change in the policy approach of the government and the external sector continued to remain under close controls. Also, minor domestic policy changes did not change the interventionist nature of economy. The continuation of extensive subsidies and the maintenance of price controls resulted in increased Central Bank financing of the government deficits. Although real growth was somewhat higher than in earlier periods, inflation was also higher during the period.

During the years of the "controlled" economy extending up to 1977, interest rates were kept artificially low to encourage investment and economic development (see, Khatkhate (1978), Preferential interest rates were provided to borrowing by sectors considered by the policy makers to be of priority.

In 1961, the nationalization of the Bank of Ceylon and the establishment of the People's bank, led to the dominance of the country's banking system by state banks. These two banks led the process of branch expansion all over the country, thereby contributing to spreading not only the banking habit but also encouraging domestic savings and entrepreneurship and resource allocation. On the negative side, these banks also contributed to expansion of credit to non-creditworthy borrowers and uneconomic public enterprises.

During the period 1961-77, annual average GDP growth amounted to 3.8 per cent, while, while growth during the import substitution phase of 1961-65 amounted to about 3.6 per cent per year. During the partial economic liberalization period of 1966-70, GDP growth improved to 5.3 per cent per annum. Growth declined to 2.9 per cent per annum during 1971-77 when government intervention increased and the external environment became unfavorable following the first oil price "shock" in 1973. Gross domestic savings (14 per cent of GDP) and investment (16 per cent of GDP) remained somewhat low.

The outward-oriented strategy introduced in the latter part of 1977 was based on market principles (see, Athukorala and Rajapatirana (1993), and various issues of the Annual Report of the Central bank of Sri Lanka). Investment increased to 27 per cent of GDP during 1978-81 because of heavy public sector infrastructure spending. As national savings remained low, the country had to depend on foreign savings. The liberalization laid the foundation for a gradual structural transformation from agriculture based economy to modern manufacturing and services based economy, and growth during the post-liberalization period amounted to about 5 per cent per annum.[2] An integral part of the economic liberalization package of November 1977 was the unification of the exchange rate and the introduction of a managed float where the exchange rate was allowed to be determined on the basis of demand and supply. In the post-liberalization period, interest rates under all subsidy schemes were raised towards the market rates, while supply and demand forces were gradually permitted to determine the market interest rates.

After reforms in 1977, the volume of activity and the variety of services provided by the commercial banking sector have increased substantially. At present 26 commercial banks operate in the country (compared with 11 in 1948). Of these 8 are locally incorporated (with 2 state banks) and 18 are branches of foreign banks. The banking sector is one of the most dynamic sectors of the economy and has adopted modern computer technology for its operations. A high level of competition among banks has led to a greater degree of efficiency and improved services. It is also noteworthy that the banking system at present is closely linked to the worldwide banking network.

With the expansion of commercial banking to rural and urban areas, the organized money market has widened. At present, the most noteworthy components of this market are the treasury bill, the interbank call money, and the foreign exchange markets. Although in the 1960s and 1970s there was no active primary or secondary market for treasury bills, opening of discount and rediscount windows by the Central Bank in 1981 has given an impetus to the development of a secondary market in treasury bills by assuring investors of the liquidity of this instrument. The starting of the sale of treasury bills under repurchase agreements (Repos) in 1993, the removal of the withholding tax on treasury bills, and the introduction of reverse repurchase agreements (Reverse Repos) in 1995, have expanded the treasury bill market.

Since independence, a number of other financial institutions have been established to cater to needs not provided for by the network of commercial banks. These include a variety of institutions relating to deposit taking, long-term lending, insurance, contractual savings, leasing, venture capital and brokerage. The main impetus to the development of these institutions came from the financial sector liberalization of 1977. Among other things, relaxation of controls on interest rates, prices, and foreign participation in the financial sector activities greatly contributed to these development.

The Licensed Specialized banks (LSB) and finance companies, whose liabilities include a considerable amount of deposits, are an important segment of the financial sector in Sri Lanka. The LSBs consists of 6 regional Development banks, the National Savings bank. National Development Bank, DFCC Bank, the State Mortgage and Investment Bank and two private savings and development bank. In addition, there are 25 finance companies registered with the Central bank that are authorized to accept deposits from the public. The significance of LSBs and finance companies in the economy has increased substantially over the years. For example, total assets of OFIs increased by more than threefold from 1990 to 1998. Although these units do not offer checking facilities, they provide a variety of services similar to those of commercial banks. An important characteristics of LSBs in Lanka is that most of their liabilities are medium-term to long-term in nature.

With the rapid growth of the financial sector and financial innovations in a relatively deregulated environment, in recent years, the distinction between the licensed commercial banks (LCB) and other financial institutions (OFI) has become quite blurred, making it important to widen the institutional categories, which could be the focus of monetary policy (Central Bank of Sri Lanka Annual Report, 1999). Sri Lanka's financial system consists of the banking system, OFIs and the unorganized financial sector. The banking system consisting of the monetary authorities and commercial banks continues to be the core of the financial system. The main variables considered hitherto in determining monetary policy in the country such as narrow money (M1) and broad money (M2) are compiled from information from the banking system. Graph 1 shows the development of these important variables over the period 1950-2000. While the ratio of M1/GDP has declined steadily, M2/GDP has increased during this period, indicating a substantial degree of financial "deepening" in Sri Lanka. One of the significant changes that has been introduced in the second half of 1990s was the inclusion of foreign currency banking units (FCBUs) of commercial banks in the monetary survey. FCBUs were excluded from the computation of broad monetary aggregates in earlier years.

Furthermore, in view of recent developments in the financial sector, the Central Bank has taken steps to present

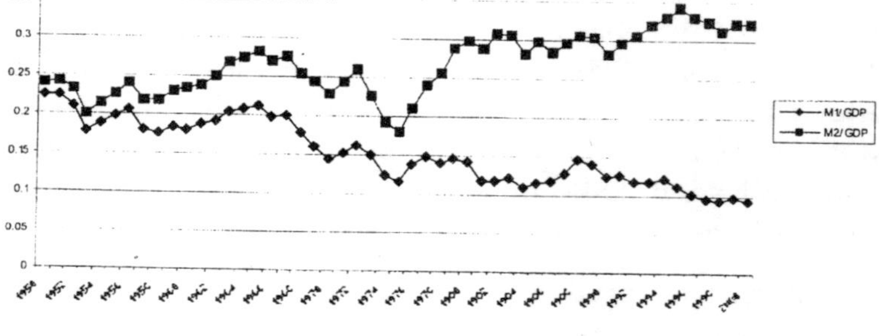

Figure 1. Sri Lanka: Financial Deepening, 1950-2000

information on a broader consolidated financial survey. A preliminary financial survey that consolidates the operations of the monetary authorities, licensed commercial banks, licensed specialized banks and the 25 finance companies has been compiled recently (CBR, 1999). This is designed to provide a more comprehensive view of the operations of the financial sector for formulating policies. The new monetary aggregate in the expanded financial survey is called M4 and includes, among other components, liabilities of other financial intermediaries.

Theoretical and Empirical Aspects of Money Demand

Economic theory suggests that money may be demanded for at least two reasons: (a) as an inventory to smooth differences between income ad expenditure streams, and (b) as one among several assets in a portfolio (Baumol (1952), Tobin (1956), Friedman (1956)). The demand for nominal money balances for transaction purposes depends on the volume of such transactions and the price level. Holdings of money as an asset are determined by relative returns vis-a-vis other assets. Considering both aspects, the long-run money demand may be specified as follows:

$$Md/P = F(y, R) \tag{1}$$

where Md - nominal money balances

P - price level

Y - scale variable denoting volume of transactions

R - a set of returns of different assets.

It is supposed that money demand varies with variations in the scale variable (usually a proxy for income or output). Money demand is assumed to be positively correlated with those returns relating to financial assets included in the monetary aggregate under consideration, while it is supposed to be negatively correlated with assets excluded from that aggregate (see, Goldfeld and Sichel (1990), Laidler (1993)).

Equation (1) is usually written in log linear form with interest rates expressed in either logs or levels:

$$(md - p) = ao + a1\ y + a2\ Rout + a3\ Rin + a4\ dp \qquad (2)$$

where ao, al, a3, a4 - parameters

Rin - rates of return on assets included in monetary aggregate

Rout - rates of return on assets excluded from monetary aggregate.

In the quantity theory f money expressed by the Fisher equation al = 1, while in the Baumol-Tobin framework al = 0.5. Typically, a2 $\leq$ and a4 ≤ 0, while a3 ≥ 0.

The inflation variable dp measures the return to holding goods and as the latter is an alternative to holding money, the coefficient a4 is expected to be negative (Cagan 1956) on inclusion of dp in equation.

From the above equations, it is clear that the definition of the monetary aggregate is crucial for determining the rates of return that can be considered "in" or "out). Considering the traditional definitions of money and the rates of return (interest rates) for which data had been compiled and reported in Sri Lanka over the last 50 years, it is possible to postulate the following model for empirical testing:

$$(md - p) = ao + al\ y + a2\ RT + a3\ RB + a4\ dp \qquad (3)$$

where RB – Treasury Bill rate

RT - Interest rate on Time Deposits.

Using a single interest rate and a set of spreads, it is possible to write (for illustrative purposes):

$$(md - p) = ao + a1\ y + b2\ RT + b3\ (RB-RT) + a4\ dp \qquad (4)$$

In this formulation, the coefficient b2 captures the total effect of interest rates, while the spread (RB-RT) captures the incremental effects of the "in" rate relative to the Treasury Bill rate.

In addition, the availability of foreign currency assets in a country widens the scope for portfolio diversification by domestic investors. Thus, the rate of return on foreign assets has a considerable influence on the demand for domestic money (McKenzie (1992)). If foreign bonds are an investment alternative, the return on such assets adjusted for the expected exchange rate depreciation should be important explanatory variable of the demand for domestic money (see, Leventakis (1993)). It would be reasonable to expect that a depreciation of the domestic currency would lower the demand for it. However, considering the practical difficulties of separating out the currency substitution and capital mobility effects, the exchange rate can be taken as a good proxy for capturing portfolio shifts between domestic and foreign money, and (4) can be written as follows:

$$(md - p) = ao + al\ y + b2\ RT + b3\ (RB\text{-}RT) + a4\ dp + a5\ ER \quad (5)$$

where ER–an appropriately defined exchange rate variable.

Cointegration and Error Correction Models

Cointegration provides both analytical and statistical foundations for assessing the long-run relationship among non-stationary economic variables: for example, many income, prices and rates of interest considered in this study. Appropriate selection of variables as well as estimation techniques are crucial for obtaining meaningful results. In the procedure proposed by Engle and Granger (1987), residuals from a static regression of integrated variabels are tested for a unit root, typically by using the ADF statistic (1981). If the null hypothesis of a unit root is rejected, the static regression is interpreted as a cointegrating relation, and the residuals can be considered to be the equilibrium error correction term in the specification of a dynamic short-run model. While this procedure is easy to implement and is intuitively appealing, it has low power to detect cointegration and the long-run coefficient estimates from the static regression could be biased in finite samples.

An alternative is the Johansen (1988) procedure, which is asymptotically fully efficient is based on a maximum likelihood systems technique for determining the number of cointegrating vectors, where inferences could be made about these vectors. identifying the different cointegrating relations among the variables in a money demand equation, which is of considerable interest to macroeconomic policy, must be done in a simultaneous equation context (Bischoff and Belay 2001)). From a statistical perspective, estimating the cointegrating vectors and testing which equations they enter is necessary for evaluating weak exogeneity (Erickson, 1998). The error correction formulation is a convenient framework to jointly study long-run and short-run dynamics, and can be considered as a dynamic generalization of partial-adjustment models.

Johansen's maximum likelihood procedure has been used in this study to identify cointegration among real money balances, real output, inflation, and several different interest rates.3

Variables and their Time Series Properties

It seems to be generally accepted that most macroeconomic time series data are non-stationary and that regressions with such data produced spurious results (Granger, C.W.J. and P. Newbold (1974). Following standard practice, the ADF test is employed for checking time series data for stationarity. In the ADF test the null hypothesis is non-stationarity of a variable. This study also uses a relatively more powerful test called KPSS that is based on testing the null of stationarity versus an alternative of a unit root. (Kwiatkowski, D., Philips, P.C.B., Schmidt, P. Shin, Y., 1992).

The data for two proxy variables for inflation and four interest rates for which data are available for the whole period 1950-2000 are shown in graphs 2 and 3.

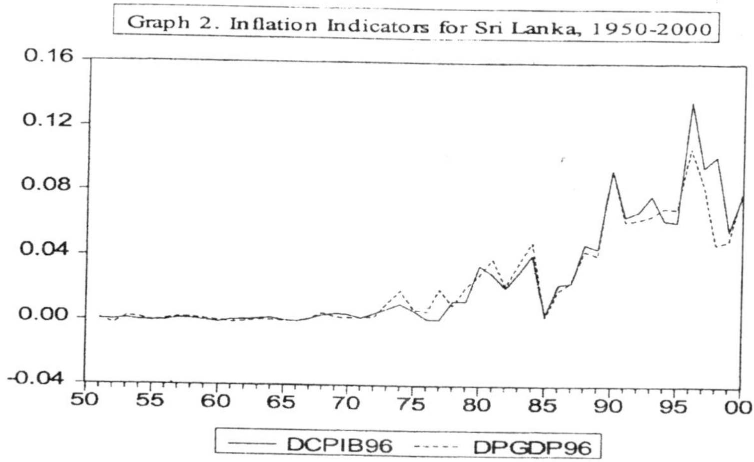

Figure 2. Inflation Indicators for Sri Lanka, 1950-2000

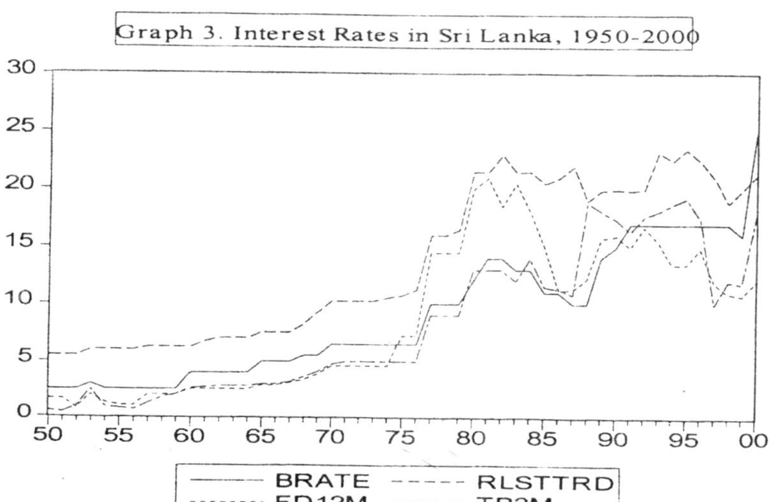

Figure 3. Interest Rates in Sri Lanka, 1950-2000

The results of the ADF tests are reported in table 1 while those of the KPSS test are shown in tables 2 and 3. Test results are reported for variables in their primary form (i.e. as shown in published records) and for several transformations of primary data. These results show that all variables included in this study are non-stationary in levels (irrespective of whether the variables are considered in primary form or log transformations) and are stationary after first differencing. This result also holds for variables that were constructed using a formula. The results of the ADF tests are confirmed by KPSS tests.

Table 1. ADF Tests Results

			Critical Values	
Variable	*ADF statistic*	*Specifications*	*–1%*	*5%*
RM1	–2.8144	T,I,1 lag	–4.1540	–3.5025
RM2	–0.8690	T,I,2 lags	–4.1584	–3.5045
RGDP1	1.8063	T,I,5 lags	–4.1728	-3.5112
CPIB96	-2.5631	T,I,1 lag	-4.1584	-3.5045
PGDPB96	1.1650	T,I,4 lags	-4.1678	-3.5088
BRATE	-2.7603	T,I,3 lags	-4.1630	-3.5066
FD12M	-2.4326	T,I,3 lags	-4.1630	-3.5066
TB3M	-3.3033	T,I,2 lags	-4.1584	-3.5045
RLSTTRD	-2.3207	T,I,3 lags	-4.1630	-3.5066
NUS$	2,2055	T,I,1 lags	-4.1540	-3.5025
dRM1	-5.9065	T,I,1 lags	-4.1584	-3.5045
dRM2	-4.1634	T,I,2 lags	-4.1630	-3.5066
DRGDP1	-5.0624	T,I,1 lag	-4.1540	-3.5025
DCPIB96	-3.8768	T,I,1 lag	-4.1540	-3.5025
dpgdpb96	-4.0371	T,I,1 lag	-4.1540	-3.5025
DBRATE	-4.1612	T,I,5 lags	-4.1781	-3.5136

(Table Contd.)

Table 1 : Contd.

dFD12M	-4.5877	T,I,1 lag	-4.1584	-3.5045
dTB3M	-5.5321	T,I,2 lags	-4.1630	-3.5066
DRLSTTRD	-4.4426	T,I,1 lag	-4.1584	-3.5045
DNUS$	-4.2267	T,I,1 lag	-4.1584	-3.5045
TBRTE	-1.7484	T,I,5 lags	-4.1728	-3.5112
TDCPI	-2.5090	T,I,2 lags	-4.1630	-3.5066
TERDEP	-3.2099	T,I,3 lags	-41678	-3.5088
TFD12M	-1.8415	T,I,3 lags	-4.1678	-3.5088
TNUS$	-2.1576	T,I,5 lags	-4.1728	-3.5112
TRLSTRD	-0.8192	T,I,3 lags	-4.1678	-3.5088
TTB3M	-3.0717	T,I,3 lags	-4.1678	-3.5088
DTBRTE	-4.7037	T,I,5 lags	-4.1781	-3.5136
DTDCPI	-5.2386	T,I,2 lags	-4.1678	-3.5088
DTERDEP	-5.9901	T,I,3 lags	-4.1728	-3.5112
DTFD12M	-5.7529	T,I,4 lags	-4.1728	-35112
dTNUS$	-3.5409	T,I,1 lag	-4.1584	-3.5045
DTRLSTRD	-5.1807	T,I,1 lag	-4.1540	-3.5025
DTTB3M	-4.1281	T,I,1 lag	-4.1540	-3.5025
LRM1	-3.3315	T,I,1 lag	-4.1540	-3.5025
LRM2	-2.6950	T,1,4 lags	-4.1728	-3.5112
LRGDP1	-2.6841	T,I,4 lags	-4.1678	-3.5088
LCPIB96	-2.3059	T,I,3 lags	-4.1630	-3.5066
LPGDPB96	-2.3815	T,I,4 lags	-4.1728	-3.5112
DLRMI	-4.2455	T,I,3 lags	-4.1678	-3.5088
DLRM2	-4.3866	T,I,2 lags	-4.1630	-3.5066
DLRGDP1	-3.5842	T,I,4 lags	-4.1728	-3.5112
DLCPIB96	-3.2482	T,I,2 lags	-4.1630	-3.5066
dLPGDPB96	-3.1470	I,1 lag	-3.5713	-2.9228

Note: For definitions of variables, see appendix.

Table 2: KPSS Tests on Primary Variables, 1950-2000

(a) KPSS test (no trend)-Lag Truncation

Series name	*0*	*1*	2	3	4	5
LRM2	5.0712	2.6018	1.7704	1.3544	1.1058	0.9409
LRM1	5.0157	2.5758	1.7542	1.3422	1.0956	0.9315
LRGDP1	5.1054	2.6294	1.7941	1.3757	1.1248	0.9579
CPIB96	3.6625	1.9202	1.3304	1.0359	0.8603	0.7443
BRATE	4.6562	2.4922	1.7201	1.3269	1.0897	0.9315
FD12M	3.8754	1.9932	1.3602	1.0441	0.8564	0.7332
TB3M	4.5561	2.3903	1.6415	1.2626	1.0297	0.8740
RLSTTRD	4.7448	2,4292	1.6485	1.2570	1.0231	0.8684
NUS$	4.1934	2,1896	1.5100	1.1682	0.9627	0.8258

(b) KPSS test (with linear trend)–Lag truncation

Series name	*0*	*1*	2	3	4	5
LRM2	0.4010	0.2170	0.1574	0.1285	0.1115	0.1008
LRM1	0.2970	0.1705	0.1313	0.1121	0.1008	0.0936
LRGDP1	0.7976	0.4290	0.3050	0.2443	0.2090	0.1867
CPIB96	1.1102	0.5838	0.4061	0.3180	0.2660	0.2321
BRATE	0.3389	0.2315	0.1846	0.1621	0.1524	0.1499
FD12M	0.4864	0.2620	0.1869	0.1501	0.1296	0.1173
TB3M	0.3038	0.1830	0.1416	0.1236	0.1132	0.1071
RLSTTRD	0.4511	0.2453	0.1749	0.1407	0.1215	0.1097
NUS$	1.1990	0.6348	0.4429	0.3465	0.2887	0.2504

(c) KPSS test (no trend)-Lag truncation

Series name	*0*	*1*	2	3	4	5
D(BRATE)	0.2219	0.2323	0.2365	0.2412	0.2562	0.2772
D(FD12M)	0.1304	0.1234	0.1203	0.1080	0.1035	0.1076

D(TB3M)	0.0365	0.0412	0.0434	0.0557	0.0638	0.0766
D(RLSTTRD)	0.1052	0.1128	0.1091	0.1021	0.1005	0.1043
DNUS$	2.9217	1.8787	1.4147	1.1433	0.9767	0.8591

(d) KPSS test (with linear trend)-Lag truncation

Series name	*0*	*1*	*2*	*3*	*4*	*5*
D(BRATE)	0.0487	0.0514	0.0528	0.0547	0.0593	0.0658
D(FD12M)	0.1044	0.0994	0.0976	0.0879	0.0845	0.0883
D(TB3M)	0.0316	0.0357	0.0374	0.0479	0.0547	0.0656
D(RLSTTRD)	0.1036	0.1112	0.1078	0.1009	0.0994	0.1031
DNUS$	0.1730	0.1635	0.1584	0.1487	0.1482	0.1482

Critical values for no trend	Critical values with linear trend
10% critical value 0.347	10% critical value 0.119
5% critical value 0.463	5% critical value 0.146
1% critical value 0.739	1% critical value 0.216

Table 3: KPSS Tests on Alternative Definition of Variables, 1950-2000

(a) KPSS test (no trend)-Lag truncation

Series name	*0*	*1*	*2*	*3*	*4*	*5*
TBRTE	1.4411	0.8504	0.6439	0.5447	0.4889	0.4527
TFD12M	4.3051	2.2648	1.5493	1.1913	0.9741	0.8312
TTB3M	3,9434	2,1203	1,5066	1.1882	0.9834	0.8427
TRLSTRD	4.8874	2,5007	1.6988	1.2974	1.0567	0.8967

(b) KPSS (with linear-trend)-Lag truncation

TBRTE	0.1328	0.0836	0.0691	0.0664	0.0715	0.0839
TFD12M	0.7974	0.4909	0.3614	0.2892	0.2434	0.2151
TTB3M	0.7435	0.4433	0.3493	0.2996	0.2610	0.2307
TRLSTRD	0.8544	0.4530	0.3177	0.2505	0.2109	0.1850

(c) KPSS trest (no trend)-Lag truncation

D(TBRTE)	0.0889	0.1059	0.1193	0.1281	0.1417	0.1404
D(TFD12M)	0.0508	0.0921	0.1267	0.1563	0.1328	0.1471
D(TTB3M)	0.1606	0.1681	0.2185	0.3038	0.3921	0.4065
D(TRLSTRD)	0.3255	0.3079	0.3086	0.2900	0.2756	0.2738

(d) KPSS test (with linear trend)–Lag trunction

D(TBRTE)	0.3046	0.0419	0.0482	0.0527	0.0597	0.0603
D(TFD12M)	0.0265	0.0486	0.0687	0.0871	0.0744	0.0850
D(TTDB3M)	0.0189	0.0206	0.0286	0.0438	0.0650	0.0744
D(TRLSTRD)	0.1214	0.1197	0.1262	0.1224	0.1194	0.1194

(e) KPSS test (no trend)–Lag truncation

TDCPI	3.7246	2.0279	1.4021	1.0894	0.9001	0.7767
TERDEP	4.0868	2.3298	1.6334	1.2690	1.0467	0.8932
TNUS$	4.9567	2.5238	1.7080	1.3002	1.0564	0.8945
D(TRLSTRD)	0.3255	0.3079	0.3086	0.2900	0.2756	0.2738

(f) KPSS test (with linear trend)–Lag truncation

TDCPI	0.6640	0.4314	0.3243	0.2703	0.2352	0.2120
TERDEP	0.1561	0.1504	0.1358	0.1262	0.1224	0.1142
TNUS$	0.6122	0.3225	0.2244	0.1759	0.1476	0.1294
D(TTB3M)	0.0189	0.0206	0.0286	0.0438	0.0650	0.0744
	0.1214	0.1197	0.1262	0.1224	0.1194	0.1224

(g) KPSS test (no trend)–Lag trunction

D(TDCPI)	0.0369	0.0680	0.0760	0.1027	0.1116	0.1695
D(TERDEP)	0.0137	0.0312	0.0427	00516	0.0840	0.0776
D(TNUS$)	0.2837	0.2676	0.2276	0.2029	0.1899	0.1752
D(TRLSTRD)	0.3255	0.3079	0.3086	0.2900	0.2756	0.2738

(h) KPSS test (with linear trend)–Lag truncation

D(TDCPI)	0.0169	0.0313	0.0353	0.0486	0.0542	0.0874
D(TERDEP)	0.0117	0.0267	0.0366	0.0443	0.0726	0.0671
D(TNUS$)	0.2523	0.2393	0.2041	0.1824	0.1712	0.1583
D(TRLSTRD)	0.1214	0.1197	0.1262	0.1224	0.1194	0.1224

Critical values-no trend	Critical values-linear trend
10% critical value 0.347	10% critical value 0.119
5% critical value 0.463	5% critical value 0.146
1% critical value 0.739	1% critical value 0.216

Empirical Estimates

A number of different VARs were specified and estimated and several cointegrating vectors were identified using the multivariate system estimation procedure of Johansen (Johansen (1988)). The results are summarized in tables 4, 5 and 6. Although a large number of experiments were conducted with different specifications including lag lengths, to save space, the summary tables include only the more interesting cases (details of the results are available from the author). Cointegrating vectors corresponding to each of the VARs have been extracted in table 6. Note that only the normalized cointegrating vectors around the relevant monetary aggregate are reported.

The full system was specified to include the endogenous variables LRM1 (or LRM2), LRGDP1, TDCPI, TERDEP, TFD12M and exogenous variables DUMLIB and TRLSTRD.[4] The dummy for liberalization was included to account for the policy regime changes that were introduced at the end of 1977. VARs were estimated for lag lengths ranging from 5 to 1 year and cointegration tests were conducted with different assumptions about deterministic trends in the data or in the VAR. The results reported in table 4 for VAR#1 relate to the case where it is assumed that there is no deterministic trend in the cointegrating equation or the test

VAR of order 5. The likelihood ratio indicates two cointegrating equations at the 1 per cent level, one of which is shown in table 6. The asymptotic standard errors in parenthesis show that the coefficients of the included variables are highly significant and have the expected sign. Thus, inflation and exchange rate depreciation seemed to have had a strong influence on agents to shift out of narrow money to holdings of real assets and foreign currency. The only exception here is the interest rate variable TFD12M, which is the 12 month fixed deposit rate and which relates to assets not included in narrow money. As such, it would not be unrealistic to expect this rate to have an inverse relationship with narrow money. The "income" elasticity of narrow money is estimated to be around 1.4. Under the assumptions of an intercept in the cointegrating equation, but no intercept in the VAR, it was possible to find a similar cointegrating vector when the number of lags considered was 2. The estimate of income elasticity is marginally lower, but the coefficient estimates for the inflation, exchange rate, and interest rate variables are substantially different in magnitude and all three variables are no longer significant at the 5 per cent level (???). In VAR#3, TRLSTRD (interest rate on lending secured by stock in trade) is eliminated from the list of exogenous variables (i.e. only the liberalization dummy–DUMLIB, is included). In addition, allowing for an intercept in the cointegrating equation and the test VAR, the likelihood ratio test indicates a cointegrating vector, which is reported in table... line#3. It turns out that under these assumptions, all variables in the cointegrating equation are significant and have the correct sign. The resulting estimate for the income elasticity of the demand for money is 1.5, marginally higher than in the cases of VARs#1 and #2. In VAR#4, the liberalization dummy (DUMLIB) is dropped from the list of exogenous variables. Although it is possible to find a significant cointegrating equation (assuming no deterministic trend in the CE or test VAR), the exchange rate depreciation variable carries the wrong sign. On a priori grounds, one could consider that the inflation rate (real assets substitution) and the exchange rate depreciation (currency substitution) to have a relatively bigger influence on narrow money demand than an interest rate on quasi-money (i.e. the TFD12M variable). VAR#5 contain results pertaining to the exclusion of the interest rate on 12 month deposits from the analysis. It is still possible to find cointegration among narrow money, inflation and the interest rate. However, while the income elasticity drops to about 0.8, neither the inflation nor the exchange rate depreciation variable are significant. Furthermore, the latter carries the wrong sign, indicating that the omission of the interest rate variable leads to misspecification of the demand for narrow money.

Table 4. Johansen's Cointegration Tests (with narrow money)

VAR Number 1, Series: LRM1 LRGDP1 TDCPI TERDEP TFD12M
Exogenous series: DUMLB TRLSTRD
Test assumption: No intercept or trend in the cointegrating equation or test VAR

VAR Number	*Lags in VAR*	*Eigenvalue*	*Likelihood Ratio*	*5 per cent Critical Value*	*1 per cent Critical Value*	*Hypothesized No. of CE(s)*
#1	5	0.8407	160.31	59.46	66.52	None**

VAR Number 2, Series: LRM1 LRGDP1 TDCPI TERDEP TFD12M
Exogenous series: DUMLIB TRLSTRD
Test assumption: Intercept (No trend in cointegrating equation); No intercept in VAR

VAR Number	*Lags in VAR*	*Eigenvalue*	*Likelihood Ratio*	*5 per cent Critical Value*	*1 per cent Critical Value*	*Hypothesized No. of CE(s)*
#2	2	0.4320	80.83	76.07	84.45	None*

VAR Number 3, Series: LRM1 LRGDPI TDCPI TERDEP TFD12M
Exogenous series: DUMLIB
Test assumption: Intercept (No trend) in cointegrating equation and test VAR

VAR Number	*Lags in VAR*	*Eigenvalue*	*Likelihood Ratio*	*5 per cent Critical Value*	*1 per cent Critical Value*	*Hypothesized No. of CE(s)*
#3	5	0.8330	166.91	68.52	76.07	None**

VAR Number 4, Series: LRM1 LRGDP1 TDCPI TERDEP TFD12M
Test assumption: No intercept or trend in the cointegrating equation or test VAR

VAR Number	*Lags in VAR*	*Eigenvalue*	*Likelihood Ratio*	*5 per cent Critical Value*	*1 per cent Critical Value*	*Hypothesized No. of CE(s)*
#4	5	0.7712	143.93	59.46	66.52	None**

VAR Number 5, Series: LRM1 LRGDPI TDCPI
TERDEP
Test assumption: No intercept or trend in the cointegrating equation or test VAR

VAR Number	*Lags in VAR*	*Eigenvalue*	*Likelihood Ratio*	*5 per cent Critical Value*	*1 per cent Critical Value*	*Hypothesized No. of CE(s)*
#5	5	0.4899	60.89	38.89	45.58	None**

Table 5: Johansen's Cointegration Tests (with broad money)

VAR Number 6, Series: LRM2 LRGDP1 TDCPI TERDEP TFD12M
Exogenous series: DUMLIB TRLSTRD
Test assumption: No intercept or trend in the cointegrating equation or test VAR

VAR Number	*Lags in VAR*	*Eigenvalue*	*Likelihood Ratio*	*5 per cent Critical Value*	*1 per cent Critical Value*	*Hypothesized No. of CE(s)*
#6	2	0.5067	73.93	59.46	66.52	None**

VAR Number 7, Series: LRM2 LRGDP1 TDCPI TERDEP TFD12M
Exogenous series: DUMLIB
Test assumption: Intercept (No trend) in cointegrating equation and test VAR

VAR Number	*Lags in VAR*	*Eigenvalue*	*Likelihood Ratio*	*5 per cent Critical Value*	*1 per cent Critical Value*	*Hypothesized No. of CE(s)*
#7	2	0.4869	75.07	68.52	76.07	None**

VAR Number 8, Series LRM2 LRGDP1 TDCPI TERDEP TFD12M
Test assumption: Intercept (No trend in cointegrating equation); No intercept in VAR

VAR Number	*Lags in VAR*	*Eigenvalue*	*Likelihood Ratio*	*5 per cent Critical Value*	*1 per cent Critical Value*	*Hypothesized No. of CE(s)*
#8	4	0.739898	134,6803	76.07	84.45	None**

VAR Number 9, Series: LRM2 LRGDP1 TDCFI TERDEP TFD12M
Test assumption: No intercept of trend in the cointegrating equation or test VAR

		Eigenvalue	*Likelihood Ratio*	*5 per cent Critical Value*	*1 per cent Critical Value*	*Hypothesized No. of CE(s)*
#9	3	0.4293	45.36	39.89	45.58	None**

Table 5 reports Johansen's cointegration tests on using VARs #6 to #9 where LRM2, the log of broad money, had been substituted for LRM1. Although tests were run on VARs with 1 to 5 lags, the results reported are those where some economically meanigful magnitude and signs of the related coefficients were obtained VAR #6 includes the full set of endogenous and exogenous variables similar to the case of VAR#1. Under the assumption of no intercept or trend in the CE or test VAR, the cointegrating equation #6 shown in table 5 was obtained, when the lag length considered was 2 years. The income elasticity of broad money of 1.7 is highly significant, and the exchange rate depreciation and interest rate variables are significant at 5 per cent level. Although the inflation variable carried the right sign, it is insignificant. For VAR#7, the interest rate TRLSTRD is omitted from the exogenous variables. Assuming an intercept (no trend) in CE and the VAR enables the recovery of the cointegrating equation #7. However, the estimate of income elasticity is substantially higher and the rest of the coefficients become insignificant. In addition, the interest rate variable has reversed sign. In VAR #8, the liberalization dummy is omitted, and a cointegrating equation is found for a system with 4 lags, under the assumptions of no intercept (no trend) in the CE and no intercept in the VAR. While the income elasticity is substantially reduced, the other coefficients become significant, but the interest rate variable has the wrong sign. VAR#9, considers a popular version of a model tried out for other countries (........), by dropping the interest rate variable. While the exchange rate depreciation variable has become highly significant, the inflation variable has become insignificant. Referring to a case where a parallel exchange rate market existed, Adams (1995) conjectured that a positive coefficient may reflect liquidity preference such that agents respond to an expected depreciation of the parallel market rate by shifting out of domestic financial assets in aggregate, but nevertheless simultaneously increase their money balances to operate in the cash-only parallel exchange market. In the case of Sri Lanka, a parallel market for foreign exchange existed during the period of the so-called Foreign exchange Entitlement Certificates Scheme (FEECS), which was a multiple exchange rate system) 1968 to November, 1977. Note also that from 1950 to 1978, Sri Lanka followed a basically fixed exchange rate system. In the case of Sri Lanka, part of the problem may be arising out of the fact that the TERDEP may not be capturing fully the effects of the multiple exchange rate system. Although several different definitions of this variable were tried out, none yielded any results different to those reported in the tables.

Tests of Exogeneity of the Regressors

Exogeneity of the regressors has important implications.[5] If the regressors are weakly exogenous, single equation estimation could be justified (Johansen 1992). Also, as Ericsson 91992) has pointed out, empirical presence of super exogeneity "immunizes the conditional model" from the well-known Lucas critique. Exogeneity can be tested in several ways: by testing the constancy of parameters in the marginal models and by testing the independence between the repressors and the residuals in the conditional model (Bardsen, 1992). According to Hendry (1988), if the conditional model (the demand for money model in the given case) has constant parameters but the equations for the regressors (the marginal models) have non-constant parameters, then the conditional model parameters could not depend on those of the marginal model. Engle and Hendy (1990) have shown that in the case of constancy of marginal

Table 6: Cointegrating Equations, Sri Lanka: 1950-2000

VAR Number	*Lags In VAR*	*Normalized*	*Cointegrating*	*Coefficient*				*Log likelihood*
#1	5	LRM1	LRGDP1	TDCPI	TERDEP	TFD12M		
		1,0000	-1.3712	7.5982	1.4386	-0.5624		541.4155
			(0.1785)	(1.6759)	(0.2895	(02693)		
#2	2	LRM1	LRGDP1	TDCPI	TERDEP	TFD12M	C	
		1,0000	-1.2879	1.4324	1.8090	-1.7603	-3.8513	454.0535
			(0.43040	(3.8384)	(0.7929)	(1.1014)	(3.7161)	
#3	5	LRM1	LRGDP1	TDCPI	TERDEP	TFD12M	C	
		1,0000	-1.5009	8.4662	1.9122	0.7750	3.2406	538.6380
			(0.2174)	(1.8984)	(0.4145)	(0.4212)		
#4	5	LRM1	LRGDP1	TDCPI	TERDEP	TFD12M		
		1,0000	-1.0767	12.2487	-0.8866	3.6879		508.4310
			(01356)	(3.1784)	(0.1788)	(1.1128)		

(*Table Contd.*)

Table 6: Contd.

#5	5	LRM1	LRGDP1	TDCPI	TERDEP			
		1,0000	-0.8381	5.4944	-1.3955			361.3373
			(0.1820)	(5.2108)	(0.7677)			
#6	2	LRM2	LRGDP1	TDCPI	TERDEP	TFD12M		
		1,0000	-1.7392	1.4955	2.5697	-1.3372		462.6369
			(0.4102)	(3.3776)	(0.9608)	(0.6318)		*
#7	2	LRM2	LRGDP1	TDCPI	TERDEP	TFD12M	C	
		1.0000	-2.5632	3.9123	5.4241	0.5379	7.7584	461.0301
			(1.2986)	(6.8209)	(3.8987)	(1.6468)		
*8	4	LRM2	LRGDP1	TDCPI	TERDEP	TFD12M	C	
		1,0000	-1.9209	14.1952	-0.9228	4.3374	3.0832	490.2222
			(0.4624)	(5.4202)	(0.2612)	(1.5652)	(1.3510)	
#9	3	LRM2	LRGDP1	TDCPI	TERDEP			
		1,0000	-0.6551	1.1606	-1.4655			343.3944
			(0.0134)	(1.4693)	(0.1400)			

Note: 1. For definitions of variables, see the appendix
2. Figures in parenthesis are the asymptotic standard errores.

model parameters, it is necessary to test for the independence between the regressors and the residual, which amounts to testing the significance of the residuals from the marginal models in the conditional model. If the parameters of the conditional model are invariant to changes in the marginal models, then such changes should not add any explanatory power.

Test for the constancy (or otherwise) of the marginal models were carried out first on the basis of univariate ARMA models for each of the regressors in the money demand model. Secondly, the information set was extended with the additional of several new instruments, and a new set of marginal models was estimated. The results for the latter set are reported in table 7 and sequential F-tests using the Chow forecast test are given in charts 1 to 4.

Considering the Chow forest tests (see charts 1 to 4), constancy of the parameters cannot be rejected for the marginal models related to LRGDP1 (log of GDP) and TFD12M (the 12-month deposit interest rate). However, the sequential Chow forest tests suggest that the marginal model parameters are no constant in the cases of TDCPI (the inflation variable) and TERDEP (the exchange rate variable). This is perhaps not that surprising, considering the fact that the liberalization policies initiated in 1978 have had a profound effect on inflation, in terms of a regime shift in that year and further volatility especially in the immediate post-liberalization period. Furthermore, an important part of the liberalization package of 1978 was the unification of the exchange rate and establishment of a managed float determined by a basket of currencies. These changes appear to be correctly captured by the marginal models for inflation and the exchange rate.

As Bardsen (1992) has pointed out, a critical element in this testing procedure is the specification of marginal models. A number of specification tests were carried out to ascertain the properties of the marginal models and the results are also reported in panel table 7. Results of the Ramsey RESET test point to a number of specification problems in all the marginal models considered in this study.[6] The ARCH-test results indicate that autoregressive conditional heteroskedasticity is a problem for only the marginal model for the 12-month deposit interest rate. This result is also confirmed by White's heteroskedasticity test. The Chow tests were supplemented by a Wald test for structural change with unequal subsample variances. For the purposes of the test, the sample period of 1950-2000 was subdivided into two periods, 1950-77 and 1978-2000. The Wald statistics for each of the marginal models are reported. These results show that constancy of parameters can be rejected for LRGDP1 (log of GDP) and TERDEP (exchange rate depreciation) variables at the 1 per cent level.

With these constraints on the rebustness and validity of the marginal models in the background, the two models for narrow money (LRM1) and broad money (LRM2) are tested next for invariance using the residuals from the marginal models described above (see panel B or table 7). In the narrow money model, none of the residuals from the marginal models are significant at even the 10 per cent level, indicating "exogeneity" of GDP, inflation, exchange rate depreciation, and 12-month deposit interest rate in explaining variations in narrow money. A similar result is obtained for the conditional model for broad money, with the notable exception of the significance of the residuals from the marginal model for 12-month deposit rate. Thus, for the model for broad money at least, it turns out that the variations in the marginal model for 12-month deposit interest rate has a significant influence in explaining the variations in broad money (LRM2), which is perhaps not surprising, considering the fat that the bulk of the quasi-money component of broad money is crucially dependent on this interest rate. Also, for broad money therefore, a single equation analysis may miss this joint dependence of the conditional and marginal models.

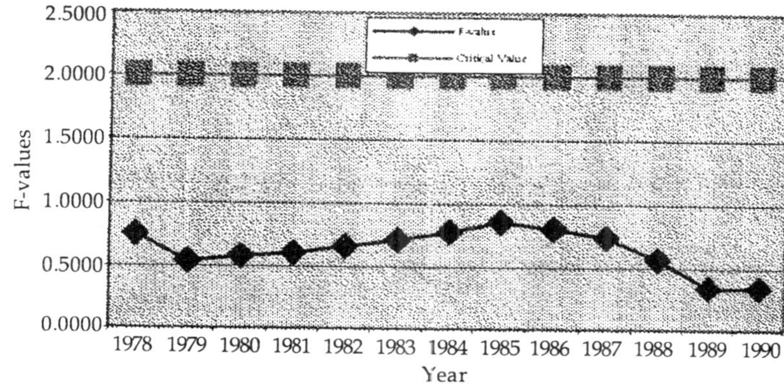

Chart 1. Chow Forecast Test for LRGDPI

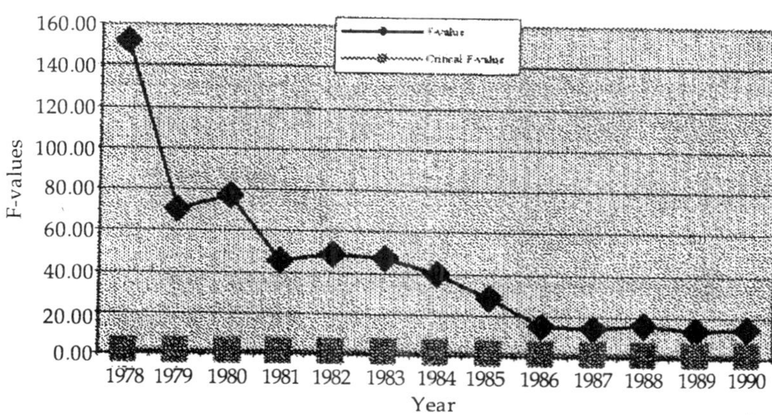

Chart 2. Chow Forecast Test for TDCP1

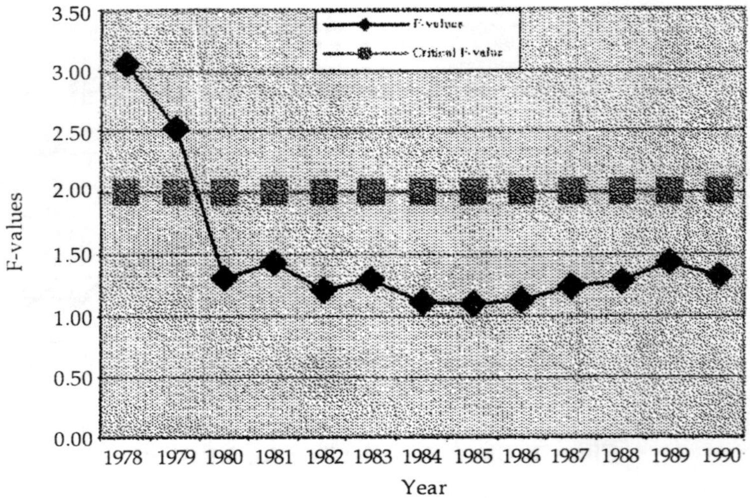

Chart 3. Chow Forecast Test for TERDEP

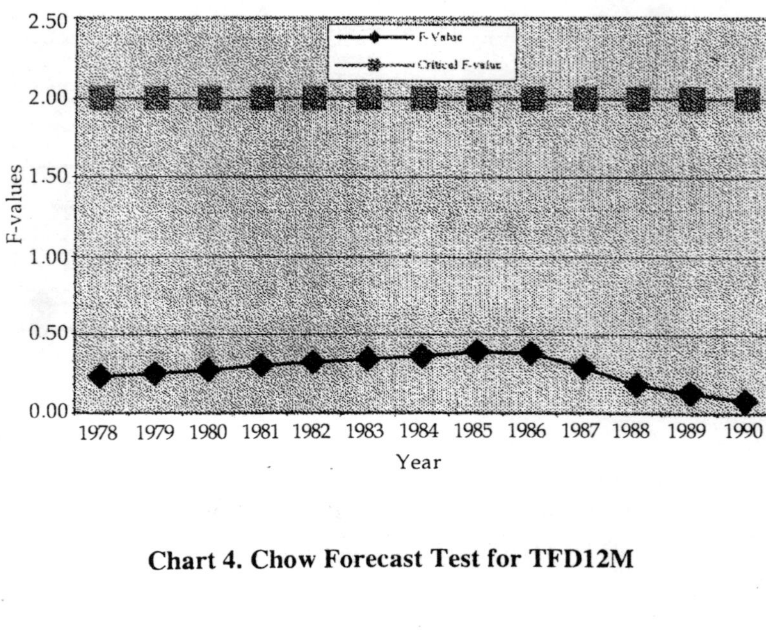

Chart 4. Chow Forecast Test for TFD12M

Table 7: A. Marginal Models for LRGDP1, TDCPI, TERDEP, TFD12M

Variables	*LARGDP1*		*TDCPI*		*TERDEP*		*TFD12M*
Sample (adjusted)	*1951-2000 Coefficients*		*1952-2000 Coefficients*		*1952-2000 Coefficients*		*1951-2000 Coefficients*
C	-0.0159 (-0.3207)	C	-0.030 (-0.5485)	C	-0.0868 (-1.2355)	C	0.1749 (2.7854)
LRGDP1 (-1)	1.0031 (87.7338)	TDCPI(-1)	0.8447 (10.8207)	TERDEP(-1)	0.6415 (6.5264)	TFD12M(-1)	0.6305 (5.6001)
LOG (QM90)	0.0025 (0.1809)	BUDY	-0.0011 (-1.2294)	BUDY	-0.0350 (-2.8659)	GDDY	0.0024 (2.4375)
LOG (QX90)	0.0081 (0.3469)	CABY	0.0003 (0.3497)	CABY	0.0178 (1.4475)	GFDY	0.0014 (2.0603)
Adjusted R-squared	0.9987		0.7434		0.6563		0.8704
S.E. of Regression	0.0248		-0.9841		0.2026		0.0505
Sum squared resid	0.0283		-0.9886		1.8474		0.1174
Log likelihood	116.0		135.5		10.8		80.4
Durbin-Watson stat	2.0589		2.6876		2.4772		2.4156

Table 7: Contd.

Mean dependent var	5.6680	0.0244	0.3623	0.8192
S.D. Dependent var	0.6908	0.0314	0.3456	0.1403
Akaike info criterion	-4.4799	-5.3681	-0.2769	-3.0567
Schwarz criterion	-4.3269	-5.2136	-0.1225	-2.9037
F-statistic	12663.6	47.3	31.6	110.7
Ramsey RESET Test	6.9847	3.4530	13.5988	11.3373
Probability	0.0006	0.0248	0.0000	0.0000
White Heteroskedasticity Test	7.1408	10.5663	9.6636	21.1256
	0.6225	0.3066	0.3784	0.0121
ARCH Test	2.8916	1.1011	0.3807	15.6001
	0.4086	0.7768	0.9442	0.0014

B. Significance of Residduals from Marginal Models in LRM1 and LRM2 equations

Marginal models	*LRGDP1*	*TDCP1* *t-Statitic*	*TERDEP*	*TFD12M*
LRM1	-0.8490	0.9039	-1.4420	-1.5759
LRM2	-0.9425	0.5196	-0.8798	-1.8393

Error Correction Models and the Short-run

The main emphasis of this study had been on the identification of the long-run cointegrating vectors of the demand for money relationship in Sri Lanka. Cointegration is a necessary and sufficient condition for the representation of economic time series in an error correction model (ECM), which combines both the short-run dynamics and long-run equilibrium relations. in fact, this specification restricts the long-run behaviour of the endogenous variables to converge to their cointegrating relationships while allowing a wide range of short-run dynamics, which are captured by the error correction term, the significance of which can be tested using conventional tests. Similarly, the lagged difference terms in the ECM could be tested. For illustrative purposes, two such ECMs are presented in table 8.

In the ECM for LRM1, the error correction term carries the right sign and indicates almost a 30 per cent gradual (partial) adjustment in the short-run money demand arising from a correction of the deviation from long-run equilibrium in the previous period. It is evident that this error correction coefficient is significant at the 1 per cent level. It is interesting to note that dynamics of exchange rate changes over the previous three year period seem to significantly affect the shortrun money demand. Changes in output in the previous two year period, similarly affect the short-run money demand. As could be expected, the dynamics of fixed deposit interest rate changes have no influence on the short-run demand for narrow money (LRM1). The dummy variable for liberalization is highly significant.

The ECM for LRM2 is relatively less successful in explaining the short-run dynamics associated with broad money. First, the error correction term had the wrong sign and is also not significient. None of the dynamic terms related to the exchange rate depreciation, read output, and inflation are significant. As expected, the fixed deposit interest rate terms possess some explanatory power,

Table 8. Error Corection Models for M1 and M2

	D(LRM1)	*(continuation for lags 4&5)=>*	*D(LRM1)*		*D(LRM2)*
ECM1	-0.2813 (-1.9990)			ECM2	0.0054 (0.0863)
D(LRM1(-3)	0.2081 (1.0323)			D(LRM2(-1))	0.3733 (2.0644)
D(LRM1(-2))	-0.5546 (-2.4001)	D(LRM1(-4)	-0.0438 (-0.2108)	D(LRM2(-2)	-0.1819 (-1.0340)
D(LRM1-3))	-0.0587 (-0.2512)	D(LRM1(-5)	0.0788 (0.4075)		
D(LRGDP1(-1)	-0.5571 (-0.7854)			D(LRGDP1(-1))	0.7860 (1.5078)
D(LRGDP1(1-2))	-1.8235 (-2.7091)	D(LRGDP1(-4)	0.17362 (0.2322)	D(LRGDP1(1-2))	0.1953 (0.3706)
D(LRGDP1(-3))	-0.4639 (-0.6876)	D(LRGDP1(-5))	-1.6539 (-2.6115)		
D(TDCPI(-1))	0.4680 (0.3396)			D(TDCP1(-1))	0.5275 (0.6056)
D(TDCPI(-2))	-2.0917 (-1.2997)	D(TDCPI(-4)	-1.0285 (-0.6467)	D(5DCPI(-2))	-0.6533 (-0.7562)

(Table Contd.)

Table 8. Contd.

	D(LRMQ)	(continuation for lags 4&5)=>	D(LRM1)		D(LRM2)
D(TDCPI(-3))	-1.0733	D(TDCPI(-5)	1.4944		
	(-0.6401)		(1.1603)		
D(TERDEP(-1))	0.4851			D(TERDEP(-1))	0.0646
	(2.8123)				(0.4793)
D(TERDEP(-2))	0.3987	D(TERDER(-4))	0.3613	D(TERDEP(-2))	0.0392
	(2.8871)		(3.1784)		(0.4503)
D(TERDEP(-3))	0.3759	D(TERDEP(-5))	0.2612		
	(2.9802)		(3.1174)		
D(TFD12M(-1))	-1.1226			D(TFD12M(-1))	0.7383
	(-1.8136)				(2.3852)
D(TFD12M(-2))	-0.4145	D(TFD12M(-4))	-0.3451	D(TFD12M(-2)	0.3279
	(-0.8154)		(-0.7334)		(1.2930)
D(TFD12M(-3))	-0.2920	D(TFD12M(-5))	0.13431		
	(-0.5833)		(0.3981)		
DUMLIB	0.2216			DUMLIB	-0.0093
	(2.0221)				(-0.1061)
TRLSTRD	-1.0379			TRLSTRD	0.0309
	(-1.6961)				(0.0689)

Table 8. Contd.

	D(LRMQ)	*(continuation for lags 4&5)=>*	*D(LRM1)*	*D(LRM2)*
R-squared	0.7320			0.2960
Adj. R-squared	0.2798			0.0475
Sum sq. resides	0.0761			0.1834
S.E. equation	0.0690			0.0734
F-statistic	1.6187			1.1913
Log likelihood	77.4712			63.6528
Akaike AIC	-2.2487			-2.1554
Schwarz SC	-1.1133			-1.6437
Mean dependent	0.0323			0.0609
S.D. dependent	0.0813			0.0752
VAR System indicators				
Log Likelihood	541.4155			462.6369
Akaike Information Criteria	-18.0189			-16.7080
Schwarz Criteria	-12.1392			-13.9524

especially the term with a lag of one period. A surprising result is that the liberalisation dummy is not significant in spite of the a priori expectation that liberalisation has had a profound impact on the diversification of the asset portfolios and the expansion of the conventional definitions of broad money in the country. These results for LRM2 are a pointer towards further work for in-depth investigations of the demand for broad money in the country.

Some Concluding Remarks

Monetary policy acquires a great deal of significance in an economy that has undergone a process of rapid liberalization and where the process continues to transform the character of the financial sector. In this context, the estimate of the parameters of a reliable demand for money function is of crucial importance. By investigating the behaviour of the related aggregate variables during the period 1950-2000, this study has attempted to provide such an estimate for a long-run money demand function for Sri Lanka.

Using Johansen's multivariate system procedure, which is being widely used by researchers, several long-run money demand relationships were identified for Sri Lanka for the period 1950-2000. Notwithstanding a number of structural changes that have taken place in the financial and real sectors of the Sri Lanka economy, the results of the study appear to support relatively stable money demand during this period, more for M1 than for M2. The long-run income elasticity for M1 is estimated to be in the range 1.0 -1.4 while the range for M2 is around 1.7-2.0. The relatively higher income elasticity for M2 may be a reflection of the greater portfolio choices made available especially after the economic liberalization of end 1977. It is also seen that inflation and exchange rate depreciation have been important factors that affected the portfolio choices of agents of the Sri Lankan economy over the last half-a century.

Two error-correction models are also given to demonstrate the logical transition from cointegration to error-correction models. in future research, it is intended to investigate these error-correction models in considerable detail. While the ECM for M1 seems to be in conformity with expectations, the results for M2 point towards the need for further investigation.

From a broader monetary policy perspective, the demand for money for M1 seems to be stable in Sri Lanka. However, the demand for M2 may need to be examined in terms of the individual components (assets) that constitute quasi-money (M2-M1) and the relative returns associated with them. Further, given the recent development in the financial sector, the Central bank of Sri Lanka seems to be moving in the right direction of not only considering quasi-money, but a broad range of other assets that fit into a wider concept of money such as M4. Due to lack of information for the entire period of this study, these other assets were not included in the current study.

Notes

1. Thanks are due to Michael Lewin, Oscar Nunez-Sandoval (World Bank), and Sarath Rajapatirana (American Enterprise Institute) for helpful comments. However, the author is responsible for any remaining errors.
2. During the first few years after liberalization, i.e. 1978-81, the economy grew by 6.5 per cent. Although growth stabilized around 5 per cent per year during the next 6 years, internal political uncertainty and civil disturbances and drought of 1987 led to a declaration of growth during 1987-89. With private investment and foreign direct investment picking up in the 1990s, growth improved to over 5 per cent per annum.
3. Although several different single equation models were tested using ordinary least squares (OLD), two-stage least squares (2SLS) and generalized method of moments (GMM), this study reports results only for the vector autoregression estimates.
4. The results from VAR analysis are sensitive to the choice and lag length and the number of variables included. The Akaike

Information Criterion and the Schawartz. Criterion and usually used for determining lag length. In using these criteria, the search had been limited to the range of lags from 1 to 5 years. The higher lags increase the severity of the degree-of-freedom problem. Furthermore, imposing reasonable restrictions seems to improve results of VAR analysis. In fact, on these grounds, in the current study, the choice of the interest rate variable had been made on some a priori considerations and had been limited to one particular rate.

5. Ericsson (1992) says that "valid exogeneity assumptions may permit simpler modeling strategies, reduce computational expenses, and help isolate invariants of the economic mechanism Invalid exogeneity assumptions may lead to inefficient or inconsistent inferences and result in misleading forecasts and policy simulations".

6. Ramsey's RESERT is a general test for the following omitted variables, incorrect functional form, measurement error in independent variables, simultaneous equation bias, and serially correlated disturbances. Under such specification error, LS estimators are biased and inconsistent, and conventional inference procedures will be invalid.

7. 'As Ericsson (1998) has pointed out, Granger causality is not invariant to the addition of new variables to the system.

References

1. Adam Christopher, (1999), Financial Liberalisation and Currency Demand in Zambia, Journal of African Economies, Volume 8, Number 3, pp. 268-306.

2. Adam Christopher, (1999), Liberalisation, Policy Reform and the Demand for Money in Africa, Journal of African Economies, Volume 8, Number 3, pp. 263-267.

3. Athukorala, Premachandra and Sarath Rajapatirana, (1993), Liberalization of the Domestic Financial Market Theorietcal issues With Evidence from Sri Lanka, International Economic Journal, Vol. 7, No. 4.

4. Athukorala, Premachandra and Sarath Rajapatirana, (1991), The Domestic Financial market and the Trade Liberalisation Outcome: The Evidence from Sri Lanka, Policy Research and External Affairs Working Paper No. 590, Washington DC, The World bank.

5. Banerjee A, Dolab J.J., Henry D.F., and Smith G.W., (1986), Exploring Equilibrium Relationship in Econometrics Through

Static Models. Some Monte Carlo Evidence. Oxford Bulletin of Economics and Statistics, 48, 3:253-277.

6. Baumol W.J., (1952), The transactions demand for cash: An inventory theoretic approach. Quarterly Journal of Economics, 66, 4, pp. 545-556.

7. Bischoff Charles W., and Haleform Belay, (2001), The Problem of identification of the money demand function, Journal of Money, Credit and Banking, 33, 2(May, Part 1).

8. Central bank of Sri Lanka, (2001), Special statistical Appendix, Trends in Key Economic Variables, 1950-2000. The Annual Report of the Central Bank of Sri Lanka, 2000.

9. Central Bank of Sri Lanka, (2000), The Annual Report of the Central Bank of Sri Lanka, 1999.

10. Chowdhury Abdur R., (1997), The financial structure and the demand for money in Thailand, Applied Economics, 29, 401-409.

11. Colombage, S.S., (1978), The behaviour of certain monetary variables in Sri Lanka, Staff Studies, Central Bank of Sri Lanka, Vol. 7, No. 2.

12. Dheerasinghe, Rupa, (1988), Error correction approach to the demand for money in Sri Lanka, Staff Studies, Central bank of Sri Lanka, Vol. 18, No. 1 & 2. Colombo.

13. Friedman M. (1956). The quantity theory of money-A restatement. Chapter I, in Friedman M. (ed). Studies in the quantity theory of money. Chicago University Press, Chicago, pp. 1-21.

14. Engle, R.F., Granger C.W.J., (1987), Co-integration and Error Correction: Representation, Estimation and Testing. Econometrica, 55, 2-251-276.

15. Ericsson, Neil R., (1998), Empirical modeling of money demand. Empirical Economics, 23: 295-315.

16. Ericsson, Neil R., and Sunil Sharma, (1998), Broad money demand and financial liberalization in Greece Empirical Economics, 23: 417-436.

17. Goldfeld, Stephen M, and Daniel E. Sichel, (1990), "The demand for Money" in handbook of Monetary Economics, Volume I, ed. by Benjamin M. Friedman and Frank H. Hahn, New York, North-Holland, pp. 300-56.

18. Granger, C.W.J. and P. Newbold, (1974), Spurious Regressions in Econometrics, Journal of Econometrics, 2, 111-120.

19. International Monetary Fund, "Theoretical aspects of the design of Fund-supported adjustment programs," Occasional paper, September, (1987).

20. International Monetary Fun, "The Monetary Approach to the Balance of Payments," IMF, Washington DC, (1977).

21. Jayatissa, R.A., (1984), Monetary analysis of exchange market pressure in Sri Lanka, 1972-85, Staff Studies, Central bank of Sri Lanka, Vol. 14. No.! & 2, pp. 49-64.

22. Laidler, David, (1993), The Demand for Money: Theories and Evidence, 4th ed. New York Harper-Collins.

23. Johansen S, (1988), Statistical analysis of cointegration vectors. Journal of Economic Dynamics and Control, 12, 2/3, 231-254.

24. Johansen, S., and K. Juselius, (1990), "Maximum Likelihood Estimation and Inference on Cointegration—With applications to the Demand for Money," Oxford Bulletin of Economics and Statistics, 52, pp. 169-210.

25. Hendry D.F., Pagan A.,R., Sargan J.D., (1984), Dynamic specification. Chapter 18 in Griliches, Z., Intriligator M.D. (eds.) handbook of econometrics, Volume 2, North-Holland, Amsterdam, pp. 1023-1100.

26. Khatkhate, Deena R. Warren L. Coats, Jr. and Klaus-Walter Riechel, (1978), "The Sri Lanka Financial System and a Framework for Monetary Policy," IMF, mimeographed.

27. Karunatilaka, H.N.S., (1973), Central Banking and Monetary Policy in Sri Lanka, Colombo.

28. Karunatilaka, H.N.S., (1974), Inflation and the Sri Lanka Economy, Staff Studies, Central bank of Sri Lanka, Vol. 14, No. 2, pp. 185-197.

29. Karunatilaka, H.N.S., (1974), Fiscal and monetary policy in Sri Lanka with special reference to the period after 1977, Sri Lanka Economic Journal, Vol. q.

30. Kremerz J.J.M., Ericsson N.R., and Dolado J.J., (1992), The power of cointegration tests. Oxford Bulletin of Economics and Statistics, 48, 3:325-348.

31. Kwiatkowski, D., Philips, P.C.B., Schmidt, P., Shin, Y., (1992), Testing the null hypothesis of stationarity against the alternative of a unit root. Journal of Econometrics, 54, 159-178.

32. Leventakis, J.A., (1993), Modelling money demand in open economies over the modern floating rate period. Applied Economics, 25, 1005-1012.

33. McKenzie, C.R., (1992), Money demand in an open economy. Journal of Japanese and International Economies, 6, 176-198.

34. Mussa, Michael, and Miguel Savastano, The IMF Approach to Economic Stabilization, IMF Working Paper, WP/99/104, July (1999).

35. Perera, Nelson, (1988), Demand for money in Sri Lanka 1960-1984. Indian Economic Journal, 36: pp. 18-32.

36. Rahman Hafizur, and Shekar Bose, (1998), An econometric analysis of the demand for moony in Bangladesh. Journal of Quantitative Economics, Vol. 14, No. 2 July 1998, 11-22.

37. Ranaweera, T.W.Y., (1971), Demand for money in Ceylon (1950-69), Staff Studies, Central bank of Sri Lanka, Vol. 1, No. 2, pp. 100-123.

38. Philips A.W., (1954), Stabilization policy in a closed economy. Economic Journal, 64, 254, pp. 290-323.

39. Siddiki Jalal U., (2000), Demand for money in Bangladesh: a cointegration analysis. Applied Economics, 32, 1977-1984.

40. Sims, Christopher A, (1980), Macroeconomics and Reality, Econometrica, January, pp. 1-47.

41. Sims, Christopher A, (1986), Are Forecasting Models Usable for Policy Analysis, Federal Reserve bank of Mineapolis Quarterly Review, 10 (Winter), pp. 2-16.

42. Tobin J, (1956). The interest elasticity of transactions demand for cash. Review of Economics and Statistics, 38, 3, pp. 241-247.

43. Weliwita, Ananda, and E.B. Ekanayake, (1998), Demand for money in Sri Lanka during the post-1977 period: a cointegration and error-correction analysis. Applied Economics, 30, pp. 1219-29.

APPENDIX 1

Variables:

M1–narrow money (currency + demand deposits)

M2–broad money (time and savings deposits in commercial banks)

GDP–Gross Domestic Product at market prices

PGDB96–Implicit GDP deflator with base 1996

CPIB96-Consumer Price Index with base 1996

BRATE–Bank rate: i.e. the rate charged by the Central bank of advances to commercial banks

FD12M–Interest rate on 12-month fixed deposits in commercial banks

TB3M–the yield on 91-day Treasury bills

RLSTTRD–lending rate of commercial banks relating to loans secured by stock in trade

NUS$–Nominal exchange rate Rupees per US$

TERDEP–rate of depreciation of nominal exchange rate

L–in front of a variable indicates logarithm of variable

d–in front of a variable indicates first difference of variable

T–in front of a variable indicates a transformation of the primary variable as follows:

$$TDCPI = dCPI/(1+dCPI)$$

A similar transformation was applied to all interest rates.

All primary variables were taken from the "Special Statistical Appendix, Trends in Key Economic Variable, 1950-2000", The Annual Report of the Central Bank of Sri Lanka, 2000.

APPENDIX 2

Granger Causality Tests

Pair wise Granger causality tests, using various lags ranging from 2 to 5 years, conducted in order to further investigate the relationship among variables. In general, except for a limited number of cases, the results for lags exceeding 3 years did not produce any information. Thus, the following discussion is based mostly on the causality tests using 2 year lags in the relevant testing equations. It is seen that the null hypothesis that real GDP (i.e. the log of real GDP–LRGDP1) does not Granger cause the log of real narrow money (LRM1) can be rejected at the 5 per cent level.

However, the hypothesis that LRM1 does not Granger cause real GDP cannot be rejected. This overall conclusion is not changed in the test where broad money was used (LRM2). Considering the pair wise relationship between log of real money and inflation, the hypothesis that inflation (represented by TDCPI) does not Granger cause LRM1 (LRM2) cannot be rejected while the hypothesis that real money (LRM1 or LRM2) does not Granger cause inflation (TDCPI) can be rejected (at the 1 per cent level in the case of LRM1 and 5 per cent level for LRM2). Furthermore, the hypothesis that real money does not Granger cause exchange rate depreciation (represented by TERDEP) is strongly rejected, while the causality in the opposite direction fails to be rejected by a narrow margin at the 5 per cent level. This result holds for both LRM1 and LRM2. As regards the growth-inflation relationship, that inflation (TDSCPI) does not Granger cause real GDP growth (LRGDP1) cannot be rejected while the hypothesis that real GDP growth does not cause inflation is rejected at the 5 per cent level. The results concerning the pair wise tests on GDP growth and the exchange rate depreciation seem to be some what inconclusive and they seem to suggest causality running in both directions. Similarly, it is not possible to find any conclusive evidence on the causal patterns with respect to inflation and exchange rate depreciation.

6

Determinants of Demand for Money in India

Arun Kumar Giri*

Introduction

Demand for money plays a major role in macroeconomic analysis, especially in selecting appropriate monetary policy actions. Particularly, money demand elasticity have been considered of crucial importance for operation and effictiveness of monetary policy. Consequently, a steady stream of theoretical and empirical research has been carried out worldwide over the past several decades. The interest has, however, heightened in recent years, triggered primarily by the concern among the central banks and researchers on the impact of the movement toward flexible exchange rate regime, globalisation of capital markets, ongoing domestic financial liberalization, financial innovation and technological and institutional developments.

Empirical research in this area centres around a few interesting issues. They include: (i) empirical definition of money, (ii) choice of appropriate scale and opportunity cost variables, (iii) role of adjustment and expected lags, (iii) estimation of functional forms and temporal stability (Laidler, 1969). Starting from the pioneering work of Iriving

* Faculty, Economics and Finance Group, Birla Institute of Technology and Science, Pilani, Rajasthan, India-333031.

Fisher to the relatively recent Buffer Stock model, the literature covering the various issues has been voluminous. Nevertheless, most of the issues remains unresolved. Moreover, the issues assumes importance in the context of economic, financial and institutional changes. Therefore, it is felt necessary in the present context to revisit demand for money in the context of Indian Economy where such changes have taken place in the recent years. It is felt that such a changes would throw some light on how accurately and reliably the effects of monetary policy could be explained and predicted.

A standard formulation of macro money demand function relates demand for money balances as an increasing function of a "scale" variable and a decreasing function of an "opportunity" cost variable. In other words, demand for money depends on the "cost" and "return" from its holding. When money is held, the rate of return on alternative assets in which money could have been held, represents the cost aspects. The return aspects constitutes the stream of invisible services that money holding provides. The quantum of services is assumed to be proportional to the amount of balances held. Rational economic units maximise the return with respect to a budget constraint provided by wealth or income. The maximisation process thus gives rise to a demand for money function in terms of a "constraint" and an "opportunity" cost variable. The former reflects the "return" side while the latter the "cost" side of the money holding. The constraint variable is also known as scale variable and is positively related to demand for money. The opportunity cost variable which reflects the rate of return on alternative assets, is negatively related to demand for money. The two sets of variables, i.e., the scale and opportunity cost variables together are called the "determinants of demand for money". Wealth, expected income/income are the proxies for the scale variable. Interest rate (short and long term), expected rate of price change etc. are the proxies for opportunity cost of holding money.

There has not been consensus about the choice/identification of the determinants of the demand for money function. While transaction theories favour real income (as a measure of transaction) as a proxy for scale variable and short term interest rate as a measure of opportunity cost of holding money, asset theories favour expected income/wealth as proxy for scale variable and have not ignored the role of long term interest as measure of opportunity cost of holding money. Similarly, rate of inflation, inflationary expectations etc. also influence the demand for money as a measure of opportunity cost of holding money. Thus, the selection of determinants is an empirical question.

The General Framework

There is a diverse spectrum of money demand theories emphasising the transactions, speculative, precautionary and utility considerations. These theories implicitly, address a broad range of hypothesis. One significant aspect, however, is that they share common important elements among almost all of them. In general, they bring forth relationship between the quantity of money demanded and a set of few important economic variables liking money to the real sector of the economy (Judd and Scadding, 1982). What set apart among these theories is that although they consider similar variables to explain the demand for money, they frequently differ in the specific role assigned to each. Consequently one consensus that emerges from the literature is that the empirical work is motivated by a blend of theories.

Different theories of money demand discussed in the literature can be broadly classified under two heads: (a) transaction theories and (b) asset or portfolio theories. Transaction theories emphasizes money's role as a medium of exchange and money is essentially an inventory held for transaction purpose. The inventory-theoretic models of W. J. Baumol and J. Tobin are the two seminal contributions to the micro foundation of the transaction theory. These theories assume the receipts and expenditures streams to the exogenous and further, money and bonds are the only two stores of value available for the household.

Under the portfolio approach, in addition to pecuniary gain, services like liquidity and safety are considered part of money's non-pecuniary yield. Money and other assets are viewed as alternative ways of holding wealth, each yielding a mix of explicit and implicit returns of services. A rational household maximises returns by way of holding a judicious portfolio of assets.

The general specification begins with the following functional relationship for the long-term demand for money:

$$M/P = f(S, OC)$$

Whether the demand for real balance M/P is a function of the chosen scale variable (S) to represent the economic activity and the opportunity cost of holding money (OC). M stands for selected monetary aggregate in nominal term and P for the price. Like theoretical models, the empirical models generally specify the money demand as a function of real balances.

A Review of Empirical Studies

The determinants to be included in the demand for money function for developed economy has been an issue has been extensively discussed and resolved by and large (Brunner and Meltzer, 1963; Laidler, 1966; Meltzer, 1963 and Starleaf and Reimer, 1967). The explanatory variables are usually some definition of wealth or income as the scale variable and some interest rate as the opportunity cost of holding money. There is a general agreement about the importance of the first variable, though there is considerable debate as to whether the appropriate constraint imposed on the money balances is current income, permanent income or wealth or a combination of these, However, there has been considerable disagreement regarding the interest rate however defined, as the appropriate opportunity cost variable. Friedman (1959) showed no close relationship between the demand for money and rate of interest. However, Laidler (1977) pointed out that this way have been due to an erroneous measurement of the relationship between the demand for money and permanent income.

The appropriateness of some other variables as the opportunity cost of holding money was suggested by Cagan (1956) in his study of demand for money during hyper-inflation. Following Cagan (1956) and Friedman (1959), and the associate upsurge of interest in the demand for money, the empirical studies focussed more generally upon the theoretical studies to suggest appropriate determinants. Here we look at the empirical findings on elasticies and related issues as to which variables should be included as determinants in the money demand function. More specifically, the focus will be on several key issues such as: (i) choice of an appropriate monetary aggregates, (ii) a proper measure of scale variable, (ii) proxies for short term interest rate, long term interest rate or opportunity cost variables (iv) other suitable determinants viz., stock prices, exchange rate, market capitalisation etc.

In re-evaluating the performance of the money demand specification and finding suitable determinants of the function, it is useful to consider the measurement and specification issues on a variable-by-variable basis. We begin our review with the dependent variable money.

Definition of Money

Rather obviously, an important issue in the empirical estimation of money demand is the selection of an explicit measure of money. Even if the choice is guided by theoretical considerations/framework, such choices are often less than clear cut. Moreover, what passes for money can be readily altered by changing financial institutions. In the United States at least, such changes, promoted by private financial innovation and deregulation, have had major implications for the definition of money.

The question of an appropriate definition of money to be included in the money demand function has been discussed in literature by Artis and Lewis (1976), Brunner and Meltzer (1963), Melitz (1963), Meltzer (1963), Kavaragh and Walters (1963) and Laidler (1966, 1969). Laidler (1977) in his survey, discussed these and other studies on this issue and concluded that a narrow definition of money (currency and demand deposits) may be preferred for quarterly data and that either a broad or a narrow definition is appropriate when annual data are analysed. The issue centres on choosing an appropriate definition so that stable demand for money function can be shown to exist under differing institutional arrangements and economic and political conditions.

In the quest for a stable money demand function it remains an open question as to which definition of money is appropriate. In this context, Meltzer (1963) argued that money should be so defined that the demand for the same should remain stable under differing institutional arrangements and under changing social, political and economic conditions. Laidler (1969) also suggested the controllability criterion. According to him, if the behaviour of an economy is to be influenced in desired direction by manipulating the quantity of money, the necessary preconditions are that the monetary authorities must be able to control the volume of the set of assets that most closely corresponds to the money stock, and at the same time, the demand function for this stock of assets must be stable enough for the consequences of changing its volume to be predictable with a high degree of reliability.

The Proponents of use of narrow money (Laidler, 1966; Melitz, 1963) argue that the supply of currency varies in response to the public's demand for it and demand deposits also responds similarly, because individuals rearrange their holdings quickly and at low cost by varying their interest bearing deposits; and therefore substitution takes place between demand deposits and other forms of wealth (including time deposits). These movements directly affect the supply of demand deposits A general rise in the interest rate cause substitution effect to take place between m1 and other assets and the inclusion of time deposits in the definition of money.

In the later period, Gordon (1984), Rose (1985), and Roley (1985) employing a cross interest elasticity from a single equation money demand regression, identified narrow money (ml) to give a stable money demand function, because it avoids all complexities of the near money which are not final means of payments. Contrary to this, Friedman and Meiselmen (1963) and Mayer (1976) concluded that broad money (m2) (ml + time deposits of the commercial banks) is the most closely correlated monetary aggregate with national income and hence most appropriate definition for stable demand for money.

It may be noted that different behavioural relationships may hold good for different components of the money stock. This idea was first stressed in the UK by Coghlan (1978) who argued that, "there is no general theory of the demand for money which is applicable regardless of the definition of money adopted". If this is so, we cannot expect to isolate stable demand functions for broad money aggregate involving components as different as, for example, currency and time deposit. This approach was advanced even earlier in the US particularly by Goldfeld (1973) who, having modelled the demand for narrow and broad money, argued strongly to disaggregate the broad money aggregate.

Extending the innovative line of approach introduced by Chetty (1969), Offenbacher (1979) and Subrahmanyam (1980) among others suggested how monetary assets should be selected for inclusion in an empirical definition of money. However, due to difference in the coverage of assets, the sample period and the method employed, the above studies have considered appropriate all the aggregates-ml to a much broader aggregate that includes S & L shares, mutual saving deposits, 91 treasury bills etc.. Finally, even the microeconomics theory of monetary aggregation by Barnet (1982, 1987) for US also proved unsuccessful. The alleged superiority of the Divisia and other superlative monetary aggregates could not be convincingly established.

In their drive to arrive at a stable demand for money function, researchers who are unhappy with the official definition of money have attempted to construct their own aggregates. Research on these lines has been in two diametrically opposite directions. They regarded the official definitions of even "narrow" money as too broad, atleast from a purely transaction point of view. This concern has led some to suggest for using a disaggregated approach in which separate empirical demand functions are estimated for each monetary assets. This side-steps the definition issue and at the same time permits the use of econometric techniques that takes account of the interrelated nature of the demand functions. However, due to the difference in the coverage of assets, sample periods and method employed, different studies justified different monetary aggregates. On the whole the appropriate definition of money proposed by different studies range from currency to very broad monetary aggregates. Still the issues of an appropriate monetary aggregate has been complicated by the appearance of new financial instruments brought about by deregulation and such effort remain unresolved.

It is also difficult to reach a firm conclusion about an appropriate definition of money to be used in developing countries like India. The relative importance of the precautionary motive due to inherent instabilities in the economy and lack of other liquid assets would seem to indicate the narrower definition. While the low percapita income and the high cost of foregoing interest on cash and demand deposits would seem to favour the broader definition (m2 or m3). The fact that demand or current deposits in a country like India also pay interest would also seem to place the onus on the narrower definition. Hence, the suitable definition of money is an empirical question to be investigated.

Choice of Scale Variable

The choice of scale variable in demand for money functions is closely linked to the definition of money employed. For narrow definitions of money, believed mainly to serve the transitory motive, it can be argued that current measured income is the appropriate scale variable. However, for broader definitions of money some measure of wealth, either non-human wealth only or total wealth (proxies by permanent income) is likely to be more appropriate.

The issue of an appropriate proxy for the scale variables has been examined in great detail in the developed economies. It has been felt that the use of permanent income, expected income or wealth has been more appropriate than the use of current income (Brunner and Meltzer, 1963; Laidler, 1966, 1970 and Starleaf and Reimer, 1967).

The likely superiority of wealth measures as scale variables was demonstrated as early as in 1963 by Meltzer (1963) who, by using the US annual data for the period 1900 to 1958, compared the stability over different decade but containing alternative scale variables: non-human wealth, permanent income and measured income. He found that the wealth variable produced a more stable demand for money function than the income variable no matter what definition was used for money. Such a conclusion was supported by Brunner and Meltzer (1963) and Laidler (1966). Chow (1966) however indicated that permanent income was more important than current income in the long run and current income more important in the short run studies.

Until recently, lack of data on private sector financial wealth for most of the countries meant that in many cases the choice of scale variable in practice lay between measured and permanent income. Choice was most frequently made on the basis that permanent income can be regarded as the distributed lag function of present and past measured income levels. However, researchers found that the estimation was not simple and hence measured income rather than permanent income could still be the appropriate scale variable.

The first serious attempt to resolve this problem was by Feige (1967) who attempted the money demand function using US data for 1915-63. Feige found that estimates of the partial adjustment parameter were not significantly different from unity, where the estimates of permanent income were 0.37 for narrow money and 0.30 for broad money. These results suggested that at least for annual data, the adjustment of actual to desired balance could be treated as instantaneous. Thus, the importance of lagged income variables indeed appeared to be the result of permanent income being the appropriate scale variable.

Availability of reliable data on private sector wealth in recent times for some economies had led to more direct attempts for modelling the non-human wealth as a scale variable. Grice and Barnett (1984) in their study of the UK demand for broad money aggregate, m3, included the gross financial wealth of non-bank private sector in their equation along with income variable. Using quarterly data and general to specific approach, they concluded that the influence of financial wealth on money demand could not be ignored. The long-run wealth elasticities were well in excess of unity. Despite the importance of wealth, income still had a role to play. The study is therefore, unusual in that it finds a significant role for two scale variables.

In more recent years, research on scale variables has focused on the following two aspects of the transaction measures: (i) the construction of more comprehensive measure of transactions; and (ii) the disaggregation of transactions into various components, reflecting the notion that not all transactions are equally "money intensive".

The construction of more comprehensive measure of transaction is motivated by the fact that despite the appearance of gross in GNP it is much less inclusive of all sales of intermediate goods, transfers, purchases of existing goods and financial transactions, all of which may contribute to the demand for money. On the other side GNP may overstate transactions because it includes imputed items. While these shortcoming of GNP have long been recognised, thorny data problems have discouraged the construction of more general transaction measures. As a proxy for such a measure, some researchers have used data on gross debits to demand deposits accounts. While in some instances substituting debits for GNP improved things, the effect was small and not robust (Judd and Scadding, 1982).

In recent years, however, there have been some noticeable advances in constructing general measures of transactions precautionary by Cramer (1986) and Corrado and Spindt (1986). Since only limited data are presently available, it is too early to tell if these new data will improve the performance of money demand functions.

Whatever measure of transaction is chosen, there remains the question of whether it might usefully be disaggregated into several scale variables. Thus, for instance, if real GNP is the basic scale variable, one might separately enter various components of GNP on the ground that these component are likely to generate different payment needs. On the whole, while there is some promising indications of disaggragations (Radecki and Wenninger, 1985 and Mankiw and Summers, 1986), there is no firm evidence that disaggregation of GNP yields a dramatic improvement in the behaviour of the aggregate money demand. The case of disaggregation, however, appears a bit stronger when coupled with the disaggregation of money into types of holder (e.g. consumer, business) and types of deposits.

With regard to income as a scale variable, and the income elasticity of demand for money, there are two conflicting forces in developing economies which would determine how the income elasticities varies vis-a-vis developed countries. The preponderance of other liquid assets in developed economies would seem to indicate a lower income elasticity in developed rather than developing economies. However, as against this force, causing a higher income elasticity in developing countries, owing to lower percapita income levels, people would not be willing to forego the premium received from holding assets. This tendency would be, in turn, counteracted by the fact that due to the greater degree of uncertainty and instability in developing countries, the precautionary motive may dominate the other motives in these countries implying a higher income elasticity. The issue can only be resolved by the empirical investigation.

Choice of Opportunity Cost and Other Variables

The choice of certain measures of opportunity cost of holding money largely depends on the theoretical perspective under consideration. Neo Keynesians tend to regard short term interest rates as the most relevant one for narrow definition of money when transactory motive is dominant, and only consider long term interest rates in the context of broad money aggregates. If the holding of money is viewed as part of general portfolio decision process, then clearly rates of return on all alternative financial assets are relevant (Laidler, 1969). Moneterists, however, have always maintained that rates of return on all alternative assets are relevant even for narrow money. For them, money is an effective substitute for all assets-both financial and physical.

Inflationary Expectations

There has been some disaggrement as to whether the interest rate variable, however defined, can be a suitable opportunity cost variable. The appropriateness of some other variable as the opportunity cost of holding money was raised by Cagan (1956). Expected inflation as an opportunity cost variable has been included in several money demand specifications (Cagan, (1956), Frowen and Arestis (1976) and Sapiro (1973).

The inclusion of expected inflation as an argument does not differ from the inclusion of interest rate in that the increase in this variable also increases the cost of holding money. In countries with well developed financial markets, the expected rate of inflation is reflected in the nominal interest rate since the latter will rise when inflation is expected, compensating the lenders for the loss of purchasing power of money due to inflation. Thus, while the issue of including inflationary expectations in the money demand function is important during the period of high inflation, in developed economies, with well developed capital markets in which the nominal interest rates are free to move to reflect expected inflation, the nominal interest rate is a relevant argument in the money demand specification. The rule of thumb proposed by Modigliani, of which variable to include, states that if the expected rate of inflation exceeds the nominal interest rate, the expected rate should be included; if not then the nominal interest rate is the appropriate rate, Dornbusch and Fischer (1981). Adekunle (1986), Melitz (1976) and Sapiro (1973) used expected inflation in the money demand function that also contained nominal interest rate as a variable.

However, this issue regarding the appropriate opportunity cost variable has added significance for the developing countries for the following reasons: (i) The wide divergence of rates of interest in the organised and unorganised money markets (ii) a multiplicity of unorganised market interest rates and a lack of time series data on them, (iii) underdeveloped financial markets and few organised dealings in commercial paper and bills.

All these factors would substantiate the importance of physical assets as substitutes for money. While the substitution effects of physical assets are important for both developed and developing countries, because of lack of other financial assets, the importance of real asset substitutes is enhanced in developing countries. One of the important characteristics which make people hold money is its function as a store of value. When prices are expected to rise its function as a store of value reduces and money holder shift money into physical assets as a store of value. The lack of other appropriate financial assets makes this movement into physical assets the preponderant one.

Thus, contrary to the experience in money demand relationships for developing countries like the US, where, despite theoretical specifications, the expected rate of change of prices is not found to play a significant role (Brunner and Meltzer, 1963), Cagan (1965) suggested that such an opportunity cost variable is particularly relevant to the demand for money during times of rapid and highly variable rates of inflation. However, the issue of appropriate opportunity cost variable (s) including inflationary expectations as a proxy should be investigated.

Rate of Inflation

To model the effects of inflation, researchers have traditionally assumed that including nominal interest would be sufficient to take care of the opportunity cost of holding money. More recently, however, some researchers (Baba et. el., 1988; Hetzel and Mehra, 1989) have began to directly include inflation rate in additional to nominal interest rate in their empirical models.

Theoretically, inflation may directly enter into the empirical models of money demand which concerns the issue of money substitutes and opportunity cost. Short term interest rate is included in the money demand function on the assumption that the only alternative to holding money is to hold short term bonds. Economists like Cagan (1959), Frankel (1977) and Friedman (1959) have pointed out that during the period of high inflation rate, assets other than short term bonds may serve as substitutes for money. During the period, price rise becomes taxing, individuals may accelerate their purchases of real goods and services rather than hold money or they may chose to hold in physical assets-land or gold. The idea is that these are immune to the devaluating effect of inflation. So, the implication for the empirical models of demand for money is hat when certain physical goods that yield their returns in kind, serve as substitute for money holding, then the nominal return on these assets - inflation in the present case, should be included as a determinant in the money demand function separately from the nominal interest rate.

Variable Expectations and Variability of Rate of Inflation

The use of inflationary expectations in the money demand specification is clearly established after the work of Cagan (1959) and Friedman (1969). There has been series of work, modelling the variable in the money demand function. Though there has not been any consensus about the findings of various studies there is one thing common to most of the studies—the use of "adaptive expectation hypothesis" for deriving observation on the unobserved expected variables. The underlying assumption has been that the process of forming expectations has been static. However, the notable expectations are the works of Khan (1977) and Koot (1975). The empirical literature on the estimation and specification of the demand for money has given little attention to the possibility that the variability of the rate of inflation may affect the demand for real cash balances. Khein (1977) has presented a formal framework to deal with the problem and the research work on his issue at the empirical level are attempted by Blejer (1979), Frankel (1977) and Khan (1977).

The role of variability of expected rate of inflation in the money demand function has been explained by Blejer

(1979). According to her, the variability of expected rate of inflation can have a dual effect on the demand for money. This variable which represents uncertainty on the price front is positively related to demand for money if people want to hold more money as a precautionary measure. On the contrary, it will give rise to the fear of loss of value of the assets whose value is not constant in real terms and hence, induce people to diversify the portfolio composition by reducing demand for money. Hence, it is of interest to capture the net effect of variability of expected rate of inflation on demand for money which is considered an important determinant in the context of economies where price stability has been elusive.

Klein (1977) measured variability by 5 term moving standard deviation from the 10 term moving mean of the annual rate of inflation. He obtained a positive and significant effect of this variable on the United States demand for money. Frankel (1977), studying German hyperinflation, does not obtain significant results using the variance of the prediction error. Khan (1977) estimated the Cagan's model of demand for money for six hyper-inflation countries (Austria, Germany, Greece, Hungary, Poland and Russia) allowing the coefficient of expectation to vary with the level and change in the rate of inflation. The results indicated a considerable support for the hypothesis that the level and variability of rate of inflation have an effect on the change in expectation of inflation and hence the usefulness of incorporating variability of rate of inflation in the model. The effect on the demand for real cash balances of change in the variability of rate of inflation was tested by estimating the money demand function of three Latin American countries -Argentina, Brazil and Chile by Blejer (1979) for the annual data period: 1951-1975. The result indicated that all the coefficients of variability of rate of inflation were negative and statistically significant. The results suggested that in highly inflationary situations, the greater financial risk implied by the increased instability of the rate has a negative effect on the demand or money, which is not fully offset by the positive effect of greater variability may have on the precautionary demand.

The above discussion clearly suggests that the time varying character of inflationary expectations and variability of rate of inflation have to be modelled in the conventional money demand analysis especially in developing countries to capture the dynamic behaviour of the prices.

Stock Market Prices

In the existing literature, it has been shown (Hamburger, 1977; Laidler, 1980), that dividend/price ratio variable has a place in the money demand specifications Such an idea is based upon Friedman's belief that money is a substitute for all assets, both real and financial, so that rates of return on the whole range of assets are relevant. Hamburger (1977) used a dividend/price ratio variable as a measure or "real rate" on all equities including durable goods for the US economy. The study found the rates of return on equities as an important determinant of demand for money even when narrow monetary aggregate was adopted.

Since then there has been considerable investigation on the relation between money and stock prices. In the literature, the relation has been treated in more than one way: first by treating volume of financial transaction as an argument in the demand for money function on the ground that such transaction would absorb money and hence reduce the income velocity. (Cramer, 1986 and Wenninger and Radecki, 1986). On the other hand, by treating the earning or dividend yield on securities as one of the returns alternative to money in a portfolio (Hamburger, 1977). The empirical results have supported the direction of effect suggested by the theory but the magnitude of the effect is small. There has not been a serious attempt to relate the levels of stock prices to demand for money except Friedman (1988). The role of stock market in influencing money demand is analysed by Friedman by using quarterly US data for the period: 1961-1986. The study found that the real quantity of money relative to income is found to be negatively related to the real stock prices and positively related to the real stock prices lagged three periods It has been suggested that the former represents the substitution effect and the latter as wealth effect.

Market Capitalisation

Since the mid 1970s attempts have been made to find out whether innovation and institutional changes in financial markets have caused shift in demand for money functions. However, it has been difficult to model financial innovation due to the limitation of data availability for appropriate variables. It has been proposed that in the empirical estimation of money demand function, the financial saving of the community in the form of financial assets other than money could be captured under capitalisation of stocks. Hence, market capitalisation could be an useful surrogate for financial innovations in money demand function to capture the portfolio decision of the agents in a situation of financial innovation.

Croker (1990) estimated money demand function by incorporating a measure of financial assets of private non-financial sectors in Japan as a proxy for wealth variable. This variable was hypothesised to capture private portfolio decisions among financial assets. The study concluded that the demand for money function for broad money explained both secular trend in the income velocity during 1970s and 1980s and the acceleration in the decline in velocity during 1986-88. The acceleration in the broad money velocity was attributed to the wealth effect that caused a rapid expansion in the demand for all assets. This effect was strongly guided by the rapid pace of financial liberalisation in Japan.

However, a priori, market capitalisation may have both wealth as well as substitution effects. The relative strength of these two is however an empirical question.

Exchange Rate

Like the rates of return on equities or dividend yield on the domestic capital market which are treated as useful determinants, there is also evidence that in more open economies, interest rate relating in the international capital markets should be regarded as a relevant opportunity cost variable. Hamburger (1977) found that three month rate on Euro dollar deposits to be a significant variable in the UK demand for money function, thus confirming the openness of UK economy and the close substitutability between UK domestic money and Euro dollar deposits. Hamburger also provided evidence that the Euro dollar rate might be important in the west Germany's demand for money function.

Recently, exchange rate has been used (Branson and Buiter, 1983; Bahmani and Pourheydarian, 1990) as an appropriate determinant in the money demand specifications. This has been found to be relevant on the ground that most of the economies have gradually opened up and integrated globally to reflect the interest rate differentials between the trading countries. Theoretically, the role of exchange rate in effecting real money holding may be rationalised in either of two diametrically opposite ways: (a) a depreciation of domestic currency may lead to a decline in demand for real money balance through a decline in real wealth; (b) a depreciation may result in an increase in wealth on account of net debtor's position in terms of ownership claims on the rest of the world and hence increase the demand for real cash. The evidence is in line with the results obtained by Bahamani-Oskooee (1991) for the UK and Bahmani-Oskooee and Pourheydarian (1990). The above discussion suggested that the economies which have gradually opened up and integrated globally, the exchange rate variable may be treaded as a suitable determinant in the money demand function.

Review of Studies Conducted In India

From the money demand studies conducted for India, it is found that the influence of real income on demand for money, whether macro level (Bhattacharya, 1974; Gupta, 1973; Mammen, 1970) or sectoral level studies (Rangarajan, 1965; Saravane, 1971) was significant. This is compatible with the view that in a developing economy like India, money demand would respond more to changes in scale factor i.e., income (Gujarati, 1968; Gupta, 1973; Vasudevan, 1979), permanent income (Gupta, 1987; Mammen, 1970) than to those relating to the opportunity cost of holding money i.e., interest rates-short term or long term (Gujarati, 1968; Mammen, 1970). However, price is also a significant variable in some studies (Vasudevan 1979). The studies (Gujarati, 1968; Kamath, 1984; Mammen, 1970 and Singh, 1984) confirmed the interest inelasticity of demand for money suggested that the interest inelasticity of the demand for money is due to the administered interest rate that prevailed during the major period of these studies. However, some studies do find contradictory evidence on the interest rate money demand relationship (Gupta, 1970, Shahi, 1977). In the household sector, shifts have occurred from the pure cash holding to quasi-money assets when interest rates are relatively high. In respect of the business sector, firms hold liquid assets in alternative forms and economise on cash balances.

Up to mid 1970s, the studies on demand for money included mainly measured income, permanent income as proxies for the scale variable and yield on debentures, yield on government securities, treasury bill rate, deposit rate and call money rate as measures of interest rates. However, studies since mid 1970s started modelling the money demand function with new set of determinants to study the effect of financial innovation, structural deregulation and globalisation. Studies (Bhole, 1985; Kamaiah and Pual, 1979; Pual 1992; Singh et al 1982; Trivedi, 1980) have included inflationary expectation as a suitable proxy for opportunity cost of holding money in Indian context. Stock prices was included as an extra explanatory variable in the money demand specification and found to be significant (Joshi and Sagar, 1995; Paul, 1992). Few recent studies also found exchange rate variable to be significant determinant in the money demand specification (Joshi and Sagar, 1995 and Nag and Upadhyay, 1993). Studies (Kamaiah and Subrahmanyam, 1982 Pual, 1981) also incorporate the variability of rate of inflation to capture the effect of volatility of inflation on the demand for real cash holding. Further, the roles of stock market and exchange rate have been recognised as instruments in a new channel of monetary transmission mechanism through which monetary policy operation could be guided. Based on the foregoing discussion and the survey of evidence, it is highly motivating to pursue a study to detect the new transmission mechanism under the situation of financial innovation, structural deregulation and globalisation of Indian economy.

Choice of Determinants for the Present Study

Based on the above discussion, the present study has selected the following determinants of demand for money function to capture the effect of the development in the money/securities and external market in the recent past.

Rate of Interest

While modelling demand for money, researchers are confronted with the problem of multiplicity of interest rates. In fact, there are instances of more than one interest rate in the typical money demand function (Mahajan, 1979). However, most of the Indian studies have included a single interest rate in the function. They are treasury bill rate

(Sastry, 1962; Gujurati, 1968), yield on Government securities (Gujurati, 1968), deposit rate (Singh 1969), 91-treasury bill rate (Gupta, 1987), Call money rate (Jadhav, 1994). Ideally interest rate should be market clearing one, which can be considered as the opportunity cost of holding money. However, when interest rate is administered, it losses its explanatory power.

With a move towards deregulation, a particular interest rate may be administered and market determined, partly for a particular time period. However, in India money market instruments like call money, commercial paper, certificate of deposits are market determined. Deposit and lending rates have been rationalised as a prelude to complete deregulation. Major chunk of treasury bills are sold on auction basis. Again, the recent institutional arrangements have important role to play in widening and deepening the money/securities market in India. All these arrangements are primarily aimed at providing basic infrastructure for the emergence of interest rate mechanism as the focal point of intervention. So, in the context of recent changes in the money market in India, interest rate have become a relevant proxy for opportunity cost variable in the money demand function.

For the present purpose, however, we could not get any interest rate which is market determined throughout the sample period. Among all the available interest rates, the cell money rate seem to have been somewhat market related for maximum number of period of our sample. The average call money rate at Bombay is therefore chosen as a useful surrogate for the opportunity cost in our study. We have also tried out one year deposits rate as an alternative opportunity cost variable in our study under the presumption that the authorities might have taken into consideration the prevailing market condition in fixing the one year deposit rate. That other alternative interest rates included in this study are treasury bill rate and yield on debentures.

Rate of Inflation and Inflationary Expectations

Most of the studies related to countries like US, UK and Canada which has been relatively free from the high rates of inflation in the past, have generally concentrated on investigating the demand for many function with either of the interest rates (short term of long term) as the relevant opportunity cost variable. However, in India, studies on demand for money published during last two decades, have included inflationary expectations as a useful proxy for opportunity cost variable in the money demand function (Kamaiah and Pual, 1979; 1979; Trivedi, 1980; Paul, 1992; Sing *et. al.* 1982; Bhole, 1985). Due to the presence of special characteristics of Indian economy, where capital market was not organised (at least in the early period of the sample), the existence of unorganised securities market, the presence of wide divergence of rates of interest rate in the organised and unorganised money market, and absence of appropriate financial assets, there is a strong case for considering the substitute relationship between money and real assets including non-perishable consumer goods as operationally more meaningful. Hence, the net adjustment in the above particular category of assets is more representative as compared to the yield on paper securities traded in the organised market.

Moreover, in terms of the inflation performance, the decades of sixties, seventies, eighties and the present, the rate has been predominantly high. During the sixties, the increase in price was particularly sharp at 6.3 per cent in seventies, money supply accelerated to 17.7 per cent per annum with a preponderant effect on prices as inflation rose on an average to 9.0 per cent. In the subsequent decade, though there was marginal decline in the rate compared to the previous decade, still it remained at 8.0 per cent. In 1990s, (up to 1996-97) again there was significant pick up in the rate to 9.6 per cent.

The evidence of high inflation rate and the existence of unorganised money/securities market and the absence of suitable financial assets, there is a strong case for including inflation rate and inflationary expectations as the relevant proxy for opportunity cost and an extra determinant in the money demand function. In the present study, we have considered both the variables in formulating alternative money demand specifications.

Variability of Rate of Inflation

The use of inflation and inflationary expectations in the money demand function has been clearly established after the work of Friedman (1968) and Cagan (1969). Further, after the work of Blejer (1979), Khan (1977), the empirical literature has emphasised on using variability of rate of inflation as an extra determinant in the money demand function. In India, there are few attempts to substantiate the use of variability of rate of inflation in the money demand function (Kamaiah and Subrahmanyam, 1982; Paul.1981). Again it is necessary to note that the average inflation rate was consistently high, the volatility of it was prominent. During the past four decades, the inflation fluctuated from as high as 25.15 per cent to as low as –12.7 per cent. And also the year to year fluctuation in the rate were prominent. These trends confirm that price stability is an elusive phenomenon in India. To capture the effect of volatile nature of the inflationary movement on demand for real cash, the present study has included the variable in the alternative money demand specifications.

Exchange Rate

Of late, the exchange rate has been used by researchers (Joshi and Sagar, 1995, Nag and Upadhyay, 1993) as a relevant determinant in the money demand function. This is used in the view of the fact that when countries are opened up globally, the exchange rate would reflect the interest rate differential between the trading countries and hence the portfolio decision will be affected. In a developing country like India, where external sector has witnessed far reaching changes including substantial elimination of qualitative controls on imports, reduction in tariffs, a market determined exchange rate system, convertibility on the current account, encouragement to foreign direct investment and greater access to the external capital markets, would certainly have a bearing on the portfolio decision. The above deregulatory measures have an exapnsionary impact on the money supply and at the same time greater access to international capital market. It may mean that the corporate bodies have greater access to funds at rates lower than the domestic interest rates. The innovations have exposed the policy makers to the vulnerability of exchange rate movements. Large scale cross-border movements of capital and increasing tempo of globalisation, in fact, have thrown new challenges for the policy makers to manage liquidity on day-to-day basis. In the present study we have chose the real effective exchange rate as an explanatory variable under the identification presumption as preferred to earlier, in respect of interest rate.

Stock Market Price and Market Capitalisation

After the serious attempt of Friedman (1988) to relate the level of stock prices to the demand for money, studies conducted in India have reformulated their money demand function by including stock market prices as one of the determinants (Paul, 1992 and Joshi and Sagar, 1995). The capital market in India which was laying as a dormant segment of the financial system has undergone metaphoric transformation since the mid eighties involving multi-dimensional growth. The magnitude of growth have been rapid in terms of funds mobilised, the turnover on the stock exchange, the amount of market capitalisation and expansion of investor population. The development of capital market during the 1980s, signifies the widening and the deepening of the market. Since the mid eighties, debenture emerged as a powerful instrument of resource mobilisation in the primary markets. Introduction of public sector bonds since 1985-86, imparted an additional dimension to the market. The growth in the secondary market was also impressive since 1984-85 in terms of increase in the number of institutions, listed companies, their paid-up capitals and market capitalisation. The capital market also witnessed the emergence of several specialised institutions such as SEBI, CRISIL, CARE, ICRA and OCTEI.

The above development in the India stock market thus have brought about a new element in which the demand for money should include the stock prices and market capitalisation to capture the effect on the variation of cash holdings. The present study has used both RBI share index and BSE index and market capitalisation in the money demand specifications.

Scale Variable

The issue concerning the selection of appropriate scale variable is closely linked to the definition of money used and the nature of study-whether long run or short-run. In India, most of the studies have used income (Gujarati, 1968; Gupta, 1973, Joshi and Sagar, 1995; Prasad, 1994; Vasudevan 1979) or permanent income (Gupta, 1987; Mammen, 1970 Paul 1981) as the relevant proxy for scale variable. However, the present study takes only the measured income (Gross Domestic Product) as the scale variable for annual data and Index of Industrial Production for monthly data money demand function.

Monetary Aggregates

The question for appropriate definition of money to be included in the money demand function has been discussed in the literature and concluded that choice depends on the frequency of data used (monthly quarterly or annual), the appropriate scale variable used, coverage of assets, sample period, and method used. The choice ranges from ml to broader definition, or construction of new aggregates (divisia) or individual components - currency, demand deposits. In India, there have been several attempt over the years to estimate the demand for money considering either narrow definition or broad definition of money. Further, in some studies, the demand for money has been analysed by its major components viz., currency, demand deposits and time deposits. However, the present study has included both narrow monetary aggregates, ml (currency + demand deposits + other deposits) and broad monetary aggregates, m3 (ml + time deposits).

Present Study and Methodology

The present study is an empirical study of macro (aggregate) demand for money in India for the period: 1960-61 to 2000-01 and as such does not derived motivation from any of the approaches in isolation. Hence, a standard formulation of the function is adopted in which the salient feature of various conventional approaches have been adopted. Accordingly, demand for money specifications have been formulated with suitable determinants.

In the present study, money has been defined in two ways viz., "narrow" money (ml) and "broad" money (m3) both in real terms. The present study has been carried out on annual data for the period spanning from 1960-61 to 2000-01. For the annual data specifications the real domestic product (RGDP) is chosen to represent the "scale" variable. The opportunity cost is measured by call money rate (CALLRATE), 1-3 year deposit rate (DPRATE), treasury bill rate (TBRATE), yield on debenture (DYRATE), rate of inflation based on WPI (WINEL) and inflationary expectations (IE), market capitalisation (RMCAR) and RBI share index (RSHIDX) as measure of stock market, real effective exchange rate (REER) are also included in the study. The variability of rate of inflation (VRI) as a measure of uncertainty on the price front has also been considered while searching for the determinants of the demand for money. The variable are described in table 1. The Formulated money demand regressions have been estimated using OLS method.

Table 1: Description of Variables

Variables	*Definition*
RM1	Real narrow money which comprises of currency with the public,
	demand deposit with banks and other deposits with RBI
RM3	Real broad money which includes m1 and time deposits with banks
RGDP	Real gross domestic product at factor cost at 1980-81 prices
CALLRATE	Weighted average of call money rate at Mumbai, average of weeks
DPRATE	1-3 year deposit rate
IE	Inflationary expectations
VRI	Variability of rate of inflation
TBRATE	Treasury Bill rate
DYRATE	Yield on debentures
WINFL	Inflation rate based on whole sale price index (WPI) with base 1980-81 = 100
RMCAP	Real market capitalization (Stock markets)
REER	Real effective exchange rate (36 country trade weighted)
RSHIDX	RBI share price index

Note: The variables IE and VRI are not directly observable. The adaptive expectation hypothesis by Cagan (1956) has been used for generating these variables.

Keeping in mind the study of Bank of England and the subsequent debate has generated, some econometric refinements in respect of estimated money demand functions have been carried out by employing some diagnostic tests in the present study. For this purpose, the non-parametric

RUNs test is used to detect autocorrelation problem. The problem of hetrosecedasticity is checked by using Breusch-Pagan (B-P-G) and Harvey tests. The chi-Square test is used to check normality of the residuals. Ramsey's RESET test is employed for investigating into possible misspecificaions.

Empirical Results: OLS Estimates

A number of alternative formulations (specifications with various combinations of determinants) both for m1 and m3 have been estimated. After extensive regressions (experiments), a set of alternative specifications have been identified. These are reported in table 2 and 3 for annual data.

Table 2: Money Demand Specifications: 1960-61 to 2000-01 and 1970-71 to 2000-01

S.No.	*Dependent Variable*	*Independent Variables*
1.	LRM1	LRGDP, DPRATE, LRMCAP
2.	LRM1	LRGDP, CALLRATE, VRI, LRMCAP
3.	LRM1	LRGDP, WINFL, LREER
4.	LRM1	LRGDP, IE
5.	LRM1	LRDGDP, IE, VRI
6.	LRM1	LRGDP, IE, LREER
7.	LRM3	LRGDP, DPRATE, LRMCAP
8.	LRM3	LRGDP, CALLRATE, VRI, LRMCAP
9.	LRM3	LRGDP, WINFL, LREER
10.	LRM3	LRGDP, IE
11.	LRM33	LRGDP, IE, VRI
12.	LRM3	LRGDP, IE, LREER

Results for the Total Period: 1960-61 to 2000-01

Table 4 contains the OLS estimates of alternative money demand specification presented in table 2 (a). In the table, the first six equations have real narrow money (ml) and the

Table 3: Money Demand Specifications: 1970-71 to 2000-01

S.No.	*Dependent Variable*	*Independent Variables*
1	LRM1	LRGDP, DYRATE, LRSHIDK
2.	LRM1	LRGDP, DYRATE, VRI, LRMCAP
3.	LRM1	LRGDP, DPRATE, LRSHIDX
4.	LRM1	LRGDP, DPRATE, VRI, LRMCAP
5.	LRM1	LRGDP, TBRATE, LRSHIDX
6.	LRM1	LRGDP, TBRATE, VRI, LRMCAP
7.	LRM3	LRGDP, DYRATE, LRSHIDK
8.	LRM3	LRGDP, DYRATE, VRI, LRMCAP
9.	LRM3	LRGDP, DPRATE, LRSHIDX
10.	LRM3	LRGDP, DPRATE, VRI, LRSHIDX
11.	LRM3	LRGDP, TBRATE, LRSHIDX
12.	LRM3	LRGDP, TBRATE, VRI, LRMCAP

next six real broad money (m3) as the dependent variable. Both are measured in logs. The estimated t-ratios are presented in the parentheses below respective coefficients. In the first specification, it is shown that the real income variable (LRGDP) is highly significant with appropriate sign. The interest rate variable (DPRATE) comes out with expected negative sign though not significant. The market capitalisation (LRMCAP) is highly significant with positive sign. The income coefficients are significant at 1 per cent level. The estimated $\bar{R}2$ is 0.98. In the second specification, deposit rate is replaced by call money rate (CALLRATE). A measure of variability of expected rate of inflation (VRI) is included as an additional determinant in the specification. Both income and market capitalisation are found to be significant at 1 per cent level. Here also LRMCAP comes out with a positive sign. Call money rate comes out with a negative coefficient without being significant. Further, VRI

Table 4: OLS Estimates of Demand for Money Functions: Annual Data 1960-61 to 2000-01

	Independent Variables										
Dependent Variable	Constant	LRGDP	DPRATE	CALLRATE	WINEL	IE	VRI	LREER	LRMCAP	$\bar{R}^2$	D.W.
LRM1	-2.4652	0.8754* (8.9674)	-0.0249 (-1.5349)						0.1294* (6.5911)	0.98	1.05
LRM1	-1.6547	0.7754* (11.2656)		-0.0063 (-1.3246)			0.0022 (0.2924)		0.1342* (4.4178)	0.98	9.98
LRM1	-9.6782	1.5643* (10.0553)			-0.0022 (-0.7429)			0.4537** (2.4751)		0.96	0.62
LRM1	-3.6754	1.0843* (24.0156)				-0.0195* (-3.0235)				0.97	0.41
LRM1	-2.7895	1.0435* (34.3312)				-0.0207* (-3.8547)	-0.0241* (-3.8868)			0.98	0.55

(Table Contd.)

Table 4: Contd.

LRM1	-8.6785	1.4250*				-0.0169*		0.3660		0.97	0.61
		(11.1412)				(-2.7221)		(2.1584)			
LRM3	-9.8754	1.5721*	-0.0263						0.0268	0.98	0.76
		(13.9054)	(-1.2502)						(1.0492)		
LRM3	-8.5054	1.5244*		-0.0060			0.0087		0.0478	0.97	0.68
		(17.7222)		(-0.9855)			(0.8862)		(1.3359)		
LRM3	-13.6574	1.9361*			-0.0023			0.3131		0.98	0.88
		(15.0891)			(-0.8614)			(1.9039)			
LRM3	-9.8765	1.7269*				-0.0173*				0.99	0.71
		(42.2891)				(-3.1039)					
LRM3	-9.7654	1.7252*				-0.0173*	-0.0010			0.99	0.71
		(38.9694)				(-3.0617)	(-0.1576)				
LRM3	-12.8734	1.8284*				-0.0153*		0.2319		0.99	0.89
		(15.2667)				(-2.8207)		(1.5295)			

Note: t-values are presented in the parentheses.
* indicates significance at 1 per cent level
** indicates significance at 5 per cent level.

is not significant even at 5 per cent level, though it posses a positive sign. The goodness of fit is statistically sound. The third specification introduces inflation rate (WINFL) based on whole sale price index as a proxy for opportunity cost variable. Though the variable comes out with the expected sign, it lacks statistical significance. The real effective exchange rate (REER) shows positive influence on holding real cash balances. The specification in terms of R2 seems to be quite satisfactory. In subsequent specifications (specification (4) to (6)), inflationary expectations is introduced as a proxy for opportunity cost variable. In the fourth specification, both income and inflationary expectation (IE) variables are significant at 1 per cent level with appropriate sign. In the fifth specification, variability of rate of inflation (VRI) is added to the specification. Here also LRGDP and IE are found to be significant at 1 per cent level. VRI is shown to be highly significant with a negative sign. The sixth specification as well shows that LRGDP and IE are significant determinants of the money demand function. Thus the overall results from specification (4) to (6) show says that in addition to income, inflationary expectations (IE) and variability of expected rate of inflation (VRI) have been shown to be significant determinants of ml.

The results of m3 aggregate (equations (7) to (12) of table 2 (a)) are more or less similar to those of ml. In equation (7) (the first specification for m3), deposit rate (DPRATE) has also a negative coefficient without being statistically significant. Market capitalisation (LRMCAP) also comes out with a positive coefficient without being statistically significant. In equation (8), CALLRATE as a proxy for opportunity cost variable comes out with expected sign without being significant. The financial wealth variable (LRMCAP) shows a positive elasticity without being significant. Results from equation (9) show the statistical insignificance of estimated coefficient of inflation (WINFL) and exchange rate variable (LREER) in m3 specification.

However, the inflation coefficient possess expected negative sign. Specification (10) to (12), however, vindicate the empirical appropriateness of surrogating the opportunity cost of holding money by IE in the broad (m3) money demand functions. Further, VRI though comes out with the same negative coefficient, however, lacks statistical significance. All the estimated specifications (7) to (12) are found to fit the data quite well, as reflected in the high $\bar{R}2$ values.

The results in table 4 shows that the income elasticity of demand for real cash balances ranges from 0.72 to 1.42 for the m1 specifications while it ranges from 1.52 to 1.82 for m3 specifications. In all the cases, save two cases where it is less than one, it is greater than unity indicating diseconomies of holding real cash. It is worth noting here that for m1 definition of money in all cases, including interest rate variable leads to reduction in income elasticity parameter below unity. Whereas, the inclusion of price variable (inflation or inflationary expectations) leads to changing the income elasticity magnitude from below unity to above unity for all the specifications. The m3 functions have higher income elasticity with magnitude greater than unity. Here also the specifications containing interest rate variable as one of the determinants reflects lower income elasticity compared to the specifications without it. It is also evident that the interest rate coefficients are low and statistically not significant though having the proper algebraic sign. The numeric values being very small supports Friedman's idea that interest rate is an unimportant variable.

From the above findings for the sample period: 1960-61 to 2000-01, a few implications may be drawn. First, the long run income elasticity is greater than unity in most of the equations implying that a proportionate changes in income requires a more than proportionate change in money balances to sustain it. Secondly, the lack of significant evidence in respect of influence of rate of interest on demand for money in India may be attributed to the less developed money market and lack of representative rate of interest due to thorny data problem. Further, the absence of an active speculative market especially in the early part of the sample period seems to be responsible for the inconsistent and insignificant evidence of rate of interest in the demand for money in India. This is somewhat convincing, as the finding refers to the total period starting from 1960-61. Thirdly, the evidence on inflationary expectations shows that people do adjust their portfolio with non-money assets as inflation rises. With an underdeveloped financial market, lack of appropriate financial assets, a few commercial papers and bills in a developing country like India, especially during the early periods, would substantiate the importance of physical assets as substitute for money. A positive elasticity for real effective exchange rate implies that the exchange rate depreciation reduces the real wealth and hence the demand for real cash balances. A positive and significant elasticity on market capitalisation reveals that people do demand more cash balances in the face of increasing financial wealth.

Results for the sub-Period: 1970-71 to 2000-01

The regression estimates for sub-period: 1970-71 to 2000-01 are presented in tables 5 and 6 Table 5 presents the estimates of alternative money demand specifications that are presented in table 1.2(a) for the sub-period 1970-71 to 2000-01. In the first specification, DPRATE comes out with insignificant coefficient though holds proper sign. The LRMCAP though loses significance, still remained significant at 5 per cent level in explaining the variation in demand for real cash. In the second specification, CALLRATE remained statistically insignificant and the coefficients of VRI and LARMACAP bear positive sign though not significant. Surprisingly, in the third specification, (inflation rate) bear a positive sign for the sub-period. In the remaining three specifications for ml money (specifications (4), (5) and (6), the IE variable loses its significance though possesses appropriate sign. This variable is significant at 5 per cent level for specification (4) and (5). However, the VRI variable comes out with the appropriate negative sign without being significant satirically.

The second half of the table 5 contains estimates of equations for m3 aggregates. They shows that again the interest rate variables are statistically insignificant in explaining the money demand variation. However, the inflation rate variable turned out with a negative coefficient for m3 function. Here, the LRMACAP bears negative sign though not statistically significant, In specifications (10), (11) and (12), IE though bear a negative sign, is statistically less significant compared to the ml specifications as well as to the total sample results. For m3 specifications, VRI carries a positive coefficient, confirming the evidence in favour of precautionary motive of holding money.

From the sub-sample results it is evident that income elasticity is large compared to the overall period elasticity and statistically highly significant. The coefficients are greater than unity for all ml and m3 specifications. It ranges from 1.18 to 1.21 for ml, and from 1.65 to 2.08 for m3 functions. When compared to the overall period, the interest rte variable remained to be statistically insignificant, IE less significant. Evidence on the financial wealth (LRMCAP) has not been consistent particularly for m3 functions. The estimated elasticities of exchange rate (LREER) do not exhibit significant differences between the whole period and the sub-period.

Table 6 presents OLS estimates of the models involving some additional variables which seen more relevant for this sub-period. The estimates are for the specifications as listed in table 2 (b). The additional variables include, treasury bill rate (TBRATE), deposit yield rate (DYRATE) and RBI ordinary share price index (LRSHIDX). The result shows that the new proxies for interest rate i.e., TBRATE, DYRATE are even not significant statistically. However, they show

Table 5: OLS Estimates of Demand for Money Functions: Annual Data: 1970-71 to 2000-01

Dependent Variable	Constant	LRGDP	DPRATE	CALLRATE	WINFL	IE	VRI	LREER	LRMCAP	$\bar{R}^2$	D.W.
		Independent Variables									
LRM1	-4.4898	1.2023* (10.4411)	-0.0177 (-1.0948)						0.0659* (2.6177)	0.98	1.26
LRM1	-3.9190	1.1861* (12.0886)		-0.0063 (-1.4452)			-0.0001 (-0.0112)		0.0669** (2.2612)	0.98	1.32
LRM1	-6.4313	1.2096* (11.4930)			-0.0012 (-0.4902)			0.0689 (0.3979)		0.96	0.89
LRM1	-5.4903	1.2149* (36.8443)				-0.0102* (-2.6585)				0.98	0.93
LRM1	-4.7801	1.1914* (28.1878)				-0.0125* (-2.6576)	-0.0109 (-1.8109)			0.98	0.97

(Table Contd.)

Table 5: Contd.

LRM1	-6.3380	1.2100*				-0.0101**		0.0690		0.98	0.92
		(12.3637)				(-2.0109)		(0.4326)			
LRM3	-12.1644	2.0857*	-0.0119						-0.0525	0.98	1.15
		(14.1776)	(-0.6003)						(-1.6899)		
LRM3	-11.8453	1.9745*		-0.0066			0.0041		-0.0405	0.98	1.22
		(17.1358)		(-1.2618)			(0.4741)		(-1.1259)		
LRM3	-13.3894	1.9608*			-0.007			0.2838		0.98	0.92
		(14.6946)			(-0.2794)			(1.4733)			
LRM3	-9.8343	1.6579*				-0.0131**				0.99	0.88
		(43.4672)				(-2.3379)					
LRM3	-10.3053	1.8719*				-0.0115	0.0073			0.99	0.99
		(36.3374)				(-1.9922)	(1.0155)				
LRM3	-13.1401	1.9541*				-0.0128**		0.2692		0.99	1.01
		(16.4139)				(-2.3728)		(1.5693)			

Note: t-values are presented in the parentheses.
* indicates significance at 1 per cent level.
** indicates significance at 5 per cent level.

Table 6: OLS Estimates of Demand for Money Functions: Annual Data: 1970-71 to 2000-01

	Independent Variables									
Dependent Variable	*Constant*	*LRGDP*	*DYRATE*	*DPRATE*	*TBRATE*	*VRI*	*LRSHIDX*	*LRMCAP*	R^2	*D.W.*
LRM1	-4.7338	1.2607* (6.4787)	-0.0145 (-1.4263)				0.0395 (0.6864)		0.98	0.99
LRM1	-4.7888	1.2499* (7.2708)	-0.0112 (-0.9022)			0.0013 (0.1772)		0.0365 (0.8349)	0.98	1.03
LRM1	-3.4684	1.1257* (7.4955)		-0.0176 (-1.0555)			0.1013 (2.8441)		0.96	1.19
LRM1	-4.4791	1.1998* (9.9219)		-0.0176 (-1.0559)		0.006 (0.0912)		0.0673* (2.8200)	0.98	1.26
LRM1	-2.7517	1.0559* (7.3562)			-0.0009 (-0.0861)		0.0951 (2.3051)		0.98	1.01

(Table Contd.)

Table 6: Contd.

LRM1	-3.6570	1.1137* (11.2541)			-0.0050 (-0.4235)	0.0026 (0.3286)		0.0746** (2.3231)	0.98	1.12
LRM3	-11.5201	1.9280* (8.1447)	-0.0092 (-0.9777)				-0.0608 (-0.8709)		0.98	1.09
LRM3	-10.8019	1.8591* (8.8808)	-0.0777 (0.5125)			0.0055 (0.6317)		-0.0234 (-0.4410)	0.98	1.08
LRM3	-13.1961	2.0983* (11.6543)		-0.0114 (-0.5698)			-0.0809 (-1.6422)		0.98	1.13
LRM3	-12.0819	1.9968* (13.4736)		-0.0108 (-0.5330)		0.0051 (0.5682)		-0.0413 (-1.1123)	0.98	1.14
LRM3	-12.4882	2.0276* (12.1201)			-0.0090 (0.7009)		-0.0728 (-1.1854)		0.98	1.12
LRM3	-11.5457	1.9285* (16.4717)			-0.0131 (-0.9323)	0.0085 (0.9217)		-0.0171 (-0.3713)	0.98	1.12

Note: t-values are presented in the parentheses.
* indicates significance at 1 per cent level.
** indicates significance at 5 per cent level.

negative influence on the narrow money holding. It is to be noted that the share price index LRSHIDX and LMRCAP positively explain the ml demand for money whereas, it has a negative impact on the m3 money demand. The income elasticity for ml is found to be around unity while for m3 it is above the Freidman's limit of 1.8.

Implications of OLS Estimation Results

Following are the implications drawn from the regression estimates based on the annual data:

(i) The income elasticity is large and statistically significant. This result is in conformity with the monetary experience of developing economies. Large value of income elasticity indicate that the transaction demand for money is more important. The elasticity is more than unity in most of the cases (more than unity in all cases for the sample period 1970-71 to 2000-01) implying that there are no economies of scale in holding money and a proportionate change in income requires more than proportionate change in money to sustain it. Income elasticities of demand for money are found to be significantly greater than one and neighbourhood of two supports the monetarists hypothesis that money holding is a luxury in India.

(ii) The statistical insignificance of the interest rate variables as a proxy for the opportunity cost of holding money does not seems to be a suitable variable for monetary management in India. This may be attributed to the presence of less developed money market, lack of representative interest rate and/or data problem for a useful interest rate. As Kamath (1984) in his study of demand for money in India has put forward the following hypothesis, "Physical assets served as substitute for money in

developing countries rather than financial assets since there are few alternative financial assets available for wealth holders due to the underdeveloped financial markets",

(*iii*) On the basis of the above hypothesis, the study introduced inflationary expectations under the economic logic that this variable which represents the return on one of the ways in which wealth could be held, will work as a useful surrogate to the opportunity cost variable in a developing country like India. The significance of inflationary expectation reflects the tendency of reallocatign non-money assets into the portfolio in the situation of continuous price rise. This also substantiate the important characteristics of money as a store of value. When price are expected to rise, its function as a store of value reduces and money holders shift out of money into physical assets as a store of value.

(*iv*) The positive effect of the financial wealth variable reflects the wealth effect dominating the substitution effect in Indian money/securities market. Again, the real stock prices are positively related to the money demand supporting the presence of wealth effect of stock prices in holding real money balances.

(*v*) A positive sign on the real effective exchange rate implies that a depreciation of the domestic currency decreases the demand for real balances. This could mean that by raising the price level, exchange rate depreciating reduce real wealth and hence demand for real money balances. The effect more than offsets the absorption reducing effect of exchange rate depreciation through a rise in wealth on account of the net debtor's positions in terms of ownership claims on rest of the world.

Diagnostic Tests

In most of the previous studies in India, money demand functions are estimated using the OLS method without paying due attention to the possible econometric problem that arises out of violation of the standard OLS assumptions. Hence, to have a more accurate conclusions, It is felt necessary to carry out some diagnostic tests on the estimated models. For this purpose, we have performed the non-parametric Run's test to detect the auto correlation problem. The problem of heteroscedasticity is checked by using both Breusch-Pagan (B-P-G) and Harvey text. The $\chi 2$ test is used to check normality of the residuals and the study made use of Ramsey's RESET test for investigating into possible misspecification in the function. The description of these tests are given in the methodology section of this chapter. The results of these tests are presented in Table 7, 8 and 9 for annual data.

Table 7 presents diagnostic test result for 12 alternative specification for the period: 1960-61 to 2000-01. From the test statistics of B-P-G and Harvey test for heteroscedasticity, it is revealed that all the test statistics, except for specifications (10) and (11), fall within the 5 per cent acceptance region. Hence, it may be safely concluded that most of the specifications are free from the heterocsedasticity problem. From $\chi 2$ test of normality of residuals, it is found that all the specifications have normal residuals. The presence of homoscedasticity in the estimated equations does not rule out the possibility of autocorrelated errors in time series data. Hence testing for autocorrlelation is also carried out in this study using non-parametric Run's test. The calculated Runs for all the specifications are equal to or less than the critical values of Runs at 0.05 level of significance. Hence, the null hypothesis of random sequence of error is rejected for all the specifications. Thus, the formulated models for ml or m3 seem to suffer from autoceorrelated error.

To check the possible misspecification in the money demand function, we have applied Ramsey's RESET test. The

Table 7: Diagnostic Tests: Annual Data: 1960-61 to 2000-01

Specifications *	*Runs Test of Autocorrelation (RUNS)*	*CHI-Sq Test Normality (χ^2 Values)*	*BPG Test Heteroscedastcity (χ^2 Values)*	*Harvey Heteroscedasticity (χ^2 Values)*	*RESET Misspecificatio (F Values)*
1	11 runs (21p, 15n)	1.4959 (2)	0.1244 (3)	1.8203 93)	0.0051 (1.31)
2	11 rus (16p, 20n)	1.0959 (2)	1.3712 (4)	4.7621 (4)	0.2214 (1,30)
3	11. runs (17p, 19n)	1.4804 (2)	1.1760 (3)	1.3890 (3)	36.3330 (1,32)
4	9 runs (20p, 16n)	0.6826 (2)	4.4312 (2)	0.6511 (2)	52.6361 (1, 32)
5	7 RUNS (19P, 17N)	0.4978 (2)	6.8250 (3)	0.2500 (3)	46.258 (1.31)

Table 7: Contd.

6	13 runs (20p, 16n)	1.4137 (2)	2.1270 (3)	1.9730 (3)	40.056 (1,31)
7	10 runs (21p, 15n)	0.8608 (2)	3.8830 (3)	3.8112 (3)	1.2676 (1.31)
8	8 runs (19p, 17n)	0.6365 (2)	5.5500 (4)	9.0666 (4)	0.2219 (1, 30)
9	12 runs (17p, 19n)	0.1972 (2)	6.2900 (3)	7.4300 (3)	0.6784 (1, 31)
10	14 runs (18p, 18n)	0.2489 (1)	8.5420 (2)	9.4771 (2)	1.6276 (1, 32)
11	14 rus (18p, 18n)	0.2444 (2)	8.6691 (3)	11.5821 (3)	1.8498 (1, 31)
12	12 runs (19p, 17n)	0.5152 (2)	7.6332 (3)	5.6241 (3)	0.7447 (1, 31)

Note: p and n inside parentheses of column (2) refer to positive and negative runs respectively.
Degrees of freedom are presented inside parentheses.
*Specifications (1) to (12) are the same as listed in table 1.2(a)

Table 8: Diagnostic Tests: Annual Data: 1970-71 to 2000-01

Specifications *	*Runs Test of Autocorrelation (RUNS)*	*CHI-Sq Test Normality (χ^2 Values)*	*BPG Test Heteroscedastcity (χ^2 Values)*	*Harvey Heteroscedasticity (χ^2 Values)*	*RESET Misspecificatio (F Values)*
1	11 runs (14p, 12n)	0.0939 (2)	2.1303 (3)	2.6941 (3)	0.1884 (1.21)
2	11 runs (14P, 12N)	0.0438 (2)	0.4832 (4)	2.7921 (4)	1.6731 (1,20)
3	9 runs (13p, 13n)	0.3579 (2)	8.0830 (3)	9.1221 (3)	4.7842 (1,21)
4	11 runs (11p, 15n)	1.5071 (2)	1.3971 (2)	0.9952 (2)	0.9818 (1,22)
4	11 runs (11p, 15n)	1.5046 (2)	2.0991 (3)	1.7781 (3)	1.0155 (1,21)

Table 8: Contd.

6	11 runs (11p, 15n)	1.5045 (2)	1.4400 (3)	1.1370 (3)	1.1695 (1,21)
7	11 runs (11p, 15n)	0.5350 (2)	2.8242 (3)	0.3992 (3)	5.2323 (1.21)
8	11 runs (12p, 14n)	0.5900 (2)	1.5630 (4)	2.3861 (4)	8.0946 (1,20)
9	11 runs (12p, 14n)	0.7202 (2)	3.5270 (3)	1.8901 (3)	7.2491 (1,21)
10	7 runs (12p, 14n)	0.4843 (1)	5.5362 (2)	1.7612 (2)	14.8321 (1,22)
11	7 runs (11p, 15n)	0.4786 (2)	4.7761 (3)	3.7453 (3)	13.2381 (1,21)
12	11 runs (13p, 13n)	0.7278 (2)	3.7573 (3)	1.5721 (3)	11.5691 (1,21)

Note: p and n inside parentheses of column (2) refer to positive and negative runs respectively.
Degrees of freedom are presented inside parentheses.
*Specifications (1) to (12) are the same as listed in table 1.2(a)

Table 9: Diagnostic Tests: Annual Data: 1970-71 to 2000-01

Specifications *	*Runs Test of Autocorrelation (RUNS)*	*CHI-Sq Test Normality (χ^2 Values)*	*BPG Test Heteroscedastcity (χ^2 Values)*	*Harvey Heteroscedasticity (χ^2 Values)*	*RESET Misspecificatio (F Values)*
1	11 runs (15p, 11n)	0.7584 (2)	3.7022 (3)	5.2881 (3)	0.9261 (1, 21)
2	11 runs (13p, 13n)	.3455 (2)	4.4291 (4)	8.6392 (4)	1.6562 (1, 20)
3	9 runs (15p, 11n)	0.1768 (2)	3.7602 (3)	1.9850 (3)	0.0073 (1, 21)
4	11 runs (12p, 14n)	0.1688 (2)	2.2253 (4)	3.0163 (4)	0.3945 (1, 22)
5	7 runs (13p, 13n)	0.1522 (2)	6.1330 (3)	3.3280 (3)	0.2120 (1, 21)

Table 9: Contd.

6	11 runs (12p, 14n)	0.2947 (2)	3.8562 (4)	3.5480 (4)	0.1767 (1, 21)
7	11 runs (12p, 14n)	3.0329 (2)	3.1350 (3)	5.0352 (3)	4.2099 (1, 21)
8	11 runs (12p, 14n)	0.8979 (2)	3.8820 (4)	2.3231 (4)	6.0308 (1, 20)
9	9 runs (12p, 14n)	1.0587 (2)	2.6301 (3)	0.4380 93)	5.2775 (1, 21)
10	11 runs (11p, 15)	0.2399 (1)	3.0150 (4)	1.6921 (4)	6.0336 (1, 20)
11	9 runs (13p, 13n)	1.8626 (2)	2.4421 (3)	1.0211 (3)	4.2139 (1, 21)
12	11 runs (10p. 16n)	0.6389 (2)	2.8572 (4)	12.3912 (4)	5.8466 (1, 20)

Note: p and n inside parentheses of column (2) refer to positive and negative runs respectively.
Degrees of freedom are presented inside parentheses.
*Specifications (13) to (24) are the same as listed in table 1.2(b)

estimated F-values for the RESET test shows that for specifications (3), (4), (5) and (6), the calculated values are more that the 5 per cent critical values. However, for all m3 specifications (specification (7) to (12)), the calculated values are well within the critical limit. From the above, it is clear that most of the m1 specifications suffers from misspecification error in contrast to the m3 specifications. The misspecification in the m1 money demand functions may be due to omission of some relevant interest rate variable or the way inflationary expectation is modelled.

Table 8 and 9 presents the estimated statistics of various diagnostic test for the specifications listed in table 1.2(a) and 1.2(b) for the sub-period: 1970-71 to 2000-01. First, we will analyse the results presented in table 8 (specifications (1) to (12). From the Run's text it is known that except specifications (10) and (11), all other are free from auto correlation problem. In all these cases, the estimated Run's fall within the critical range of runs at the 0.05 level of significance. From the B-P-G and Harvey test, it is known that all, save one (specification (3)) are free from heteroscedasticity problem. In other worlds, for all most all the specifications, the residuals have equal variance or spread. From the $\chi 2$ test of normality, it is seen that none of the equations confirm non-normal errors. Further, through Ramsey's RESET test it is confirmed that all the ml money demand specifications, except specification (3), are free from misspecification. However, in contrast to the evidence for ml specification, all the m3 specification are found to be misspecified. Table 9 presents the diagnostic results for the remaining specifications (specifications (13) to (24) for the period: 1970-71 to 200-01. The result from Run's test show that all but specification (17), are free from autocorrelation error. From the B-P-G test, it is found that all the specifications are free from heteroscedasticity problem. Further, from Harvey test it is confirmed that only specification (14) and (24) suffer from the problem of heteroscedasticity. $\chi 2$ test confirms normality of residuals for all specifications. From the F-values of RESET test we could reject the hypothesis of no-mispecification for all ml money demand functions. However, the test statistics revealed that all the m3 functions are misspecified.

The main findings of the diagnostic tests for the total as well as sub-periods together for the annual data as follows:

(i) The $\chi 2$ test of normality of residuals shows that the money demand functions have normal residuals.

(ii) The B-P-G and Harvey tests show that the problem of heteroscedasticity is not present in most of the money demand specifications.

(iii) The non-parametric Run's test reveals that for the total period, most of the specifications considered are having auto correlated errors. Whereas, for the sub-period data, very few suffer from the problem of randomnes of errors.

(iv) The Ramsey's RESET test for total sample shows that most of the m1 specifications suffer from misspecification. In contrast, the result for sub-period show that all the m3 specifications are mis-specified.

Concluding Remarks

The main focus of this chapter is to re-evaluate the performance of the money demand specifications in the context of identifying suitable determinants. The major concern of this effort is to find out appropriate channel of monetary transmission mechanism or the routes of the effects of monetary policy operations. The major conclusions that emerge from this analytical and empirical study are as follows.

The income elasticity of the demand for money is positive, statistically significant and in most of the cases greater than unity. This result clearly suggests that there is no economies of scale in holding money and a proportionate change in the income requires more than proportionate change in money to sustain it. Again, the result suggests that money is considered to be a luxury asset in India. This result may be ascribed to the fact that people are willing to forego the premium received from holding assets in illiquid form. Moreover, the large value of income elasticity indicates that transaction demand for money is important. The statistical insignificance of the interest rate variables implies that interest rate can not be a suitable variable for monetary management variable in India. This implies that interest rate fail to become an appropriate proxy for opportunity cost variable in the context of India. The results obtained from fitting inflationary expectations as an opportunity cost variable suggest an expected sign and statistically significant. This suggests the importance of physical assets in people's portfolio in the country like India.

The insignificant influence of the rate of interest on the demand for money in India may be attributed to the less developed money and capital markets and lack of a representative interest rate. This may be true as our study period starts from 1960s onwards. Moreover, the lack of speculative demand for money (which is mainly a function of rate of interest) also seems to be responsible for the insignificant effect of rate of interest on the demand for money in India.

The demand for real cash balances is positively and significantly related to the movement of real stock prices. The positive relation appears to reflect a wealth and/or transaction effect. Further, in Indian context, the transaction effect cannot be ruled out and difficult to be separated from the wealth effect. The result also suggest that the demand side has been influenced more directly with the development in the capital market having pronounced bearing on the money market.

The effects of exchange rate on the level of real money balances show different results for annual and monthly money demand specifications. For annual data it confirms the positive effect whereas for the monthly demand specifications it confirms negative effects (absorption reducing effect). This suggests either of the following reasons: (i) the absorption effect is only a temporary short run phenomenon, which peters out in the long run and even on an annual basis, or (ii) the absorption reducing effect is only a recent phenomenon of the 1980s and 1990, which may even continue in future.

From the above conclusions, the following implications may be drawn for the effective operation of monetary policy in India. The ineffectiveness of the interest rate shows the lack of response mechanism through the changes in the interest rate. Under such a situation, monetary authorities should go for a complete deregulation of interest rate. Further, the results indicates that the expectations about future price level plays a crucial role in determining the demand for money. The results also show that, exchange rate is gradually emerging as an alternative route through which monetary impulses could be transmitted to the economy. The asset prices of the capital market provides sufficient clues for becoming the channels of transmitting the monetary policy operations. The market capitalisation used as an explanatory variable turned out to be positive and significant. This suggests that long term assets market has emerged as a possible channel of monetary transmission which supports the hypothesis that money is required for investment purposes.

References

1. Adekunle, J.O., (1968), "The Demand for Money: Evidence from Developed and Less developed Economies", *IMF Staff Papers*, Vol. 15, pp. 220-2y.

2. Artis, M.J. and Lewis, M.K., (1976), "The Demand for Money in the UK", *Manchester School of Economics*, Vol. 44, pp. 147-181.

3. Baba, Y, Hendry, D.F. and Starr, R.M., (1988), "U.S. Money Demand, 1960-1984", *Discussion Paper, NO 88(8),* University of California, San Diego (December).

4. Bahmani-Oskooee, M., (1991), "The Demand for Money in Open Economy", *Applied Economics,* Vol. 22, pp. 917-925.

5. Bahmani-Oṣkooee, M. and Pourhui-Darian, (1990), "Effects of Exchange Sensitivity of Demand for Money in an Open Economy: The UK, *Applied Economics,* Vol. 22.

6. Barnett, W.A., (1982), "Divisia Monetary Aggregate: Their Compilation, Data and Historical Behaviour", *Fedral Reserve Board Staff Study, No. 116,* Washington Publication S. services, Fedral Reserve Board.

7. Barnett, W.A., (1987), "The Microeconomic Theory of Monetary Aggregation" in W.A. Barnett and K.J. Singleton (eds.), *New Approaches to Monetary Economics,* Cambridge: Cambridge University Press, pp. 115-168.

8. Baumol, W.J., (1952), "The transaction demand for Cash: An inventory Theoretic Approach", Quarterly Journal of Economics, yy.

9. Bhattacharya, B.B., (1974), "Demand and Supply of Money in a Developing Economy: A Structural Analysis for India", *The Review of Economic and Statistics,* Vol. 56, pp. 502-510.

10. Bhole, L.M., (1985), *"Impacts of Monetary Policy",* Himalayan Publishing House; Bombay.

11. Biswas, D., (1962), "The Indian Money Market: An analysis of Demand for Money", *Indian Economic Journals,* Vol. 9, pp. 308-323.

12. Blejer, M.I., (1979), "The Demand for Money and the Variability of the Rate of Inflation: Some Empirical Results,", *International Economic Journal,* Vol. 47, pp. 579-591.

14. Branson, W.H. and Buiter, W.H., (1983), Monetary and Fiscal Policy with Flexible Exchange Rates, in J.S. Bhandari and R.H. Putram (eds.), *Economic Independence and Flexible Exchange Rate,* M.I.T. Press.

15. Brunner, K. and Meltzer, A., (1963), "Predicting Velocity: Implication for Theory and Policy", *Journal of Finance,* Vol. 18, pp. 319-354.

16. Brunner, K. and Meltzer, A., (1971), "The use of Money: Money in the Theory of Exchange Economy", *American Economic Review.* Vol. 61, pp. 784-805.

17. Cagan, P., (1956), "The Monetary Dynamics of Hyper Inflation, in M. Friedman (eds.) *Studies in Quantity Theory of Money,* Chicago: Chicago University Press.

18. Carr. J. and Darby, M., (1981), "The Role of Money Supply Shocks in the Short run Demand for money, *Journal of Monetary economics,* Vol. 8, pp. 183-199.

19. Chetty, V.K., (1969), "On the Nearness of Near Moneys", *American Economic Review,* Vol. 73, pp. 270-281.

20. Chow, G.C., (1966), "On the Long run and Short run Demand for Money", *Journal of Political Economy,* April, pp. 111-131.

21. Coghlan, R., (1978), "A Transaction Demand for Money", *Bank of England Quarterly Bulletin,* Vol. 18, pp. 48-60.

22. Corrado, C. and Spindt, P., (1986), "The measurement and Analysis of Monetary Transaction, *Mimeo.*

23. Cramer, J.S., (1981), "The Volume of Transaction and Payments in the United Kingdom, 1968-1977, *Oxford Economic Papers,* Vol. 33, pp. 234-255.

24. Cramer, J.A., (1986), "The Volume of Transaction and the circulation of Money in the United States: 1950-1979, *Journal of Business and Economics Statistics,* Vol. 4, pp. 225-232.

25. Croker, R., (1990), "Wealth, Financial Liberalisation and the Demand for Money in Japan", *IMF Staff Papers,* Vol. 73, pp. 270-281.

26. Dornbush, R.S. and Fischer, S.S, (1981), "*Macroeconomics,* Mcgraw Hill: Newyork (2nd eds.).

27. Fiege, E.L., (1967), "Expectation and Adjustments in the Monetary Sector", *American Economic Review,* Vol. 57, pp. 462-473.

28. Fisher, I (1911), "The Purchasig Power of Money, New York.

29. Frankel, J.A., (1977), "The Forward exchange rate and the Demand for Money: The German Hyperinflation, *American Economic Review,* Vol. 67, pp. 653-670.

30. Friedman, M., (1956), "The Quantity Theory of Money: A Restatement, in M. Friedman (ed.), *Studies in the Quantity Theory of Money,* Chicago: University of Chicago Press.

31. Friedman, M., (1959), The Demand for Money: Some theoretical and Empirical Results", *Journal of Political Economy,* Vol. 67, pp. 327-350.

32. Friedman, M., (1988), "Money and Capital Market, *Journal of Political Economy,* Vol. 92, pp. 221-245.

33. Friedman, M. and Meiselman, D., (1963), "The Relative Stability of Monetary Velocity and the Investment Multiplier in the United States, 1897-1958", in *Stabilisation Policies,* Prentice Hall.

34. Frowen, S.F. and Arestis, P., (1976), "Some Investigations of Demand and Supply Functions for Money in the Federal Republic of Germany, 1965-1974". *Weltwirtshaftliches Archiv,* Vol. 112, pp. 136-164.

35. Goldfeld, S.M., (1973), "The Demand for Money Revisited", *Brooking Papers on Economic Activity,* Vol. 3, pp. 577-638.

36. Goldfeld, S.M., (1976), "The Case of Missing Money, *Brooking Papers on Economic Activity,* Vol. 3, pp. 683-739.

37. Goldfeld, S.M. and Sichel, D., (1987), "Money Demand: The Effects of Inflation and Alternative Adjustment Mechisms, *Review of Economic and Statics,* Vol. 69, p. 511-515.

38. Gordon, R.J., (1984), "The Short-run demand for Money: A Reconsideration, *Journal of Money, Credit and Banking,* Vol. 16, p. 403-434.

39. Grice, J. and Bennett, A., (1984), "Wealth and the Demand for M3 in the United Kingdom 1963-1978", *Manchester School.*

40. Gujarti, D.S., (1968), "The Demand for Money in India", *Journal of Development Studies,* Vol. 5, pp. 59-64.

41. Gupta, G.S., (1973), "A Monetary Policy Model for India", *Sankhya,* Series B, December.

42. Gupta, G.S., (1987), "Demand for Money: An Empirical Estimation of Unsettled Issues for India, *Prajnan,* Vol. 15, pp. 463-476.

43. Gupta, K.L., (1970), "The Demand for Money in India; Further Evidence", *Journal of Development Studies,* Vol. 6, pp. 159-168.

44. Gupta, S.B., (1979), "Monetary Planning for India", *Oxford University Press,* New Delhi.

45. Hetzel, L.R. and Mehra, Y.P., (1989), "The Behaviour of Money Demand in 1980s", *Journal of Money, Credit and Banking,* Vol. 21, pp. 455-463.

46. Hamburger, M.J., (1977), "behaviour of the Money Stocks; Is there a Puzzle?", *Journal of Monetary Economics,* Vol. 3, pp. 263-288.

47. Jadhav, N., (1994), "*Monetary Economics for India,* MacMillan: New Delhi, Chapter 5.

48. Joshi, H. and Saggar, M., (1995), "The Demand for Money in India, Stability Revisited", *RBI Occasional Papers,* Vol. 16, pp. 79-97.

49. Judd, J.P. and Scadding, J.L., (1982), "The Search for the a Stable Money Demand Function; A Survey of Post-1973 Literature", *Journal of Economic Literature,* Vol. 20, pp. 993-1023.

50. Kamaiah, B. and Paul, M.T., (1979), "An Empirical Study of Velocity of Money Function in India: 1951-52 to 1974-75", *Vishleshan,* Vol. 5, pp. 314-324.

51. Kamaiah, B. and Subrahmanyam, G., (1982), "Variability of Expectations and the Demand for Money in India, 1951-1978", *Margin,* Vol. 14, pp. 61-67.

52. Kamaiah, B. and Paul, T. and Others, (1987), "Velocity of Money in India, A Time Series Analysis, Working Paper, NIBM.

53. Kamath, S.J., (1984), The Demand for Money in India—1951-76: Theoretical aspects and Empirical Evidence", *Indian Journal of Economics,* Vol. 65, pp. 131-172.

54. Kavanagh, N.J. and Walters, A.A., (1963), "The Demand for Money in the United Kingdom, 1877-1961: Preliminary Findings, in H.G. Johson et al. Readings in British Monetary Economics, Oxford: Clarendon Press.

55. Khan, M., (1977), "The Variability of Expectations in Hyperinflation", *Journal of Political Economy,* Vol. 85, pp. 817-827.

56. Khatan, C.P. and Waghmare, R.R., (1971), "Monetary Adjustment in India", *Indian Economic Journal,* Vol. 18, pp. 496-513.

57. Klein, B., (1974), "Comptitive Interest Payments on bank deposits and long run demand for money, *America Economic Review,* Vol. 64, pp. 931-949.

58. Klein, B., (1977), "The Demand for Quality adjusted Cash balances: Price Uncertainty in the US Demand for Money function", *Journal of Political Economy,* Vol. 85, pp. 691-715.

59. Koot, R.S., (1975), "Non-Constant Coefficient of Expectation and the recent Development for Money, *Journal of Monetary Economic,* Vol. 1, pp. 375-382.

60. Laidler, D., (1966), "The Rate of Interest and the Demand for Money: Some Empirical Evidence", *Journal of Political Economy,* Vol. 74, pp. 55-68.

61. Laidler, D., (1969), "The Definition of Money: Theoretical and Empirical Problems", *Journal of Money Credit and Banking,* Vol. 1, pp. 508-525.

62. Laidler, D., (1977), *"The Demand for Money: Theories and Evidences"*, Second Edition, New York: Dun-Donelly.

63. Laidler, D., (1980), "The Demand for Money in United States yet Again", in *Brunner, Kand Meltzer, A. (ed.). The State of Macroeconomics, Carnegie Rochester Conference Series on Public Policy,* Vol. 12, Amsterdam: North-Holland.

64. Mahajan, Y.L., (1979), "Stability of Demand for Money in India", *Indian Economic Journal,* Vol. 27, pp. 59-109.

65 Mammen, T., (1970), "The Monetary Sector of India: An Econometric Study", *Indian Economic Journal,* Vol. 18, pp. 482-495.

66. Mayer, L.H., (1976), "Alternative Definitions of Money Stocks and the Demand for Money", *Federal Reserve Bank of New York Monthly Review,* pp. 266-274.

67. Melitz, J., (1976), "Inflationary Expectations and The French Demand for Money: 1959-1970", *The Manchestor School,* Vol. 44, pp. 17-41.

68. Meltzer, A.H., (1963), "Demand for Money: The Evidence from Time Series", *Journal of Political Economy,* Vol. 71, pp. 219-246.

69. Mankiw,.G. and Summers, L.H., (1986), "Money Demand and the Effects of Fiscal Policies", *Journal of Money Credit and banking,* Vol. 18, pp. 415-438.

70. Mundell, R.A., (1963), "Capital Mobility and stabilization Policy under Fixed and Flexible Exchange Rates", *Canadian Journal of Economics and Political Science,* November.

71. Nag, A.K., and Upadhyay, G., 1993, "Estimation of Money Demand Function: A Cointegration Approach", *RBI Occasional Papers,* Vol. 14, pp. 47-66.

72. Offenbacher, E.K., (1979), "The Substitution of Monetary Assets", *Mimeographed.*

73. Paul, M.T., (1981), "The Demand for Money and the Variability of rate of Inflation: India 1951-52 to 1977-78", *Indian Journal of Economics,* Vol. 29, p. 65-74.

74. Paul, M.T., (1992), "Demand for Money, Inflation Expectation and Stock Market", *Indian Economic Journal,* Vol. 44, pp. 37-40.

75. Paul, M.T. and Kulkarni, K. (1987), "Supply Shock and Demand for Money in India", *Asian Economic Review,* Vol. 29, pp. 1-16.

76. Prasad, R., (1994), "Determinants of Demand for Money in India", *Indian Journal of Economics,* Vol. 74, pp. 457-470.

77. Rangarajan, C., (1965), "Demand for Money: Some Empirical Estimates Relating to India, *5th Indian Econometric Conference,* Delhi.

78. Radecki, L.J. and Wenninger, J., (1985), "Recent Instability in M1 Velocity", *Federal Reserve bank of New York Quarterly Review*, Vol. 10, pp. 16-22.

79. Rasche, R.H., (1987), "M1 Velocity and Money Demand Function: Do Stable Relation Exist? in *Empirical Studies of Velocity, Real Exchange Rates, Unemployment and Productivity, Edited by Karl Barunner and Allen Meltzer*, pp. 9-88.

80. Roley, V.V., (1985), "Money Demand Predictability", *Journal of Money Credit and Banking*, Vol. 17, pp. 611-641.

81. Rose, A.K., (1985), "Alternative Approach to American Demand for Money", *Journal of Money Credit and Banking*, Vol. 17, pp. 439-455."

82. Sampath, R.K. and Hussain, Z., (1981), "Demand for Money in India", *Indian Economic Journal*, Vol. 29, pp. 17-36.

83. Sapiro, A.A., (1973), "Inflation, lags and the Demand for Money", *International Economic Review*, Vol. 14, pp. 81-96.

84. Sarvane, N., (1971), "The Demand for Money—Sectoral Approach", *Vikash Publications: New Delhi*.

85. Sastry, V.K., (1962), *"Demand for and Supply of Money in India"*, Indian Economic Journal, *pp. 29-38.*

86. Shah, V.C., (1961), *"Demand for Money in India, 1948-59", Indian Economic Review*, Vol. pp. 352-361.

87. Shahi, M., A., (1977), "The Demand for Money: Some Empirical Evidence from Developing Countries, 1960-1974", *Indian Economic Journal*, Vol. 24, pp. 357-368.

88. Sharma, R.L., (1978), "The Demand for Money in India: A Empirical Analysis, *Indian Economic Review*, Vol. 13, pp. 34-43.

89. Singh, A.P., Shetty, S.L. and Venkatachalalam, T.R., (1982), "Monetary Policy in India: Issues ad Evidence", Supplement to the RBI Occasional Papers, 3.

90. Sigh, B., (1969), "Price Stability and Money Supply during Fourth Five Year Plan", *Indian Economic Journal*, Vol., 17, pp. 469-477.

91. Sigh, T., (1984), "Determinants of Demand for Money in India", *Indian Journal of Economics*, Vol. 65, pp. 83-97.

92. Starleaf, D.R. and Reimer, R.S., (1967), "The keynesian Demand function for money: Some statistical tests, *journal of Finance*, Vol. 22, pp. 71-76.

93. Subrahmanyam, G., (1980), "Empirical Definition of Money", Unpublished Ph.D., Thesis, SUNY at Buffalo, Buffalo, USA.

94. Tobin, J., (1956), "The Interest Rate Elasticity of Transaction Demand for Cash", *Review of Economics and Statistics,* Vol. 84, pp. 593-612.

95. Trivedi, M.S., (1979), "Role of Inflationary Expectations in a Simple Model of Demand for Money in India: 1951-52 to 1974-75", *Artha Vikas,* Vol. 15, pp. 43-66.

96. Trivedi, M.S., (1980), "Inflationary Expectations and Demand for Money in India—1951 to 1975", *Indian Economic Journal,* Vol. 28, pp. 62-76.

97. Vasudevan, A., (1977), "Demand for Money in India: A Survey of Literature", *Reserve Bank of India occasional Papers,* Vol. 2, pp. 38-83.

98. Vasudevan, A., (1979), "Demand for Money in India: 1961-62 to 1976-77", *Economic and Political Weekly,* Vol. 14, pp. 1170-1172.

99. Weiinger, J. and Radecki, L.J., (1986), Financial transaction and Demand for m1, *Federal Reserve,* Vol. 11, pp. 24-29.

7

Globalization and Challenges to Bank Regulation in India: Post 1991 Period

Kishore G. Kulkarni*
Meenakshi Rishi**

Introduction

Bank regulation in India has been a daunting task for the Reserve bank of India (RBI hereafter) ever since the major banks were nationalized in 1969. There have been more challenges due to bank transactions, recent declines in interest rates, and bank deregulation prompted since 1991 by Mr. Narasimham and the ability of customers to explore other non banking financial markets.

Indian banks were nationalised in 1969 with the aim of shifting the banks' business. The purpose of nationalisation was to ensure that the banking sector would shift from "class" banking to "mass" banking, from urban banking to rural banking, from profit making motive to service motive, from big customers to small customers, from short term finance to development finance, and from self-interest to social welfare perspectives. While some of these shifts are not mutually exclusive, their effectiveness and validity are at best debatable. What is not debatable however is the fact that since

* Professor, Metropolitan State College of Denver, CO 80217-3362, USA.
** Associate Professor, College of Business Administration, Ohio Northern University, Ada, OH 45810, USA.

nationalization there has been tremendous growth in financial intermediation in the Indian banking sector. According to Dhingra (2001) the household sector's gross saving in the form of financial assets has increased from 5.5 per cent of Net Domestic Product (NDP) in 1965 to 12.5 per cent of NDP in 1990. The population per bank branch has declined from 65,000 in 1969 to 14,500 in 1999. Table 1 highlights the magnitude of growth in 19 biggest banks in India in terms of branches, deposits and advances. As the figures indicate, Indian banks have shown growth not only in terms of number of branches but also in terms of deposits attracted and loans offered over a 50 year period (1947 to 1997).

Despite such tremendous growth in advances, the performance of Indian banks has been largely lackluster since the 1980s characterized by low profitability, high and growing non-performing assets and low capital base. Poor internal controls, lack of proper disclosure norms and stiff competition from better equipped and better managed foreign banks also exposed numerous problems of Indian banks. Fortunately (or unfortunately) Indian banks are not the only ones going through major changes in recent times. Other countries have been opening their economies for a longer time and with a greater speed. The trend of changes in bank functioning is thus in a way, universal.

In this context, Middleton (1996) notes, "Twenty years ago bankers operated in the world of beneficially regulated markets and comfortable cartels which restricted competition, reduced risk and virtually guaranteed attractive profits. As the old insult would have it, the successful banker needed only to the formula 3, 6, 3, namely, 'borrow at 3 per cent, lend at 6 per cent, and be on the golf course by 3 PM'. This pleasant world has been ruptured by the three forces of de-regulation, technology and growing customer sophistication, which coupled with increased volatility in markets and interest rates, has made banking a much less predictable and hence riskier occupation (Middleton, 1996, p. 278)."

Table 1: Indian Banking: Magnitude of Growth (Deposits and Advances are in Rs. crores)

Name	*Branches*		*Deposits*		*Advances*	
	1947	*1997*	*1947*	*1997*	*1947*	*1997*
State Bank of India	362	8883	287	110701	77	62233
Bank of Baroda	38	2493	33	32156	11	16532
Bank of India	31	2474	69	31973	27	18337
Punjab National Bank	196	3765	60	30806	23	14067
Canara Bank	40	2262	5	31445	1	14413
Central Bank of India	285	3087	123	23051	43	8790
Union Bank of India	5	2030	5	20197	1	9612
Indian Overseas Bank	43	1365	7	15973	8	7254
Indian Bank	70	1472	18	13315	3	7873
Syndicate Bank	58	1611	3	14946	2	5832
UCO Bank	57	1796	35	12614	1	4612
Allahabad Bank	70	1863	26	11541	13	4938
Oriental Bank of Commerce	15	773	68	10054	39	4886
Dena Bank	47	143	7	7861	1	4044
Vijaya Bank	13	835	0.3	6827	.27	2734
bank of Maharashtra.	17	1147	2	7365	1	3111
Andhra Bank	41	974	4	7091	3	2907
Punjab and Sind Bank	3	704	3	6400	63	3550
Corporation Bank	32	507	2	6673	1	3015

Source: Dhingra (2001), page 789

In the Indian case specifically, a BOP crisis in 1991 propelled the government to adopt an overall strategy of economic liberalization. Banking sector reforms and financial liberalisation were deemed to be a necessary element of this overall strategy that was oriented toward a liberalization of the real sector of the economy. Thus, the Ministry of Finance commissioned two independent reviews of its banking system. The first commission was called the Committee on Financial System. (Narsimham Report 1991), the second review was submitted by Khan Report. In 1992 several key recommendations of the Narasimham and the Khan reports were accepted and the process of banking sector privatization and reform was formally initiated in the economy.

This paper aims to critically examine the post-reform performance of the Indian banking sector and to identify challenges faced by Indian banks in the current context of global banking. The following section (2) summarizes the key aspects of the 1991-92 banking sector reforms. Section 3 utilizes key indicators of bank performance and profitability to assess the post-reform state of the Indian banking sector. Section 3 concludes the paper by raising the issue of emerging challenges for the sector.

The Banking Sector Reform

The banking Sector reforms of 1992 were aimed at increasing the profitability and efficiency of the public sector banks as well as improving their safety and soundness. In response to the Narasimhan and Khan Reports, many state-owned banks were partially privatized via public issues since 1993. However, as displayed, the strong central government share of equity capital in India's public sector banks continues to be substantial. In 1998, the Committee on Banking Sector Reforms (a successor to the Narsimham Committee) recommended that the minimum shareholding by the government of the RBI equity in nationalized banks be brought down to 33 per cent of total assets. Other features of the reform package were concerned with the following five aspects,

(*a*) The reforms recommended a gradual reduction in the cash reserve ratio (CRR) and the statutory

Table 2: Comparison of central government holdings by major Indian banks after public issue

Bank Name	*Date of Public Issues*	*Current Government Percentage Holding After Public Issue (per cent)*
State Bank of India	December 1993	66.34
State Bank of Bikaner	November 1997	75
State Bank of Baroda	December 1996	66.88
State Bank of Travancore	January 1998	76
Bank of India	February 1997	77
Corporation Bank	October 1997	66.33
Oriental Bank	October 1994	66.48
Dena Bank	December 1996	71

Source: Reserve Bank of India.

liquidity ratio (SLR) to minimise the implicit taxation of the banking system and to beef up its profitability.

(b) Interest rate deregulation was an important element of the bank reform process and was intended to enable commercial banks to compete for funds on par with the capital market and other intermediaries that were not subjected to interest rate controls or to tight credit allocation mechanisms.

(c) Entry of private banks was deregulated in January 1993 and the RBI was charged with the responsibility of financial viability of the new entrants.

(d) Financial soundness and credibility of the banking system also required overhauling the capital adequacy norms and bringing those more in line with international standards as recommended by the BIS (Bank of international settlements). Pursuant

to this, a strategy to introduce the attainment of capital-to-risk-weighted-assets ratio (CRAR) of 8 per cent was adopted. The CRAR was raised to 9 per cent in March 2000.

(*e*) An overall strengthening of the institutional framework for supervision and monitoring was the final element of the reform process. Under this head, both off-site and on-site monitoring mechanisms were put in place and a Board of Financial Supervision was set up in November 1994. In order to be more open to customer needs, a Banking Ombudsman Scheme was instituted in 1995.

A Post-reform Assessment

As of March 2000, the total number of commercial banks in India were 101 of which 27 were Public Sector Banks (PBS), 24 were old private banks, 8 were new private banks and 42 were foreign banks. These banks had total assets worth 11,104 billion Rupees and network of 55,855 branches scattered all over the country. Despite the large number of foreign banks operating in the country, they controlled only 7.5 per cent of the total assets. The banking market is still very much dominated by the Public Sector Banks which controlled the largest share of total assets (about 80 per cent).

A post-reform assessment of the Indian banking sector is organized along the following indicators of performance.

Income: The income of all scheduled commercial banks (SCBs) increased form roughly Rs. 1 trillion to Rs. 1.153 trillion from 1999 to 2000, an increase of 15.3 per cent. As the deposit interest rates and prime lending rates declined in this period, this increased income was mainly from the "non-interest items" such as profit on sale of investments, commission, exchange, brokerage, lease income and profit on exchange transactions. In fact, in this period the interest income declined from 9.2 per cent of the total income to 9 per cent. Again, the dominant banks were PSBs that earned Rs. 909 billion (roughly 79 per cent of the total income earned by all banks). In comparison to this performance by Indian banks, the foreign banks recorded increase in income of only 6.3 per cent, in fact their interest income declined by 3 per cent.

Profitability: Although the question of profitability is moot, especially with regard to the performance of PSBs in India, the latter have been under pressure to increase their profitability. Also, as some public sector banks are listed on the stock exchange and more banks are expected to mobilize funds from the capital market, improvements in profitability become important signals of good performance to existing and prospective investors. Despite the thrust towards profitability, it is hard to discern any significant trends in post-reform profitability of Indian banks. However, as Table 3 shows, net profitability of foreign banks is much higher than the profitability of SCBs even though both sectors showed increased profitability over 1999-2000. The most impressive growth in profitability is in State bank of India (SBI, 82.6 per cent), Old Private banks (110.3 per cent) and Foreign Banks (83.3 per cent). In 2000, major PSBs that reported a drop in their profitability were bank of India, Indian Overseas bank, Dena Bank and Union Bank.

Table 3: Net Profits of Scheduled Commercial Banks

	SBI	*Natl Banks*	*PSB*	*Old Private*	*New Private*	*Private*	*Foreign*	*All SCBs*
1999	14.66	17.88	32.54	3.11	3.97	7.09	5.28	44.90
2000	26.77	24.37	51.14	6.55	5.69	12.25	9.68	73.06
Growth	82.6	36.3	57.2	110.3	43.4	72.8	83.3	62.7

Source: Report on Trend and Progress of Banking.

Return on Assets: A four year trend (from 1997 to 2000) of return on assets indicates that SCBs in India have a declining interest income, a somewhat unchanged non-interest income, a declining total income, somewhat unchanged interest expenditure and operating expenditure resulting in declining operating profits and net profits as a percentage of total assets (ICRA, 2001).

Spreads: Another distinguishing feature of Banks's performance is the decline in spread experienced by PSBs in year 2000 as well as in last decade. Interestingly, while PSBs experienced decline in spread, the foreign banks showed a significant improvement in their spread. The spread is higher when there is a decline in yield in relation to the cost of funds. The primary reason for increased cost was that over the last three years the interest rates in India have declined and 84 per cent of the deposits in commercial banks were for the duration of longer than six months that were attracting higher (older) rates. The proportion of term deposits for longer than six months duration was higher for Indian banks than for foreign banks.

Capital Adequacy: There are basically five ways for Indian PSBs to acquire capital (1) capital injection by the Government of India (2) tapping the private equity capital market domestically (3) tapping private equity market abroad (4) private placement of subordinated bonds and (5) internal capital generation. In March 1993, only one PSB had a CRAR of above 8 per cent, but by March of 2000 only 4 SCBs had CRARs of less than 9 per cent. This is impressive but must be tempered by the fact that most PSBs have been aided in achieving their capital adequacy norms through substantial infusions of capital by the Government. This suggests that PSBs need to diversify their sources of funding avenues and tap non-Governmental avenues more aggressively.

Asset Quality: The asset quality is tested most significantly by observing the share of Non-Performing Assets (NPAs hereafter) in the total assets of a bank. In India, NPAs are defined as a proportion of total advances and usually refers to a credit facility where interest has remained unpaid for a period of four quarters. Indian banking law defines a loan default as one that is unpaid for over two quarters, compared with the international standard of one quarter. Despite this liberal definition, the proliferation of NPAs is currently one of the most critical features of Indian banking. Table 4 reports the net NPAs as a percentage of net advances offered by Public Sector banks, Old Private Sector Banks, New Private Sector Banks and Foreign Banks. As can be observed, foreign banks have only roughly 2.2 per cent of its net advances in NPA category while the Indian banks (old private or public) are struggling to keep that ratio below 7 per cent. Among the factors that have been held responsible for the persistence of NPAs are inadequate credit appraisal skills and inadequate loan recovery by public sector banks (Sarkar, 1999).

Table 4: Net Non-Performing Assets (as a percentage of Net Advances)

	March 31 1998	*March 31 1999*	*March 31 2000*
Public Sector Banks	8.2	8.1	7.4
Old Private sector Banks	6.5	8.4	7.3
New Private Sector Banks	2.6	4.1	2.9
Foreign Banks	2.2	2.0	2.4
All Banks	7.3	7.5	6.8

Source: Report on Trend and Progress of Banking in India, 1999-2000.

Competition: There have been limited signs of competition within the banking sector. The post reform emphasis on deregulation and privatization is beginning to bear modest, yet favorable outcomes. Since 1994, there have been nine new entrants into the banking system. There are signs of service competition as well, with banks making increasing use of computer and telecommunication technology to provide better banking services. The reform process also emphasized the need to increase *outside* competition (financial disintermediation) for the Indian banking sector. This process of financial disintermediation has resulted in an impressive growth of non-bank financial companies (NBFCs) and the capital market in India. On 1992, a Securities and Exchange Board of India (SEBI) was set up to ensure transparency in the Indian capital market.

A post reform assessment of India's banking sector suggests a slow but steady pace of improvement. However, the progress on asset quality has been marginal at best due to the proliferation of NPAs in the banking sector, especially PSBs. Thus, while there have been substantial benefits in the wake of the 1991-92 reforms, several challenges and obstacles have also emerged in the process. The next section discusses some of these challenges and emphasizes the need for a "second generation" reforms designed to address the same.

Emerging Challenges and Obstacles

Globalization of the banking industry presents Indian banks with a unique set of challenges. Banks are under pressure from both the liability as well as the asset side of their balance sheets. Banks can no longer take their liabilities for granted as investors are increasingly seeking alternate institutions to supply their funds to. Likewise, the advent of competition has resulted in business seeking non-bank funding to raise capital. With shrinking liabilities, banks might themselves have to tap the capital markets for funds. As credit rating agencies typically downgrade banks, banks may have to pay higher interest rates to secure funds while simultaneously losing asset base to NBFCs and the capital market. This twin whammy puts pressure on banks's interest margins, a pressure that may be eased by resorting to simultaneous cost cutting and revenue generation measures. Cost cutting in the Indian case has manifested itself in recent mergers, and acquisitions. Banks have also been tapping the capital markets but with limited success, perhaps due to a poor record of dealing with the NPA problem.

The public sector banks of India are also experiencing difficulties due to the extensive regulations in which they are forced to operate. Such regulations hinder their ability to compete at a global level against banks that do not submit to widespread regulations and restrictions. For example, while both the foreign and public sector banks in India are required to meet priority sector obligations, PSBs have a quota for these obligations that is eight per cent higher than that of the foreign banks. However, new entrants to India's banking system suggest that the NPS need not be a permanent feature of the Indian banking sector. Recent studies (Ajit and Bangar, 1998; Rajaraman et al., 1999) have demonstrated that private sector banks have higher capital adequacy ratios and lower NPAs than PSBs.

The PSBs of India are also experiencing difficulties due to the extensive regulations in which they are forced to operate. Such regulations hinder their ability to compete at a global level against banks that do not submit to widespread regulations and restrictions. For example, while both the foreign and public sector banks in India are required to meet priority sector obligations, public sector banks have a quota for these obligations that is eight per cent higher than that of the foreign banks.

Other obstacles to the success of banking reform in India are primarily structural and include: overstaffing, trade unions, disadvantage with regard to competition, extreme administrative regulations, and an administrative structure that is much more intricate than necessary (Sarkar 1999). Overstaffing of the banks is a key component of the problems being posed to the public sector banking industry. Ratios of employees to assets indicate the significant overstaffing of Indian banks, especially in comparison the same ratios in foreign banks. Rampant trade unionism is often cited as another impediment to bank profitability (Sarkar 1999).

While outside sources have caused difficulties for the public sector banks, internal sources, such as problems within the administrative structure have also deterred from profitability. Administrators are unable to make decisions in the interests of their banks because they must submit to governmental rules and regulations. This has been especially problematic with the hiring of new employees. The banks are required to follow bureaucratic rules that prevent them from hiring the best candidates for available positions. Furthermore, the geographical separation of the public banks in India creates difficulties with coordination and supervision of the banks. Recent expansions have separated the banks and spread them throughout the entire country.

In the final analysis it can only be said that globalization is bound to increase the pressures on the banking sector. Such pressures are expected to even intensify as the Government moves to full capital account convertibility and inefficient banks become progressively more vulnerable to the winds of international competition. The evidence from the East Asian banking crisis is indicative of the strong linkages between financial fragility and its consequences on the real sector of the economy. The admittedly limited but nevertheless significant findings if this paper emphasize that the Indian banking sector has to reassess its performance under this backdrop of globalization and design an agenda for a "second generation' of reforms.

References

1. Ajit, D., and Bangar, R.D., (1998), "The role and performance of private sector banks in India, 1991-92 to 1996-97," *Political Economy Journal of India*, no. 7, pp. 7-20.

2. Dhingra, Ishwar C., (2001), "The Indian Economy: Environment and Policy", *Financial System and Commercial banking in India*, Sutlan Chand and Sons, 14th Edition, 2000, pp. 764-790.

3. ICRA Information Services, (2001), "banks and Financial Institution," *The Indian Bank Industry Study*, New Delhi, August, pp. 1-31.

4. Middleton, P.D., (1996), "Globalization and International Competition", in N. Jadahv Ed., *Challenges to Indian Banking: Competition, Globalization and Financial Markets*, Second Edition, Macmillan India Limited, Delhi, pp. 277-283.

5. Narasimham Committee Report, (1991), *Reserve Bank of India*, November 16.

6. Rajaraman, I., S. Bhaumik, and N. Bhatia, (1999), "NPA variations across Indian commercial banking', *Economic and Political Weekly*, Vol. XXIV, No. 34.

7. Sarkar, J., (1999), "India's Banking Sector: Current Status, Emerging Challenges and Policy Imperatives in a Globalized Environment," in James Hanson and Sanjay Kathuria (ed.) India: *A Financial Sector for the Twenty-First Century*, Oxford University Press.

8

Stock Return, Money Supply and Market Efficiency: Indian Evidence

Amanulla S*

Introduction

The stock return predictability has been the subject of extensive research in the past and the different empirical models were proposed by various researchers to predict stock return variability. The earlier studies [Molodovsky *et al* (1965) Malkiel and Cragg(1970), Piper and Fruhan(1981) and Fischer and Jordan(1993)], possibly grouped as *Fundamental School*, strongly believes that the stock return does have a strong linkages with certain fundamental factors and hence, an attempt of tracking these fundamental factors may provide a possible explanation of stock return variability.[1] However, this stock return-fundamental factor relation is criticized by various researchers based on the reason that the stock return variability is, largely, influenced by the forces of demand and supply in stock market. Hence, they trust the predictability of stock return with help of the behavioural chart of past return sequence [Seligman(1962), Pinches(1970), Plummer(1990)]. In essence, this group,

* Reader, School of Management, Pondicherry University, Pondicherry-605 014.

generally referred as *Technical School,* rests on the belief that the past price sequence of stock do have information content to predict the stock return variability.[2] If fundamental school or technical school helps to earn extra-normal profits *consistently,* then the market participant will tend to exploit this opportunity. In other words, 'the knowledge of fundamental linkages' or 'the ability to read the stock price movement' may provide a convenient edge in earning extra-normal profit.

Generally financial economists used *financial variables* such as P/E ratio, dividend, market price, pay-out ratio, etc., in predicting stock return variability. Though the use of these variables may help the stock market participant in micro-level stock return prediction, there are certain macro-economic factors that also affect the stock return variability. In order to capture the ability of the macro-economic factors on stock return prediction, earlier research studies have related stock return to *macro-economic factors* such as Gross National Product, Index of Industrial Production, Money Supply, Wholesale Price Index, Call Money rate and budget deficit and so on. In simple words, besides the financial variables, financial economists believed that the macro-economic factors have predictive information content to explain the stock return variability. The various studies provided mixed evidence in support of stock return-macro-economic relation [Castanias(1979), Fama(1981), Huang and Kracaw(1984), and Murthy(1994)].

Though financial economists related stock return to macro-variables, the monetary economists differ in proposing the possible linkage between stock return and macro-variables, more specifically with *monetary variables.* They strongly support the proposition that the changes in monetary variables call for a change in stock return. Further they believe that the monetary variable lead stock return in time. Hence, the possible lagged monetary relationship may provide some clues for stock return predictability. In simple terms, the monetarists claims that the stock return variability can be explained with monetary variables.

If the market is said to be an efficient, then it instantaneously incorporates all available information on its price, leaving no scope for providing extra-normal profit by any strategy based on technical school or fundamental school. Whether the information may be financial variables or monetary variables, the stock market does not distinguish the same but absorbs and process all the information on its price. Thus, the current price fully reflect all available information and the stock market participants may not have any additional information to predict the stock return variability. Hence, the monetarists' claim, that the monetary variables do have predictive information content of stock return, may not also give any superior information in predicting stock return in an efficient stock market.

Though various studies provided mixed evidence between the stock return-monetary variable relation, this study attempts to investigate how the monetary variables may provide the possible and recent explanation of stock return variation. More specifically, this study attempts to relate the stock return to changes in growth rate of money supply and may search for the possible evidence in Indian stock market. The rest of the paper is organized as follows: section-I deals about the theoretical linkages between stock return and money supply; the methodology, data and its sources are given in section II. The empirical evidence is discussed in Section-III and the Section-IV concludes the paper.

Stock Return, Money Supply and Market Efficiency: Theoretical Linkages

The investigation of stock price-money supply relation is pursued by earlier studies in two different directions. For instance, monetary economists [Hamburger(1966, 1977) Friedman(1988)], attempt to find the money supply variation with help of stock return and hence, proposed a testable form of money supply as a function of stock price. In other words, the efforts were made to explain the variability of money supply with help of stock return.[3] But financial economists focuses on the stock return variability with help of predictive information content of money supply [Keran(1971), Sprinkel and Genetski(1977)]. In testable form, the stock return is a function of changes in money supply[4]. However, this paper attempts to investigate the second form, i.e., stock return as a function of money supply, and attempts to find-out the possible explanation of stock return variability with help of changes in money supply. The following sub-sections presents two different propositions under the second category.

1. *Monetary Portfolio (MP) Model*

Though the researchers agree on the stock return predictability with help of changes in money supply, they do differ in their testable propositions. For instance, the studies such as Brunner(1961), Friedman(1961), Friedman and Schwartz(1963), Rozeff(1974) proposed a model viz., Monetary Portfolio(MP) model[5] to investigate the stock return variability. The MP model rests on the foundation that the investor will hold money as one asset in his portfolio of assets. In other words, besides other investment avenues such as stocks, long-term bonds, real assets and capital assets, the investor will also hold some proportion of his funds in the form of Money. In a macro-framework, if there is a monetary disturbances such as unexpected increase or decrease of the growth of rates of money supply, it affects total investors' portfolio, more specifically investor's desired money balance. In such case, the expected return from investor's portfolio will be affected and hence, the investors attempt to re-balance his existing portfolio of assets in such a way to get a desired return from his portfolio. However, the portfolio rebalancing is not done instantaneously by investors due to lag in information transmission of money supply changes. Hence, the response by investors, at a large for portfolio re-balancing, is sufficiently delayed. In essence, the stock return responds to monetary disturbance with sufficiently longer time lag.[6] The earlier studies employed MP model include: Sprinkel(1964), Palmer(1970), Homa and Jaffee(1971), Keran(1971), Reilly and Lewis(1971), Hamburger and Kochin(1972), Meigs(1972), Bernanke and Gertler(1999) and Sellin(2001).

Based on the empirical investigation by various studies on MP model, it is possible to state that: (i) the monetary policy changes affects the stock return variability; (ii) the monetary variables lead the stock return in time[7]. Especially, by employing graphical and regression analysis, the studies such as Sprinkel(1974) and Homa and Jaffee(1971) evidenced that there was a lagged relationships of stock prices to monetary variables and also devised a trading strategy to earn higher profit as compared to simple buy-and-hold strategy. In other words, the monetary variables have the predictive information content to explain the stock return variation and hence, there is a possibility for investor to use this lagged stock return relationship for devising profitable trading strategies. Hence various researchers attempted to predict the stock return with the help of past changes in money supply. More specifically, researchers searched the existence of causality from past changes in money supply to stock return. The presence of causality from changes in money supply to stock return implies the possibility of predicting stock return with help of changes in money supply. The empirical test of this proposition exists in volume.[8]

2. *Efficient Market (EM) Model*

The stock market is said to be efficient only if all the available information is instantaneously absorbed and processed on its price, leaving no scope for any possibility for earning extra-normal return [Fama(1970, 1991)]. In similar line, the efficient market (EM) model rests on the beliefs that the current stock return, in an efficient market, contains all available information. Hence, no market participant has any additional information and hence, he may not have any ability to predict the stock return. However, the MP model strongly supports that the past changes in money supply may provide predictive information content to explain the stock return variation. The stock return predictability with help of money supply indicates that the stock market is not rational information processor of money supply [Lucas(1972), Huang and Castanias(1979) and Huang and Kracaw(1984)]. It essentially asserts that the stock market is not efficient and hence, provides the possibility of predicting the stock return. Thus, the support for MP model may viewed as the rejection of EM model.

Though the MP model contradicts the EM Model, the efforts are also made to find-out the possible explanations through various theoretical and empirical investigations. Pursuing on this line, Cooper(1972) and Rozeff(1974) had provided sufficient theoretical background to resolve the conflict, at least partially, between EM and MP model,. For instance, Cooper(1972) supported that the lead/lag of stock returns and money growth rates are consistent with efficient markets by employing spectral methods. Rozeff(1974) provided a theoretical explanation for the conflict between MP and EM model. For instance, the MP model is based on the principles that: (i) monetary disturbance affects stock return; and (ii) the monetary change affects stock return with lag. According to Rozeff(1974), the EM does not conflict with principle (i) but contradicts the principle (ii). In other words, the basic premise of EM model is that the stock return contains all available information in market and hence, current changes in monetary disturbance is also expected to be absorbed and immediately incorporated in current stock return, i.e., *contemporaneous relationship*. If the stock market is efficient in processing the current changes in monetary variables rapidly on its price, then such a model may be acceptable to both EM and MP models. But the claim that monetary variables affect stock return with lag is seriously questioned by EM model. In an efficient market, it is not possible for a lagged changes in growth rates of money to affect the current changes in stock return. Hence, the power of lagged monetary variables to predict current stock return was refuted by EM Model.

If the changes in growth rates of money supply affects the stock return *contemporaneously*, then EM model and MP model does not differ each other in their propositions. However, If the changes in growth rates of money affects the stock return with time lag, then EM model contradicts the MP model. Rozeff(1974) referred the model based on con*temporaneously* relationship as *'Non-predictive Monetary Portfolio Model'*. And, the model based on *lagged relationship,* is denoted as *'Predictive Monetary Portfolio Model'*. In case of contemporaneous relationship, it is not possible for an investor to predict stock return with the changes in money supply and hence, EM model does support with Non-predictive MP model. As the existence of lagged relation, of monetary changes with stock return, provides to earn extra-normal profit, EM model directly contradicts with Predictive MP model. This paper attempts to test the presence of predictive MP model or non-predictive MP model in Indian stock market. For this purpose, the specific empirical model is to be proposed and the following section presents the same.

Empirical Model

This papers attempts to test the stock return variability with help of changes in money supply as per Rozeff(1974) methodology. In order to test the predictive MP model, this paper proposes the following functional form:

$$R_t = a_0 + \sum_{i=0}^{n} a_i (g_t - g_{t-i}) + e_t \qquad \ldots(1)$$

where; $R_t = \left(\frac{p_t - p_{t-1}}{p_{t-1}} \right)$; p_t and p_{t-1} are stock price at time t and t-1 respectively; $g_t = \left(\frac{m_t}{m_{t-1}} \right)$; a_0 and a_i are co-efficients and e_t is error term. Equation (1) relates current stock return to current and lagged changes in growth rates of money supply. The equation (1) also addresses the '*contemporaneous*' stock return relationship as well as lagged changes of '*predictive*' and '*non-predictive*' model.

The existence of contemporaneous relationship is assured if

$$a_i = 0; \qquad i = 1, 2, ..n \qquad ...(2)$$

Equation (2) states that the zero-explanatory power, of each of lagged changes in growth rates of money supply, 'strongly' supports the non-predictive MP model (i.e., strong restriction), implying the presence of EM Model. However, it is also quite possible that the sum of lagged changes in money supply may be equal to zero and it may be represented as;

$$\sum_{i=1}^{n} a_i = 0 \qquad ...(3)$$

Equation (3) specifies the weak restriction to ensure the contemporaneous relationship between stock return and money supply. In order to assure the presence of predictive MP model, the lagged changes in growth rates of money supply are expected to be statistically significant (F-test). The acceptance of the hypothesis that the lagged error terms contribute significantly to explain the stock return ensures predictive MP model.

Data and Sources

This paper attempts to use the monthly data on stock price indices viz., BSE Sensitive Index, BSE National Index, narrow money supply (m1) and board money supply (M3). The selection of BSE Sensitive index is based on the reason that it contains 30 highly sensitive stocks that 'instantaneously' reflect the changes in stock market. However, the BSE national index is selected due to broad based index. The period covered from 1990:1 –2001:9. The data collected from Handbook of statistics on Indian Economy, published by Reserve Bank of India.

Empirical Evidence

This study attempts to test the predictive power of monetary variable to explain the stock return variability by carrying out regression specified in equation (1). For this purpose, (i) the return from the BSE sensitive index is regressed on the narrow money supply (m1) and broad money supply (m3) individually; and further, (ii) the return BSE national index is regressed on the narrow money supply (m1) and broad money supply (m3) individually. In order to find-out the changes over the study period, this study carries out these regression in two sub-sample periods viz., 1990:5-1995:3 and 1995:4-2001:9 as well as full sample period.

The test of strong and weak restriction of lagged money changes is carried out through F-test and the results are presented in Table-1. In case of full sample period, the null of hypothesis of zero-individual m1 lagged co-efficients (i.e., strong restriction $a_i = 0$) is not rejected in BSE national index. But the individual m1 lagged co-efficients is statistically significant in BSE sensitive index at 10% significance level. Hence, it asserts that m1 is having predictive information content to explain the BSE sensitive index while it fails to do so in BSE national index. But the lagged m3 co-efficients do not have any explanatory power to explain the return variability in BSE sensitive index as well as BSE national index. The 'weak restriction' that the sum of lagged co-efficients is zero, is accepted in m1 and m3. Thus, it evidences that there is a 'contemporaneous relationship' between money supply (m1 as well as m3) and stock market indices.

Table 1: Test Statistics (F-Test)

	BSE-S		BSE-N	
	$a_i = 0;$	$\sum_{i=1}^{n} a_i = 0$	$a_i = 0;$	$\sum_{i=1}^{n} a_i = 0$
1990:5 – 2001:9				
M1(6)	2.066 -0.062	0.483 -0.488	1.806 -0.103	0.563 -0.455
M3(6)	0.987 -0.473	0.462 -0.498	0.778 -0.588	0.391 -0.532
1990:5-1995:3				
M1(6)	1.987 -0.087	0.664 -0.419	2.067 -0.076	0.79 -0.378
M3(6)	1.613 -0.166	0.208 -0.651	1.652 -0.155	0.244 -0.623
1995:4-2001:9				
M1(6)	1.565 -0.17	6.319 -0.014	1.289 -0.274	5.221 -0.025
M3(6)	0.881 -0.512	4.414 -0.039	0.532 -0.781	2.614 -0.11

Notes: BSE-S: BSE sensitive Index; BSE-N: BSE National Index; M1(6): narrow money supply with 6 lags; M3(6): Broad money supply with six lag; The figures in the parenthesis refers to significance level.

The results from sub-sample period 1990:5 – 1995:3, by and large, confirms the outcome of full sample period with the exception that the lagged individual m1 co-efficient is statistically significant in explaining the return variability of BSE national index (i.e., strong restriction). The outcome of sub-sample period 1995:4 – 2001:9 accepts the null hypothesis of zero explanatory power of the individual lagged money supply changes, thereby suggesting the existence of contemporaneous relationship between stock price and money supply. The presence of 'contemporaneous relationship is acceptable within the framework of MP model as well as EM model. This period further suggests that weak restriction, i.e., the null of sum of lagged co-efficients is zero, is rejected and hence, supports that the money supply (i.e., m1 and m3) has power to explain the stock return variability. This outcome strongly refutes the EM model.

Conclusion

This paper attempts to test whether monetary variables has any power in explaining the stock variability. For this purpose, the study used monetary portfolio (MP) model. The data used in the study include: BSE-sensitive index, BSE national index, narrow money supply (m1) and broad money supply (m3). Excepting few cases, the results from full sample and sub-sample periods largely suggest that the null hypothesis of weak (i.e., the sum of lagged money supply is zero) and strong condition (i.e., the individual lagged money supply is zero) could not be rejected in case of BSE –Sensitive Index as well as BSE National index. Hence, it supports that the stock return has 'contemporaneous relationship' with money supply and hence, the monetary portfolio (MP) model as well as efficient market model (EM) are accepted in Indian context.

Notes

1. In Indian context, the various factors such as growth rate of market price, dividend pay-out ratio, leverage, firm size, price/earning (P/E) ratio, time factor and etc., were identified as fundamental factors, capable of explaining the stock return variability [For details, refer Sharma(1989), Barua and Raghunathan(1990), Sundaram(1991), Obaidullah(1991), Zahir(1992)].

2. The literature review on Fundamental school, Technical School and Efficient Market Hypothesis in Indian context is presented in Barua and Raghunathan(1987), and Amanulla and Kamaiah(1995-96).
3. The Indian studies focuses on this direction includes: Paul and Kamaiah(1992), Paul(1992), and Apte(1997).
4. The studies such as Murthy(1994), Sahadevan and Thiripalraju(1995), Roy *et al* (2000) and *Amanulla* and Kamaiah(2001) focused on this direction in Indian context.
5. The term 'Monetary Portfolio' (MP) Model was coined by Rozeff(1974). The same proposition was coined differently by Cooper(1972) as 'Simple Quantity' Model; and by Burger(1971) as 'The Portfolio Theory of Monetary Policy'.
6. It also produces impacts in prices of other assets. For instance, Rozeff(1974) supports that the increased money growth rates also results in producing higher price increase in durable goods as compared to non-durable goods and makes the latter cheaper. Further he also asserted the price increase (with lag). of non-durables will affect the current production of goods and services.
7. This is otherwise referred as 'Lagged Information Hypothesis' by Huang and Kracaw(1984).
8. For further details, please refer Friedman(1988), Lucas(1972), Clark(1973), Castanias(1979), Huang and Kracaw(1984). The Indian studies on this topic include: Brahmananda *et al* (1992), Sahadevan and Thiripalraju(1995), Apte(1997), and Roy *et al(2001).*

Reference

Amanulla , S and Kamaiah, B(1995-96), "Stock Market Efficiency: A Review of Indian Evidence", *Prajanan*, 24, 3, 257-280.

Amanulla , S and Kamaiah, B(2001), "Price Integration in Indian Stock Market: A Test of Market Efficiency", *Asian-African Journal of Economics and Econometrics*, 1, 1, 9-39.

Apte, P G(1997), "Money, Stock Prices and Industrial Activity in India: Long-run Relationship and Causality", *Indian Economic Review*, 32, 2, 179-198.

Barua S K and Raghunathan, V(1990), "Soaring Stock Prices: Defying Fundamentals", *Economic and Political Weekly*, 25, 46, 2559-2561.

Bernanke B and Gertler, M(1999), "Monetary Policy and Asset Price Volatility", *Federak Reserve Bank of Kansas City Economic Review*, Fourth Quarter, 17-51.

Brahmananda, P R, Anjaneyulu, D, Barman, R D and Sastry, D V S(1992), "The Changing Monetary Process in the Indian Economy", Study 4, Development Research Group, Department of Economic Analysis and Policy, Reserve Bank of India, Mumbai.

Brunner, K(1961), "Some Major Problems in Monetary Theory", *American Economic Review Proceedings*, May, 47-56.

Burger, A E(1971): *The Money Supply Process*, Wadsworth: Belmont, Calif

Castanias, R P II(1979), "Macro-information and the Variability of Stock Market Prices", *Journal of Finance*, 34, 2, 439-450.

Clark P K(1973) "A Subordinated Stochastic Process Model with Finite Variance for Speculative Prices", *Econometrica*, 41, 135-155.

Cooper, R V L(1974), "Efficient Capital Markets and The Quantity Theory of Money", *Journal of Finance*, 29, 887-908.

Fama, E(1970), "Efficient Capital Markets: A Review of Theory and Empirical Work", *Journal of Finance*, 25, 382-417

Fama, E(1981), "Stock Returns, Real Activity, Inflation and Money", *American Economic Review*, 71, 4, 545-565.

Fama, E(1991), "Efficient Capital Market-II" *Journal of Finance, Journal of Finance*, XLVL, 5, 1575-1617.

Fischer D E and Jordan, R J(1993): *Security Analysis and Portfolio Management*, New Delhi: Prentice Hall.

Friedman, M(1988), "Money and Stock Market", *Journal of Political Economy*, 96, 2, 221-245.

Hamburger, M J(1966), "The Demand for Money by Households, Money Substitutes, and Monetary Policy", *Journal of Political Economy*, , 74, 600-623.

Hamburger, M J(1977), "Behaviour of the Money Stock: Is There a Puzzle?" *Journal of Monetary Economics*, 3, 265-88.

Huang, R D and Kracaw W A(1984), "Stock Market Returns and Real Activity: A Note", *Journal of Finance*, 39, 1, 267-273.

Keran, M W(1971), "Expectations, Money and The Stock Market", *Federal Reserve Bank St. Louis Review*, 53, 16-32.

Lucas, R E(1972), "Expectations and the Neutrality of Money", *Journal of Economic Theory*, 4, 103-124.

Malkiel, B G and Cragg, J G(1970), "Expectations and the Structure of Share Prices", *American Economic Review*, 60, 601-17.

Molodovsky, N, May, C. and Chuttiner, S(1965) "Common Stock Valuation: Theory and Tables", *Financial Analysts Journal*, 20, 104-123.

Murthy, Y S R(1994), "Share Prices and Economic Activity in India: A Multiple Regression Approach", *Decision*, 21, 1, 87-96.

Obaidullah M(1991), "The Price/Earnings Ratio Anomaly in Indian Stock Market", *Decision*, 18, 183.

Paul, M T and Kamaiah, B(1992), "Stock Prices and Demand for Money: The Indian Case", *Prajnan*, 21, 3, 309-323.

Paul, M T(1992), "Demand for Money, Inflationary Expectations and Stock Market", *Indian Economic Journal*, 40, 1, 36-62.

Pinches, G E(1970), "The Random Walk Hypothesis and Technical Analysis", *Financial Analysts Journal*, 26, 2, 104-110.

Piper, T R and Fruhan, W E Jr(1981), "Is Your Stock Worth its Market Price", *Harvard Business Review*, 59, 3, 124-132.

Plummer, T(1990): *Forecasting Financial Markets: Technical Analysis and the Dynamics of Prices*, John Wiley & Sons, New York.

Roy, A, Amanulla, S and Kamaiah, B(2000), "Indian Stock Market: A Test of Semi-strong Form of Efficiency", *International Journal of Development Banking*, 18, 2, 17-26.

Rozeff, M S(1974), "Money and Stock Prices", *Journal of Financial Economics*, 1, 3, 245-302.

Sahadevan, K G and Thiripalraju, M(1995), "Money and Stock Prices: Some Empirical Evidence on Their Lead-lag Relationship", *Indian Journal of Finance and Research*, 4, 1, 11-29

Seligman, D(1962), "Playing the Market with Charts", *Fortune*, 65, 2, 118.

Sellin, P(2001), "Monetary Policy and The Stock Market: Theory and Empirical Evidence", *Journal of Economic Surveys*, 15, 4, 491-537.

Sharma, R K(1989), "Factors Affecting Relative Prices of Equity Shares: An Empirical Analysis", *The Chartered Accountant*, 38, 110-114, 121.

Sprinkel, B W and Genetski, R J(1977): *Winning With Money: A Guide for Your Future*, Homewood Ill: Dow Jones-Irwin.

Sundaram, S M(1991), "Soaring Stock Prices", *Economic and Political Weekly*, 26, 18, 1184.

Zahir, M A(1992), "Factors Affecting Equity Prices in India", *The Chartered Accountant*, 40, 9, 743-748.

9

Stock Market Volatility in India

Puja Padhi[*]

Introduction

Risk generally implies the possibility that actual or realized returns will be less than what were expected. All kinds of investment, be they financial or real assets, have an element of risk associated with them. It is therefore logical that risk and return expectations have a positive proportional relationship—the higher the risk, the greater the return expectation of the investor. Risk precisely, is the degree of fluctuation in actual returns around the average expectation of investors. Expected return is the mean or central tendency of the probability distribution of one period returns. Variance and its square root, the standard deviation, measure the total variability of returns and hence the total risk. Variance as the measure of dispersion takes into account the possibility of returns deviating from the expected return on either side—both above and below.

Volatility is the most basic statistical measure of risk. It can be used to measure the market risk of a single instrument or an entire portfolio of instruments. The volatility of an asset indicates the variability of its returns.

* Research Scholar, Department of Economics, University of Hyderabad, Hyderabad 500 046.

Most academic studies have defined volatility in terms of statistical measure of the variability of percentage price changes or rates of return. Most often statistical measure of volatility is the standard deviation of return. Because it is used as a standard measure of risk in theories of portfolio selection. Many investors, defined volatility as episodes of extreme or rapid price movements within certain days. An important aspect of volatility is its emphasis on the variability, rather than the direction of price movements, which could be upward, downward or flat. Thus, volatility, as a concept, can be treated as synonymous with variability in general or variance in particular.

Although there is a plethora of research concerning stock market volatility, most of the studies have been done for stock markets of the developed world. The few studies that have been done on the Indian market have left many issues untouched. For instance days of the week variations, seasonality, size effect, noise trading, sign and size of sign, co-movement have been found in the developed and some of the developing markets. However, this facet has not been explored for the Indian market. Most of the studies conducted in India have dealt only with stock price Indices. Because of the weighted nature of the Indices, volatilities of the individual stocks tend to average out. So apart from the market indices, individual stocks should also be considered for analyzing volatility. For arriving at volatility forecast model, ARCH and GARCH class of models have been developed for most of the developed market. But, their application to the Indian stock market has not been explored. The present study is an attempt to investigate some vital aspects and issues relating to stock market volatility in India. Days of the week effect, size of the firm on stock return analysis, week end effect, January effect, size and sign of shocks, noise trading, co movement are some of the important issues relating to the stock return behaviour. The present study tries to make an attempt to select some of the aspects to analyze the stock market volatility.

In the backdrop of above discussion, this essay attempts to address the issues of 'volatility in the Indian stock market'. Section II, discusses, stock return volatility, Section III, the days of week effect and Section IV, gives the concluding remarks.

Stock Return Volatility

Stock returns are characterized by statistical distribution. Most of the high frequency financial time series are found deviating from normality. They exhibit characteristics such as skewness and excess kurtosis. This means that the size of the up moves is not the same as the size of the down moves and more returns are to be found in the distribution's tails found in a normal distribution. High—frequency financial time series such as stock return series, exhibit a tendency to revert to their long—term mean (Lo and Mackinlay 1988). The basi assumption of normality has been tested using BSE 500 stocks existing during 1991-2001. Marisetty and Alayur (2002) found that there is significant positive skewness in India's stock returns. They found that this asymmetry has persisted over the years. This result brings in a new paradigm in the risk analysis of India's stocks. Their research points out that Indian investors might accept higher variance investment over a low variance investment with the same expected returns because it offers a higher probability of extraordinary payoffs. Statistically significant positive skewness captures such behaviour.

Every time the returns deviate from the mean, either in the positive or in the negative direction, they would tend to move in opposite direction, i.e. back towards the mean. This is synonymous with negative autocorrelation. Also, another interesting property of such time series is that clusters of positive moves are followed by clusters of negative moves, meaning that there is positive autocorrelation in the returns. Negative autocorrelation cancels out up moves and down moves over a passage of time, yielding lower volatility over time. Positive autocorrelation, on the other hand, reinforces the moves in one direction and results in higher volatility overtime.

The introduction of the ARCH models has inspired many researchers in financial economics to model volatility and examined its persistence over time. However in India, with the exception of the study by Amanulla (1997), there has not been any attempt to model volatility in ARCH/ GARCH framework. Amanulla, study contrasted the traditional CAPM with conditional CAPM when the return follow either ARCH or GARCH process.

Volatility and its persistence based on daily returns of 30 BLUE chip securities traded on Bombay Stock Exchange (BSE) were empirically estimated by Mohanty *et. al* (2000). Before estimating ARCH/GARCH models to capture volatility the results of the diagnostic statistics show the coefficient of skewness, in no cases equal to zero and hence indicate that return distribution is skewed. The kurtoses of all the return distributions are greater than three, thereby indicating leptokurtic distribution and the Bera Jarqua (BJ) statistics, which exceeds critical chi-square value with 2 degree of freedom in all cases, reject the normality of the underlying distribution. The Ljung Box (LB) statistics shows the significance of both the residual and squred residual. The Augmented Dicky—Fuller (ADF) test indicates that return series are stationary in nature. To sum up, stock returns are not identically and independently distributed and this may lead to conclude that return variance process is time varying and heteroskedastic in nature and hence ARCH formulation would be appropriate. The coefficient of ARCH (5) model (α_0 to α_1 (i = 1 ..... 5) are estimated for total return of each securities. The coefficient from market point of view may be interpreted as follows: the volatility of the previous trading day is carried over to the current period and it persists over a period of three days in most cases, as most of the coefficient are significant upto lag 4. At the same time GARCH model also conveys the important application for persistence of variance as represented by the sum of coefficients of lagged squared disturbances α and that of past variance β. The sum $(\alpha + \beta)$ approaches unity $(\alpha + \beta > 0.8)$ in 23 cases. Which thus shows that volatility is persisting on most of the cases and the sum quantifies the degree of persistence.

Volatility is central to many investment decisions in new product areas and is the critical variable in options. Most option-pricing model including Black-Scholes (1973) require a volatility input defined as the standard deviation of log relative prices. Option traders typically make option quotes in terms of volatility rather than dollar or rupee value. Financial markets have been giving importance to volatility. Since volatility is a standard measure of financial vulnerability, it plays a key role in assessing risk/return trade-off. Extreme stock return volatility could disrupt the smooth functioning of the financial system and lead to structural or regulatory changes.

Based on measurement of stock market volatility for the period 1935 to 1992, Roy and Kamakar (1995) focus on the measurement of the average level of volatility in the Indian stock market and whether it has increased in the current period. Market volatility has been measured for a span of 58 years. It is said that an assessment based on an analysis of this period can be truly called as an average measure of volatility of the stock market. The current level of volatility has been compared with this average measure in order to understand whether it is above or below the historical level. Volatility has been measured by the standard deviation of the rate of return. Their sample data consists of two sets of index numbers. The first set comprises of the 'Capital' stock and share index complied and published by the *Capital* Magazine on a monthly basis for the period January 1935 to December 1960. The second set is composed of 'the Economic Time Index Number of Ordinary Share Prices' compiled and published on a daily basis for the period 1961 to 1992. For the period 1935-92, volatility has been measured using standard deviation of monthly returns within each year. For each year, monthly prices have been converted into natural logarithms and the mean return and standard deviation have been calculated from log differences between months within each year. Their decade-wise analysis shows that violent changes in share price cluster around the boom of the 40's and share mania of the 80's that continued up to 1992. For a relatively current period, 1961-92, volatility has been measured based on daily returns within each month. Their analyses show that out of a total of 25 volatile month, only 2 pertain to the claim period of the 60's and the 70's. In the 90's the year 1992 is the most current and volatile year in the history of Indian capital market.

The nature and trend of the stock return volatility in the Indian stock market and assess the role of "carry forward system" in causing variations in the volatility levels was examined by Goyal (1995). His study focuses on what constituents the stock market volatility and how the stock market volatility is related to the volatility in some of the macroeconomic indicators. Analysis carried out through vector autoregressive (VAR) model reveals a significant influence of industrial output and money supply on stock returns and of changes in stock returns on industrial output. Volatility of stock returns have been estimated on daily basis from May 1993 to December 1994 and on monthly basis for a period of 8 years from 1986 to 1994. Two sets of estimate have been prepared based on BSE Sensitive (Sensex) and BSE National (Natex) indices.

The effect of market microstructure on the stock market volatility was analyzed by Reddy (1997-98). The influence of establishment of NSE and the introduction of BSE On Line Trading (BOLT) on the volatility of securities traded on the BSE has been analyzed. Fragmentation that has resulted with the establishment of the NSE and the introduction of BOLT has been hypothesized to lead to an increase in the volatility of securities traded on the BSE. Stock market daily trading data relating to about 3000 securities traded on the BSE for the period October 1994 to 1995 form the database. The data has been accessed from on-line corporate databases like Metastock, Capitaline Ole' and CIMM. For estimating volatility, three measures of volatility have been used. These are-standard deviation of closing prices, standard deviation of returns and the extreme value estimator intended to capture the extreme movements of prices or returns of securities based on difference between the highest and the lowest price. The results of the influence of establishment of the NSE on the volatility in the BSE are mixed. Volatility as measured by standard deviation of returns shows no increase, while the standard deviation of closing prices and the extreme value estimator of volatility show an increase. Thus, it is stated that though the establishment of the NSE fragmented the stock market structure in India, it has not been really affected the working of the BSE, as his analysis could not find sufficient evidence for an increase in the volatility of the securities traded on BSE.

The relation between stock returns and stock market volatility was examined by French *et al.* (1987). They have found evidence that the expected market risk premium is positively related to the predictable volatility of stock returns. There is also evidence that unexpected stock market returns are negatively related to the unexpected change in the volatility of stock returns. This negative relation provides an indirect evidence of a positive relation between expected risk premiums and volatility. The study uses two statistical approaches to investigate the relation between expected stock returns and volatility. In the first, they use the daily returns of the Standard and Poor (S&P) Composite Portfolio to estimate the monthly standard deviation (volatility) from January 1928 through December 1984. They decompose these estimates into predictable and unpredictable components using univariate autoregressive integrated moving average models. Regressions of monthly excess holding period returns on the predictable component provide little evidence of a positive relation between *ex ante* volatility and expected risk premiums. There is a strong negative relation, however, between excess holding period returns and unpredictable component of volatility.

New evidence about the time series behaviour of stock market returns and summarizes the results of applying some new time series models to daily return series was presented by Akgiray (1989). The data used in the study were obtained from the Center for Research in Security Prices (CRSP), and they obtained 6030 daily returns on the CRSP value-weighted and equal-weighted indices covering the period from January 1963 to December 1986. The 24-year period is divided into four different periods of 6 years each and each period is analyzed separately. In particular, generalized autoregressive conditional heteroskedastic GARCH (1, 1) process fit to the data very satisfactorily.

Whether the class of autoregressive conditional heteroskedastic models (ARCH) introduced by Engle (1982) and its generalized versions (GARCH) by Bollerslev (1986) can adequately describe stock price behaviour in European capital markets, which are generally much smaller and thinner than the American ones was investigated by Corhay and Taurani (1994). There, the objective was to model non-linear dependencies in stock returns. The five countries selected for this are—France, Germany, Italy, the Netherlands and the United Kingdom. The indices for five European stock markets are collected from DATASTREAM for the period 1 January 1980 to 30 September 1990. All the indices except for Netherlands are value-weighted. The statistical findings confirm the fact that daily stock return are not normally distributed and are leptokurtic and skewed. The results indicate that conditional heteroskedastic is a prime feature of daily returns behaviour of five European equity indices.

The GARCH (1, 1) class of model is appropriate for studying the behaviour of stock returns on small equity markets.

An overview of the GARCH family of variance models and examines the behaviour of Australian aggregate stock market volatility over the period 1988-91 using the GARCH framework was presented by Nicholls and Tonuri (1995). The study considers daily returns on the Australian Fifty Leaders Statex—Actuaries Accumulation Index from 4 January 1988 to 31 December 1991 inclusive, of a series of 1023 observations in total. It has been stated that stock return data is typically negatively skewed, leptokurtic or heavily tailed and sharply peaked about the mean when compared with the normal distribution, and it shows evidence of autocorrelation in the returns and squared returns. Because of these empirical observations it has been stated that the use of a GARCH type model might be appropriate to describe the evolution of variance for this set of datas. GARCH type models attempt to incorporate such asymmetry in their structure by featuring the property of leptokurtosis and volatility clustering (i.e., autocorrelation) in the squares of stock return.

The study by Kaur (2002) investigated the return volatility exhibited by two major market indices viz. BSE Sensex and S&P CNX Nifty during the period 1990-2000, it is found that the stock market volatility was the highest during 1992 followed by 1990 and 2000 respectively. It fell sharply after 1992 and continued till 1995, after which it started rising again. Volatility increased from 1997-98, and reached highest in 2002. The largest number of spikes occurred in the years 1992, 1990 and 2000, the three most volatile years. The increased volatility in the year 2000 can be attributed to the worldwide infotech boom. It is found that volatility has varied across months in a year. Among the months, April has been the most volatile followed by March and February. This could be due to the most significant economic event in a year namely the presentation of the

Union Budget, which is usually presented on the last day of February. The volatility of the Indian market is quite high compared to the major developed markets and even some of the emerging Asian and Latin American markets like Malaysia, South Korea. Thailand and Chile. In analyzing the presence of the Day of the Week effect in the return of the market indices, it is found that Monday returns have the highest volatility and Friday returns lowest. The differences are statistically significant in the case of Nifty as well as Sensex. However there is no definite pattern in the weekday returns. Though the returns are the lowest on Tuesday for both the indices, the highest return for sensex occurs on Monday while for Nifty it is on Wednesday. The "higher the risk, higher the return" paradigm thus does not hold consistently. It is found from both the indices that the volatility on trading days preceded by a holiday is significantly different (higher) than those preceded by a working day. Thus, the phenomenon that Monday have higher volatility is found to be caused by the closed market effect (as Monday is preceded by two holidays) and not by the virtue of Day of the week effect. The closed market or the holiday effect is future substantiated by the fact that open-to-open returns are more volatile than close-to-close returns. Return volatility is greater at the opening of trading than at the close. This empirical study reveals that the GARCH(1, 1) model fits the sensex return data best.

Following French *et. al. ex ante* measures of volatility using ARCH and GARCH are estimated and the relationship between equity premium and volatility for the composite BSE sensex is empirically tested by Pattanaik and Chatterjee (2000). They observed negative relationship between the *ex ante* volatility and statistically insignificant relationship with the unpredictable component of return volatility. It indicates that even the indirect tests of the return—risk relationship do not hold good in India. The negative return-risk relationship could be explained to some extent by the nature of investors operating in the market as well as their asymmetrical response to bearish and bullish phases of the market.

Days of the Week Effect

The volatility of equity returns during exchange trading and non-trading hours was analyzed by French and Roll (1986). This study found that equity returns are more volatile during exchange trading than during non-trading hours. The variance of returns from the open-to-close of trading on an average day is over six times larger than the variance of close-to-open returns over a weekend, even though the weekend is eleven times longer. on an hourly basis, the variance when the exchanges are open is between 13 and 100 times larger than on the non-trading period considered. Using daily returns provided by the Center for Research in Security Prices (CRSP) for all common stocks listed on the New York Stock Exchange and the American Stock Exchange between 1963-82, they calculated return variances for weekdays, weekends, holidays and holiday weekends. These estimates were used to compute multiple-to-single-day variance ratios for each stock in each sub-period. (The 20-years period is broken into two-year sub-periods.) To examine whether the relation between trading and non-trading variances is a function of firm size. They sorted firms into quintiles based on their equity values at the beginning of each sub-period. They found no obvious relation between the estimated variance ratios and the size of the firm. The estimated variance ratio implies that trading hours are more volatile than non-trading hours. Among non-trading hours, weekends have lower volatility than normal holidays and holiday's weekends have the least volatility of all.

The behaviour of open-to-open and close=to-close returns of NYSE stocks was compared by Amihud and Mendelson's (1987), given the differences in execution methods applied in the opening and closing transactions. The empirical investigation employed the price data from the opening and closing transactions in active NYSE stocks, utilizing the fact that each of these transaction series is generated by a different trading mechanism. The clearing house transaction series is represented by the opening transaction, where as the closing transaction represents the dealership market. They then compared the effect of trading mechanism on the behaviour of the returns on the same stocks in the same market during the same time period. They interpreted the results using a model where prices follow a lagged partial adjustment process with noise. Their results show that the trading mechanism has a significant effect on a number of characteristics on stock returns. First, the distribution of open-to-open returns has greater variance than that of close-to-close returns. While both show deviation from normality, the opening return distribution exhibits greater peakedness and flatter tails than that of the closing return. Second, the serial correlation pattern is quite different in two return series. Further employing an ARIMA (1,1) model they find that opening returns exhibit higher residual noise and stronger dependence on past returns, reflecting stronger deviations from the random walk form of market efficiency hypothesis. Taken as a whole, this evidence suggests that trading at the opening exposes the trader to a greater variance (volatility) than at the close, reflecting the differences between the trading mechanisms.

Volatility has been measured by the standard deviation of rates of return to a broad stock market index such as the Standard and Poor's 500 by Schwert (1990). Three return series—daily returns, monthly returns and 15-minute returns- have been used to calculate different volatility estimates. The various estimates of standard deviation show that volatility, as measured using the standard deviation of rates of return has been stable since the mid-19th century in the United States. The major exception was the great depression period from 1929 to 1939. It is also observed that the high levels of volatility following Black Monday (October 19, 1897) were short-lived; the burst of volatility on Friday the 13th (October 13, 1989) was even more temporary. The conclusions are the same whether volatility is measured from monthly returns, daily returns or 15-minute returns. Thus apart from October 1987 and October 1989, volatility was not particularly high in 1980's.

The study by Lockwood and Linn (1990) examined the stability of the variance of returns on the Dow Jones Industrial Average (DJIA) for the period 1964-89. The market volatility is assessed using returns computed from opening, closing and intra-day hourly values of DJIA. Returns are computed as the natural logarithm of the DJIA value relative times 100 for the trading and non-trading periods for each day.

(a) The overnight period from close of the previous trading day to open of the subsequent trading days (e.g., overnight Monday is the period from close Friday to open Monday);

(b) The intraday period from open to close;

(c) The period from the open of the previous trading day to open of the subsequent trading days;

(d) The period from the close of the previous trading day to close of the subsequent trading days; and

(e) Several hourly intra-day periods (e.g., 1000 hrs.-1100 hrs. 1200 hrs, etc.)

Results indicate that hourly intra-day return variances are heterogeneous and ordered, falling from the opening hour until the early afternoon and rising thereafter. Results also indicate that market volatility is significantly higher during intraday *versus* overnight periods. Market return variance is shown to be significantly higher for open-to open versus close-to-close periods during the pre-NASDAQ, options, and commission periods but is shown to be significantly lower for open-to-open versus close-to-close periods during the future period.

The seasonal variation pattern in return volatility was examined by Ho and Cheung (1994). Using Leven test, it was found that there exists day-of-the-week variations in volatility in most of the emerging Asian sock markets. The data for the study consists of the daily stock price indexes of the eight Asian markets including Hong Kong, Japan, Korea, Malaysia, the Philippines, Singapore, Taiwan and Thailand. The period from January 1975 to December 1989 is used to compile daily returns. Volatility is measured by the standard deviation (SD) of the returns. It was confirmed in the study that the days-of-the week variation in volatility measured in terms of standard deviation was the most pronounced for most of the emerging Asian markets, including Hong Kong, Korea, Malaysia, Singapore, Taiwan. Generally speaking, the Monday returns have the highest volatility for all the emerging Asian markets with the exception of Korea (its Tuesday in the case of Korea). However, out of the five markets that have a significant day-of-the-week effect in variance, three had the lowest volatility on the last trading day.

Evidence on seasonality in daily and weekly return variances was reported by McInish and Ord (1985). That have been documented using intraday data is that, volatility is higher when the market is open than when it is closed. They documented a U-shaped pattern in return volatility during the trading day, that is, volatility is highest at the beginning and the end of the trading days, Jain and Joh (1988) show that the trading volume is different within and across days. They provide evidence of an inverted U-shape in volume across days. Monday and Friday have the lowest volume, and the most active periods are in the middle of week.

Conclusion

From the above review, it has been observed that trading hours are more volatile than non trading hours. Among non-trading hours, weekends have lower volatility than normal holidays and holidays's weekend have least volatility of all. Trading at the opening exposes the trader to a greater variance (volatility) than at close, reflecting the differences between the trading mechanism. After analyzing the different trading and non-trading periods for each day, open-to-open return has more volatility compared to close-to-close periods. It shows a U-shaped pattern in return volatility during the trading days, that is, volatility is the highest at the beginning and end of the trading days. There is a positive relationship between *ex ante* volatility and expected risk premium. In India volatility has been the highest during 1992 followed by 1990 and 2000 respectively. It fell sharply after 1992 and continued till 1992, after which it started again. The largest number of spikes occurred in the year 1992, 1990, 2000, the three most volatile years.

References

1. Akgiray, V, (1989), "Conditional Heteroskedasticity in Time Series of Stock Returns: Evidence and Forests, *Journal of Business,* 62, 1, 55-80.
2. Amanulla, S, (1997), "Indian Stock Market: Asset Price Behaviour and Stock Market Efficiency", Ph.D. Dissertation, University of Hyderabad, Hyderabad.
3. Amihud, Y and Mendelson, H., (1987), "Trading Mechanisms and Stock Returns: An Empirical Investigation", *The Journal of Finance,* XLII, 3,533-55.
4. Black, F. and Scholes, M., (1973), "The Pricing of Options and Corporate Liabilities. *Journal of Political Economy,* 81, 634-54.
5. Corhay, A and Tourani, A.R., (1994), "Statistical properties of Daily Stock Returns: Evidence From European Stock Markets, *Journal of Business Finance and Accounting,* 21(2), 271-82.
6. French, K.R. Schwert, W.G. and Stambaugh, R.F., (1987), "Expected Stock Return and Volatility", *Journal of Financial Economics,* 19, 3-29.

7. Goyal, R., (1995), "Volatility in Stock Returns", *Reserve Bank of India Occasional Papers,* 16, 3, 175-195.

8. Ho, Y.K. and Cheung, Y., (1994), "Seasonal Pattern in Volatility in Asian Stock Markets", *Applied Financial Economics,* 4, 61-67.

9. Jain P. and G. Joh, (1988), "The Interdependence Between Hourly Prices and Trading Volume", *Journal of Financial and Quantitative Analysis.*

10. Kaur H (2002), Stock Market Volatility in India (ed) book, Deep and Deep publication. New Delhi.

11. Lo, A and Mackinlay, C (1988), "Stock Market Prices Do Not Follow Random Walks: Evidence from a Specification Test", *Review of Financial Studies,* 1, 41-66

12. Lockwood, L.G and Linn, S.C (1990), "An Examination of stock Market Return Volatility During Overnight and Intra-day periods, -1964-89", *The Journal of Finance,* XLV, 2,591-601

13. Marisetty BV.B and V. Alayur (2002), "Asymmetry in India Stock Returns An Empirical Investigation", *The ICFAI Journal of Applied Finance,* 8, 3.

14. McInish, T and R Wood (1992), "An Analysis of Intraday Pattern in bid\ask Spreads of NYSE stock, *Journal of Finance,* 47, 753-64.

15. Mohant P.B and B. Kamaiah (2002), "Volatility and its Persistence in the India Stock Market: A Case Study of 30 Scrips", *Journal of Foreign Exchange and International Finance,* XIII,4,289-303

16. Nicholls, D and Tonuri, D(1995), "Modelling Stock Market Volatility in Australia", *Journal of Business Finance and Accounting,* 22(3), 377-95

17. Pattanaik S and Chatterjee (2000), "Stock Returns and Volatility in India: An Empirical Puzzle? " *Reserve Bank of India Occasional Papers,* 21,1

18. Reddy Y.S (1977-98), "Effects of Micro structure on Stock Market Liquidity and Volatility", *Prajnan,* XXVI, 2, 217-31

19. Roy, M.K, and Karmakar, M,(1995), "Stock Market Volatility, Roots and Results", *Vikalpa,*20,1,37-48

20. Schwert, W.G (1990), "Stock Market Volatility", *Financial Analysts Journal,* 6, 23-34

10

An Overview of Non-Voting Share

S. Aravanan*

Why to remain with only two kinds of shares, viz. equity shares and preference shares-Indian corporate sector you have one more kind of share in the form of Non Voting Shares (NVS) was the message which Thiru Palaniappan Chidambaram the then Finance Minister gave while presenting the 50th Budget (1996-97) of the Union of India. I do not know what message Thiru R.K. Shanmugam Chettiar gave to the corporate sector when he presented the first budget of India. But in the Golden Jubille Budget Thiru Chidambaram made the corporate sector—at least a section of it—jubilant by giving them the power to issue NVS, though it was later withdrawn.

In a sense the decision to permit companies to issue NVS was in response to persistent demand from a section of the industry which felt the industrial playing field was not quite as level as it should be vis-a-vis foreign entities. On its part, SEBI during the tenure of its previous chairman Mr. S.S. Nadkarni had taken the first step regarding NVS and had suggested to the Finance Ministry that corporates should be allowed to come out with such shares. On this background in this article certain issues in favour of NVS are discussed.

* Selection Grade Lecturer, Department of Commerce, Pondicherry University, Pondicherry–605014.

Of the two kinds of shares a company can have equity shares and preference shares - NVS belong to the equity category but without voting rights. No doubt the holder of the NVS is one of the owners of the company but a (voting) powerless owner. Here a question arises as to who will be willing to buy an equity share which has no voting right? I would like to answer this question taking my own my case. I am an average investor holding shares in around 30 companies. But I never even bothered to go through the Annual General Meeting notices whenever I received the same from the companies, leave alone attending the meetings. I am concerned only with consistent dividend and a handsome capital appreciation. Majority of the holders of voting shares are, I believe, like me only. When majority of the shareholders are not interested in attending the AGMs, majority of those who do attend are not serious about the AGMs. D.H. Pai Panandikar, R.P.G. Group Adviser once expressed: "AGMs are amusing and tell a lot about the average investor. More time is spent on the content of the lunch packet than on the annual report or accounts. Normally no one exercises the voting rights. Generally it is the management that runs the company on its own". Mr. Anil Nanda, Joint Managing Director Escorts Ltd., in an interview opined: "The investor is not concerned whether a share has a voting right or not. Left to him he will choose a share with higher returns, if need be by leaving his voting right. So it is a myth that NVS would mar democracy". By giving a higher dividend and offering at a lower price, NVS can be made an attractive instrument of money raising by companies.

A natural question that would emerge in this context is that why managements should be keen about NVS when the voting shareholders are not serious about exercising their voting rights. Definitely there are times when the voting right of shareholders assume importance, says D.H. Pai. These are times when for instance the threat of a takeover or a split in the family threatens to cause a split in the management. This was seen in the case of the ITC-BAT imbroglio. This sort of threat comes from those who have or can buy large chunks of equity. Those who have this capability include the FIs and FIIs. One way to prevent the further expansion of the voting power in the hands of these corporate raiders is to make it attractive for them to hold NVS. Can they be tempted? They should be tempted.

A criticism against NVS is that FIIS do not favour the proposal and one FII has gone to the extent of saying that it would hammer the scrip of that company which proposes to issue NVS. Because further issue of capital would result in decrease in earnings and intrinsic worth of existing shares. But Sir Robert Wade-Gery, Vice-Chairman of leading investment bank Barclays de Zoette Wedd thought otherwise: "From FIIs view point there is no real disadvantage about not being able to vote. On the other hand, they do abhor lack of liquidity in NVS. The lack of a vote does not bother them. From the promoters view point having the ability to raise capital through NVS is helpful, provided they can find willing buyers because if you have an ownership structure which you do not want to upset then this is an alternative. It is simply one more option open to issuers. In my books, anything that increases the legal range of options which they have is good". Similar opinion was given by Surjit S. Bhalla that NVS was a non issue because it was only one of several methods a firm had of raising money in the market place. In fact FIIs must feel happy over NVS because through NVS they can increase their holding of the voting shares of a company since NVS is considered as part of issued and paid up capital of company.

NVS is a cheaper source of finance. A company must raise fresh funds when it needs them. One way of raising funds is using of devious ways to retain control while getting additional funds. Another way is going in for costly borrowings. There is also an alternative of not arranging fresh funds at all and thus losing opportunities and competitiveness. While borrowing is the least damaging of these options the best thing would be to find an instrument which reduces the cost of finance. NVS is that instrument. To illustrate let us assume a company borrows Rs. 8 crores from a bank at a rate of 12 per cent. It has to pay the bank as interest Rs. 96 lakhs in a year. If it succeeds in raising funds through NVS at say Rs. 80 per share when the market price of the normal voting shares of the company is Rs. 100 per share (Face value Rs. 10 per share), then it has to issue 10,00,000 shares of Rs. 10 each at a premium of Rs. 70 per share. If the company declared a handsome dividend of say 50 per cent then on the NVS it has to pay a dividend of Rs. 50 lakhs. But as interest payment is tax deductible, the company gets a tax advantage of Rs. 33.6 lakhs (35 per cent of Rs. 96 lakhs) which should be deducted from the interest cost of Rs. 96 lakhs. But the resultant Rs. 62.4 lakhs of cost on the borrowing is still much higher i.e. Rs. 12.4 lakhs higher than the Rs. 50 lakhs cost on the NVS. If the company follows a conservative dividend policy its cost on NVS will be much lesser than Rs. 50 lakhs.

NVS can also help to keep corporate predators at bay. Now the promoters in India are anxious over the probable dilution of their hold over their companies owing to direct influx of equity capital into the corporate enterprises through overseas investments. With the conversion of GDRs issued by the companies into equity shares at a later date the foreign stake in Indian companies will increase. One expert had even gone to the extent of saying that there was a danger of ICICI becoming a foreign financial institution when its GDRs got converted into equity shares. Though there is a cap on investment by all FIIs in the equity stock of a company, this with GDR converted equity may pose a potential threat to Indian stake of Indian companies. In this situation NVS has a role to play.

The NVS concept has been thought of as a solution to what the Indian promoters see as an unfair advantage enjoyed by foreign enterprises in competing in the market place. In fact in 1992-93 when the first phase of liberalisation of foreign investment in India was allowed the Indian corporate guardians launched the idea of NVS as part of the level playing field. The thirst of Indian companies for such issue was obvious when Reliance, TISCO and a few other passed resolutions for the issue of NVS even a few years back. From another point of view of increasing capital without dilution of managerial control NVS can prove extremely useful. Whatever one says on record it is a fact that no promoter likes to dilute his stake in his company. Most experts are unanimous that companies which desire to expand their capital but are afraid of dilution of control will find NVS more than useful. Also companies where promoter's holding is thin may prefer this route of raising capital.

Will earnings be diluted? This is a most relevant question raised in connection with NVS. The answer is a comfortable 'No'. Earnings will not be any more diluted by an issue of NVS than they will be by an issue of voting shares. What will be the effect of an issue of voting shares of earnings, the same will be the effect that of NVS. In fact NVS should be compared with borrowing rather than with voting shares. Why should investors buy such shares? Are not bonds better? Eventhough many write that gentlemen prefer bonds, whatever rates bonds or other form of debt offer to investors today they only give a fixed return. That too in the present low interest rate regime the rate of interest is very less. Hence it is right time that NVS comes into the picture. NVS like normal equity will offer capital appreciation through bonus shares as well as increase in market prices because they also carry greater risk than debt. In an expanding phase, earnings will take care of themselves. NVS would be best suited for investors aiming at returns over a longer time frame.

Another issue pointed against NVS—will NVS lead to a decline in share prices? Some may say 'yes' and may point in proof that share prices plunged after the presentation of the Union Budget (1996-97) and the main reasons cited for this were: MAT and NVS. But what happened to the market a few months after the presentation of 1996-97 budget. It had further crashed and had almost came down to 3000 points (BSE sensex) around the second week of October 1996. Then what caused the downfall—certainly NVS was not the villain. Markets generally reward over time good policy and punish bad policy. Let the investors decide their own fate. The role of the government is to prepare the ground for market action and provide a level playing field and that was what Thiru. P. Chidambaram had done. In this connection Surjit S. Bhalla sarcastically remarked. Most likely the NVS policy is unlikely to affect the price of tomatoes or the 'permanent price' of any stock.

Thus NVS command clear advantages. To retain these advantages and/or at least to maintain the level of 'deuce' with other financial instruments the following precautions and suggestions should be considered:

(i) NVS should carry with it a prescribed higher rate of dividend or it should be offered at a discount or both should be given. SEBI while recommending NVS had suggested that to make such shares popular with shareholders a higher dividend by around 2 per cent should be permitted. In developing countries there has been evidences of NVS quoting at a 5-7 per cent discount to the price of voting shares. Both—higher dividend and lower price—raise the cost of NVS vis-a-vis ordinary shares. Hence NVS should be issued only if the benefit arising out of the project on hand is more than the higher cost of NVS.

(ii) NVS belongs to equity share category. As any holder of equity shares, NVS holders should be

prepared to bear a certain amount of risk. In this context the then Finance Secretary Montek Singh's remarks are relevant: It is upto the investor to scrutunize the company carefully before putting his money into equity. So the investors should make a thorough analysis of the fundamentals of the investee company before investing in its NVS. The equity analysts should carefully evaluate NVS issues in financial newspapers. The institutional investors must educate the investors. Despite such information if investors buy bad issues they are investing for their own economic burial.

(iii) Only strong performance and growth oriented companies with good dividend record should issue NVS. Says T.P. Ostwal, Chartered Accountant, "only blue chip companies can succeed in raising capital through this route". Companies with dubious track records of dividend payment should be debarred from issuing such scrips. If they do issue markets should give them a fitting reply by hammering down the prices of their scrips.

(iv) There ought to be a punishing mechanism. If a firm issuing NVS does not declare a dividend for 2 out of 3 succeeding years then the NVS should be converted into voting shares. This sort of restrictions will serve the purpose of ensuring that only the cream of corporate India issue NVS. The rest should think twice, even thrice, why any number of times. Though the Department of Company Affairs as a policy matter decided that NVS would not be convertible into voting shares even if the issuing company defaults on payment of dividend steps must be taken by SEBI to convince DCA and Finance Ministry to penalise

the defaulting companies by ordering for conversion of NVS into voting shares. In fact it was SEBI, while recommending NVS to Finance Ministry which suggested as a measure of caution that if the company failed to declare dividends generally for two consecutive years the NVS would automatically be converted into voting shares. Hence SEBI must ensure that its suggestion is implemented.

(v) The listing requirements as per Section 73 of the Companies Act should be made applicable to the issue of NVS.

(vi) SEBI and DCA should formulate guidelines on payment of additional dividend on NVS and on their pricing. Especially SEBI should show a great deal of imagination and flexibility by evolving the necessary guidelines and regulations before the corporate sector plans NVS issues. SEBI should continue to play its role of protecting its beloved specie—the small investor in the matter of NVS also. In this connection it would be quite relevant to recall what D.R. Mehta, the then SEBI Chairman, said: "The regulator is nobody's friend except that of investor's". Let SEBI play its friendly and protective role in the matter of NVS also.

Though NVS is yet to see the light of the day in India yet industry circles prefer NVS. The following were some of the reactions in favour of NVS.

The Confederation of Indian Industry which supported the NVS proposal from the very beginning was optimistic that the provision for introduction of NVS would be incorporated when comprehensive amendments to the Companies Act are introduced. The M.D. of Maruti Udyog Limited did not see any reason to drop it. He stated 'The argument that NVS would be used to promote the interest of the promoters did not hold water for the promoter cannot compel the small investor to buy these shares. If the public and financial institutions do not support the NVS, the issue will flop. Let the market decide'. In the same spirit Chairman, Escorts Limited reacted that NVS was a good option for raising capital from overseas. With takeover threats surrounding the various companies NVS is a good option and this is rightly underlined by M.D. of Apollo Types who felt that NVS should be allowed as Indian Companies were witnessing the prospect of takeover from the global corporations which have astronomical buying power. Chairman of the Raunaq Group was apprehensive about the effect of non inclusion of NVS on the share markets. He joined with the CII and with Director, Unitech Limited in emphasising that the NVS should have been included in the amendments to the Company Law Bill. They were positive that shareholders' interest would not be affected in any case since no good company can ignore the shareholders' interest.

Now encouraging news are coming that the committee appointed for reviewing the existing Companies Act have recommended for the introduction of NVS in the draft Companies Act. If the recommendation is accepted the industries circle will definitely welcome it with three cheers.

Indian capital market is a developing market and as is the characteristic of any developing market in our market also there are a number of imperfections. Trial and error method only can help in achieving perfection. Every now and then Indian corporate is trying with one or other new instrument to raise money. Now a recent addition is mortgage backed security which the Indian Housing finance companies are floating. Likewise let NVS be a new addition. Further this new addition is very much required now because with Banks and Small Savings Schemes offering a very low rate of interest of 6 to 8 per cent the only source of investment which could give a handsome return is equity shares in the form of dividend. And conceptually the rate of dividend on NVS should be greater than that of equity shares. Hence when this high yielding security is introduced the entire investing community would be immensely pleased. Hence let us give a welcoming hand to this prospective entrant and wish it a good success.

11

Theories of International Investmemt: A Selective Survey of Literature

Dinkar N. Nayak*

This article Surveys the literature on the inter-country movements of Capital.[1] There is a vast list of theories explaining why firms move and operate in other countries. Some theories suggest that the internationalisation of capital can be explained through the theory of international trade, mainly due to the fact that trade is one of the mode of transferring capital to other countries. Others explain the movement of capital in terms of foreign direct investment.[2] Some of these theories have assumed perfect market conditions while others have developed their views on this basis of imperfect market framework. There are also theories which do not fall in the general equilibrium theory of international trade or investment. A selective survey of these divergent views is the main objective of this paper.

International Trade Theories

International trade theories has been dominated by (a) the theory of absolute cost advantage (b) the concept of comparative cost advantage and (c) the theory of difference in factor endowments.

* Reader, Department of Business Economics, Faculty of Commerce, M.S. University of Baroda, Vadodara 390002.

The theory of Absolute Cost Advantage

It was Adam Smith who clearly stated that a country could gain by trade (Sodersten and reed, 1994: 4-5). A tailor does not make his own shoes, he exchanges a suit for shoes. Thereby both the tailor and the shoemaker gain. In the same way, Smith argued, a country could gain by trading with other countries.

Adam Smith Explained the theory of absolute advantage in a two-country, two commodity and one factor model. If country A produces one unit of good X with the help of 10 units of labour or one unit of good Y with the help of 20 units of labour, and if country B produces one unit of good X with the help of 20 units of labour or one unit of good Y with the help of 10 units of labour, then the country A has absolute advantage in producing good X and country B in producing good Y. This means that country A shall specialize in the production of good X and export it to country B. Country B will specialize in the production of good Y and export it to country A. Thus both countries will benefit from trade.

However, this theory fails to explain the occurrence of trade between countries if, a country produces both the goods with absolute advantage. It was left to Ricardo to produce a stronger argument from benefits of trade contained in the theory of comparative advantage.

The Theory of Comparative Topic Cost Advantage

The theory of absolute cost advantage is limited by the fact that it fails to explain the occurrence of trade between two countries even if one particular country produces both the goods with absolute cost advantage. This limitations led David Ricardo to set out the theory of comparative cost advantage (Haberler, 1950).

Ricardo not only postulated immobility of labour and land from one country to another, but also that of free capital in form of invisible funds. Hence international trade would consist of produced and reproducible commodities only. Different countries would be endowed with different types and qualities of land and labour. The accumulated stocks of capital would also be different. Given the difference in endowments of land, labour and accumulated capital, different countries would have different cost of producing different commodities. Some products would be cheaper in some countries than in others and some products would be costlier in some countries than in others. This being so, some countries would have an advantage in some products while others would produce some other commodities at a lower cost. Hence, it would be advantageous for countries to trade their cheaper products with others in exchange for products which they themselves may produce at a higher cost.

Heckscher-Ohlin Approach

The theory of comparative cost advantage was rejected by Heckscher-Ohlin (Bhagwati, 1964). According to them the difference in comparative cost advantage between two countries results not only from the difference in the quality of labour but also from the differences in the relative scarcity (as reflected in their relative prices) of factors of production in and in the propotion in which the different factors are required in the production of different commodities. A country which employs more of the factors that are relatively abundant in the production of a commodity can produce it cheaper than another country and hence it will enjoy comparative cost advantage in the production of this commodity. Thus a capital abundant country would export capital intensive products to a labour abundant country and import labour intensive products from it. The capital-intensive country would adopt capital-intensive techniques for the same commodities. A labour abundant country on the other hand would export labour intensive products to capital intensive countries and import capital intensive products from them. It will also employ labour intensive technique for production of similar commodities. Similarly is the case with land intensive products though it is difficult to define land intensity than capital intensity (Brahmananda, 1997:9)

Samuelson (1939) and Jones (1957) by abstracting the theory from all the factors other than strict differences in factor endowments (relating to two factors) between the trading countries, have further developed the theory of comparative cost of Heckscher-Ohlin. This theory has been widely accepted for explaining the existence of trade. It also has been tested empircally by Leontief (1966).

The Trade Theories Applied to International Investment

Several writers have attempted to explain international investment with the help of the trade theory. Here it need to be emphasized that in the classical model of static comparative advantage there is no room for international investment at all. With immobility of factors of production but completely free movement of goods, there is little incentive for international investment especially in direct form (Kindleberger, 1969: 15-45). But in the present times with production by firms outside national boundries accounting for more than 25 per cent of the world's output (UN, 1998), these assumptions are no longer valid.

It was Mundel (1957) who first attempted to incorporate capital movements into trade theory. Using Hekcher-Ohlin-Samuelson model, Mundel stated that trade and capital movements are substitutes for each other and that the factor price ratio equalisation implies the equalisation of commodity price ratio. Corden (1974) by quoting Mundel is of the firm opinion that "it is possible to use various bits of analysis derived from trade theory to study location decisions of the multinational corporations (MNCs)[3] and their effects on trade flows". Similarly Hirsch (1976) while admitting that assumptions of trade theory are not consistent with the theory of international investment, feels that international investment takes place in a world which admits revenue producing factors, such as firm specific advantages. Lall (1976) is also in favour of enlarging the trade theory in order to take into account the industrial organizational factors that have led to the phenomenal growth of MNCs.

International Investment Theories Assuming A perfect Competitive Market

It Was MacDougall (1958) who tried to develop a model in a perfectly competitive market to explain the effects of and the reason for foreign investment. His theory was further elaborated by Kemp (1964). They by assuming a two country model and the price of capital being equal to its marginal productivity stated that when capital moves freely from an investing country to the host country, the marginal productivity of capital tends to be equalized between the two countries. Even though the output of the investing country falls subsequent to foreign investment, the national income doesnot decline because the country receives a positive return on the capital invested abroad. So long as the receipt from foreign investment is greater than the loss of output, the investing country will continue to invest abroad as the national income is higher than what it was before foreign investment. A greater investment in the host country is also beneficial to it because there is an increase in national income.

The end result of foreign investment, thus, benefits both the two countries in terms of efficient use of resources and increase in welfare.

However MacDougall-kemp model is unhelpful in explaining the growth and causes of international investment in a realistic way as it assumes competitive factor and commodity market, which does not exist in real world. Morever, this model doesnot deal exclusively with foreign direct investment. Later analyses of international investment have, therefore, turned to explanation of foreign investment which explicity take market imperfect into account and pay greater attention to industrial structure, the production and dissemation of technology and the role of product differentiation in order to examine the phenomenon of international investment.

International Investment Theories Assuming Market Imperfections

The Oligopolistic Theory of Investment

The Oligopolistic theory takes the help of such diverse fields of study as theories of firm, location, monopolistic competition, innovation and exchange instability to come out with a comprehensive view of the actual process of international investment. The oligopolistic theory also known as intangible asset approach of investment was first advanced by Hymer (1960)[4] and later expounded by Kindleberger (1969), Caves (1971) and Knickerbocker (1973).

The essence of the oligopolistic theory is that firms operating abroad and over long distance suffer from an instrinsic disadvantage due to the differences in language, difficulties of communication or lack of knowledge of local laws and market conditions. These disadvantages must be sufficiently offset by some sort of market power as to make international investment profitable.[5] The sources of market power, monopolistic advantage in Kindleberger's terms or the firm specific advantage in Hymer's terms are in the form of a larger or cheaper source of capital superior management, patent protected superior technology, better marketing skill, easy access to raw materials and economies of scale. Since the market is imperfect, the international firms are able to take the advantage of their market power and reap good profit by investing internationally.

There are many who support this theory of international investment. Graham and Krugman (1989) stated that it is the technological advantage possessed by European firms that has made them to invest in USA in the past. However, critics like Robock and Simmond (1983) argue that possessing of technological advantage doesnot necessarily mean investment abroad. The international firms may very well exploit their market power through exports or licensing. But there are number of factors which influence the choice between direct investment and export such as cost of production, local government policy, local market conditions, the oligopolistic reaction of rival firms etc. (Corden, 1974). Similarly the choice between direct investment and licensing will depend upon factors such as the size of the market, the riskness of investment, the secrecy and novelty of the technology, the host government's policy and the range of technologies and products involved (Baranson, 1970).

The Location Theory

The oligopolistic theory explains "What motives a firm to go international. The location theory on the other hand explains "Where" international investment will occur. The location theory is concerned with both supply and demand oriented variables influencing the spatial distribution of production processes. Assuming a certain size and distribution of markets and that each firm is a profit maximizer operating in situation of price taker, production will be located in a place where the costs are lowest (Greenhut, 1952). This in turn will depend on the availability and cost of factor inputs, the efficiency at which these factors are converted into outputs and the costs movement from the point of production to that of marketing.

As opposed to this approach demand oriented theories assume production costs to be independent of location and assert that the distribution of markets and the location of rivals will govern the setting up of production units (Losch, 1954). This theory is essentially an extension of the oligopoly theory of international investment. Each location will gaurantee an element of spatial monopoly and the extent of this monopoly will depend on the character of market, the location strategy, the efficiency of competitors and the transport costs. It will also depend upon the character of production i.e. whether or not a firm is operating under the conditions of economies of scale as this will affect the extent to which firms tend to cluster or disperse and the number of firms involved.

However, the location theory tends to confine itself to explaining the location of plants of single product, national firms (Dunning, 1973). Further many of the unique quality connected with multinational firms such as its ability to shift inputs like human capital, information and knowledge across national boundries at negligible or zero cost are igonored. Product acceptability is also assumed to be interdependent of the location of supply. For these reason, the location theory provides only a partial answer to the question "where" international investment will take place.

The Product Topic Cycle

Theory in contrast to the above theories it was Vernon (1966) who with the help the data from US multinational firms tried to explain "when" international investment will take place. This theory is known as the Product Cycle theory.

According to Vernon most of the products follow a three-stage life cycle. The First stage is known as the "innovation" stage. In order to have a lead in the market, the firm with the help of research and development will innovate a product and initial production will be located in the country of innovation and mostly sold in local market. In this stage the quality of the product rather than the price will determine the demand because the demand is assumed to be price-inelastic.

In the second or the "maturing product" stage the demand for the new product increases substantially in other developed countries and it turns price-elastic. Competitors begin to appear at this stage to supply the product at a lower price due to lower distribution cost. The product of the innovator is often costlier as it involves transportation cost and other barries to entry especially tarrif imposed by host country's government. Thus in order to compete with rivals and sormount the barriers to entry the innovator decides to produce the product in the host country. This leads to international investment.

At the final "standardize product" stage, the product becomes standardized and its production becomes widely know, therefore, production will shift to a low cost location or to a developing country where labour cost is low. The product is then exported back to the country of origin or to other developed markets.

This theory explains the early post world war-II expansion of US firms in other countries. But the different stages of the product life cycle do no necessarily follow in the same order. In fact Vernon (1979) himself pointed in his latter writings that the firms have been found moving to developing countries in the second stage itself. Further, the assumption of barriers to export causes a firm to set up production base in other countries is not always true. For the US firms have not set up subsidiaries in all foreign countries where they have been exporting (Bhagwati, 1972a): Morever there is contradiction in development in the second stage which is anti-trade oriented while the third stage is trade oriented.

Internalization Theory

Buckley and Casson (1976) provide an explanation for international investment by linking the oliogopolist theories with the location theory. Like Hymer they also assume market imperfection in the sense that an international firm possesses firm specific advantages. While in the views of Buckley and Casson the imperfection relates to the transaction cost that leads to internationalization of intermediate products mainly in the form of knowledge and expertise.

The involvement in research and development and training of manpower by a firm will lead to the emergence of new knowledge, processes and expertise. But it becomes difficult to transmit this knowledge and expertise to other firms because of market imperfection and high transport cost. However, these intermediate products can be easily transferred at a low cost to different units of the same firm located at different places. The intra-firm transmission rather than inter-firm transmission makes the subsidiaries to earn higher profit than the rival firms. This provides a motivation for a firm to go international. The internalization approach of international investment is similar to the appropriability approach of Magee (1979) which emphasizes on the potential returns to technology enhancement as the prime motive behind internationalization of firms.

The opponents of this theory argue that the intra-firm transaction cost may not always be low. If subsidiaries are located in an unfamiliar location and if the cultural difference between the home country and the host country is large, internalization process will become costly because the firms will have to spend money to make their product adaptable to local environment (Kogut and Parkinson, 1993; Franke etal. 1991). Buckley (1988) himself was aware of this limitation in his latter writtings.

The Eclectic Approach

The eclectic approach which is often referred to as the OLI paradigm, as profounded by Dunning (1977) combines the oligopolistic theory, the location theory and the internationalization theory to explain international investment in an imperfect market set up.

According to Dunning at any given point of time, the stock of foreign assets owned by a multinational firms is dependent on the ownership advantages (O), the locational consideration (L), and the extent to which these advantages are marketed within the various units of the firm i.e. the internalisation gains (I).

The essential element in the eclectic theory is that all three types of conditions must be met before there will be foreign investment i.e. all the three conditions are necessary, but no one is sufficient. Suppose for example that a firm has an ownership advantage. If locational consideration indicate that production within the foreign market would be more profitable than producing at home and exporting, but there are no internalisation advantage than it would be more profitable for the home firm to license its ownership advantage to the foreign firm. If on the other hand, there were internalisation gains but no locational advantages on another country than the firm be better off if it produces at home and export to the foreign market.

Dunning is also conscious of the fact that the configuration of the OLI advantage differs from country to country and products to products. And ultimately, it is the difference in configuration of OLI advantages that will determine the direction and pattern of foreign investment.

The eclectic paradigm is widely accepted than the other imperfect market based theories of international investment. It has also been empirically tested by Dunning (1980) himself with satisfactory results.

Theories Based on Relative Strength of Currency

It was Aliber (1970) who first developed the theory of international investment based on the relative strength of a currency. He recognizes some of the specific aspect of foreign investment which are absent from domestic investment. Of these, investment in a different currency area is the most obvious. Aliber is not concerned with explaining investment in the same currency area, e.g. UK investment in Australia, but only where assets are in different currency.

He postulated that firms from strong-currency country will shift to weaker-currency country because a firm from strong currency country has a competitive advantage over the weak currency firms partly because the market demands a premium for bearing uncertainty about exchange risk and partly because the market does not attach a currency premium to foreign income of the source country firm. As a result, the home country firms are motivated to invest abroad to capitalize on the same stream of expected earnings at a higher rate than the host country firms. Aliber hypothesis has been empirically tested to explain foreign investment in United States, United Kingdom and Canada.

Another theory based on the strength of the currency was developed by Froot and Stein (1991). According to them, a depreciation in the real value of a country's currency lower the wealth of its residents vis-a-vas the wealth of foreign residents, this gives foreigners an edge in buying control of productive corporate assets of the domestic firms. However, the authors have stressed that this factor is one of the many determinants of foreign investment in USA. De Mello (1997) in the same vein, stated that exchange rates affect foreign investment in so far as they affect a firm's cash flow, expected profitability and the attractiveness of domestic assets to foreigners.

Caves (1988) has also tested empirically the theory based on the strength of currency. He found a significant negative correlation between the level of exchange rate and the level of foreign investment in the United States.

But however, valid such an explanation may be for foreign investment in the developed countries, it fails to explain international investment in the same currency areas. It also does not seem to be particularly relevant to that in developing countries with highly imperfect or non existence capital markets and with heavily regulated foreign exchange.[6]

Other Theories

Politico-Economic Theories

One approach to explain the extent and character of international investment is to ask the multinational companies themselves to identify the reasons for their behaviour. In one such survey conducted by Basi (1966) it was revealed the executives of 159 firm out of 214 firms reported political stability in host country as the most important variable affecting their foreign investment decisions.

Fatehi-Sedah and Safi Zedah (1989) have also found that political risk and instability in host country adversely affect the level of foreign investment inflow. In contrast to this Tallman (1988) opines that political risk in the home country has a favourable impact on outward foreign investment.

However, Schneider and Frey (1985) are of the opinion that political factors are only supporting factor for international investment. The economic determinant cannot be ignored in explaining foreign investment.

The Geo-business Theory

Robock and Simmonds (1983): have come out with a "geo-business" theory by integrating different factors to explain why firms invest abroad. These factors are:

(*a*) Conditioning variables,

(*b*) Motivational variables, and

(*c*) Control variables.

Factors which are product specific, country specific and inter-nation specific are included in the conditioning variables. As explained in the oligopolistic theories, the product specific factors can be explained in terms of economies of scale, product differentiation, managerial skills, patented product processes etc. Adverse conditions in the home country like lack of demand, poor resources, anti-business government policies and the favourable conditions in the host country such as high growth rate, availability of natural resources and economic and political stability are the country specific variables which encourages the internationalization of firms. The operations of international finance, monetary and trade system that encourage or discourage international investments are included in internation variables.

The motivational variables indicates whether a firm has the motive to exploit its conditioning variables or not. The motivational variables are either exclusive to the firm or those based on the firm's competitive relationship with other firms. In the first case the firm must be aware of foreign opportunities and its own capability. In the second case, the variables include the firm's competitive position and reaction of its competitors.

Lastly, the control variables in the form of government policies in the home and the host country will also affect foreign investment. This many be exerted in various ways, both by direct controls and those affecting the values of the variables which influence decision-taking by firms to invest overseas (Dunning, 1973). For instance, if the policies of the host government are anti-foreign investment then investment will be affected adversely even if other factors mentioned above are favourable. Similarly, it will be difficult for a firm to invest abroad if the source-country government restricts the outflow of foreign exchange. Thus all these factors together will determine international production.

Theories Explaining Foreign Investment from Third World Countries

Various theories discussed above related mostly to foreign investment from the western developed countries like USA. But during the past two decades a large number of multinational firms have emerged from the developing countries like Taiwan and Korea-the so called newly industrialized countries. This being so, some changes are needed to be made in the existing theories to explain the growth of the third world multinationals and their investment abroad (Sharan, 1985). These countries have generally imported technology from developed countries. But as the technology imported is more suited for a very large market, the firms tend to export the products after meeting the local demand. Once the consumer abroad become familiar with product and market is gradually established i.e. when the products become mature, the firms prefer to set up subsidiaries abroad to produce it locally rather than export it. In some cases the affiliates are set up even in those countries from where the technology originates. Thus, the firms from third world countries, also experience the product cycle theory (Ting, 1982).

Sometimes firms in developing world modify the product or change the technology in order to suit the consumer and thereby enjoy an oligopolistic advantage, not only this firms from developing countries use technology which are more suitable for local condition and consumption habits of the consumers of other developing countries. Thus the firm specific advantage as mentioned by Hymer is also applicable to the firms from these countries (Ting 1982). A firm may also move to other developing countries where they find cheap natural resources. Therefore, the locational advantage mentioned in the location theory can also be applied to firms from developing countries (Sharan, 1995). In some countries like China a positive impact is expected when the domestic currency is relatively weak compared to that of the foreign investor (Wang and Swain, 1995). Thus Currency Based Theory is also Relevant to the Countries of the Third World.

Apart from the economic variables, the domestic turmoil and the subsequent labour disputes may also have a considerable impact on outward investments from developing countries. Teha (1998) mentions that domestic labour disputes have significantly influenced Korea's foreign investment in North American and countries in Asia. The labour disputes have led to rapid increase in wages and uncertainty in production which have undermined Korea s comparative advantage in labour intensive industries and reduced profitability even in capital-intensive industries. Thus Korean labour intensive industries have been relocated in Asian countries with lower wages and negligible labour problems. In contrast, North American, where union power is low and technologies is high has attracted capital intensive firms from Korea.

Conclusion

A great deal of theories exists to explain the "why", "when" and "where" international investment occurs. Starting with international trade theories and other theories in the conditions of perfect market the other theories have gone through different market conditions. Most of the theories are developed in an imperfect market setup to explain investment from developed countries. In spite of their different approach, these theories are unanimous in their view that a firm moves abroad to reap the benefit of some advantage enjoyed by them in form of locational, firm specific or internationalization of market. At the same time some theories suggest that government policy in the host country is also vitally important to attract foreign investment. The theories mentioned above, however, needs some modification to incorporate such factors like labour disputes for explaining international investment from third world countries. In certain cases weak currency in the host country also cause larger flow of foreign investment.

Notes

1. In the present paper the terms international investment, international movements of capital, foreign investment and foreign direct investment have been used interchangeably.
2. Foreign direct investment (FDI) is conventionally defined as a form of international inter-firm cooperation that involves a significant equity stake in, or effective management control of, foreign enterprises. See De Mello (1997).
3. MNC also referred to as Multinational firm (MNFs) or Multinational Enterprises (MNEs) are those enterprises which

operates in atleast six foreign countries. Since FDI takes place mainly through MNCs, the theory of FDI is also a theory of MNCs. See Ahoroni (1971).

4. Hymer put forward his theory first in 1960 in his doctoral dessertation to M.I.T. His thesis was published in 1976.

5. Market power refers to the ability of particular firms, acting singly or in collusion, to dominate their respective markets, to be more secure or even to be less efficient, than in a situation with more effective competition. See Lall (1976).

6. But in certain developing countries like China a possitive impact in inflow of foreign investment is witnessed when the domestic currency is relatively weak compared to that of the foreign investor. See Wang and Swain (1995).

References

1. Aharoni, Y., (1971) "The definition of a Multinational Corporation", *Quartely Review of Economics and Business,* Autumn, pp. 101-120.

2. Aliber, R.Z., (1970), "A Theory of Direct Investment" in C.P. Kindleberger (e. d.) *The International Corporation,* Cambridge: MIT Press.

3. Baranson, J., (1970), "Technology Transfer through the International Firm, *American Economic Review,* May, pp. 435-440.

4. Basi, R. S., (1966), *Determinants of US Direct Investment in Foreign Countries,* Kent:Kent University Press.

5. Bhagwati, J., (1964), "The Pure Theory of International Trade: A Survey", Economic Journal, LXXIV, PP. 1-84.

6. Bhagwati, J., (1972), "The Internationalization of Capital", *Journal of Economic Issues,* March, pp. 28-36.

7. Bhagwati, J., (1972a), "Book Review Raymond Vernon, Sovereignty at Bay : The Multinational spread of US Enterprises, 1971", *Journal of International Evonomics,* 25, pp. 456-457.

8. Brahmananda, P. R., (1997), "Factor Mobility, Globalisation, Multi-National Corporations, Convergence and the Consequent Revolution in International Trade Theory", *The Indian Economic Journal,* 44, pp. 7-12.

9. Buckley, P.J. and Casson, M., (1970), *The Future of the Multinational Enterprise,* London: Macmillan.

10. Buckley, P.J., (1988), "The Limits of Explanation : Testing the Interntionalization Theory of the Multinational Enterprise", *Journal of International Business Studies,* 29, pp. 181-1993.

11. Caves. R.E., (1971), "International Corporations: The Industrial Economics of Foreign Investment", *Economica*, pp. 1-27.

12. Caves, R.E., (1988), *Exchange Rate Movements and Foreign Direct Investment in United States*, Discussion Paper: 1383, Harvard Insurance of Economic Research.

13. Corden, W.M., (1974), "The Theory of International Trade", in J. H. Dunning (ed.), *Economic Analysis and the Multinational Enterprise*, New York: Praeger.

14. De Mello, L.R., (1997), "Foreign Direct Investment in Developing Countries and Growth", *The Journal of Developments Studies*, 134 (1), pp. 1-31.

15. Dunning, J.H., (1973), "The Determinants of International Production", *Oxford Economic papers*, pp. 289-336.

16. Dunning J.H., (1977), "Trade, Location of Economic Activity and the MNE: A search for an Eclectic Approach" in B.H. Ohlin and P.K. Wijkman (eds.), *The International Allocation of Economic Activity*, London: Macmillan, pp. 77-80.

17. Dunning J.H., (1980), "Towards an Eclectic Theory of International Production", *Journal of International Business*, XI, pp., 9-31

18. Fetehi-Sedah, K and Safizedah, M.H., (1989), "Association between Political Instability and Flow of Foreign Direct Investment *Management International Review*, 29, pp. 33-45.

19. Franke, R.H, Hofstade, G and Bond, M.H., (1991), "Cultural Roots of Economic Performance : *A Research Note", Strategic management Journal, 12, pp. 165-175.*

20. Froot, K.A. and Stein, J.M., (1991), "Exchange Rates and Foreign Direct Investment : An Imperfect Capital Markets Approach", *The Quarterly Journal of Economics*, 4, pp. 1191-1217.

21. Graham, E.M. and Krugman, P.R., (1989), *Foreign Direct Investments in the United States*, Washington, DC: Institute for International Economics, pp. 36-40.

22. Greenhut, M., (1952), "The Size and Shape of the Market Area of the Firm", *Southern Economic Journal*, July, pp. 35-46.

23. Haberler, G.U., (1950), *The theory of International Trade*, London: William Hudge and Co.

24. Hirsch, S., (1967), *Location of Industry and International Competitiveness*, London: Oxford University Press.

25. Hymer, S.H., (1976), *The International Operations of National Firms:* A Study of Direct Investment, Cambridge : MIT Press.

26. Jones. R.W., (1957), " Factor Proportions and the Heckscher – Ohlin Theorem", *Review of Economic Studies*, 25, pp. 1-10.

27. Kemp. M.C., (1964), *The Theory of International Trade*, London: Prentice Hall.

28. Kindleberger, C.P., (1969), *American Business abroad*, New Haven: Yale University Press.

29. Knickerbocker, F.T., (1973), *Oligopolistic Reaction and the Multinational Enterprise*, Boston: Harvard University Press.

30. Kogut, B and Parkinson, D., (1993), "The diffusion of American Organizing Principles to Europe" in B. Kogut (ed.), *Country Competitiveness and the Organization of Work*, London: Oxford University Press.

31. Lall, S., (1976), "Theories of Direct Private Foreign Investment and Multinational Behaviour" *Economic and Political Weekly*, XI, pp. 1331-1340.

32. Leontif, W.W., (1966), "Domestic Production and Foreign Trade", *Input-output Economics*, pp. 68-99.

33. Losch, A., (1954), *The Economics of Location*, New Haven: Hale University Press.

34. MacDougal, G.D.A., (1958), "The Benefits and Costs of Private Foreign Investment Abroad: A Theoritical Approach", *Economic Record*, 36, pp. 13-20.

35. Magee, S.P., (1979), "Information and the Multinational Corporation : An Appropriability Theory of Direct Foreign Investment" in D.R. Lessard (ed.), *International Financial Management*, Boston: Warren Gorham & Lamont, pp. 57-73.

36. Mundell, R.A., (1957), "International Trade and Factor Mobility", *American Economic Review*, 47, pp. 60-75.

37. Robock S.H. and Simmonds K., (1983), *International Business and Multinational Enterprise*, Illinois: Richard D. Irwin.

38. Samuelson, P.A., (1939), "The Gains from International Trade", *Canadian Journal of Economics and Political Science*, 5, pp. 195-205.

39. Schneider, F and Frey, B.S., (1985), "Economic and Political Determinants of Foreign Direct Investments", *World Development, 13*, pp. 161-178.

40. Sharan, V., (1985), "Internationalization of Third World Firms: An Indian Case Study", *International Marketing Review*, 2, pp. 63-71.

41. Sharan, V., (1995), Theories of International Business, 4, *Foreign Trade Review*, pp. 326-328. Soderstein Reed, 1994, *International Economics*, London: Macmillan. (1988).

42. Tallman, S.B., "Home Country Political Risk and foreign Direct Investment in the United States", *Journal of International Business Studies*, 29, pp. 219-234.

43. Teha, M.J., (1996), "Labour Disputes and Direct Foreign Investment", *Seoul Journal of Economics*, 9, pp. 175-180.

44. Teha, M.J., (1998), "Labour disputes and Direct Foreign Investment: The Experience of Korea in Transition", *Economic Development and Cultural Change*, 2, pp. 305-327.

45. Ting, W., (1982), "The Product Development Process in NIC Multinationals", *Columbia Journal of World Business*, 28, pp. 76-81.

46. U.N., (1998), *World Investment Report*, Delhi: Bookwell.

47. Vornon, R., (1966), "International Investment and International Trade in the Product Cycle", *Quarterly Journal of Economics*, 80, pp. 190-207.

48. Vernon, R., (1979), "The product cycle Hypothesis in a New International Environment", *Oxford Bulletion of Economics and Statistics*, LXI, pp. 255-267.

49. Wing, Z.Q. and Swain, N.J., (1995), "The Determinants of Foreign Direct Investment in Transforming Economies: Evidence from Hungary and China", *Weltwirtschaftsliches Archiv*, *131*, pp. 359-382.

50. Wells, L.T., (1969), "Test of the Product Life Cycle Model of International Trade", Quarterly Journal of Economics, 28, pp. 152-162.

12

An Overview of Various Theories of Exchange Rate

R. Rajendran*

The rate of exchange is the price of one currency in terms of another. The exchange rate is one of the most important prices in a country because it links domestic economy and the rest of world economy. As such, it affects relative national competitiveness.

Almost from the dawn of history, gold has been used as a medium of exchange because of the desirable properties. It is durable, storable, portable, easily recognized, divisible and easily standardized (Shapiro, A.C. 1999).

The gold standard essentially involved a commitment by the participating countries to the prices of their domestic currencies in terms of a specified amount of gold. The countries maintained these prices by being willingly to buy or sell gold to anyone at that price. Since the value of gold relative to other goods doesn't change much over long periods of time, the mandatory discipline imposed by gold standard should ensure long-run price stability for both individual countries and group of countries. Indeed, there was remarkable long-run price stability in the period before World War I when most countries were on gold standards.

* Senior Lecturer in Economics, Postgraduate and Research Department of Economics, Government Arts College, Kumbakonam.

The gold exchange standard broke down during World War I and was briefly reinstated from 1925-1931 as the gold exchange standard. Under this standard, the United States and England could hold only gold reserves but other nations could hold both gold or dollars or pounds as reserves. In 1931, England departed from gold in the wake of massive gold and capital flows, owing to an unrealistic exchange rate, and the gold standard was finished.

Fixed Exchange Rate System: (1946-1971)

Under the Bretton-woods agreement, implemented in 1946, each Government pledged to maintain a fixed rate for the currency vis-à-vis the dollar or gold. Since one ounce of gold was set equal to $35, fixing a currency's gold price was equivalent to setting the exchange rate to the dollar. The exchange rate was allowed to fluctuate only within one per cent of its stated par value.

The fixed exchange rates were maintained by official intervention in the foreign exchange markets. The intervention took the form of purchase and sales of dollars by foreign Central Banks against their own currencies, whenever the supply and demand conditions in the market caused exchange rates to deviate from the agreed-upon par values. The International Monetary Fund (IMF) stood ready to provide the necessary foreign exchange to member nations for defending their currencies against pressure resulting from temporary factors. Any dollar acquired by the monetary authorities in the process of such intervention could then be exchanged to gold at the U.S treasury, at a fixed price of $35 per ounce.

The stability of exchange rates removed a great deal of uncertainty from international trade and investment transactions, thus promoting their growth for the benefit of all the participants. Also, the functioning of the system imposed a degree of discipline on the participating nations economic policies.

In fact, Bretton-woods system was a fixed exchange rate system in name only. Of 21 major industrial countries, only the United States and Japan had no change in par values during the period 1946-1971 (Shapiro, A.C 1999).

The deathblow for the system came on August 15,1971, when president Nixon, ordered the U.S authorities to terminate convertibility even for Central Banks. At the same time he devalued the dollar to deal with America's emerging trade deficit.

Floating Exchange Rate System

In December 1971, under the Bretton-woods agreement, the dollar was devalued to 1/38 of an ounce of gold and other currencies were revalued by agreed on amounts vis-à-vis the dollar. After months of such last-ditch efforts to set new fixed rates, the world sufficiently turned to floating exchange rates in 1973.

These conditions make a system of flexible or floating exchange rates-exchange rates freely determined in an open market primarily by private dealings and like other market prices, varying from day to day which is absolutely essential for the fulfillment of our basic economic objective namely the achievement and maintenance of a free and prosperous world community engaged in unrestricted multilateral trade. (Friedman, M 1968)

Free or floating rates refer to the system where the exchange rates are determined by the conditions of demand for and supply of foreign exchange in the market. The rates are free to fluctuate according to the changes in the market demand and supply forces with no restriction on buying and selling of foreign currencies in the exchange market.

Flexible exchange rates provide a smoother adjustment mechanism through changes in exchange rates. Any adverse in country's Balance of Payments situation is corrected immediately and automatically under flexible rates. It thereby prevents from having persistent deficits and inspires confidence in the international financial system.

Both the fixed and floating exchange rate system have their own merits and demerits. What is required is a system which is fairly stable but at the same time flexible enough to accommodate small changes in accordance with the needs.

A number of theoretical models of exchange rate determination have been developed to explain the behaviour of exchange rate under different exchange rate regimes. A model which suits under one exchange rate regime may not work out under another exchange rate system. Again a model emphasises a particular variable or group of variables in deciding the external value of currency. A detailed discussion about these theoretical models proves these points. These models are generally divided into two groups they are: - i) Structural models and ii) Time series models. The mint parity theory, the purchasing power parity approach, asset marker approach which includes monetary and portfolio balance model etc., are coming under structural models. Random walk model, chaotic model etc., are coming under time series models.

Structural Models

(i) The Mint Parity Approach

The mint parity theory of determination of foreign exchange rate explains the determination of exchange rate between the currency units of the gold standard. When two countries are on the gold standard, their currency units are either made of gold of given purity and weight or are freely convertible into gold of given purity of fixed rate. Under the gold standard, countries maintain the value of their currencies in a fixed relationship to the value of gold by committing themselves to buy and sell gold at fixed prices. A nation's currency is said to be fully on the gold standard if the government of that country: (i) buys and sells gold in unlimited quantity at an officially fixed price; and (ii) permits unrestricted gold flows into and out of the country. The practical meaning of (i) and (ii) is that an individual who holds domestic currency knows in advance how much he can obtain in exchange for it and how much foreign currency the gold will buy when exposed to another country.

By mint par is meant that the foreign exchange rate is determined on the weight to weight basis of the metallic content of the two money units, allowance being given to the purity of metallic content (Vaish, M.C. and Singh, S 1978).

Before World War I and later 1920's many countries, including U.S.A and U.K followed the gold standard. Since gold standard no longer exists the scope for the application of the mint parity theory of foreign exchange rate does not exist today.

(ii) Purchasing Power Parity Approach

The Purchasing power parity theory was first developed by the scholars of the Salamanca school of Spain. Purchasing power is the disarmingly simple empirical proposition that, once converted to a common currency, national price levels should be equal (Rogoff Kenneth, 1996).

The modern origins of purchasing power parity theory trace to the debate on how to restore the world financial system after its collapse during World War I. Prior to war most countries followed the gold standard, in which their currencies were convertible to gold at fixed parities. However maintaining the gold standard became impossible and so it was abandoned.

In a series of influential articles, the Swedish economist Gustav Cassel (1921, 1922) promoted the use of purchasing power parity as means for settling relative gold parities. Though purchasing power parity had been discussed previously by classical economists such as J.S. Mill, Alfred Marshal and Ludwig Von Miser, Cassel was originally the first to treat purchasing power parity as a practical empirical theory. Cassel's writings were quite influential and purchasing power parity calculations played an important role in the debate over Britain's much criticized decision to try to restore the pre-war mint parity with the dollar in 1925. In this context, Cassel stated that given a normal freedom of trade between two countries A and B, a rate of exchange will establish itself between them and this rate will, smaller fluctuation apart, remain unaltered as no alteration in the purchasing power of either currency is made and no special hindrances are imposed upon the trade. But as soon as inflation takes place in the money of 'A', and the purchasing power of their money is, therefore, diminished, the value of the A-money in B must necessarily be reduced in the some proportion. Hence the main principle under purchasing power parity can be stated as: when two currencies have been inflated the new normal rate of exchange will be equal to the old rate multiplied by the quotient between the degrees of inflation of both countries. There will, of course, always be fluctuations from this new normal rate, and in a period of transition these fluctuations are apt to be rather wide. But the rate calculated in the way indicated must be regarded as the new parity between the currencies. This parity may be called the purchasing power parity, as it's determined by the quotients of the purchasing power of the different countries.

Today various versions of purchasing power parity are used in a wide range of applications: from charging the right initial exchange rate for a newly independent country to forecasting medium and long-term real exchange rates, and to adjusts for price differentials in international comparison of income.

Alternative Versions of Purchasing Power Parity Theory

The two versions of purchasing power parity theory are: (i) absolute version, and (ii) relative version.

Absolute Version of Purchasing Power Parity Theory

The basic building block of purchasing power parity theory is the so, called "Law of one price" (LOP). The law of one price states that once prices are converted to a common currency, the same good should be sold for the same price in different countries. Symbolically:

$$P_i = E\,P^*_i$$

$$\text{Or } E = \frac{P_i}{P^*_i}$$

Where

P_i = the domestic currency price of good i,

P^*_i = the foreign currency price, and

E = the exchange rate defined as the home currency price of foreign currency.

The biggest problem with the implemention of absolute purchasing power parity, however, is that very little data is available for measuring it. First, governments do not construct indices for an internationally standardized basket of goods. Second, government price data come in the form of indices relative to a base year. The indices give no indication of how large absolute purchasing power parity theory deviations were for the base year. To overcome these difficulties the second version has been developed and it is known as relative purchasing power parity theory.

Relative Purchasing Power Parity Theory

Relative purchasing power parity theory is the prediction that the proportionate change in the home country's price level is equal to the proportionate change in the product of the foreign price level and the exchange rate. This has been expressed in the form of the following equation.

$$\frac{\sum P_{it}}{\sum P_{it-1}} = \left(\frac{E_t}{E_{t-1}}\right)\left(\frac{\sum P^*_{it}}{\sum P^*_{it-1}}\right)$$

Where

Pi = the domestic currency price of good i,

P^*i = foreign currency price,

E = the exchange rate defined as the home currency price of foreign currency, and

T = time.

There are two possible time horizons for which purchasing power parity theory might hold. One is the long run. Under this, short run exchange rate tends towards a long run equilibrium that is purchasing power parity. Short run fluctuations in the exchange rate can occur for a variety of reasons, but once such a disturbance has occurred, the exchange rate eventually returns to the long-run purchasing power parity rate. The relative version is that the purchasing power parity theory must always hold, even in the short run. (Kruger, Anne, 1983).

The purchasing power parity theory is subjected to the following criticisms:

(i) The theory makes use of the price index number to measure the changes in the equilibrium rate of exchange and hence the theory suffers from the various limitations of the price index number.

(ii) The Theory ignores the cost of transport in international trade.

(iii) The theory ignores the effects of international capital movement on the foreign exchange market.

(iv) The purchasing power parity theory starts with given rate of exchange, but fails to explain how

that particular rate of exchange is arrived at. Thus, the theory only tells us how, with a given rate of exchange, changes in the purchasing powers of two currencies affect the exchange rate.

(v) The theory is based on the wrong assumption that the elasticity of demand for exports and imports is equal to unity; the theory is valid if the exports and imports change in the same proportion as the change in prices. But this is a very rare occurrence.

(vi) No satisfactory explanation for short-term changes in exchange rate is provided by the theory.

Though, the purchasing power parity theory approach is having certain limitations, the theory keeps resurfacing whenever exchange rates have come unfixed by wars or other events (Lindert, P. 1995). The purchasing power parity theory came into its own in the 1920's when Gustav Cassel and others directed it at the issue of how much European countries would have to change either the official exchange rate or their domestic price levels, given the world war I had driven the exchange rates off their pre-war par values and had brought varying percentages of price inflation to different countries. With the restoration of fixed exchange rate during the early post-war era, the purchasing power parity theory again faded from prominence. This is because the issue in the new system raised seemed less compelling as long as exchange rates are expected to stay fixed. After the resumption of wider spread floating exchange rate 1970's, the hypothesis was revised once again.

Asset Market Approach

Under asset market approach, the exchange market is viewed or modeled as reflecting the supply and demand for financial assets denominated in different currencies. Equilibrium in the balance of payments and exchange market exists when these financial asset markets clear; payment deficit or depreciation occurs when the relative demand for financial asset rises and vice versa.

This broad class of asset market model includes two sub sectors (Ingram, J and Munn R. 1993). They are: - i) monetary model, and ii) portfolio balance model. In the first group of asset market model problems of risk and uncertainty are ignored, thereby allowing domestic and foreign assets to be viewed as perfect substitutes in portfolios. This is monetary approach to balance of payments.

In the second group of model, domestic and foreign assets are viewed as imperfect substitutes in financial portfolios because of uncertainty and risk constraints. This is portfolio approach. A detailed analysis of these two approaches is given below.

Monetary Approach (or) monetary Model of Exchange Rate Determination

To put the new approach in perspective, it is helpful to go back to the origin of balance of payments theory in the framework of David Hume, and specifically to his contribution of the analysis of the price-specie-flow mechanism. Hume's analysis run in terms of an automatic mechanism of international adjustment motivated by money flows and consequential changes in national money price levels. The subsequent elaboration of the theory, up to and partly through the 1930' retained the general notion of automaticity.

In the 1930's, under the stimulus on the one hand of the collapse of the international regime of fixed exchange rates and the emergence of mass unemployment as a major economic problem, and on the other hand of Keynesian revolution- which altered the basic assumption of theory from wage and price flexibility with full employement to wage rigidity with normal mass unemployment-a new approach to balance of payments theory emerged, one which viewed interrelated adjustment not as an automatic process but as a policy problem for governments (Johnson, H.G., 1976).

Attention was therefore concentrated on the 'elasticity condition' required for the impact effect of a devaluation i.e. of the associated change in relative real prices-to be an improvement in the balance of payments. The condition is, for a simple and initially balanced trade, that the sum of the elasticities of home and foreign demand for imports should exceed unity ('Marshall-Lerner condition').

The so called 'elasticity approach' proved demonstrably unsatisfactory in the immediate post-war period of full and over-full employment, owing to its implicit assumption of the existence of unemployed resources that could be mobilised to produce the additional exports and imports substitutes required to satisfy a favourable impact effect.

So the alternative approach, 'absorption approach' was presented by S.S, Alexander, (1952). This approach argues that a favourable effect from devaluation, in a fully developed economy, depends not on the elasticities but on the inflation resulting from the devaluation in these conditions providing a reduction in aggregate absorption relative to aggregate productive capacity.

The presentation of 'absorption approach' as an alternative to 'elasticity approach' led to considerable controversy and extensive efforts to reconcile the two. James Meade (1953) provided a synthesis between 'the elasticity' and 'absorption approach'. Meade presented his analysis in terms of short run equilibrium analysis.

The above approaches are generally termed as current account models of exchange rate determination of 1960's (Kruger, Anne, 1983). The monetary approach represents the intellectual bridge between current account models and the modern understanding of crucial variables in exchange rate determination. The approach originated in the work of a group of economists teaching at or trained at the university of Chicago, led by Robert Mundell and Harry. G. Johnson.

According to H.G. Johnson (1976) "The purpose of monetary approach is to develop a theory of Balance of payments based on the fact that the Balance of payments is a monetary phenomenon in a monetary international economy and requires analysis in terms of monetary concept, and especially the concept of money as a stock and of monetary adjustments of actual to desired stocks, rather than in terms of international money flows as the residual of 'real' flows determined by real relative prices and income".

This approach emphasises that both the balance of payments and the exchange rates are essentially monetary phenomena (Mussa, M 1978).The monetary model is subdivided into flexible-price and sticky-price monetary models.

Flexible-price monetary Model

An important assumption of flexible price monetary model is continuous purchasing power parity (Lindert, P.H. 1995). This approach starts from the definition of exchange rate as the relative price of two monies and attempts to model that relative price in terms of relative supply of and demand for these monies (Taylor, M. 1995). The demand for money, m, is assumed to depend on real income, y, the price level 'p' and the level of nominal interest rate. With all variables except interest rates expressed in logarithms, monetary equlibria in the domestic and foreign country respectively are given by

$$mt = pt + kyt - øit \qquad \text{(i)}$$

$$mt = p^{*}t + k^{*}yt - ø^{*}i^{*}t \qquad \text{(ii)}$$

Since flexible-price monetary model assumes purchasing power parity, the purchasing power parity theory condition ie $St=Pt-P^{*}t$ - (iii) is included in the model.

Where

St = exchange rate of domestic currency in terms of one unit of foreign currency.

The domestic money supply determines the domestic price level and hence the exchange rate is determined by relative money supplies. Solving (i), (ii) and (iii) for the exchange rate gives

$$St= mt- m^{*}t+kyt- k^{*}yt+øit -ø^{*}i^{*}t \qquad \text{(iv)}$$

Equation (iv) is the fundamental flexible price monetary equation. From (iv) we can see that an increase in the domestic money supply, relative to the foreign money stock, will lead to a rise in the St - i.e., a depreciation of domestic currency in terms of foreign currency. A rise in the domestic real income, other things equal, creates an excess demand for the domestic money stock. In an attempt to increase their real money balances, domestic residents reduce expenditure and prices fall until money market equilibrium is achieved. Via purchasing power parity, foreign domestic prices (with foreign prices constant) imply an appreciation of the domestic currency in terms of the foreign currency. Similarly, a depreciation follows from an increase in the domestic interest rate and this reduces the domestic demand for money.

The very high volatility of real exchange rate during the 1970's float, conspicuously refuting the assumption of continuous purchasing power parity, led to the development of sticky price monetary model.

Sticky-Price Monetary Model

Sticky-price monetary model originally due to Dornbush, allows short-terms over-shooting of nominal and real exchange rates above their long-run equilibrium level. Dornbush accepted Chicago version only as the long-run relationship where both purchasing power parity and covered interest parity hold good. But in the short run, it is assumed that goods prices are sticky, but the asset markets adjust instantaneously to preserve the uncovered parity. This means that short run real exchange rate over shoots its long-run equilibrium. (Dornbusch, R. 1976).

Consider effects of a cut in the nominal domestic money supply. Goods prices are sticky in the short run, implies an initial fail in the real money supply and a consequent rise in interest rate in order to clear the money market. This rise in domestic interest rates then leads to a capital inflow and an appreciation of the nominal exchange rate. On the other hand, an increase in the money supply will cause a decline in the interest rate. To prevent capital outflows, the exchange rate will depreciate (in nominal terms) proportionately but because of the sticky prices, this implies a real exchange rate depreciation i.e., the real exchange rates overshoot per unit of foreign exchange. Over time, exchange rate expectations will take the following from:

$$S^e = Q(s\text{-}s) \text{ where}$$

$$0 < Q < 1$$

This means if the actual exchange rate is above the long-run equilibrium exchange rate (s), then speculators will expect 's' to fall towards s at the rate Q per period (i.e., they would expect the exchange rate to depreciate in future). This means that in the short run, due to sticky prices, the purchasing power parity theory relation between the exchange rates s and $p\text{-}p^*$ does not hold good. Moreover, $S^e = (i - i^*)$ because of the uncovered interest parity and $(i - i^*) \neq (\pi_e - \pi^*_e)$ as there are no secular inflationary expectation. So the Dornbush formulation looks as follows (Bokil, S.V. 1990).

$$\bar{s} = (m - m^*) - \varnothing (y - y^*) \qquad \text{(i)}$$

$$\bar{s} - s = \frac{1}{Q}(i - i^*)$$

$$\text{ie } s = \bar{s} - \frac{1}{Q}(i - i^*) \qquad \text{(ii)}$$

(i) and (ii) give as

$$s = (m - m)^* - \varnothing(y - y^*) - \lambda\,(i - i^*) \qquad \text{(iii)}$$

In the Dornbush model, flexible exchange rate does not insulate the economy from foreign disturbances. For overshooting to take place disturbances must be unanticipated. Anticipated events under rational expectations follow long run values and cannot cause over shooting (Bhandari, J.S. 1986).

Frankel (1979) produced a model, which is of general type. With the monetary version's assumption of the uncovered parity, which retained in the Frankel model we have the expression for the gap (s-s)

$$\Delta S_e = \overline{S} - S = \frac{1}{Q}(i + \bar{\pi}_e) - (i^* + \bar{\pi}_e^*)$$

and so,

$$S = \overline{S} + \Delta S^e$$

$$\text{ie., } S = (m - m^*) - \varnothing(\bar{y} - \bar{y}^*) + \lambda(\bar{\pi}_e - \bar{\pi}_e^x) + \frac{1}{Q}(i + \bar{\pi}_e) - (i^* + \bar{\pi}_e^z)$$

by rearranging the terms

$$S = (\overline{m} - \overline{m}^*) - \varnothing(Y - Y^x) + (\lambda + \frac{1}{Q})(\bar{\pi} - \bar{\pi}^*) - \frac{1}{Q}(i - 1^*$$

$$\text{Put } (\lambda + 1) = \beta \text{ and } -\frac{1}{Q} = \alpha$$

This gives

$S = (\overline{m} - \overline{m}^*) - \varnothing(\overline{y} - \overline{y}^*) + \beta(\pi_e - \pi_e^*) + \alpha(i - i^*)$ If $\beta = 0$, we get the Dornbush model, and if $\alpha = 0$ we get the monetary version.

So, Frankel model can make a distinction between short term and long run determinants of the exchange rate. In the short run, because of the price stickiness, deviation from the long run equilibrium value can occur and we get the Dornbush result. In the long run, the expected rate of exchange rate depreciation is given by the expected inflation differential between the domestic and foreign currency and we obtain the Chicago results. The Frankel model is also called the real interest model.

Critical Analysis of Monetary Approach

Although the monetary model is widely used in analysing payment problem, it is not without problem. Firstly, it results in central banks being blamed for payment deficit without questioning whether the central bank is actually an independent decision making agency. The money supply expands, often at an in appropriate rate, not because the central bank decides on such policy, but because it is forced to monetize large government budget deficits. The resulting balance of payments deficits should be blamed not on the central bank, which has no policy independence, but the fiscal authorities who allowed an excessive budget deficit that had to be financed by the central bank.

The next problem with the monetarists view is regarding the stability of demand for money, which means the velocity of money. A stable relationship between Gross National product (P.Q) and the demand for money, in the form of a fixed or a least a predictable velocity of money, is central to both domestic and international monetarism, but the stability is not as apparent as it was once. The monetarists' view that the demand for a national currency is a stable function of that country's Gross National Product based on the implicit assumption that each country has a monopoly in circulating money with in its national border. This may be true for paper currency but not for bank accounts. As barriers to international capital flow have declined as business has become more international, an increasingly large number of firms hold more than one currency in the forms of bank deposits. Thus, the total demand for a currency need not be a stable funciton of that country's Gross National Product. It can be far more volatile.

Despite these criticisms and problems, the monetary model is widely used in analysing the balance of payments problem and in designing adjustment programs. It is particularly useful in developing countries that are suffering from serious inflation. It's emphasis on controlling the rate of growth of the money supply is correct and countries that are designing a payment adjustment programme typically include a target for reduced growth in the money supply.

The Portfolio Approach

The monetary approach assumes perfect substitutability between domestic and foreign assets. By contrast, all variants of the portfolio approach emphasis some aspects of individual choices between holding domestic and foreign currency denominated assets. The models are differentiated chiefly in their assumptions about what the individuals can and cannot hold and about the degree of substitutability between assets.

Mundell–Flemming Model is regarded as intellectual antecedent to the portfolio approach. Flemming (1962), Mundell (1963) and others developed a Keynesian type model in which net current account balance is a function of real income and exchange rate, whereas the net capital account balance is a function of the differential interest rates between the home currency and the rest of the world. Real income, in turn is a function of monetary and fiscal policy, increasing with increase in growth expenditure and decreasing with the interest rate. The model asserts an appropriate combination of monetary and fiscal instruments could achieve the target of balance of payments and the level of real income. The basic equation of the model is as follows.

$$NCA = X(Y, E) - M(Y, E)$$

$$\frac{\partial x}{\partial y} < 0; \frac{\partial x}{\partial E} > 0; \frac{\partial m}{\partial y} > 0; \frac{\partial m}{\partial E} < 0 \qquad \text{(i)}$$

$$I = I(i); \frac{\partial I}{\partial i} > 0 \qquad \text{(ii)}$$

$$B = NCA + I \qquad \text{(iii)}$$

$$Y = \frac{1}{(G, i, E);} \frac{\partial y}{\partial G} > 0; \frac{\partial y}{\partial i} < 0 \frac{\partial x}{\partial E} > 0 \qquad \text{(iv)}$$

Where NCA is the net current account balance and x is exports (a function of Y, nominal income and E the price of foreign exchange) with partial derivatives as indicated, I is the net capital inflow to' the country (positive or negative) B is then the Balance of Payments. G is the government expenditures (or tax receipt) and 'i' is rate of interest.

For a real given income, the Balance of Payments can always be improved by raising the interest rate and the level of government expenditure (or lowering tax). For a given Balance of Payments real income can always be increased by raising both.

This model neglects the impact of increasing short-term indebtedness and the future balance of payments. Second the treatment of capital flow is unsatisfactory. This leads directly to the protfolio model.

However, the Mundell-Flemming contribution remembers the economists the important fact that the Balance of Payments consist of both current account and capital account transaction. Mundell-Flemming analysis was the precursor to the monetary approach as well as other models.

Portfolio-Balance Model

This model cannot be attributed to a single or few economists. At the early stage McKinnon (1969) and McKinnon and Oates (1966) pointed out the deficiency of capital flows as the function of interest rate in the Mundell-Flemming Model. Branson (1977) modeled the approach based on Tobin's monetary model; Dornbush (1975 a), and Frankel and Rodriguez (1975) have also contributed to the model building.

The model states that individuals allocate their wealth, which is fixed at a point of time among alternative assets, including domestic and foreign money, domestic and foreign security. The basic equations of this model are

$$M = \alpha\ (i, i^*)\ W \qquad \text{(i)}$$

$$B = \beta\ (i, i^*)\ W \qquad \text{(ii)}$$

$$EF = \gamma\ (i, i^*)\ W \qquad \text{(iii)}$$

$$W = M + B + EF \qquad \text{(iv)}$$

Where M is the domestic money, B is the supply of domestic assets, F is the net holding of foreign assets, E is the price of foreign exchange, i is the nominal interest rate and w is initial wealth. From (iv) $\alpha+\beta+\gamma$ must be unity, so that (i), (ii), (iii) are not independent.

A change in the exchange rate, E will lead to a change in total wealth and also alter demand for foreign securities F. The role of exchange rate is one of balancing asset demands and supplies, given domestic money supplies and assets.

The portfolio balance model is 'partial' due to following shortcomings. First, it abstracts from the determinants of real income and real domestic wealth and interaction between them. Second, there is no treatment at all for flow of goods and services. There is no role for expectations in this model.

Currency Substitution Models

Both the monetary and portfolio approaches assume that domestic residents do not hold foreign currency. The important point behind all the currency substitution models is that individual demand for money is defined not for domestic currency but for a group of currencies. As such individuals demand for domestic currency may or may not be a well defined and stable function. There are two types of currency substitution models. One is termed as monetary currency substitution model and the other as global currency substitution model.

Monetary Currency Substitution Model

The model, which is also termed as Calvo-Rodriguez approach (1977), interprets any current account surpluses or deficits as reflecting excess demand or supply of domestic currency relative to foreign currency. Hence capital account and capital markets are largely neglected. The key notation of the model is that the only asset, ie., money, has two components.

$$A = m + eD$$

Where 'a' is the real value of assets in terms of home goods, m is the real stock of money in term of home goods, e is the real exchange rate and D is domestically held and owned stock of foreign currency. Here it is shown that, at any point of time, real assets is a decreasing function of the real exchange rate where as change in the holding of foreign currency is an increasing function of real exchange rate.

Global Currency Substitution Model

This model views the money supply as being a worldwide phenomenon within the context of a highly integrated capital markets. Again where as monetary currency substitution model focuses on the effects of changes in the exchange rate on holding of foreign currency (and vice Versa) from the viewpoint of single currency, the global currency substitution model essentially focuses on the dependencies between monies.

Wallace (1984) has perhaps been the formest advocate of this view. According to the model, the desired composition of currency holding (in each country and in two countries world) is a function of the ratio of interest rates. The higher the home country's interest rate, the higher the fraction of money that will be held in the foreign currency because opportunity costs of holding it are lower. This, of course, assumes that individuals in both countries can and do hold securities nominally denominated in both currencies in an integrated capital market.

Time Series Models

This approach, which gained popularity during 1980's, examines the foreign exchange markets by using various tests of market efficiency that were developed to analyse the stock market behaviour. The evidence points out that the time series models often prove superior to the structural models in short-run exchange rate forecasting. The poor performance of structural models is often attributed to factors such as simultaneous equation bias, sampling error, instability of money demand equation, and misspecifications due to in consistent stochastic properties of the underlying parameters (Messee and Rogoff, 1983).

Under the time series models (TSM) exchange rate is expressed as function of time or of the past values. There are various versions of TSM and these include Random Walk model, ARIMA model (Auto regressive moving average model), Vector auto regression model (VAR) etc.

Random Walk Model

Messee and Rogoff (1983) have found that a random walk model would have outperformed all other models as a predictor of the logarithm of major currency exchange rates during the 1970's. They have also argued that owing to apparent instability of the underlying macro economic structure exchange rates are hard to predict. The failure of the structural models to predict exchange rate behaviour out of sample could be rationalized by arguing that the explanatory variables (money, income, interest rates, current account etc.) are difficult to predict (Singh, Devi 1986). However, even when uncertainty about the explanatory variables is purged by using ex-post realized values of these variables, the structural models still fail to fit the data out-of-sample as well as random walk model (Messe and Rogoff, 1983).

The random walk model, which uses the current spot rate as a predictor of all future rates, is a univariate model. A standard random walk model is defined as follows.

$$St = Lo + L1St\text{-}1$$

Where St-1 is the lagged value of exchange rate. If the co-efficient of St-1 is very close to one, exchange rate has the tendency to follow random walk.

Auto-Regressive Time series Method

The univariate Box Jenkins Auto-regressive integrated moving average model is a special class of univariate time series model that uses only the past information of the series. Though the models have been proved to be more robust than structural models in forecasting economic activity, their use has not been appreciated much in exchange rate modeling (Paul and Ashtekar, 1990).

Vector Auto Regression Model

Vector auto regressive models are atheoretical in nature, which use only observed time series properties of the data to forecast economic variables (Rani. U and Kamaiah.B, 1991). Because they are atheoretical, vector time series models can be estimated without imposing restrictions that are necessary to identify and estimate structural econometric models. This multivariate model system may be easy to estimate, but difficult to interpret due to the problem of the multi co-linearity.

Chaotic Behaviour

"Chaos is characterized as a seemingly random and irregular signal generated by deterministic process with some additional properties. The first of the property is that the deterministic process that a chaotic signal must show sensitivity to initial conditions. A second property is that a chaotic signal is associated with a strange attractor (Mark Embrechts 1994). Hentri Poin care, a physicist, found that if a system consisted a few parts that interact strongly, it could exhibit its unpredicatable behaviour. This concept is the origin of chaos theory (Chorafas, 1995).

Both in physics and finance the object of chaotic theory is to study the irregular behaviour of simple deterministic equations by providing more sophisticated tools that are close to real life. The mathematical properties of dynamic, non liner equations have been studied since the time of Poin care but the physical and to a greater extent the financial implications of chaos have not been appreciated until the work of Lorenz, Feigenbaum and Ruelle (Chorafas, 1995). This new formulation of chaotic condition provided researches with both tools and examples of chaos.

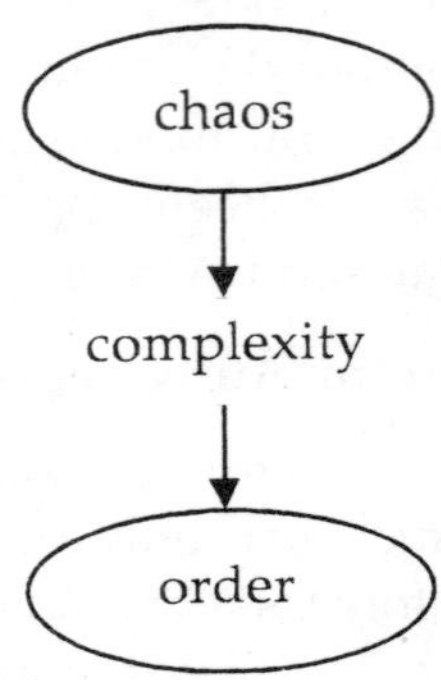

The theory of complexity interfaces between chaos and order and addresses the problem of transition as shown in the following figure.

Chaos, lack of equilibrum, has gone beyond the confines of their nineteenth century definition. They are beginning to acquire formal aspects based on mathematical relationships. In the words of D. Kelsey (1988), "it is not possible to define chaos without using a large number of technical terms. Informally chaos occurs when for a typical initial value there is both sensitive dependence on initial conditions and a periodic motion".

The implementation of chaos theory rests on a few simple principles. The essence of studies in chaotic behaviour lies in the way in which patterns change overtime. The pattern we make of chaos pulls the data into shapes that are visible and therefore detectable. Such pattern also tends to indicate that all possible pathways of disorder, nature and the markets favour only few.

Mostly liner models are used to explain and visualize the relationships that may exist between time series values. But non-liner approaches motivated by chaotic dynamics provide superior prediction capabilities as compared to linear models. A financial example helps in appreciating this reference. If banks are to manage risk and be competitive in their pricing, they have to have a good view of correlation between movement in short term interest rates and movements in the exchange rates of currencies

Typically, financial analysts apply correlation of co-variance to the interplay of two currencies and their interest rates. But no one has yet come up with a model that can comfortably predict how an interest rate movement in one currency relation to the exchange rate and interest rate of another-and for a good reason the relationship between factors is non linear.

Due to the mathematical break through that took place during the last twenty years, the recent studies have used chaos theory to examine the information content of time series.

The importance of chaotic behaviour is explained in the words of Manohar Rao – currently a transition towards a chaotic regime has been witnessed in several macro economies around the world. Many industrialized countries seem to have suddenly switched from condition of steady state growth towards those exhibiting erratic fluctuations. As a result it has become very difficult to predict several key macro economic variables. Under these circumstances non-linear dynamic system theory can provide a better description of economic behaviour (Rao Manohar, 1993).

Although chaos suggests a possibility to predict the exchange rate in short term, it also warns that the forecaster must have precise details of information that govern the market. This implies that even a very small error in precision may result in, after some time totally different predictions. (Sunderrajan and Subramaniyan, 1997).

Concluding Remarks

Empirically, both structural and non-structural models have been tested thoroughly by the economists all over the world. An analysis of the structural models reveals that the structural models not only break down in terms of serious econometric problems but also fail to perform as prediction models.

Though it is argued that non-structural model scores over traditional economic model in tracing the forex rates the fundamental factors such as money stock differentials, interest rate differentials and so forth will continue to occupy an important place in the field of exchange rate analysis. The monetary model, which emphasises the role of these fundamental factors in the derermination of exchange rate can't be completely ruled out. So it can be concluded that the structural models can not be ignored at the cost of time series models though the latter are gaining more attention now a days.

References

1. Alexander, S.S. (1952), "Effects of devaluation on a Trade Balance" ,IMF staff Papers, Vol.5, pp. 263-268.
2. Bhandari, J.S. (1986), "Exchange rate Determination and adjustments," Praeger Publications. Chicago.
3. Bokil, S.V. (1990), "New Frontiers of Research in Exchange Rate Analysis". Artha Vijnana, Vol. 32, No. 3 & 4, pp. 204-222.
4. Branson, W. (1977)," Asset Markets and Relative Prices in Exchange Rate Determination", Institute for International Economic Studies, Paper No. 96.
5. Calvo, G.A. and Rodriguez, C.A (1977), "A Model of Exchange Rate Determination Under Currency Substitution and Rational Expectation", Journal of Political Economy, Vol.85, pp. 617-625.
6. Cassel, Gustav (1922), Money and Foreign Exchange after 1914, MacMillan, New York.
7. Charafas D.N. (1995), Chaos Theory in the Financial Market, S. Chand & Company. New Delhi.
8. Dornbush, Rudiger (1975.a), A Portfolio Balance Model of the Open Economy", Journal of Monetary economics, Vol.1, pp. 3-20.
9. Dornbush, Rudiger (1976), "Expectation and Exchange Rate Dynamics", American Economic Review, Vol. 77, pp 93-106.
10 Flemming, J. Marcus (1962), "Domestic Financial Policies Under Fixed and Floating Exchange Rates",IMF Staff Paper, Vol.9, No.4, pp. 369-80.
11. Frankel, J.A. and Rodriguez, C.A. (1975), "Portfolio Equilibrium and the Balance of Payments: A monetary Approach", American Economic Review, Vol.65, No.4 , pp. 674-688.
12. Frankel, Jacob, A. (1979), "On the Mark: A Theory of Exchange Rates on the Real Interest Rate Differentials", American Economic Review, Vol.69, pp 610-622.
13. Friendman, Milton (1968), "The Case for Flexible Exchange Rates", in Caves, R.E. and Johnson, H.G. (ed) 'Readings in International Economics', Richard. D. Irwin, Inc, London.
14. Ingram, James and Munn, Robert, (1993), "International Economics", John Wiley & Sons Inc, New York.
15. Johnson, H.G. (1976), "The Monetary Approach to balance of Payments", in Frankel, Jacob and Johnson, H.G. (Ed) "The

Monetary Approach to Balance of Payments", George Allen & Irwin ltd., London.

16. Kelsey, D. (1988), "The Economics of Chaos or The Chaos of Economics", Oxford Economic Papers, No.40, pp. 1-13.

17. Kruger, Anne, E. (1983), Exchange Rate Determination, Cambridge University Press, Cambridge.

18. Lindert, Peter, H. (1995), International Economics, Richard, D. Irwin. Ince Homewool, Illions.

19. Mark, Embrechts (1994), "Basic Concepts of Non-Liner Dynamics and Chaos Theory", in G.J. Deboct (ed) "Trading on the edges, John Wiley, New York", pp. 265-279.

20. Mckinnon, R.I. (1969), "Portfolio Balance and International Payments Adjustment", in Mundell, R.A and Sweboda, A.K (ed), "Monetary Problems of the International Economy", Chicago, pp. 199-234.

21. Mckinnon, R.I. and Oates, W. (1966), "The Implications of International Economic Integration for Monetary, Fiscal and Exchange Rate Policy", No.16, Princeton Studies in International Finance.

22. Meade, James (1953), The Balance of Payments: with Mathematical Appendix, Oxford University Press, Oxford.

23. Messe, R. and Rogoff (1983), "Empirical Exchange Rate Models of the Seventies-Do They Fit Out of Sample", Journal of International Economics, Vol.14, pp. 3-24.

24. Mundell, Robert (1963), "Capital Mobility and Stabilization Policy Under Fixed and Flexible Exchange Rates", Canadian Journal of Economics and Political Science, pp. 475-85.

25. Mussa, Michael (1978), "The exchange Rate, the Balance of Payments and Monetary and fiscal Policy Under a Regime of Controlled Floating", In Frenkel, J.A. and Johnson, H.G. (Ed) "The Economics of Exchange Rates", Addison-Wesley Publishing Company. Philippines.

26. Paul, Thomas, M. and Ashtekar, Madha (1990), "Forecasting of Some Major Exchange Rates: Structural and Time Series Model's Results " ,Artha Vijnana, Vol.32, No 3,4, pp. 223-255.

27. Rani, U. and Kamiah, B. (1991), "Exchange Rate Models: A Review of Theory and Evidence", Journal of Foreign Exchange and International Finance, Vol.5, No.3, pp. 229-240.

28. Rao, Manohar (1993), "Excessive Exchange Rate Volatility: A Possible Explanation Using Chaos Theory", Journal of Foreign Exchange and International Finance, Vol.7, No:3, pp. 279-301.

29. Rogoff, Kenneth, (1996), "The Purchasing Power Parity Puzzle", Journal of Economic Literature, Vol. 34, No.2, pp. 647-668.

30. Shapiro, A.C. (1999), International Financial Management, Prentice Hall of India Pvt. Ltd., New Delhi.

31. Singh, Devi (1986), Economics of Exchanges Rate Managemet, Criterion Publications, New Delhi.

32. Sundarrajan, S. and Subramaniyan, V. (1997), "Do Exchange Rates Follow a Chaotic Path", NIIBM, Pune.

33. Taylor, Mark (1995), "The Economics of Exchange Rates", Journal of Economic Literature, Vol.33, No. 1, pp. 13-14.

34. Vaish, M.C. and Singh, S. (1978), International Economics, Oxford and IBM Publishing Company, New Delhi.

35. Wallace, Neil (1984), "Why Markets in Foreign Exchange are Different From Other Markets", in Gerald, D.G and Robert, W.K (ed), "International Finance: Concepts and Issues", Reston Publishing Company Inc, Virgeniea, pp. 332-343.

13

Euro Versus US Dollar: Invoicing Dilemma

Justin Paul*
Rushab Desai**

Introduction

A single European currency called the Euro, was created on 1 January 1999. The new currency zone cover some 300 million Europeans. The Euro represents an important structural change in the world economy. At the moment of its inception, the Euro accounted for 19.4 per cent of the world's GDP, compared with 19.6 per cent for the United State. The Euro confirmed the EU's importance as a commercial power in the world with an 18.2 per cent share of world trade, roughly equal to that of the United States. Exports from the Euro currency zone are already 25 per cent higher than those of the US and twice those of Japan. The Euro is expected to play a growing role in international trade in the future. Belgium, Austria, Finland, France, Luxembourg, Ireland, Netherlands, Germany, Portugal, Italy, and Spain were the founding members of the Euro. Greece joined in 2001. Great Britain, Denmark and Sweden have not joined the Eurozone.

* Assistant Professor, NMIMS, Vile Parle West, Mumbai-400 056, e-mail: justinpaul@hotmail.com, justinpaul@indiatimes.com
** Management Trainee, GE India

The history of Euro is summarized below.

- In 1999-The Euro became a currency in its own right.
- Jan-June 2002-Euro notes and coins put up in circulation (exchange of national currencies against Euro)*
- 1st July 2002 onwards - Euro has become the only currency of 12 European Monetary Union countries

Euro—Benefits and caveats

Benefits

- Elimination of foreign exchange transactions costs with other Eurozone countries.
- Elimination of exchange rate uncertainty of the country's currency against the Euro, which should improve the quality of information on which consumers and firms base their decisions.
- Greater price transparency when all goods are priced in Euro may lead to increased competition in the Single Market.
- Broadening and deepening of integrated European financial markets
- Maintain fiscal discipline with "Growth and Stability Pact"
- Make more urgent the need for structural reforms in Europe. Discipline argument
- An alternative to the US dollar for debt management
- The Euro will stimulate international trade
- International financial markets in Euro will develop and grow
- The Euro will develop as a reserve currency

Caveats

- The member country can no longer conduct, monetary policy on its own behalf.
- Monetary policy may work in short-run, but not in long run.
- Little room for fiscal policy as a stabilization tool in the absence of independent monetary policy
- Limited labour mobility and structural labour market rigidities imply that Europe may not be an optimal currency area.
- The exchange rate is no longer available to cushion "asymmetric shocks." For example, a decline in the demand for the country's exports, which is specific to the country, would lead to an automatic depreciation of the currency if the exchange rate is floating. This would cushion the effect on the economy. On the other hand, if the country is part of the Eurozone, there is no longer a British Pound, for example, to depreciate against other currencies, so the cushioning mechanism would be lost. Whether the economic benefits exceed the costs depend on three factors:
    1. The amount of trade integration with the other countries in the Eurozone.
    2. The amount of labour mobility with the other countries in the Eurozone.
    3. The amount of "asymmetric shocks" that hit the countries.

Trade Invoicing in Euro vs. Dollar–An Inquiry

The internal techniques that help in managing the currency risk include netting, pooling and invoicing. Out of the above-mentioned tools, selection of currency for invoicing

Euro-For & Against

Arguments for Euro	*Arguments Against Euro*
Transaction Costs	Non-Synchronicity of Business Cycles
Having to deal with only one currency will reduce the cost of converting one currency into another. This will benefit businesses as well as tourists.	Europe may not constitute an "optimum currency area" because the business cycles across the various countries do not move in synchronicity
No Exchange Rate Uncertainty	Fiscal Policy Spillovers
Eliminating exchange rates between European countries eliminates the risks of unforeseen exchange rate revaluations or devaluations.	Since there will only be a Europe-wide interest rate, individual countries that increase their debt will raise interest rates in all other countries. EU countries may have to increase their intra-EU transfer payment to help regions in need.
Transparency & Competition	Central Bank Independence
The direct comparability of prices and wages will increase competition across Europe, leading to lower prices for consumers and improved investment opportunities for businesses.	Previously, the anchor of the European Monetary System has been the independence of the German Bundesbank and its strong focus on price stability. Even though the new European Central Bank (ECB) is nominally independent, it will have to prove its independence. This will at the very least incur temporary costs as it will have to be extra-tough on inflation.
Strength	Excessive Fiscal Discipline
The new Euro will be the among the strongest currencies in the world, along with the US Dollar and the Japanese Yen. It will soon become the 2nd-most important reserve currency after the US Dollar.	When other governments exert pressure on a government to reduce borrowing, or even pay fines if the budget deficity exceeds a reference value, this may have the perverse effect of increasing an existing economic imbalance.
Capital Market	
The large Euro zone will integrate the national financial markets, leading to higher efficiency in the allocation of capital in Europe.	
No Competitive Devaluations	
One country can no longer devalue its currency against another member country in a bid to increase the competitiveness of its exporters	

the exports and imports is a tricky affair. Trade invoicing implications apply to both the domestic country and the foreign nations. Invoicing can be done in the currency of the exporter's choice. Euro opened the doors to the innumerable debates on which currency to use for invoicing. Either the exporter or the importer can gain, depending on the currency of invoice. The decision of trade invoicing in a particular currency is a very difficult task. The task was not so difficult, until the arrival of Euro. Earlier, majority of exporters world over, used to trade invoice in Dollars. This was primarily due to the fact that the Dollar was the only world currency. Moreover US was the most advanced nation and the failure and success of other economies depended on the whims and fancies of the US economy. The other economies had a direct correlation with the crests and troughs in the US economy. As a result of this almost all other currencies were depreciating against the dollar, sometimes or the other. Thus at the time of receipts of payments, the exporters used to earn a premium due to such exchange rate fluctuations.

While the decision to some extent depends on whether one is in a buyer's market or seller's market, it is quite common to see that the invoicing is done in a third-party currency, predominantly US Dollar. Since all transactions in international trade involve time lags, there always exists a possibility of a currency appreciation or depreciation and hence a firm has to forecast to decide the currency of invoice or at least understand the implications of invoicing. Generally, parties to trade prefer invoicing in a currency which is relatively stable and hence the trade predominantly gets invoiced in US Dollars. The arrival of Euro as an alternative world currency gave more options to the exporters as regards trade invoicing. The Euro started off very well against the dollar but soon lost out. The Euro today is depreciating against the Dollar. The exporters are in a real dilemma as to which currency to select for their trade invoicing. Their invoicing decisions have to be based totally on their future exchange rate expectations. But these expectations are arrived at after considering certain economic components of the concerned currencies.

International Trade and Currency Risk are essentially two sides of the same coin as it is very difficult to conceive the former without the latter. As a result, it has become increasingly important for firms to manage this risk to sustain in this competitive world. There is no better example than the recent South East Asian crisis to demonstrate how foreign currency volatility can become catastrophic. Is there a need for managing the currency risk? Can firms overcome the foreign exchange risk and perform better in international market?

Elimination of exchange risk altogether is neither feasible nor desirable, since the decision to eliminate does not assure more profits. Hence it is necessary to undertake a cost benefit analysis before taking a decision on whether to hedge or not. It is possible that international trade would find Euro an alternate currency for invoicing. Roughly, 50 per cent of the world exports is invoiced in US dollars, almost four times the share of US in world trade. On the other hand, around 20 per cent of world exports are invoiced in EU currencies and 5 per cent in Japanese Yen. Almost all-major internationally trade commodities are currently priced in US dollars. In the long run, it is expected that Euro may become an important alternate currency for the invoicing of foreign trade.

An exporter can avoid exchange risk by invoicing the trade in home currency. This decision has certain hidden costs. It is necessary to understand the implications and then take a conscious decision. It is in this context that an attempt is made to quantify the implications of the decision to select a currency for invoicing. For example, A US-based exporter has a choice to invoice in US $ or Euro for a transaction involving US $ 1,000,000. If the US $/Euro is at 1.0065 at the time of invoicing then the exporter could have invoiced for US $ 1,000,000 or Euro 993,542. It is assumed that the bill is realized after three months. The inflow will remain at US $ 1,000,000, irrespective of the changes in the rate. But the inflow in terms of US $ will undergo a change depending on the rate prevailing at the end of three months when the currency of invoice is Euro. If this rate is assumed to be US $/Euro 1.0025, then the inflow in terms of US $ will be 991,064. Thus the exporter will actually receive US $ 8,936 less as a consequence of the decision to invoice in Euro.

Case for Euro Invoicing

While the use of the Euro inside EMU is supply dominated, its use as an international currency is demand drive the therefore more competitive. The role of the Euro depends therefore on international market preferences as well as on its ability to challenge the dollar in terms of liquidity and transaction costs. It can be argued that the greater exchange rate stability within the Euro area will be offset by greater instability between the Euro and other currencies, notably the dollar, and the yen. International currencies such as the dollar against the D-Mark or the yen seem to be more volatile than the D-Mark against the yen. The European currencies which preceded the Euro were not all equally unstable against the dollar, but from now on they could become as unstable as the most unstable previous currency, usually the D-Mark.

Financial Markets

The Euro did not bolt from the starting gate, but then it was not expected to. Its progress has been most rapid in the money market, where national currencies were phased out from the outset, and a single interest rate is set by the ECB. However, the money market is not yet fully intergrated because of different national financial instruments and procedures. Many feel that the Euro may become a more attractive currency for bond issuers in future. Secondly, there are some that are of the opinion that Euro may also become an attractive currency for the investment of official reserves. Currently the US dollar is by far the most important official reserve currency worldwide. It is reported that well over half of official reserves are held in US dollar denominated assets while around one-fifth are currently held in EMU currencies. it is possible that some countries in Asia and Latin America, which traditionally have predominantly held US dollar reserves, may find it useful to consider divestment of part of their reserve holdings gradually by acquiring Euro. The shift to Euro assets by central banks around the world may among other factors be motivated by its strength, its increasing use as a transaction currency and the more liquid and deeper bond market. However, it is reasonable to expect that such a shift will take place in a manner that will be non-disruptive of currency markets. There is a feeling that Euro may increasingly be recognized as a preferred currency for financial transactions. Trade finance could be more easily available to corporate in India and elsewhere as the European banks are expected to compete for business and are expected to extend credit at cheaper rates in order to stay ahead of each other. Also, in respect of long-term financing, those corporate that have natural hedge in Euro may find it advantageous to borrow in Euro and take advantage of lower costs.

In a global currency system, it is argued is equilibrium between centripetal and centrifugal forces. The centripetal forces favour the main incumbent currency as the general medium of exchange benefiting from network externalities. The centrifugal forces depend on the store of value function of currencies, and thus on the diversification of portfolios by means of a multiplicity of currencies. It is true that major stock market movements have become more highly correlated across countries, then currency movements, notably between the Euro and the Dollar, may become more important in determining global security flows.

Futures Markets

The Euro has made good progress in the futures market. On a typical July day, 7,10,000 contracts in German Euro government bonds were traded on the German Eurex exchange, compared with 200,000 US Treasury contracts on the Chicago Board of Trade.

Exports Market

The European Union will remain one of the largest exporting zones in the world. This will boost the Euro as an international invoicing currency and means of payment. However, the preference of the EU main trading partners might also shift to the Euro when exchange rate variations are expected to be limited. For countries with relatively stable exchange rates against the Euro and closed trade links with the Euro area such as the ERM2 countries, Central and Eastern Europe and African countries, companies will have an incentive to invoice in Euro because this will remove hedging costs.

Integration of CEECs Around the Euro

The Central and Eastern European Countries (CEEC) are nearest to the Euro in geographical and trading terms. Poland and Hungary have already replaced the EMU currencies with the Euro and plan to peg their currency solely to the Euro within the next few years. The exchange rate policies of the countries with flexible arrangements have often followed the dual objective of reducing inflation and preserving competitiveness in the face of nominal appreciation pressure caused by the inflow of capital. If the Euro is used as a nominal anchor, the incentive to use it for invoicing and debt denomination will increase for those countries, thereby reinforming the international role of the Euro. Second, the use of the Euro as an anchor currency could push the international monetary system towards a bipolar framework, which in turn also has consequences for the variability of the dollar-Euro exchange rate. In a world with two currency blocs, the exchange rate between the two anchor currencies could be more volatile, as this is the only exchange rate to adjust for fundamental disequilibria between the currency blocs. All the above mentioned factors may work in congruence to appreciate Euro against the Dollar. Thus, in such a situation, investors will be better off invoicing in Euro.

Story of Invoicing

As of today, the dollar is dominant, accounting for 65 per cent of international currency reserves, with the EU currencies coming a remote second with a 21 per cent share and yen accounting for 8.1 per cent: and what counts is today and not Euro dreams of tomorrow. Popular perceptions have always placed the American dollar on a pedestal much above the pound sterling of the UK with which India has had close historical links or the yen of Japan having the second largest economy in the world. In financial circles the dollar's supremacy is taken for grated. Not surprising then, much of India's trade (exports and imports) as well as non-trade remittances are denominated in dollars.

The dollar's pre-eminence in trade matters is to be appreciated against the backdrop of India's exchange control rules that allow cross-border transactions to be denominated in many "permitted" currencies including the dollar. Permitted currencies are those which can be converted into major reserve currencies such as the dollar and the sterling. Not only should that country's rules permit such unhindered conversion but also there should be an active dealing market for those currencies. It is therefore not mandatory that a trade transaction between an exporter in the U.S. and an importer in India should be denominated only in dollars. It can be invoiced in, say, the Euro, the sterling or the yen or any other permitted currency. A trade in the U.K. can invoice his transaction to an Indian importer in sterling, dollar or any of the permitted currencies.

Invoicing in rupees is allowed—in fact it was quite significant until 1991 when it had a 7.7 per cent share in all imports. However, India's rupee denominated trade was almost exclusively with the Soviet bloc countries. (There was no other option then). With the collapse of that bloc, trade invoicing has shifted to dollars. Between 1990-91 and 1999-2000 the combined share of U.S. dollar, DM, Euro, yen and pound sterling in India's imports moved in a range of 74.2 to 96.2 per cent. The dollar's share at the start of the decade was 59.7 per cent but jumped substantially to 85.8 per cent by the end of the decade. In contrast, the proportion of DM declined from 7 per cent in 1990-91 to 4.6 per cent in 1998-99 and to 1.6 per cent in 1999-2000. The introduction of Euro was, of course, the main reason.

Since 1993-94, the dollar became the intervention currency in India. That made dollar invoicing even more acceptable. Petroleum and related imports have been traditionally deal with in dollars. Another interesting finding: on an average as much as 72 per cent of India's imports from non-U.S. destinations were designed in dollars during the 1990s. The dollar's pre-eminence is borne out in the invoicing of exports too. In 1990-91, 57.2 per cent of exports was in dollars. Rupee invoicing accounted for 27.7 per cent almost entirely due to the then flourishing trade with the Soviet bloc. Moreover, with the disintegration of the Soviet Union, trade invoicing in rupees took a backseat.

Dollar as Incumbent

In this section, we present a view, totally contrary to the above one. Here we propagate the Dollar as a currency for trade invoicing. International currency usage is habit-forming, and old habits die-hard. In deciding what international currency to use, it pays for an international trader, investor or central bank to use the same currency as other traders, investors and central banks, for that will be the currency with the deepest, most liquid markets.

Transaction costs will be lowest, and it will be possible to get in and out of the market without distributing the level of prices. Thus, a reserve currency seeking to retain its status, has the advantage of incumbency. In highly competitive markets such as the energy and metal market where demand is reactive to small price changes, pricing in an international currency is common practice. This reduces information costs for importers and exporters and transaction costs, due to high liquidity. The potential role of the Euro in such markets depends therefore on its transaction costs.

Liquidity

The Euro does not yet have the liquidity of the dollar. Dealing spreads and transaction changes are higher, because the costs of maintaining national financial markets, even in the same currency as each other, are higher than those o f a single market such as the US, centered as it is in New York, or the international dollar markets. The average size and trading turnover of Euro instruments are smaller than for their dollar equivalents. Since the willingness of market participants to hold dollar or Euro instruments depends partly on the degree of liquidity, the Euro area needs to develop greater liquidity by means of integration of national marketers, greater size of issues, and higher turnover. The single European financial market and the Euro depend on each other. They are both still in their early stages.

Bond Market

The dollar has a bigger lead over the Euro in the domestic bond markets. Although the combined Euro-II government bond market is nearly one-quarter larger than the US Treasury bond market, government guaranteed mortgage issues and corporate bonds take total domestic US bonds outstanding to well over double the total in Euro-II currencies. In view of the greater size of the US economy, and the fiscal restraint being exercised on both sides of the Atlantic, it will be a long time before domestic Euro bond issues catch up with domestic dollar bond issues.

Euro and Implications for India

Today, the international currency markets see skewed anomalies, where the dollar is the invoiced currency for 48 per cent of all global trade although it contributes only 23 per cent of the global GNP. Against this, the EU currencies account for just 31 per cent of international involving although the European Union countries have a much larger GNP. US status as a major trading partner of India may be wrested away by an unified Europe with the Euro currency emerging as the preferred invoiced currency for all trade with Europe. The dollar has been the preferred involving currency even for trade between India and European countries on account of its price transparency, wide acceptability, liquidity, low transaction cost and stability.

But the importance of European Union in India's external economy lies in the fact that not only is European Union 15, India's largest trading partner, many larger companies from these countries also have a considerable presence in this country. Many Indian companies during Post-liberalization have also gone on to raise short and long-term debt from the Euro markets. The Euro will therefore have major implications for India. Today, trade between EU and India accounts for 22 per cent of India's external trade, while invoicing in EU currencies accounts for only 7.2 per cent of the total invoicing. In the changed scenario, EMU member states are likely to insist on settlement of business transactions in the Euro. This demand for the Euro as settlement currency (as also a reserve currency) will make a stronger against the rupee, which, in turn, will help Indian exports. The hazards of invoicing in a different currency involves trade risk for both the buyer and the seller. With the introduction of the Euro as the invoicing currency, trade will become competitive. Another major likely impact will be that the Euro will co-exist with the dollar as a reserve currency of central banks on account of its large economic base and its potential for denomination of trade flows.

Exchange Rate Movements and Implication

Exchange Rate of India Rupee/major currencies
Financial year (Apr-Mar)

Year	*USD/INR*	*JPY/INR*	*CHF/INR*	*EUR/INR*	*GBP/INR*	
1990-91	13.67%	29.41%	17.20%	NA		29.91%
(Apri-Mar)	17.27 19.63	10.86 14.05	11.51 13.48		28.22	34.12
1991-92	58.13%	66.32%	50.34%	NA	55.21%	
(Apr-Mar)	19.61 31.01	14.01 23.30	13.73 20.65		34.63	53.75
1992-93	-0.70%	13.81%	-0.25%	NA		-14.42%
(Apr-Mar)	31.45 31.23	23.58 26.84	20.96 20.91		54.52	46.66
1993-94	0.54%	11.73%	5.97%	NA		-1.29%
(Apr-Mar)	31.20 31.37	27.30 30.50	20.89 22.14		47.10	46.49
1994-95	0.32%	16.87%	22.25%	NA		9.40%
(Apr-Mar)	31.37 31.47	30.15 35.24	22.03 26.93		46.17	50.51
1995-96	8.91%	-11.18%	3.78%	NA		2.63%
(Apr-Mar)	31.42 34.22	36.20 32.15	27.73 28.78		50.86	52.20
1996-97	5.74%	-8.38%	-13.16%	NA		13.24%
(Apr-Mar)	34.00 35,95	31.66 29.00	28.51 24.76		51.84	58.71
1997-98	10.09%	3.28%	4.39%	NA		12.51%
(Apr-Mar)	35.88 39.50	29.02 29.97	24.86 25.96		58.86	66.23
1998-99	7.42%	18.60%	9.59%	NA		3.47%
(Apr-Mar)	39.50 42.43	29.67 35.18	25.98 28.47		66.07	68.36
1999-2000	2.78%	15.66%	-8.19%	-8.62%		1.53%
(Apr-Mar)	42.43 43.61	35.74 41.34	28.61 26.26	45.74 41.80	68.43	69.47
2000-01	6.90%	-9.19%	3.08%	-1.34%	-4.10%	
(Apr-Mar)	43.6146.62	41.3437.54	26.1626.96	41.5841.03	69.39	66.55
2001-01	4.45%	-1.76%	7.30%	3.74%	43.34%	
(Apr-Mar)	46.62 4.795	37.54 36,89	26.97 29.09	41.03 42.62	66.55	69.57
Last 3 Years	4.55%	1.05%	0.55%		-2.38%	0.55%
Last 5 Years	5.96%	4.69%	3.09%		N.A.	3.29%
Last 10 Years	4.30%	4.38%	3.22%		N.A	2.41%

An attempt has been made to analyse the recent exchange fluctuations of Indian Rupee against US Dollar, Pound Sterling, Euro and Japanese Yen and implications on involving. When the euro was born in 1999, Indian exporters were initially reluctant to invoice their exports on euro after watching it consistently weaken against the dollar (Euro had weakened from 50 Rs. to 39 Rs. against INR and 1.17 USD to 0.90 USD against Dollar in 1999 and 2000). Those that did switch to euro invoicing did so more due to the pressure exerted on them by their buyers in the European Union. Though exports to the US presently account for less than 20 per cent of the total exports out of India, nearly 70 per cent of all invoicing is done is US dollars. Though the European Union, the UK and Japan together account for over 30 per cent of exports, invoicing in these currencies is much lower.

Table 3: Exchange Rate of INR against USD GBP, EUR, JPY (year 2002)

Currency	*August 2*	*April 1*	*% Change (over 4 months)*
US dollar	48.65	48.82	0.3
Pound Sterling	76.47	69.70	-9.7
Euro	48.06	42.06	-12.7
Japanese Yen	0.40	0.36	-11.1

Source: The Economic Times, 3rd, 5th August & 2nd April 2002.

The exchange rate movement of Indian Rupees against other currencies including Euro since the start of the fiscal year 2002 is given in table 3. While the Rupee has appreciated 0.3 per cent against the greenback since the start of the financial year, it has weakened by 9.7 per cent against the pound sterling, 12.7 per cent against the euro and 11.1 per cent against the Japanese yen. Put simply, an Indian exporter invoicing on Pound sterling has gained Rs. 6.80 per pound since the start of the fiscal year 2002. On euro invoicing, he has gained Rs. 5.40 per euro. This makes the exporters invoicing in Euro and Pound sterling laugh while the exporters invoiced in Dollar lost their competitive advantage.

Conclusion

We have one big question to answer—should nations invoice in Euro or should they invoice in Dollars? The answer to the pertinent questions remains judgmental. After going through the whole 'invoicing' experience we feel that it would be better for Indian exporters if they invoice in US dollars. The recession in US has to be looked at as a business cycle. The Eurozone has its own intrinsic problems, which will prove to be a cog in their race against the US dollar. The twelve member countries are fighting over the control of one currency and this weighs over their currency prospects. The chain cannot be stronger than the weakest link'—goes an old saying. Portugal and Greece being the weakest link here. The progress made by the stronger links—France and Germany are subsidized by Portugal and Greece. The re-established dollar standard should therefore also foresee a shock-absorbing mechanism by allowing temporary crisis-based suspensions of convertibility, followed by gradual restoration of the original parity. We are not saying that Euro will fail. What we are trying to say is that it will be quite an arduous job for Euro to overtake dollar as the world currency.

14

Does Government Spending Crowd Out Private Investment? Some Econometric Evidence from the Indian Economy

N.V. Vasudeva Murthy*

Introduction

In the area of development finance, understanding the long-run economic relationship between government spending and private investment has been a major focus of interest. For instance, economists and policy makers in this area are interested in finding out whether public or government investment in infra-structure, such as highways, streets, educational buildings, sewer and water facilities, hospitals, gas, electric and transit facilities, ports, airports and electrification of rural areas crowd in (increase) or crowd out (decrease) private investment. In the case of infrastructure

* Professor, College of Business Administration, Creighton University, 2500 California Plaza, Omaha.

Acknowledgements

Parts of this paper were completed during the author's sabbatical at the Indian Statistical Institute (ISI), Bangalore, India and the Institute for Social and Economic Change (ISEC), Bangalore during the spring of 2000. The author is grateful to Dr. Surekha Rao (ISI) and Dr. Govinda Rao (ISEC) for their valuable insights. He would like to thank Dr. Robert Pitts, Dr. Jack Krogstad, Dr. Randy Jorgensen, Mrs. Shirley Gust and Dr. John R. Wingender, Jr., for their constant support.

provision, the government should decide the optimal level of investment by equating the marginal product of public infrastructure with its marginal costs. It is well-known that in the case of goods and services, where the marginal social benefits are greater than the marginal private benefits, and where the free-rider problem in financing these goods and services is imminent and where the private investment is not forthcoming, the efficient allocation of scarce resources by the government is highly warranted. For instance, in the presence of credit market imperfections and physical and human capital externalities, private firms and individuals may not have incentives and funds to investment in education, roads and bridges [see, Zagler and Durnecker (2003). But, in those areas where the elements of externalities and publicness are not imminent, investment by the government might lead to the crowding in and crowding out of private investment. A government should not invest in projects where the private sector finds it highly profitable and willing to do so. If governments invest in an area where the private rate of return on investment is high, it is not efficient because of the sub-optimal allocation of the highly scarce government resource. This would result in crowding out effect. Also, the government by competing with the private sector in the loanable-funds market raises the interest rate(via deficit financing) which would crowd out private investment. This is also called financial crowding out effect. On the other hand, the government, by investing in infrastructure would likely to enhance the marginal productivity of capital and consequent higher rate of return on private capital will attract private investment leading to the crowding in effect. In fact, in many developing countries, the major goal of government spending is to raise the marginal productivity of the private sector's human and physical capital. Therefore, this phenomenon of crowding out or crowding in, examined especially from the supply side, has a tremendous implication for financing the private sector investment especially in a developing economy.

A survey of the literature on the impact of public capital stock on private capital shows that the empirical findings are mixed. For many developing countries, time-series data on public capital stock do not exist, the researchers use government investment spending (public sector real domestic capital formation).The empirical studies of Aschsauer (1989), Erenburg and Wohart (1995), Easterly and Rebelo (1993), Servan (1996), Odedokun (1997), Mamatzakis (1999), Ahmed and Miller (2000), Ghura and Goodwin (2000), Mamatzakis (2001) and Wang (2001) provide us with empirical evidence to support that government spending does crowd in private investment. In this case, the evidence implies that government investment or capital complements private capital or investment. On the other hand, the empirical investigations by Bailey (1971), Barro (1981), Monadjemi (1993), Nazmi and Ramirej (1997), Looney and Frederiken (1997), Herrera and Garcia (2000), Everhart and Sumlinski (2001) and Rossiter (2002) indicate the government spending (public capital) crowd-out private investment and thus they are substitutes rather than complements. Rossiter(2002) presents evidence which shows that while public investment in equipment crowd out, public investment in structures crowd in private investment.

While there have been several studies dealing with the phenomenon of crowding in and crowding out effect of government spending on private investment in developing economies, the prominent among them are, Ahmed and Miller (2000) for the developing world, Ghura and Goodwin (2000) which focuses on a sample of developing countries including Asian Latin American and Sub-Saharan Africa, Herrera and Garcia (2000) dealing with Latin America and East Asia, Everhart and Sumlinski (2001) dealing with a sample of 62 developing countries, Wang (2002) using of annual data for East Asian, both developing and industrialized countries, and Mamtazakis (2001) incorporating 1950-1998 time series data on Greece, no studies on the Indian economy, with the exception of Servan (1996), are found. Servan (1996), conducting a cointegration analysis using annual data on the Indian data for period of 1960-1961 and 1993-1994, contends that there has been a crowding out effect of public capital stock of infrastructure does crowd in. Although, Servan's efforts are commendable, his study suffers from the sample size problem. The degrees of freedom, left, in his cointegration analysis may not be sufficient to draw strong conclusions. As evident in Table 1, in the Indian economy public sector real gross capital formation as a per cent of total gross domestic capital formation has been more than 30 per cent on average over the period 1950-2000. It can by observed form Table 1 that although the share of public investment has been remarkable, the share of private investment in total investment has been rising, especially during the 1990-2000 period.

Table 1. Real gross Domestic Capital Formation in The Indian Economy (% of RGDP)

	1950-1951	*1960-1961*	*1970-1971*	*1980-1981*	*1990-1991*	*1999-2000*
Total	10.93	15.50	17.10	20.59	26.78	25.14
Private	8.04	8.24	10.20	11.34	16.30	17.43
Public	2.89	7.26	6.91	9.30	10.39	7.71

Source: Government of India, *Economic Survey 2001-2002.*

The present paper attempts to address this problem by applying the maximum likelihood technique of Johansen and Juselius (1990), to test whether government spending crowd out or crowd in private investment, using the data on the relevant variables of interest in the Indian economy for the period, 1950-2000. Hakkio and Rush (1991) demonstrate that for cointegration analysis, what matters most is the span of the data and not the frequency of data [also see, Shiller and Perron 1985)]. Furthermore, in this paper the Johansen cointegration test statistics are corrected for small sample biases using the Reimers (1992) adjustment procedure.

Theoretical Specification, Data and Methodology

At the very outset, the following expression for the private investment function in the Indian economy can be specified:

$$I_{p'} = F(Y, I_g\, G_c) \tag{1}$$

Where $I_{p'}$, Y, I_g and G_c are private sector real gross domestic capital formation, real gross domestic product, public sector real gross domestic capital formation and government real final consumption expenditure, respectively. Assuming linearity, dynamic adjustment towards the long-run economic equilibrium among the arguments of (1) can take place in several ways. One such simple way is to assume that the adjustment can be expressed by a vector error-correction model (VECM), as demonstrated by Johansen (1998) and Johansen and Juselius (1990), as follows:

$$\Delta X_t = \Gamma_1 \Delta X_{t-1} + \ldots \Gamma_{k-1} \Delta X_{t-k} + \Pi X_{t-k} + \varepsilon_t \tag{2}$$

Where Δ is a difference operator and k is the number of lags. In the present context, in equation (2) Γ_i represent a (4*4) matrix that contains information on the short-run adjustment of changes in X_t, and is Π is a (4*4) matrix of parameters, which indicates information on the long-run matrix of r cointegrating vectors and ε_t is a $(4 * r)$ vector of stochastic disturbance terms, assumed to be white noise. If the rank of Π is $0 < r < p$, than Π can be expressed as $\Pi = \alpha\beta'$. In the present case, β' is α (4 * 4) matrix of r cointegrating vectors and α is α $(4^* r)$ matrix of speed of adjustment factors, also called factor loadings. These factor loadings show how the system adjusts to the long-run economic equilibrium, should there be any disequilibrium in the short-run. Finding cointegration amounts to finding the existence of the number of linearly independent columns or cointegration relationships in Π. In equation (2), it is specified that

$X_t = (I_p, Y, I_g, G_c)'$. Thus the VECM in equation (2) explicitly expresses the link between the short-run and the long-run equilibrium relationships among I_p, Y, I_g and G_c. Johansen and Juselius (1990) use two statistics, the λ– max statistic and the trace statistic to determine the number of cointegrating vectors or long-run relationships in the system. While the observed λ– max statistic compares the null hypothesis of $Ho(r)$ with an alternative hypothesis of $H1\ (r + 1)$, the observed trace statistic defines the null $Ho(r)$ in contrast to an alternative hypothesis of $H1(p)$. These tests are associated with non-standard distributions and are adjusted for small samples [see Johansen and Juselius (1990), Reimers (1992) and Osterwald-Lenum (1992)].

This paper, using the Johansen-Juselius procedure discussed above, estimates the effect of disaggregated government spending investment and consumption expenditure and real gross domestic product on private capital during the period, 1950-2000. The data on private sector real gross domestic capital formation (I_p), public sector real gross domestic capital formation (I_g) are obtained from *Economic Survey 2001-2002*. The data on government real final consumption expenditure (G_c) and real gross domestic product (Y) are gathered from *Handbook of Statistics on Indian Economy Annual Series* (Reserve Bank of India, 2002). All the variables, in 1993-1994 constant prices, are expressed in natural logarithms. As mentioned above, since the data on public and private capital stock over a long period are not available for the Indian economy, and since it is customary to use the data on gross domestic capital formation as proxies for capital stock and investment in studies dealing with the topic under investigation for developing economies, the present paper has followed a consistent procedure.

Empirical Findings[1]

A pre-requisite for cointegration analysis is a determination of the order of integration of all variables used in equation (1). In the specified equation (1), integration analysis involves determining whether the variables series included in the empirical analysis are stationary in levels or in first-differences. One has to make sure that whether the observed increase in an economic time-series is driven by underlying trend or is it due to the presence of a unit root in its data generating process (d.g.p.), because if the series contains a unit root or if it represents random walk, a shock to the series will have permanent consequences and therefore the series will not revert to its mean. Moreover in conducting a regression analysis, if two series Y_t and X_t are random walks, then estimating their relationship by using the Ordinary Least Squares (OLS) results in spurious regression relationship and in that case, a cointegration analysis is warranted. If a time series X_t is stationary, 1(0), then its mean, variance and auto-covariance (at various lags) remain constant at whatever point we measure them [see, Gujarati (2003), Harris and Sollis (2003) and Maddala and Kim(1999)]. On the other hand, if a time-series X_t is non-stationary, I(1), then its mean and variance are time-variant and the series are not mean reverting. Regressing two series $Y_t \sim (1)$ and X_t (1), by using the OLS technique, in first-differences would lead to a loss of long-run information or low frequency information, and therefore, in this case, the OLS estimator will be an inefficient estimator. If both $Y_t \sim I(0)$ and $X_t \sim I(0)$, then we can estimate their relationship using the OLS estimator. Contrary to this phenomenon, if $Y_t \sim I(1)$, and $X_t \sim I(1)$ and their linear combination is $(Y_t - bX_t) \sim I(0)$, then X_t and Y_t are said to be cointegratd, reflecting their long-run economic equilibrium relationship. One has to be certain that cointegration is arising out of the underlying structural economic equilibrium relationship, but not due to a common unrelated time trend in the data generating process [see, Harris and Sollis (2003) and Enders (2004)]. Therefore, in this paper, a battery of unit root tests is conducted to discern the presence of a unit root in the variables included in the cointegration analysis. A bettery of unit root tests is undertaken, rather than a single unit root test, because often times, the conventional unit root test, such as the Dickey-Fuller test does suffer from low power.

Table 2 reports the result of the unit root test. The Augmented Dickey-Fuller test (ADF) incorporates extra lagged differenced terms in the data generating process to account for autocorrelation [see, Fuller (1976)]. The Phillips-Perror unit root test (pp) implements a non-parametric correction to the t-statistic of the ADF regression to adjust for the presence of autocorrelation which is a high possibility in the error terms when their underlying data generating process is not AR(1) [see, Phillips and Perron (1988)]. While the ADF, ADF-GLS and the PP unit root tests consider the null hypothesis of non-stationarity, the recently formulated KPSS unit root test [see, Kwiatkowski et al. (1992)] states the null hypothesis of stationarity. It is evident in Table 2 that for the level series, and ADF, PP and ADF-GLS we fail to reject the null hypothesis of the presence of a unit root in all the series. The ADF-GLS is a much more powerful test than the ADF test. Ellio et al. (1996) have formulated the ADF-GLS unit root test which is an ADF test on the detrended series. The ADF-GLS unit root test boosts the power of the ADF test [see, Harris and Sollis, (2003)]. For the level variable series, the KPSS test result reject the null of the stationarity [see, Stock and Watson (2003)]. While for the first-differenced series of all variables, the ADF, PP and ADF-GLS test result the null of the presence of a unit root, and the KPSS test results vehemently fail to reject the null of stationarity. Thus, the results presented in Table 2 confirm that the variable-series of I_p, Y, I_g and G_c in levels are non-stationary, and in first-differences they are stationary. They are said to be integrated of the order 1. Furthermore, an application of the Zivot- Andrews (1992) test for the presence of a structural break confirmed the absence of any statistically discernible structural breaks.

Table 2. Results of the Unit Root Tests

Variable	*ADF*	*ADF-GLS*	*PP*	*KPSS*
I_p	–0.96(3)	–3.95(0)	–4.64(4)*	0.21(4)
I_g	–2.54(3)	–1.80(0)	–2.41(4)	0.16(4)
Y	–0.133(1)	–0.84(0)	–0.08(2)	0.22(5)
G_c	–3.011(1)	–2.99(1)	–2.57(4)	0.22(5)
ΔI_p	–5.47(5)*	–7.65(1)	–9.43(4)*	0.06(4)*
ΔI_g	–4.0(2)*	–7.55(0)*	–91.08(4)*	0.06(4)*
ΔY	–6.201(1)*	–9.03(0)*	–10.19(4)*	0.06(4)*
ΔG_c	–4.24(0)	–4.25(0)*	–4.29(4)*	0.07(4)*

Note: Lags in parentheses. (*) indicates significance at the 5 per cent level. The critical values at the 5 per cent level of significance for the ADF, PP and ADF-GLS unit root tests are respectively, –3.51, –3.51 and –3.19. The upper critical $\hat{\eta}_t$ value for the KPSS statistic is 0.146 at the 5 per cent level.

Table 3 reports some univariate and multivariate (system) misspecification tests to confirm whether the cointegratd VAR model with a lag of 6, adequately describes changes in the data. The results are basically robust to other lag lengths. The chosen order of the VAR, a lag of 6, is high enough to ensure that autocorrelation is not present and the degrees of freedom left for estimation are large enough for the asymptotic theory to be reasonably applicable. Therefore, a sufficient amount of care has been taken to confirm that the VAR model is estimated in such a way that it is free from autocorrelation. Furthermore, the results from Table 3 show that the system-LM tests for first and fourth order residual autocorrelation are not significant, as their observed values are respectively 0.61 and 0.95 confirming that the residuals are white-noise and therefore free from serial autocorrelation. The system-test for normality indicates that the condition of normality is not met. However, the Johansen-Juselius procedure is robust to departure from normality.

Table 3: Misspecification Diagnostics of the VAR Model

Univariate		*System*
Arch (6)	Normality	Residual Autocorrelation
		LM(1), Chi. Sq (16) = 13.82
4.72	0.08	[0.61]
1.63	1.40	LM(4), Chi. Sq. (16) = 8.0
5.35	2.98	[0.95]
4.16	5.61	Normality, chi. Sq (8) = 21.65
		[0.01]
Skewness	R^2	
–0.05	0.84	
0.05	0.68	
0.06	0.55	
–0.14	0.63	

Note: For VAR, Lags = 6. P-values in brackets.

Cointegration results using the Johansen and Juselius (1990) maximum likelihood approach, with unrestricted intercepts and no trends in the VAR estimation are reported in Table 4. The presence of the deterministic terms in the present case, unrestricted intercepts and no trends, is determined by the Pantula (1989) principle [also see, Johansen (1992). The Pantula principle is a sequential procedure to simultaneously determine both cointegration rank and the deterministic component of a cointegration model.

The result reported in Table 4, show that both the observed maximum given value and trace statistics with Reimer's adjustment procedure (1992), reject the null hypothesis of no cointegration but fail to reject the null hypothesis of one cointegrating vector at the 5 per cent level, thus indicating the presence of a single cointegrating vector.

Table 4: The Johansen-Juselius Cointegration Test Results

Trace Test				*λ-Max*			
H_0	H_1	Stat.	95%	H_0	H_1	Stat.	95%
$r = 0$	$r \geq 1$	60.82*	48.85	$r = 0$	$r = 1$	36.67*	27.42
$r \leq 1$	$r \geq 2$	24.06	31.45	$r \leq 1$	$r = 2$	18.83	21.12
$r \leq 2$	$r \geq 3$	5.20	17.86	$r \leq 2$	$r = 3$	4.77	14.88
$r \leq 3$	$r \geq 4$	0.46	8.07	$r \leq 3$	$r = 4$	0.46	8.07

Note: The results are based on VAR with legs = 6. The test statistics are corrected for small sample biases using the Reimers (1992) adjustment procedure. * denotes rejection of the null hypothesis at the 5% level. Critical values from Osterwald-Lenum (1992).

Thus, in the Indian economy during the period under investigation, 1950-2000, I_p, Y, I_g and G_c do form a long run link and hence are cointegrated. Technically, this amounts to saying that there exists a single cointegrating vector. Table 5 presents the cointegrating vector, normalized on I_p, as equation (3). Since the existence of a unique cointegrating vector is consistent with, a priori criteria and satisfies an explicit formulation of the long-run economic hypothesis that underlies the cointegration analysis, no structural restrictions are imposed and tested. However, a non-testable restriction is imposed on the cointegrating vector so that it can be identified exactly. This is done by normalizing the cointegrating vector on I_p, with $\beta_1 = 1$.

Table 5: Normalized Cointegrating Vector

$$I_p = 1.39Y + 0.17I_g - 0.09G_c \quad (3)$$

[42.25]* [11.33]* [3.0]*

$\hat{\alpha}_{IP} = -0.07$; $\hat{\alpha}_Y = -0.03$; $\hat{\alpha}_{Ig} = -02$; $\hat{\alpha}_{GC} = -0.00$

[–8.64]* [–1.26] [–2.3] [–1.51]

Note: Asymptotic t-values in brackets. * denotes significance at 1 per cent level. $\hat{\alpha}_i$ are the loading factors.

The t-values of the estimated parameters shown in Table 5 indicate that the estimated parameters of interest in equation (3) are statistically significant at one per cent level. The exclusionary tests conducted on I_p, Y, I_g and G_c yield observed likelihood ratio test statistics of 34.44, 33.68, 33.06, and 9.0, respectively. The critical likelihood ratio statistic is distributed as a chi-square statistic with one degree of freedom. The observed p-values of the likelihood ratio indicate that the coefficients of interest are significantly different from zero at 5% level of significance, indicating that I_p, Y, I_g and G_c, do enter the cointegrating vector. Government investment spending does exert a significantly positive effect on private investment, indicating crowding in effect. The effect of government final consumption expenditure on private investment is significantly negative, which shows that as more resources are used for government consumption, less of them remain for private saving and investment. The real GDP has a significantly positive effect on public investment indicating the effects of acceleration principle, and the consequent impact of economic growth and increasing level of profits on private investment spending. While the *t*-values of the loading factors of I_g, Y and G_c, $\hat{\alpha}_{Ig}$, $\hat{\alpha}_y$, and $\hat{\alpha}_{GC}$, are not statistically significant, the *t*-value of the loading factor of I_p,$\hat{\alpha}_{Ip}$, is statistically significant at 1 per cent level, besides having the expected negative sign. These empirical finding show that the variables, Y, I_g and G_c are weakly exogenous, implying that the dependent variable, I_p is endogenous and therefore, private investment responds to policy intervention involving variables in the system. Weak exogeneity of I_g, Y and G_c also indicates that cointegration analysis and estimation can be conducted with a single-equation framework

Empirical findings from the results presented in Table 6 indicate that the parameters of interest are statistically significant and this observation further reinforces the finding that while private sector investment and public sector investment are complements, government final consumption expenditure and private investment are substitutes. These findings are consistent with the studies on other countries by Mamatzakis (2001), Ghura and Goodwin (2000) and Wang (2002).

Table 6: Noramlized Cointegrating vector: Conditioned on the Weakly Exogenous Variables

$I_p = 1.37Y + 0.14I_g - 0.4G_c$ (4)

[42.14]* [9.51]* [–9.51]*

$\alpha_{Ip} = 0.07$
[10.86]*

Note: *denotes significance at 1 per cent level. T-values in brackets.

Since the application of the Johansen-Juselius cointegration procedure indicates the presence of a single cointegration vector, an alternative cointegration technique, the Phillips-Hansen fully-modified method (FM-OLS) is employed to further confirm the existence of cointegration in equation (1) [see, Phillips-Hansen (1990)]. The Phillips-Hansen FM-OLS procedure (1990) is a single-equation cointegration technique which corrects for endogeneity and contemporaneous correlation in equation (1). It has been demonstrated by Hargreaves (1994) that the FM-OLS cointegration estimator is a fully efficient method of estimating long-run economic relationships, especially in small samples. The FM-OLS result are reported in Table 7.

Table 7: The FM-OLS Results

I_p = –8.10	+ 1.40Y	+ 0.21I_g	–0.13G_c
[–23.26]*	[12.10]*	[7.31]	[–2.48]**

Wald Test (H_0: $\beta_2 = 1$): *Chi. sq* = 43.89*; (5)

ADF (1) = –5.56(1)*; pp(=1) = –10.55*; ADF-GLS(1) = –6.07*; KPSS(0) = 0.50

Note: * and ** denote significance at 1 and 5 per cent levels. Asymptotic t-values in brackets. Lag in parentheses. For all unit root tests, except the KPSS test, on the residuals, regression include a constant and linear trend.

The FM-OLS results presented in Table 7, further reinforces the existence of a long-run relationship among I_p, Y, I_g and G_c. The asymptotic t-values reported in brackets indicate that the estimated parameters of Y, I_g and G_c. and the intercept are statistically significant. The magnitudes of the estimated parameters are consistent with those found using the Johansen-Juselius procedure and the results support the finding that in the Indian economy during the period under investigation, government investment spending does crowd in private investment. A Wald test on the coefficient of Y, β_2, indicates that the elasticity of private investment spending with respect to real GDP is significantly different from one. The unit root tests on the residuals from equation (5), ADF, ADF-GLS, and PP tests confirm that, the residuals are stationary at the 5 per cent level and thus suggest I_p, Y, I_g and G_c are cointegrated. Furthermore, the KPSS unit root test result, with a constant included in the regression, reinforces the same conclusion....

Table 8: An Error-Correction Model

$\Delta I_g = 0.05$	$+ 0.88\Delta Y$	$+ 0.01\Delta Ig$	$-0.55\Delta G_{C\ t-1}$	$-0.91 ECT_{t-1}$	(6)
[1.60]	[1.88]**	[0.05]	[1.72]**	[-6.23]*	
$R^2 = 0.47$;	η_I (0.19);	η_2(0.68);	η_3(0.42);	η_4(0.58)	

Note: t-values in brackets. *and **denote significance at 1 and 10 per cent levels. η_1, η_2, η_3, and η_4 are respectively, tests for the presence of serial correlation, functional form, normality and heterioscedasticity. Observed p-values in parentheses.

In order to further confirm the existence of cointegration, along the line suggested by the Granger representation theorem (Engle and Granger (1987)], a parsimonious dynamic correction model (ECM) is estimated using the OLS method and the results are presented as equation (6) in Table 8. The statistically significant lagged error-correction term (ECT_{t-1}) in equation (6), although high in magnitude, compared to that found using the Johansen-

Juselius procedure, supports the validity of the existence of a long-run economic relationship in equation (5). The estimated error-correction model passes all the diagnostic tests, including the tests for the presence of serial correlation, misspecification, non-normality and heteroscedasticity.

Finally, an alternative econometric procedure, the Variance Decomposition Analysis (VDC) is employed to examine the system dynamics, especially out-of-sample dynamics and to partition the variance of the forecast error of the variable of interest, I_p, into proportions attributable to shocks in other variables in the system, I_g, Y, I_{GC} and finally shocks in its own.

Table 9 reports the variance decomposition of the private investment. I_g account for 9.10 per cent of the forecast error variance of private investment, I_p, in the Indian economy after one year. In contrast, after on year, Y and G_C explain 8.6% and 33.20%, of the forecast error variance in I_p, respectively. After 20 years, 4.60% of the forecast variance of I_p is attributable to disturbance in I_g, while 12.34 per cent of the forecast variance is accounted for G_c. Overall, the result in Table 9 do provide some evidence that I_g does produce a positive impact on I_p, although the magnitude may be relatively small. The empirical findings from the impulse response function (IRF), the results of which are not reported

Table 9. Variance Decomposition of Private Investment

Period	I_p	Y	I_g	G_c
0	100.00	0.00	0.00	0.00
1	49.10	8.60	9.10	33.20
5	34.39	32.18	8.50	24.93
15	24.75	55.47	5.60	14.18
20	22.40	60.66	4.60	12.34

Note:Source: Author's calculations. Ordering: I_p, Y, I_g and G_C.

here, indicate overall positive response of I_p to a one standard deviation shock to I_g and a negative response of I_p to a one standard deviation shock to G_c, supporting the main findings from the cointegration analysis that where as, I_g can be deemed as a complement of I_p, G_c can be considered a substitute for I_p. The IRF measures the dynamic response path of I_p due to an unanticipated shock to I_g, Y and G_c.

Conclusion and Policy Implication

This paper presents econometric results which suggest that in the Indian economy, during the period 1950-2000, government investment and real gross domestic product affect private investment positively, thus indicating a crowding in effect. In stark contrast, government consumption expenditure exerts a negative impact on private investment. Some policy implications are that the government should continue and increase investment in infrastructure services, especially in transportation, construction of paved roads connecting the presently inaccessible rural areas, electricity generation, facilitating telephone and the Internet diffusion, that would promote accelerate economic growth, poverty alleviation and further expedite the process of economic and financial liberalization. The results presented in this paper also imply that increases in government investment would lead to increased employment in the Indian economy. Furthermore, in the Indian economy, enhanced and greater coverage of infrastructure by government investment, would instrumental in attracting foreign direct investment. While the empirical findings show that fiscal policy, specifically government spending can be used as a capacity enhancing instrument, the policy makers have to pay special attention to the composition of public spending, as there is a high possibility that government consumption crowds out private investment. Efforts should be undertaken to ensure that excessive government consumption, which leads to higher public deficit and thus push interest rates escalating borrowing costs and thus resulting in lower private investment, is not undertaken. Therefore, the government should curtail some of its wasteful expenditure, and hence not absorb precious and scarce resources from the private sector, which could be used elsewhere in the economy for building private capital stock.

Notes

1. Unit root testing, cointegration analysis and the variance decomposition are conducted using MICROFIT 4.0 [Pesaran and Pesaran (1997)] and confirmed using EViews 4.1 (2002) and CATS (1995).

References

1. Ahmed, H. and Miller, S.M., (2000), "Crowding-out and Crowding-In Effects of the Components of Government Expenditure," *Comporary Economic Policy,* 18(1): pp. 124-133.
2. Aschauer, D.A., (1989), "Does Public Capital Crowd Out Private Capital?", *Journal of Monetary Economics* 2492): pp. 171-188.
3. Baily, M., (1971), *National Income and the Price Level,* McGraw-Hill.
4. Barro, R., (1981), "Output Effects of Government Purchases," *Journal of Political Economy,* December, pp. 1086-111.
5. Easterly, W. and Rebelo, S., (1993), "Fiscal Policy and Growth," *Journal of Monetary Economics,* 32, pp. 417-458.
6. Elliot, G.T., Rothenberg, J. and Stock, J.H., (1996), "Efficient Tests for Autoregressive Unit Root," *Econometrica,* 64, pp. 813-836.
7. Enders, W., (2004), *Applied Economic Time Series,* John Wiley & Sons.
8. Engle, R.F. and Granger, C.W.J., (1987), "Cointegration and Error-Correction: Representation, Estijation and Testing", *Econometrica,* 55, pp. 251-276.
9. Erenburg, S. and Wohart, M., (1995), "Public and Private Investment: Are there Casual Linkage?", *Journal of Macroeconomics,* 17, pp. 1-30.
10. Everhart, S.S. and Sumlinski, M.A., (2001), "Trends in Private Investment in Development Countries, Statistics for 1971-2000, and the Impact on Private Investment of Corruption and the Quality of Public Investment," *International Finance Corproation.*

11. Fuller, W.A., (1976), *Introduction to Statistical Time Series*, Wiley, New York.

12. Ghura, D. and Goodwin, B., (2000), "Determinants of Private Investment: A Cross-Regional Empirical Investigation," *Applied Economics*, 32(14): pp. 1819-1829.

13. Government of India, (2002), *Economic Survey* 2001-2002.

14. Gujarati, D. (2003), *Basic Econometrics*, Mc-Graw-Hill, New York.

15. Hakkio, C.S. and Rush, M., (1991), "Cointegration: How Short is Long-run?", *Journal of International Money and Finance*, 10, pp. 571-581.

16. Hansen, H. and Juselius, K., (1995), *CATS in RATS: Cointegration of Time Series*, Estima, Evanston, IL.

17. Hargreaves, C.P., (1994), *Nonstationary Time Series Analysis and Cointegration*, Oxford University Press, Oxford, England.

18. Harris, R. and Sollis, R., (2003), *Applied Time Series Modelling and Forecasting*, John Wiley & Sons.

19. Herrera, S. and Garcia, C., (2000), "Aggregate Investment and Foreign Direct Investment in Latin America and East Asia: Is There a Crowding-Out Effect," *World Bank Working Paper*, Washington, D.C.

20. Johansen, S. and Juselius, K., (1990), "Maximum Likelihood Estimation and Inference on Cointegration–with Applications to the Demand for Money, *Oxford Bullen for Economics and Statitics*, 52, pp. 169-210.

21. Johansen, S., (1992), "Cointegration in Partial Systems and the Efficiency of Single Equation Analysis," *Journal of Econometrics*.

22. Kwiatkowski, D., P.C.B. Phillips, P. Schmidt, and Y. Shin, (1992), "Testing the Null Hypothesis of Stationarity Against the Alternative of a Unit Root: How Sure are We that Economic Time Series have A Unit Root," *Journal of Econometrics*, pp. 159-178.

23. Looney, R.E. and Frederiken, P.C., (1997), "Government Investment and Follow-on Private Sector Investment in Pakistan, 1972-1995," *Journal of Economic Development*, 22, pp. 91-100.

24. Maddala, G.S. and Kim, I.M., (1999), *Unit Roots Cointegration and Structural Change*, Cambridge University Press, Cambridge.

25. Mamatzakis, E.C., (1999), "Testing for Long-run Relationship Between infrastructure and Private Capital Productivity: A Time Series Analysis for the Greek Industry," *Applied Economic Letters*, pp. 243-246.

26. Mamatzakis, E.C., (2001), "Public Investment Private Investment: Evidence from Greece," *International Economic Journal*, 15, pp. 33-46.

27. Monadjemi, M.S., (1993), "Fiscal Policy and Private Investment Expenditure: A Study of Australia and the United States," *Applied Economics*, pp. 143-148.

28. Nazmi and Ramirez, (1997), "Public and Private Investment and Economic Growth in Mexico," *Contemporary Econometric Policy*, 15, pp. 65-75.

29. Odedokun, M.O., (1997), "Relative Effects of Public Versus Private Investment Spending on Economic Efficiency and Growth in Development Countries," *Applied Economics*, 29, pp. 1325-1336.

30. Osterwald-Lenum, M., (1992), "Practitioner's Corner: A Note with Quantiles of the Asymptotic Distribution of the Maximum Likelihood Cointegration Rank Test Statistics," *Oxford Bulletin of Economics and Statistics*, pp. 461-472.

31. Pantula, and Sastry, G., (1989), "Testing for Unit Roots in Time Series Data," *Econometric Theory*, pp. 256-271.

32. Pesaran, M. and Pesaran, B., (1997), *Working with Microfit 4.0: Interactive Economic Analysis*, Camfit Data Limited, United Kingdom.

33. Phillips, P.C.B. and Hansen, B.E., (1990), "Statistical Inference in Instrumental Variabels Regression with I(1) Process," *Review of Economic Studies*, 57, pp. 90-125.

34. Phillips, P.C.B. and Perron, P., (1988), "Testing for a Unit Root in Time-Series Regression," *Biometrika*, 75, pp. 335-346.

35. Quantitative Microsoftware, (2002), *Eviews 4.1*, Irvine, CA.

36. Reimers, H.E., (1992), "Comparisons of Tests for Multivariate Cointegration," *Statistical Papers*, 33, pp. 335-359.

37. Reserve bank of India, (2002), *Handbook of Statistics, on Indian Economy, Annual Series*, (Table 2).

38. Rossiter, R., (2002), "Structural Cointegration Analysis of Private and Public Investment," *International Journal of Business and Economics*, 1, pp. 59-67.

39. Servan, L., (1996), "Does Public Capital Crowd-out Private Capital? Evidence from India," *World Bank Policy Research Working Paper*, 1613 (May).

40. Shiller, R. and Perron, P., (1985), "Testing the Random Walk Hypothesis: Power versus Frequency of Observations," *Economics Letters*, 18, pp. 381-386.

41. Stock and Watson, (2003), *Introduction to Econometrics*, Addison-Wesley, New York.

42. Wang, E., (2002), "Public Infrastructure and Economic Growth: A New Approach Applied to East Asian Economies," *Journal of Policy Modeling*, 25(5), pp. 411-435.

43. Zagler, M. and Durnecker, G., (2003), "Fiscal Policy and Economic Growth," 17(3), pp. 397-418.

44. Zivot, E. and Andrews, D.W.K., (1992), "Further Evidence on the Great Crash, the Oil-Price Shock, and the Unit-Root Hypothesis," *Journal of Business and Economic Statistics*, 10(3), pp. 251-270.

15

Causal Nexus Between Fiscal Deficits and Macro-Economic Variables in Indian States

K. Sham Bhat*
Tripura Sundari**
Prachitha, J.***

The most reliable indicator of overall macro-economic health and sickness in both developed and developing economies is the size of their respective government deficits. As per the Ricardian Equivalence Proposition [Leiderman and Blejer (1988) and Seater (1933)], the size of a country's fiscal deficit or its national debts, at any point of time is irrelevant to any economic issue of consequences. This proposition holds well under the existence of complete inter-temporal markets whereby agents can borrow and lend freely their current and future income through time. Empirical evidence tend to reject the proposition which means that we live in a non-Ricardian world wherein there are borrowing constraints and the size of the fiscal deficits and its cumulated stock does matter. High deficits show up in at least one type of macro-economic

* Professor and Head, Department of Economics, Pondicherry University, Pondicherry-14
** Ph.D., Scholar, Department of Economics, Pondicherry University, Pondicherry-14
*** M.S., Scholar, Department of Economics, Pondicherry University, Pondicherry-14.

imbalance-either through inflation, a shortage of foreign exchange, crowding out of the private sector or a foreign debt crisis.

The developing countries are always beset with over-indebtedness and hence, the debt crisis, high inflation, poor investment performance and low economic growth. The persistent high fiscal deficits in these countries received the blame for all these economic ills. The type of imbalance created by the deficits depends on the modes in which the deficit is financed; these being printing currency, running down foreign exchange reserves and domestic borrowing or foreign borrowing. Over-reliance on any one of these sources can create macro-economic imbalances.

When resources are used productively it can generate a future stream of income to cover the servicing costs of debt incurred in financing the deficits. Thus deficits by themselves cannot imply macro-economic problems. Therefore, it is only a prudent fiscal policy that can maintain consistency with other macro-economic objectives of controlling inflation, promoting private investment and maintaining external credit worthiness.

Governments have been incurring deficits for a long time due to their increased intervention in the form of simulative fiscal policies to redress the problems of unemployment, to overcome cyclical fluctuations in the economy and to undertake the role of 'welfare state'. In the process, there are chances for the macro-economic variables such as private savings, private investment, government investment, money supply, inflation rate, government bond yield rate and gross domestic product were affected by fiscal deficit. The rationale behind the relationship between fiscal deficit and macro-economic variables relationship are as follows:

Private Saving

The impact of budget deficits on private saving has been a subject of recurrent interest in developing countries where fiscal policies has the overriding importance for domestic capital formation and growth. There are competing theories, which attempt to establish direct or indirect relationship between the two. Certain theoretical framework which owes its origin to the Ricardian Equivalence theory argued that no relationship between the two variables exist and perhaps this has made the relationship the most controversial issue in macroeconomics.

The three major routes through which fiscal deficits could have implication for private saving are:

(i) As per Keynesian analysis, fiscal deficits increase aggregate absorption in the economy and therefore reduce the saving potential in the economy. As per the Neo-classical Life-cycle Theory (Ando, Modigliani, Brumberg, 1954), fiscal deficits increase private consumption not to the extent anticipated by the Keynesian school, because the private agents discount future tax liability with their disposable income. Under the Ricardian paradigm, a completely different result emerges. The deficit will reduce private consumption if the private sector is forward looking and discounts the future tax liability in order to repay and service the debt incurred for financing the deficit.

(ii) The impact of budget deficit on private saving stems from direct complementary and substitution possibilities between private and public expenditures. In developing countries 'direct crowding out' is generally found as public and private sector investments and consumption are complementary and final impact could be a deterioration of private financial balance and reduced national savings. If private expenditure is a substitute for public expenditure, the opposite would happen.

(iii) deficits could be positively associated with private savings if they are due to the growing fiscal incentives meant for promoting saving activities in the economy.

Private Investment and Consumption Expenditure

Fiscal policies affect private investment through three major channels. They are: (a) Public Investment, (b) Public Deficit, and (c) User cost of capital. Public capital is a close substitute for private capital, which can bring down the rate of return on private investment. The greater the complementarity of private and public capital, the public investment is more likely to have a net positive effect on private investment. Further, when interest rates are not regulated, deficit financing through domestic borrowing tends to push up the real interest rate which crowds out private investment. Fiscal policies affect private consumption and saving through two major channels. They are: (i) disposable income, and (ii) rate of return. An increase in deficit due to cut in current taxes boosts private consumption as per Keynesian hypothesis (1936) that consumers increase spending when their current income rises. However, according to the Permanent Income hypothesis (Friedman, 1957), only permanent tax cuts significantly affects consumer spending. The effect of real interest rates cause consumers to substitute consumption for the future rather than consuming in the present. It also induces consumers to feel richer thus making them spend in both the periods.

Government Investment and Consumption Expenditure

According to Buchanan and Wagner (1977), federal deficits increase federal spending because they reduce the perceived price of federal services to the current generation and therefore increase the demand for those services. In developed countries, there is growing need for government services to help the less fortunate while in developing countries; governments perform diverse roles in order to achieve a number of socio-economic objectives. Besides, in every country, the government plays a major role in directing resources either directly through its intervention and establishing its own enterprises or indirectly through taxes, subsidies and other regulations and also providing defence and social infrastructure. All these activities of the Government raise its investment and consumption expenditures thereby increasing the deficits.

Money Supply

The relationship between deficits and money supply depends upon the nature in which the deficit is financed. When the government engages in money financing of the deficit by borrowing from the Central Bank, the fiscal deficit-money supply relationship is brought into focus. The Central Bank will purchase government's debt securities and create high-powered money to finance the deficit. The validation hypothesis of Dornbush and Fischer (1990) states that the Central Bank favours normal interest rate stability over the rate of growth of money supply and the self-perpetuating hypothesis of inflation-induced deficits and deficits induced inflation by Sarma (1982) and Jadhav (1994) support the existence of a relationship between fiscal deficits and money supply.

Inflation

The over-reliance on money creation to finance the deficits forms the base for inflation to creep up. Various factors such as unstable demand for money, exchange rate depreciation and widespread indexation blur the relation between money financing and inflation. Buchanan and Wagner (1977) have offered the monetarist explanation of the relation between fiscal deficit and inflation, which are considered to be conventional. According to them federal deficits increase the pressure on the monetary authorities to increase the money supply, if the Central Bank does not purchase the federal debt, instruments in response to an increase in the federal deficits. The additional government borrowings is likely to increase the interest rates which may increase the velocity of money and real output. The effect of both these variables lead to an increase in the rate of inflation. On the other hand increase in inflation leads to increase in the cost of government services. This will result to an increase in deficit.

Government Bond Yield Rate

When the monetary policy is not adaptive, the sales of Government bonds increases. To induce people to buy large quantities of bonds than before, it must discount the bonds such that the rate of interest rate on government bonds must rise. Traditional theories suggest two ways by which deficits can affect the real interest rates:

(i) Keynesian IS-LM analysis states that if the public treats governments securities as net wealth then it would increase aggregate demand by increasing private consumption. Here the linkages work through goods and services market.

(ii) The assets markets approach where the supply and demand for government securities determines its market yield. Besides, run in government bond yield rate enhances the cost of the bond. This will increase the deficit of the government.

Gross Domestic Product

The excess expenditures are undertaken with the ultimate goal of the development of an economy or to raise its income levels, but there has been a lot of contradictory views right from the origin of economic theory on the relationship between the Adam Smith in his 'The Wealth of Nations' and other classical economists favoured a small public sector and relied on private initiative to generate growth. Keynes (1936) advocated the policy of increased government expenditures especially during fluctuations in the economy thereby bringing in economic stabilization and hence the growth of the economy. In the views of Wagner it is an increase in the income levels of a nation that decides the size of the public sector.

The above theoretical relationship reveals a contradictory view on the nature of causation between the states fiscal deficit and macro-economic variables. The causation may run into four categories. They are: (i) fiscal deficit leads to macro-economic variables, (b) macro-economic variables leads to fiscal deficits, (c) Bi-directional relationship between the two, and (d) Independent relationship between fiscal deficit and macro-economic variables. These possible alternative ways of theoretical results calls for an investigation of earlier literature that will be immensely useful in identifying the gap of the study.

Niskanen (1978) conducted empirical tests to analyse the individual impact of the increase in federal spending and the higher rate of inflation on the rising federal deficits in the United States using annual time-series data for the year 1947-1976. Two separate models were framed for both the variables and estimated using Ordinary Least Squares. The results showed that in the case of increase in federal spending, the rising deficits significantly increase the total federal spending as the demand for federal services increases with the increase in income. Added to this, an increase in adult population and also on account of the increase in real unit cost of federal services with the increase in real private sector wages have contributed to the rise in the demand for federal services. But rising inflation rate is not having any relationship with the federal deficits.

Tanzi (1986) made an attempt to analyse empirically the relationship between interest rates and several other variables, including the fiscal variables, for the U.S. economy. The study was conducted for 1960-80 and 1960-84 separately as several policy changes had taken place during the period 1980-84. In a simple model of interest rate determination with non-fiscal variables such as inflation and the level of economic activity, called the 'gap' and three fiscal measures of deficits and public debt expressed as percentages of GNP, it was observed that the fiscal deficits weigh heavily in the determination of real interest rates. For the period 1960-84, the changes in tax rules have contributed to rise in short-run interest rates, while, in the long run, the interest rates reduced because additional investments lead to higher capital stock and falling rate of returns to investment, thus, reducing further capital spending and hence, low interest rates.

Khan and Lizondo (1987) examined the effects of a reduction in the fiscal deficit on the real exchange rate by formulating a simple theoretical model which combined several arguments made on the subject. They focused on the use of fiscal policies to sustain the effects of a nominal devaluation on the real exchange rate. It was observed that the magnitude of a change in the real exchange rate depends not only on the size of the devaluation and the degree of fiscal adjustment, but also on the means by which the fiscal deficit is reduced. It was suggested that if the fiscal deficit is eliminated by increasing taxes, the required depreciation of the domestic currency will be larger rather than that which is achieved by lowering government expenditures. The depreciation would be still smaller if the cuts in expenditure fell on traded rather than non-traded goods. Thus, it was inferred that the authorities have to ensure that consistency is maintained between the size of the nominal devaluation and the way the fiscal deficit is reduced.

Thomas and Abderrezak (1988) tried to analyse the effect of budget deficit on the government bond yield, that is, the long-term interest rates for the U.S. economy using quarterly data for the period 1970-86. To conduct the analysis, a model of longterm interest rates has been formulated with expected inflation, expected structural deficits as percentage of GNP, growth rate of real GNP and growth rate of liquidity as explanatory variables. Cochran-Orcutt transformation technique was employed to remove serial correlation in residuals and the estimates were obtained using Ordinary Least Square method. The parameter estimates of the expected deficits exerted a statisticaly significant impact on the government bond yields. In alternative experiments, it was also seen that these bond yields are highly sensitive to the forthcoming deficits. Granger Causality tests were conducted which showed that agents in financial markets are forward-looking and foresee the major changes in the structural deficits. Hence, larger expected deficits increase long-term interest rates.

Rangarajan, Basu and Jadhav (1989) examined the dynamic nexus between widening government deficits an the resultant rapid expansion of domestic debt in India during late 1970s and early 80s. The study called for the reconstruction of the data-base by replacing it with analytically meaningful measures of domestic debt and deficits and also for a strong methodological base. Thus, attention was paid to the different modes of financing the deficits in the framework of inter temporal budget constraint and the macro-economic consequences therein. In the 'debt-financing scenario', the future time profile of 'debt-financing' to GDP ratio was estimated, thereby allowing the government deficit to evolve passively and for the domestic borrowings to finance it. The net RBI credit to government and external financing were maintained at their current ratios to GDP. The over-all debt-GDP ratio was projected to increase very rapidly in the future, reaching as much as 150 per cent by 1999-2000. This would create a corresponding net interest burden which would lead to a squeeze on budgetary capital outlays, thereby, stifling economic growth. In 'monetary financing scenario' the macroeconomic consequences on the economy was assessed, when the government deficit is allowed to evolve passively and is financed by resorting to net RBI credit while maintaining the domestic 'debt-financing' and foreign financing at their current ratios to GDP. Application of this framework to Indian data demonstrated that such an attempt would lead to a vicious circle of large deficit, higher monetary financing, more inflation, larger deficits and so on.

Gupta and Moazzami (1991) aimed at reassessing the impact of budget deficits on the interest rates in the long-run in the United States. The main focus of the analysis was to test the Ricardian Equivalence proposition. The idea behind this analysis was to obtain direct estimates of the permanent or long-run effects of budget deficits on interest rates. Quarterly data was employed and estimates were obtained using Instrumental Variable method. The results seemed to have a significant and positive long run effect of the budget deficits on the interest rates which was quite contradictory to the Ricardian equivalence proposition. Thus, application to other countries or other time periòds or alternative models will be needed before the results are to be considered definitive.

Poterba (1994) explored the underlying causes for the fiscal stress in the U.S. State governments during the late 1980s and analysed the effects of budgetary institutions and politics on the unexpected fiscal shocks by obtaining new estimates for these shocks. He enquired into the dynamics of state taxes and spending for 1988-92 which led to substantial state budget deficits. Regression equations were run to analyse the effects of deficit shocks on state spending and taxes. Since, the deficit shock variable can be endogenous, a time-series model for state spending and revenues using lagged spending, lagged expenditure and lagged state personal income as explanatory variables was framed which yielded alternative estimates of the fiscal shock and this was used as an instrumental variable. The study revealed that the more restrictive state fixed institutions like no-deficit-carry-over rules and tax and expenditure limitations are correlated with more rapid fiscal adjustment to unexpected deficits. Regarding political factors, it was found that when a single party controls the state house and the governorship, deficit adjustment is much faster than when party control is divided. The tax increases and spending cuts were both significantly smaller in gubernational election years, compared to other times.

Ashworth (1995) argued that the empirical relationship between budgetary deficits and government expenditure growth has to be examined by adopting a more systematic approach where the existence of a long-run equilibrium should be tested using co-integration techniques and the dynamic adjustment to this equilibrium has to be modelled using an error-correction mechanism. The study using data for the United Kingdom found a unique co-integrating vector between the real aggregate demand for government services, the tax share, income, the relative price and population. The analysis also made allowances for displacement factors which showed only short-run interventions. Further, in the short-run, only tax share and possibly, the relative price found its importance. Thus, deficit financing is a long-run phenomenon which also has a crucial short-run role for the United Kingdom.

Mohanty (1995) made an attempt to collect empirical evidence of the rising public deficits on the private savings in India under the framework of Ricardian Equivalence Theory. The test results revealed little practical evidence of Ricardian behaviour in the context of Indian economy. The study observed a 'direct crowding out' impact of government expenditure on private consumption. The tests based on 'direct crowding out' hypothesis revealed that the government consumption and transfer payments have an expansionary outcome on the consumption level, while public investment and interest payments dampen private consumption and contribute to national savings.

Joshi (1999) argued for the need of a fiscal correction at the state level to improve the deteriorating financial health of the economy. He attempted to study the existing state of finances of Uttar Pradesh, identifying its revenue surplus and revenue deficit phases and the systematic factors that have lead to adverse situation. The study covered the period 1970-71 to 1997-98 where, the revenue surplus phase was from 1970-1983 and the second phase was a revenue deficit phase. Analysing the trends in the revenue and expenditure of State, the study found a decline in the tax and non-tax revenues in the second phase. The flow of funds from the centre also witnessed a decline; but the borrowings have increased many folds over the years, which has been utilized for current consumption expenditure and no allocations were made for capital building from these borrowings. The net lending and capital outlays were decreasing year after year and hence, increasing debt burden and rising interests rates. This made the state come close to a vicious grip of an international debt trap.

Raju (2000)analysed the causal relationship between fiscal deficit and the macro-economic variables and also the direction of causality. For the analysis, data from 1952-53 to 1996-97 was used for variables such as Gross Domestic Capital formation at current prices, Government Final Consumption expenditure at current prices, High powered Money, Bank Rate, Private Final Consumption expenditure at current prices, Total Final Consumption Expenditure at current Prices, Inflation Rate and Per capita Gross Domestic Product. Co-integration technique was employed to test whether a long-run stable relationship exists between fiscal deficits and the selected macro-economic variable. The results indicated that the deficits and five macro-economic variables - capital Formation, Government Final Consumption Expenditure, High Powered Money, Money Supply and Government Bond Yield Rate enjoy co-integration relationship, and there is a unidirectional causality from the variables- Capital Formation, High Powered Money and Inflation Rate to fiscal deficit and a bi-directional causality between Government Final Consumption Expenditure and Government Bond Yield rate and fiscal deficit.

From the literature reviewed it is found that most of the studies are related to the relationships that exist between fiscal deficits and the macro-economic variables at national and international level. Few studies by Mishra and Joshi have examined the fiscal imbalances of individual States. One particular study by Raju has concentrated on the causal relationship between fiscal deficits and the macroeconomic variables at national level. The study by Easterly and Schmidt- Hebbel also support the macro-economic implications of the fiscal deficits. But, no work has been conducted to analyse the causal relationship between States' deficits and macro-economic variables at Indian state level. In addition to this, in recent times, the economist and policy makers argue for the reduction of deficits mostly in developing countries due to its ill-effects. Hence, an in-depth analysis pertaining to fiscal deficits and macro-economic variables are need of the hour to design proper fiscal policy.

On the above background, an attempt is made to analyse the direction of causation between state fiscal deficit and the macro-economic variables. The rest of the article is as follows:-Section II presents the methodology of the study. Empirical results and discussion are presented in Section III. Finally, the concluding remarks are presented in Section IV.

Section II: Methodology

Simple ratio and percentage method were employed to examine the trend of fiscal deficits in Indian states. With the aim of analyzing the existence of co-integration between fiscal deficits and the macro economic variables, Granger (1969) Causality test has been employed. The Granger (1969) test of causality states that a variable X caused another variable Y, if the variability of Y is predicted not only by the past values of Y, but also by the past values of X. Like wise, Y causes X, if the variability of X is predicted not only by the past values of X, but also the past values of Y. If X causes Y and Y does not cause X then X is said to be causing Y unidirectionally. If X causes Y and Y causes X, then there is said to be a feedback or bi-directional causality between X and Y. If X does not causes

Y and Y does not causes X, X and Y are said to be independent. Thus, for the implementation of Granger Causality test two sets of regression equations have to be estimated. They are as follows:

1. Regress the restricted equation i.e. $Y = \sum_{i-1}^{n} \alpha_i Y_{t-i} + \varepsilon_t$ and obtain the residual sum of square (RSS_R).
2. Regress the unrestricted equation as $Y = \sum_{i-1}^{n} \alpha_i Y_{t-i} + \sum_{i-1}^{n} \beta_i X_{t-i} + \varepsilon_t$ and find out the unrestricted residual sum of square (RSS_U)
3. Test the null hypothesis that H_0: $\Sigma\ \alpha_i = 0$ against an alternative hypothesis that H_1: $\Sigma\alpha_i \neq 0$ ***
4. Apply the F test to test the above hypothesis and it is given by $F \frac{(RSS_R - RSS_U)/m}{(RSS_U)/(n-k)}$ which follows F distribution with m and n-k degrees of freedom.
5. If the computed F value exceeds the critical F value at the chosen level of significance, we reject null hypothesis and accept that X causes Y.

Steps 1 to 5 should be repeated by interchanging X and Y variables in the above regression equation to test whether Y causes X.

Granger causality test assumes that data series are stationary at first order level. Besides, prima-facie casual or an independent relation between X and Y may exist under the above mentioned Granger causality test. To overcome the above defects, it is essential to verify the stationarity property of the selected time series data.

Dickey-Fuller test is employed to test the stationarity of the given time series data. A time series X_t is said to be stationary if the joint distribution of $X(t_1)$..........X(tn) is the same as the joint distribution of $X(t_1 + \tau)$. ......$X(t_n + \tau)$ for all t_1, t_2, ... t_n, τ. In other words, shifting the time origin by an amount t has no effect on the joint distribution which must therefore depend only on the intervals between t_1, t_2, ...t_n. The above definition holds for any value of n. The Dickey-Fuller test (1979,1981) is employed to examine the stationarity of the series, which requires the estimation of the following equation:

$$\Delta X_t = BX_{t-1} \sum_{i=1}^{n} d_i \Delta X_{t-1} + \varepsilon_t$$

where, n is large enough to make 'e_t' a white noise. The null hypothesis that X_t is I(0) is rejected in favour of an alternate hypothesis that X_t is I(i), provided B is significantly negative. For testing purpose, t-statistics is taken as test 'statistic' though it does not follow that t-distribution (critical value are provided by Dickey and Fuller (1979, 1981)). After confirming the stationarity of the series we are supposed to estimate the co-integration regression equation and error correction model*.

The necessary information's were collected from various issues of Reserve Bank of India bulletin State Finance and Reserve Bank of India's Handbook of Statistics of Indian Economy for the year 1970-71 to 2001-02.

Section III: Empirical Results and Discussions

Granger Causality test and Dickey-Fuller test were employed to examine the causal nexus between Fiscal deficit of Indian States and macro-economic variable for the year 1970-71 to 2001-02. Table 1 reveals the trends of Gross Fiscal Deficit of Indian states during the study period. It can be

---

* However, the explanations of these models are not presented due to the fact that both the variables (States Fiscal deficit and macro-economic variable) are not integrated in the same order.

seen that the gross fiscal deficit of Indian states was Rs. 901 crores in 1970-71, and it went upto Rs.96073 crores in 2001-02. Similar trend have been observed in terms of per capita gross fiscal deficit during the study period. Further, the gross fiscal deficit of Indian states as a percentage of state receipts remained more or less 16 per cent during 1970-71 to 1985-86, but later it slowly increased. Similarly gross fiscal deficit as a percentage of gross domestic product showed a mild increase during 1970-71 to 1995-96. It was around 2.56 per cent in 1995-96 and went up to 4.23 per cent in 2001-02. The analysis clearly reveals that the fiscal deficit of Indian states has enhanced both in absolute and relative terms during the study period, which will result to a serious concern from the policy point of view.

Table 1: Trends in states' Gross Fiscal Deficit

Fiscal Year	*Gross Fiscal Deficit (Rupees. Crores)*	*Gross Fiscal Deficit as a percentage of state receipts*	*Gross Fisal Deficit as a percentage of GDP*	*Per Capita Gross Fisal Deficit*
1970-71	901	17.90	1.97	16.65
1975-76	1102	10.64	1.32	18.15
1980-81	3713	17.06	2.58	54.68
1985-86	7521	16.15	2.71	99.62
1990-91	18787	20.61	3.30	223.92
1995-96	31426	17.42	2.65	339.01
2000-01	95277	26.21	4.6	946.15
2001-02	96073	24.11	4.33	933.47

To examine the causal nexus between States Fiscal deficit and macro-economic variables, Granger Causality test is employed. The selected macro-economic variables for the analysis is Gross Domestic Capital Formation (GDCF), Private Final Consumption Expenditure (PFCE), Government Final Consumption Expenditure (GFCE), Total Final

Consumption Expenditure (TFCE), Money Supply M_3, Inflation Rate (INFLRT), Government Bond Yield Rate (GBYR) and Gross Domestic Product (GDP). The test results are presented in table 2 to 9. Experiments were conducted upto lag 3,3. By and large, the test result indicates an independent relationship between states fiscal deficit and macro-economic variables such as government final consumption expenditure, money supply, inflation rate, government bond yield rate and gross domestic product. In respect of the causal relationship between states fiscal deficit and macro-economic variables such as gross domestic capital formation, private final consumption expenditure and total final consumption expenditure, the test results reveals one-way causation (macro-economic variables leads to states fiscal deficit) between the two in the short-run during the period of our study.

Table 2: Granger-Causality test Results Between States Fiscal Deficit and Gross Domestic Capital Formation

Lags	*FD→GDCF F-value*	*GDCF→FD F-value*	*Inference*
1,1	0.86	4.02	GDCF→FD
2,2	0.79	1.48	Independent
3,3	1.42	1.8	Independent

Table 3: Granger-Causality test Results Between States Fiscal Deficit and Private Final Consumption Expenditure

Lags	*FD→PFCE F-value*	*PFCE→FD F-value*	*Inference*
1,1	2.07	5.59	PFCE→FD
2,2	0.25	2.02	Independent
3,3	0.42	1.97	Independent

Table 4: Granger-Causality test Results Between States Fiscal Deficit and Government final consumption Expenditure

Lags	*FD→GFCE F-value*	*GFCE→FD F-value*	*Inference*
1,1	0.13	1.03	Independent
2,2	0.69	0.797	Independent
3,3	2.12	0.56	Independent

Table 5: Granger-Causality test Results Between States Fiscal Deficit and Total Final Consumption Expenditure

Lags	*FD→TFCE F-value*	*TFCE→FD F-value*	*Inference*
1,1	2.234	5.017	TFCE→FD
2,2	0.353	1.68	Independent
3,3	0.42	1.81	Independent

Table 6: Granger-Causality test Results Between States Fiscal Deficit and Money Supply

Lags	*FD→M3 F-value*	*M3→FD F-value*	*Inference*
1,1	2,338	0.1697	Independent
2,2	1.816	0.295	Independent
3,3	1.528	0.214	Independent

Table 7: Granger-Causality test Results Between States Fiscal Deficit and Inflation Rate

Lags	*FD→INFLRT F-value*	*INFLRT→FD F-value*	*Inference*
1,1	0.000005	1.074	Independent
2,2	0.72	0.465	Independent
3,3	0.509	2,183	Independent

Table 8: Granger-Causality test Results Between States Fiscal Deficit and Government Bond Yield Rate.

Lags	*FD→GBYR F-value*	*GBYR→FD F-value*	*Inference*
1,1	0.036	0.027	Indepedent
2,2	0.083	0.176	Independent
3,3	0.261	0.428	Independent

Table 9: Granger-Causality test Results Between States Fiscal Deficit and Gross Domestic Product.

Lags	*FD→GDP F-value*	*GDP→FD F-value*	*Inference*
1,1	0.757	2,448	Independent
2,2	0.286	1.316	Independent
3,3	0.16	1.007	Independent

Granger causality test results assume that data series are stationary at first order level and it fails to detect prima-facie causal relationship between the two series. Hence, the finding may be due to the assumption put forward in the test statistics. To overcome this, we attempted to examine the issue with the help of co-integration analysis. Co-integration analysis requires the stationarity of both the series in an identical order. So, Dickey-Fuller test was conducted. Dickey-Fuller test results pertaining to states fiscal deficit and selected macro-economic variables are presented in tables 10 to 18. Experiments were conducted upto second order level. The condition of Dickey-Fuller test for stationary series is that β co-efficient should be negative and statistically significant. However, the variables such as gross state fiscal deficit, private final consumption expenditure, government final consumption expenditure, and total final consumption expenditure are not in a position to satisfy the condition throughout the order selected in estimating the equation. In case of gross domestic capital formation, money supply, inflation rate, government bond yield rate and gross domestic product, the coefficients are negative and statistically significant, either in first or second order level and it indicates the existence of stationarity property in the series. However, the existence of co-integration regression equation requires an integration of States Fiscal deficit and macro-economic variable in an identical order and this condition is not satisfied. Hence, it can be concluded that State Fiscal deficit and selected macro-economic variables are independent, during the period of our study.

The main reason for an independent relationship between the two is: (i) the deficits incurred by the states due to increased expenditure are not growth oriented. They are bureaucratic or politically motivated expenditures. As they are undertaken to serve political objectives, the chances of it influencing the macro variables is less. (ii) the size or quality of most of the macro-economic variables are decided by the Centre alone. The States do not have the autonomy power to alter these variables. However hence, whatever be the increase in the expenditure of the States' the macro variables may not be affected as per the theory (iii) the Centre has adopted the reform process in the fiscal sector, which aimed at reducing the deficits and putting the economy on the rails of growth. The States are not ready to implement these policies for political reasons. The States' expenditures are still non-growth oriented and hence, there are less chances of having any relationship between the two.

The above results calls for the following policy options from the part of the state government: (i) the heavy subsidisation of power, irrigation and transport sectors in the states should be reduced, (ii) the states borrowings should be utilized for capital building and raising the rate of net lending, instead of utilizing them for consumption expenditures and non-development expenditures, (iii) the states should be free to decide their expenditure and revenue

Table 10: Dickey-Fuller test results pertaining to Gross Fiscal Deficit

Function	*Order*	*Constant*	Y_{t-1}	*Trend*	R^2	*Adj* R^2	*F*
$\log Y_t = f(\log Y_{t-1})$	0,0	0.05568 (0.74)	1.003 (52.89)*	-	0.99	0.99	2796.98*
$\log Y_t = f(\log Y_{t-1}, t)$	0,0	1.141 (2.84)*	0.606 (4.15)	0.02707 (2.74)*	0.99	0.99	1716.21*
$\Delta \log Y_t = f(\log Y_{t-1})$	1,1	0.059 (3.37)*	0.0934 (0.48)	-	0.008	–0.27	0.238
$\Delta \log Y_t = f(\log Y_{t-1}, t)$	1,1	0.0507 (1.76)	0.083 (0.42)	0.0005 (0.37)	0.013	–0.06	0.184
$\Delta^2 \log Y_t = f(\log Y_{t-1})$	2,2	–0.0042 (0.27)	–0.32 (1.79)	-	0.11	0.07	3.205
$\Delta^2 \log Y_t = f(\log Y_{t-1}, t)$	2,2	0.0006 (0.012)	–0.325 (1.176)	–0.00026 (0.14)	0.11	0.04	1.554

Note: Parenthesis shows the 't' value,* Significant at 1 per cent level, ** Significant at 5 per cent level.

Table 11: Dickey-Fuller test results pertaining to Gross Domestic capital formation

Function	*Order*	*Constant*	Y_{t-1}	*trend*	R^2	*Adj.* R^2	*F*
$\log Y_t = f(\log Y_{t-1})$	0,0	0.092 (1.84)	0.994 (95.61)*	-	0.99	0.99	9140.29*
$\log Y_t = f(\log Y_{t-1}, t)$	0,0	1.75 (2.7)*	0.545 (3.107)*	0.029 (2.56)**	0.99	0.99	5448.66*
$\Delta \log Y_t = f(\log Y_{t-1})$	1,1	0.075 (5.77)**	–0.202 (1.15)	-	0.045	0.011	1.311
$\Delta \log Y_t = f(\log Y_{t-1}, t)$	1,1	0.084 (4.56)*	–0.22 (1.17)	0.000515 (0.73)	0.063	–0.006	0.909
$\Delta^2 \log Y_t = f(\log Y_{t-1})$	2,2	0.00079 (0.097)	–0.562 (3.56)*	-	0.319	0.29	12.64*
$\Delta^2 \log Y_t = f(\log Y_{t-1}, t)$	2,2	0.0117 (0.595)	–0.565 (3.54)*	0.000607 (0.61)	0.33	0.28	6.362*

Note: Parenthesis shows the 't' value, *Significant at 1 per cent level,

** Significant at 5 per cent level.

Table 12: Dickey-Fuller test results pertaining to private final consumption expenditure.

Function	*Order*	*Constant*	Y_{t-1}	*trend*	R^2	*Adj.* R^2	*F*
$\log Y_t = f(\log Y_{t-1})$	0,0	0.036 (0.94)	1.003 (141.9)*	-	0.999	0.998	19871.62*
$\log Y_t = f(\log Y_{t-1}, t)$	0,0	1.461 (2.53)**	0.683 (5.28)*	0.01677 (2.48)**	0.999	0.999	11694.82*
$\Delta \log Y_t = f(\log Y_{t-1})$	1,1	0.0528 (5.14)*	–0.0194 (0.10)	-	0.000	–0.04	0.011
$\Delta \log Y_t = f(\log Y_{t-1}, t)$	1,1	0.052 (4.35)*	–0.0261 (0.14)	0.000095 (0.24)	0.002	–0.07	0.033
$\Delta^2 \log Y_t = f(\log Y_{t-1})$	2,2	0 (0.02)	–0.33 (1.82)	-	0.109	0.076	3.305
$\Delta^2 \log Y_t = f(\log Y_{t-1}, t)$	2,2	0.004 (0.39)	–0.34 (1.82)	0.000253 (0.44)	0.116	0.048	1.699

Note: Parenthesis shows the 't' value
*Significant at 1 per cent level, and
**Significant at 5 per cent level

Table 13: Dickey-Fuller test results pertaining to Government final consumption expenditure

Function	*Order*	*Constant*	Y_{t-1}	*Trend*	R^2	*Adj.* R^2	*F*
$\log Y_t = f(\log Y_{t-1})$	0,0	0.026 (1.22)	1.008 (213.2)*	-	0.99	0.99	45450.12*
$\log Y_t = f(\log Y_{t-1}, t)$	0,0	0.791 (2.27)**	0.787 (7.803)*	0.014 (2.20)**	0.99	0.99	25719.07*
$\Delta \log Y_t = f(\log Y_{t-1})$	1,1	0.0414 (3.68)*	0.316 (1.76)	-	0.100	0.068	3.105
$\Delta \log Y_t = f(\log Y_{t-1}, t)$	1,1	0.039 (3.48)*	0.227 (1.206)	0.00045 (1.39)	0.160	0.097	2.566
$\Delta^2 \log Y_t = f(\log Y_{t-1})$	2,2	0.001 (0.34)	−0.118 (0.68)	-	0.017	−0.02	0.460
$\Delta^2 \log Y_t = f(\log Y_{t-1}, t)$	2,2	0.0063 (0.87)	−0.115 (0.66)	0.00029 (0.798)	0.04	−0.03	0.545

Note: Parenthesis shows the 't' value

*Significant at 1 per cent level, and

**Significant at 5 per cent level.

Table 14: Dickey-Fuller test results pertaining to total final consumption expenditure

Function	*Order*	*Constant*	Y_{t-1}	*Trend*	R^2	*Adj.* R^2	*F*
$\log Y_t = f(\log Y_{t-1})$	0,0	0.0298 (0.89)	1.004 (162.5)*	-	0.99	0.99	26418.68*
$\log Y_t = f(\log Y_{t-1}, t)$	0,0	1.349 (2.48)**	0.711 (5.87)*	0.0157 (2.43)**	0.99	0.99	15441.14*
$\Delta \log Y_t = f(\log Y_{t-1},)$	1,1	0.0532 (5.135)*	–0.037 (0.02)	-	0	–0.36	0
$\Delta \log Y_t = f(\log Y_{t-1}, t)$	1,1	0.0511 (4.499)*	–0.023 (0.12)	0.00018 (0.5)	0.009	–0.06	0.125
$\Delta^2 \log Y_t = f(\log Y_{t-1},)$	2,2	0.00009 (0.02)	–0.324 (1.78)	-	0.105	0.072	3.16
$\Delta^2 \log Y_t = f(\log Y_{t-1}, t)$	2,2	0.0045 (0.45)	–0.33 (1.78)	–0.00025 (0.483)	0.113	0.045	0.625

Note: Parenthesis shows the 't' value

*Significant at 1 per cent level, and

**Significant at 5 per cent level.

Table 15: Tickey-Fuller test results pertaining to Money supply

Function	*Order*	*Constant*	Y_{t-1}	*Trend*	R^2	*Adj.* R^2	*F*
$\log Y_t = f(\log Y_{t-1})$	0,0	0.072 (1.86)	0.99 (131.0)*	-	0.99	0.99	17161.32*
$\log Y_t = f(\log Y_{t-1}, t)$	0,0	4.64 (6.51)*	−0.187 (1.01)	0.083 (6.4)*	0.99	0.99	20482.04*
$\Delta \log Y_t = f(\log Y_{t-1})$	1,1	0.107 (9.13)*	−0.548 (3.46)*	-	0.29	0.27	11.941*
$\Delta \log Y_t = f(\log Y_{t-1}, t)$	1,1	0.107 (7.42)*	−0.548 (3.39)*	−3.5E+04 (0.007)	0.29	0.25	5.757*
$\Delta^2 \log Y_t = f(\log Y_{t-1})$	2,2	−0.0002 (0.04)	−0.69 (4.90)*	-	0.47	0.45	23.989*
$\Delta^2 \log Y_t = f(\log Y_{t-1}, t)$	2,2	0.0035 (0.22)	−0.687 (4.82)*	−0.00021 (0.26)	0.47	0.43	11.614*

Note: Parenthesis shows the 't' value

*Significant at 1 per cent level, and

**Significant at 5 per cent level.

Table 16: Dickey-Fuller Test Results Pertaining to Inflation Rate

Function	*Order*	*Constant*	Y_{t-1}	*Trend*	R^2	*Adj.* R^2	*F*
$\log Y_t = f(\log Y_{t-1})$	0,0	2.191 (4.64)*	0.176 (0.99)	-	0.032	–0.001	0.973
$\log Y_t = f(\log Y_{t-1}, t)$	0,0	2.58 (6.004)*	–0.143 (0.77)	0.02616 (3.18)*	0.289	0.238	5.687*
$\Delta \log Y_t = f(\log Y_{t-1})$	1,1	0.052 (0.63)	–0.517 (3.19)*	-	0.268	0.241	10.233*
$\Delta \log Y_t = f(\log Y_{t-1}, t)$	1,1	0.092 (0.49)	–0.518 (3.15)*	–0.0023 (0.24)	0.269	0.215	4.972*
$\Delta^2 \log Y_t = f(\log Y_{t-1})$	2,2	–0.0698 (0.664)	–0.679 (5.86)*	-	0.56	0.543	34.33*
$\Delta^2 \log Y_t = f(\log Y_{t-1}, t)$	2,2	–0.332 (1.34)	–0.68 (5.90)*	0.0146 (1.170)	0.58	0.55	18.085*

Note: Parenthesis shows the 't' value.
*Significant at 1 per cent level, and
**Significant at 5 per cent level.

Table 17: Dickey-Fuller test results pertaining to Government Bond Yield Rate

Function	*Order*	*Constant*	Y_{t-1}	*Trend*	R^2	*Adj.* R^2	*F*
$\log Y_t = f(\log Y_{t-1})$	0,0	0.06055 (1.93)	0.947 (128.5)*	-	0.966	0.964	814.151*
$\log Y_t = f(\log Y_{t-1}, t)$	0,0	0.08735 (1.17)	0.908 (8.53)*	0.00062 (0.395)*	0.966	0.963	395.306*
$\Delta \log Y_t = f(\log Y_{t-1},)$	1,1	0.0153 (2.24)**	–0.0384 (0.204*)	-	0.001	–0.03	0.041
$\Delta \log Y_t = f(\log Y_{t-1}, t)$	1,1	0.02587 (2.27)**	–0.108 (0.50)	–0.0008 (1.403)	0.069	0	1.005
$\Delta^2 \log Y_t = f(\log Y_{t-1},)$	2,2	–0.00002 (0.004)	–0.491 (2.92)*	-	0.240	0.212	8.546*
$\Delta^2 \log Y_t = f(\log Y_{t-1}, t)$	2,2	0.0021 (0.144)	–0.492 (2.87)*	–0.0001 (0.161)	0.241	0.183	4.132*

Note: Parenthesis shows the 't' value
* Significant at 1 per cent level, and
** Significant at 5 per cent level.

Table 18: Dickey-Fuller test results pertaining to Gross Domestic Product

Function	*Order*	*Constant*	Y_{t-1}	*Trend*	R^2	*Adj.* R^2	*F*
$\log Y_t = f(\log Y_{t-1})$	0,0	0.546 (1.55)	0.86 (8.76)*	-	0.73	0.716	76.776*
$\log Y_t = f(\log Y_{t-1}, t)$	0,0	0.27 (5.18)*	0.028 (0.15)	0.0478 (4.81)*	0.85	0.84	79.203*
$\Delta \log Y_t = f(\log Y_{t-1},)$	1,1	0.070 (1.60)	–0.506 (3.10)*	-	0.26	0.23	9.634*
$\Delta \log Y_t = f(\log Y_{t-1}, t)$	1,1	0.0551 (0.56)	–0.507 (3.05)*	0.00083 (0.17)	0.26	0.20	4.663*
$\Delta^2 \log Y_t = f(\log Y_{t-1},)$	2,2	–0.00046 (0.007)	–0.672 (4.72)*	-	0.45	0.43	22.247*
$\Delta^2 \log Y_t = f(\log Y_{t-1}, t)$	2,2	0.0088 (0.06)	–0.672 (4.63)*	--0.00057 (0.07)	0.45	0.41	10.716*

Note: Parenthesis shows the 't' value

*Significant at 1 per cent level, and

**Significant at 5 per cent level.

themselves ad should not be influenced by what the centre gives. This can motivate the states to take efforts to raise their own revenues for their expenditure, (iv) the states should be allowed to borrow from the market, instead of making continuous resource transfers from centre to the states. In the case of very poor states, the centre can support them, but it should be under the agreement that they should be totally independent within a time frame. It is also necessary that the reforms at the central level percolate down to the states.

Section IV: Concluding Remarks

Granger Causality test and Dickey-Fuller test were employed to examine the causal nexus between States Fiscal deficit and macro-economic variables. The test result reveals an independent relation between the two. The possible reasons are: (i) the deficits incurred by the states due to increased expenditure are not growth oriented. They are bureaucratic or politically motivated expenditures. As they are undertaken to serve political objectives, the chances of its influencing on macro economic variables is less. (ii) the size or quantity of most of the macro-economic variables are decided by the Centre alone. The States do not have the autonomy power to alter these variables. Hence, whatever be the increase in the expenditure of the States' the macro variables may not be affected as per the theory. (iii) the Centre has adopted the reform process in the fiscal sector, which aimed at reducing the deficits and putting the economy on the rails of growth. The States are not ready to implement these policies for political reasons. The States' expenditures are still not-growth oriented and hence, there are less chances of having any relationship between the two.

References

1. Ashworth, John, (1995), "The empirical relationship between Budgetary Deficits and Government Expenditure growth: An examination using co-integration", *Public Finance,* Vol. 50(1).
2. Buchana, J. and Wangner R., (1977), "Democracy in Deficit", Academic Press, New York.

3. Dickey, D.A. and W.A. Fuller., (1979), "Distribution of the estimators for Autoregressive Times Series with unit root", *Journal of the American Statistical Association*, Vol. 74, pp. 427-431.

4. Dickey, D.A. and W.A. Fuller, (1981), "Likelihood Ratio Statistics for Autoregressive Time Series with a unit root", *Econometrica*, Vol. 49, pp. 1057-1072.

5. Dornbush, R. and Fisher, S., (1990), "*Macroeconomics*", fifth edition, Tata Mcgraw Hill, Singapore.

6. Easterly, William and Schmidt–Hebbel Klaus, (1993), "Fiscal Deficits and Macroeconomic Performance in Developing Countries", *World Bank Research Observer*, Vol. 8, No. 2, July, p. 211-37.

7. Granger, C.W.J., (1969) "Investigating causal relations by econometric models and cross-spectral methods", *Econometrica*, Vol. 37, pp. 427-438.

8. Gupta, Kanhaya L. and Moazzami, Bakhtiar, (1991), "Dymamic Specification and the Long-run Effect of Budget Deficits on Interest rates", *Public Finance*, Vol. XXXXVI, No. 2, pp. 208-221.

9. Jadhav, N., (1994), *Monetary Economics for India*, Macmillian, New Delhi

10. Joshi, B.M., (1999), "Fiscal Imbalances at the State level: Case study of Uttar Pradesh", *The Indian Journal of Public Administration*, Vol. 45(2), pp. 208-223.

11. Khan, Mohsin, S. and Lizondo, J. Saul, (1987), "Devaluation, Fiscal deficits and Real Exchange Rate", *World Bank Economic Review*, Vol. 1, No. 2, pp. 357-375.

12. Leiderman, Leonardo and Mario, I. Blejer, (1988), "Modeling and testing Ricardian Equivalance: a Survey", *IMF staff paper*, Vol. 35, No. 1, pp. 1-35.

13. Mohanty M.S., (1995), "Budget Deficits and Private Saving in India: Evidence on Ricardian Equivalance", *RBI Occasional papers*, Vol. 16, No. 1, pp. 1-23.

14. Niskaran, William A., (1978), "Deficits, Government Spending and Inflation", *Journal of Monetary Economics*, Vol. 4, pp. 591-602.

16

Dividend (Distribution) Tax–An Evaluation

S. Aravanan*

What Mr. P. Chidambaram had done in his dream budget 1997 and what Mr. Yashwant Sinha had retained for 4 years and what the same Mr. Sinha had undone in his 2002 Budget was redone by Mr. Jaswant Singh in his 2003 Budget-that being the dividend distribution tax.

As per Section 10 (33) (i) of the Income Tax Act, 1961 with effect from the Assessment Year 1998-99 income by way of dividend was not to be chargeable to tax in the hands of the recipients i.e. the shareholders. Instead the amounts declared, distributed or paid by way of dividends on or after June 1, 1997 by a domestic company was charged to additional income-tax at a flat rate of 10 per cent in addition to the normal income-tax chargeable on the income of the company (Dividend Distribution Tax). This position had totally been reversed on 28.02.2002 by the Finance Minister Mr. Yashwant Sinha when he presented the Union Budget for the year 2002-2003. According to Mr. Sinha the dividend was an income in the hands of the shareholders and not in the hands of the company. The incidence of tax should therefore be on the recipient (Dividend Tax). Moreover tax was levied at a flat rate of 10 per cent on the distributed

* Selection Grade Lecturer, Department of Commerce, Pondicherry University, Pondicherry–605014.

profits across the board irrespective of the marginal rate at which the recipient was otherwise taxed. The provisions were hence considered inequitous also (after 4 years). Hence he reverted to the earlier system of taxing dividend and shifted the incidence of tax on to the shareholder receiving the dividends by omitting sub clause (i) of clause (33) of Section 10. However to prevent cascading effect in the case of a company he reintroduced Section 80M of the Income Tax Act in a revised form. A deduction under this section was available to a domestic company which received dividend from another domestic company and again distributed dividend out of its profits. The amendments were to take effect from 1st April 2002 and accordingly were applied from the Assessment year 2003-2004.

But the ministerial swap that took place between Mr. Yashwant Sinha and Mr. Jaswant Singh had its impact on dividend (distribution) tax. In his Budget for the financial year 2003-2004, Mr. Singh had again reverted to the system of taxing the dividend distributed by the company in the hands of the company and relieved the individual shareholders- the recipients of dividends from the clutches of dividend tax and Section 80M had been omitted. On this background, the purpose of this article is to analyse the impact of the two extreme ways of tax relating to dividend i.e. dividend distribution tax on India Inc. and dividend tax on shareholders.

Dividend Tax Systems

The choice between the various ways of taxing distributed profits in relation to how retained profits are taxed has been much discussed over the last three decades. Different countries have chosen different systems since the mid-1960s, but they have changed them in different ways. The tax treatment of dividends paid by companies to their owners varies from one country to another country depending upon the system of taxation of dividend followed by each country. Basically three systems of taxation of dividends are prevailing at present-classical system, dual rate system and imputation system. Classical system suffers from double taxation in that first tax is levied on the company's profits and again on the dividends distributed to the shareholders. Under the dual rate system tax is charged at a lower rate on the distributed profits than the tax rate charged on the retained profits of the company. The imputation system is a system where the shareholder is given credit for a part or whole of the tax on the distributed profits. In countries like USA and Netherlands classical system is followed. In countries like Canada, Japan and UK partial shareholder dividend relief (partial imputation) is given and in countries like France, Germany, Italy, Sweden, Hongkong, Singapore and Mauritius shareholders get credit to the full extent (full imputation) of the tax paid by the companies on profits.

In our country upto June 1, 1997 classical system was followed; from June 1, 1997 to 31-03-2002 dual rate system was adopted, then from 01-04-2002 we reverted to classical system and again from 01-04-2003 dual rate system was introduced. The same is the case with Section 80M. Earlier we had it, then we were deprived of it., again the same had been reintroduced with effect from 01-04-2002 and now the same has been omitted with effect from 01-04-2003. That is why some sarcastically comment about Budgets as: what is given by the right hand is taken by the left hand - what is introduced in the current year will be withdrawn in the next year and again will be reintroduced in the third year and so on. This exactly happened in the case of tax on dividends and Section 80M.

Impact of Removal of Dividend Distribution Tax With Effect From 01-04-2002

The removal of dividend distribution tax and taxing of dividends in the hands of shareholders might have increased the level of revenues to the government as shareholders in the higher tax brackets of 20 per cent and 30 per cent had to shell out more tax on the dividends they received whereas under the system of dividend distribution tax, the tax on dividends was 10 per cent. However shareholders in the lower tax bracket of 10 per cent may stand to be on an equal footing without any additional tax outgo. Why, the tax liability on account of dividend in the case of small shareholders whose taxable income was less than Rs.50000 was NIL and in this way they gained also. From the point of view of companies, high dividends payers such as ONGC, VSNL, Hindustan Lever, IOC, Reliance Industries, ICICI, HPCL, MTNL, ITC, SBI,BPCL, Tata Power and GAIL among others would have found more cash in the kitty as dividend tax need not be paid by them. An estimate of the Economic Times (01/03/2002) indicated the impact of the abolition of distribution tax as a saving of a whopping Rs.885 crores for top 25 dividend paying companies. Of the top 10 companies in the sample, 7 companies paying an aggregate of more than Rs.500 crores as dividend tax are owned by the government. But a natural question arises here: whether savings in tax would lead to higher payout to shareholders? The answer to this question depends upon the investment climate for a year.

If the corporates feel that the investment climate for the year is not good they might declare higher dividend on the hope that the investors-shareholders would have had better investment avenues at their disposal. If the companies think that investment climate is improving then they may resort to a conservative payout despite the savings due to removal of dividend distribution tax.

How the stock markets reacted? The market did not welcome the reversal of dividend distribution tax provision. To quote an instance, when Mr. Sinha had just completed reading the proposal relating to dividend tax a collective groan was triggered in the main dealing room of Motilal Oswal Securities Firm in Mumbai and as though by magic the room of the firm came alive and silent phones sprang to life with full of sell calls. Sensex dipped by 143 points on the day of the budget. The main reason cited for this dipping was that the taxing of dividend in investor hands would lead to an exodus from Mutual Funds by corporates who had parked their money there for tax free dividend. As far as reintroduction of Section 80M was concerned on the day of the budget doubts were raised as to whether 80M benefits would be available to corporate investments in Mutual Funds. However on March 3, 2002 Union Revenue Secretary had clarified that in case there was a need to extend the 80M benefits to Mutual Funds the Government would take care of the issue by moving suitable amendments. This clarification helped fuel a rally in bond prices that day. These two reactions stand as an evidence to the 2001Nobel Laurette Stiglitz's information defines capital market–informaiton is the essence of capital market.

In his budget speech Mr. Sinha had proposed to revert to the earlier system as the present levy of distribution tax at a flat rate of 10 per cent was inequitous. The fact which Mr. Sinha had forgotten in this context was the question of double taxation of dividends. When the receipts by a coparcener from a Hindu Undivided Family is exempt from tax (Section 10 (2) of the Income Tax Act), the share of profit of a partner from the firm is exempt from tax (Section 10 (2A) of the Income Tax Act.), on the same footing the dividend in the hands of shareholders should not be taxed. Say a company has a profit of Rs.100 before ax. (Assessment year 2003-2004) First a tax of Rs. 36.75 (including surcharge) would be paid as corporate tax and then the remaining amount of Rs.63.25 when distributed as dividend would be liable for tax. In the case of a person who is falling in the highest tax bracket the tax would come to an additional Rs.19.92 (including surcharge) thus making the overall tax collection to Rs.56.67. There is another anomalous situation. A small investor falling in the 30 per cent tax bracket would pay tax on dividends at 31.5 per cent which would be significantly higher than what a foreign company would pay as the latter can avail of he benefits of Double Taxation Avoidance Agreements. Thus a lot of investors who benefits from good dividends declared by blue chip companies stand to lose. How John D. Rockfeller would have reacted in this context who once was quoted to have said, "The only thing that gives me pleasure is to see my dividends coming in".

Procedural Complications

Besides being detrimental to the interest of investors in the higher tax brackets of 20% and 30% the shifting of dividend tax incidence to recipients had complicated the administrative procedure also. The system of collecting tax on dividend from the company introduced in the Finance Act 1997 was simple to operate. Then the object was to prevent leakage of revenue which was achieved. The Explanatory Memorandum to the Finance Bill 1997 concluded with the remark that the procedure of taxing the recipients would be too cumbersome and involved a lot of paper work. These inconveniences all came back. Prior to 1997 the tax at source on dividend on shares of companies and the income of the mutual funds was applicable only on the dividend/unit income exceeding Rs.2500 and Rs.10000 respectively. But as per the budget for 2002-03 dividend paid out whether from a company or a mutual fund in excess of Rs.1000/- should have tax deducted at source. Who was the hardest hit by this: no doubt the small tax payer. Further the compliance cost of paying tax to the government: printing, issuing the and posting of TDS certificate to shareholders in millions was tedious and the paper work was gigantic. From the point of view of recipients, filing of the annual tax return became a bulky and troublesome exercise. This was so because for a person to claim benefit of TDS he had to produce the TDS certificate.

However there was a consolation prize available to the shareholders through Section 14A of the Income Tax Act which remained untouched. Section 14A says that expenditure incurred to earn an exempt income does not qualify for deduction. So under the earlier disposition if an investor incurred certain expenses to earn dividend income, the same expense could not be deducted from the income in arriving at his taxable income. But the dividend income for the fiscal 2001-02 was no longer exempt, the expenditure qualified for deduction.

Though Mr. Sinha had taxed dividend in the hands of the recipients he had given a concession to corporate shareholders and also to individual shareholders by reintroducing Section 80M.Deduction under Section 80M was available to a domestic company which received dividend from another domestic company in the previous year and distributed the whole or part of such dividend to its own shareholders on or before the date of filing return for that previous year. The amount of deduction would be equal to the amount of such dividend income distributed by the recipient domestic company among its own shareholders. Suppose an Indian company received Rs.2 crores as dividend income from another Indian company and distributed the entire Rs.2 crores to its own shareholders in the Assessment year 2003-2004 then by virtue of Section 80M its Tax Savings was 36.75 per cent (including surcharge) of Rs.2 crores i.e. Rs.73.5 lakhs. Again from the shareholders point of view their overall income had increased by Rs.2 crores minus the relevant tax payable depending upon the tax rate applicable to them. Thus Section 80M was advantageous both to the Indian companies and their shareholders. Mr. Jaswant Singh had omitted this Section with effect from 01-04-2003 i.e. from the Assessment year 2004-2005.

Impact of Reintroduction of Dividend Distribution Tax

When Mr. Jaswant Singh presented the Budget for 2003-2004 he had reintroduced the additional dividend distribution tax on companies at 12.5 per cent and had spared the shareholders i.e. he dividend income is tax free in their hands. The expectation of Indian Corporate Sector and the wish of the Kelkar Task Force was for tax-free dividends in the hands of the shareholders together with tax-free distribution of dividends. However Mr. Sinha had only conceded to the first wish. For corporates it was a double hit, since even Section 80M of the Income Tax Act, which attempted to make the effect of this distribution cost, tax neutral, has been omitted. Therefore, if a domestic company receives dividend and pays out dividend from its profits, then no deduction will be available to it. An estimate suggested an additional burden of Rs.1438.9 crores on the bottom line of the top 25 dividend paying companies. Table 1 gives the details in this regard.

Table 1: Impact of Reintroduction of Dividend Distribution Tax

Company	*Dividend*	*Dividend Tax*
VSNL	2493.8	311.7
ONGC	1996.3	249.5
HLL	1100.6	137.6
IOC	856.5	107.1
RIL	663.3	82.9
GAIL	380.5	47.6
Hero Honda	339.5	42.4
HPCL	359.3	42.4
ITC	334.1	41.8
BPCL	330.0	41.3
SBI	315.8	39.5
HDFC	304.3	38.0
MTNL	283.5	35.4
NALCO	257.7	32.2

(*Table Contd.*)

Table 1: Contd...

NLC	226.5	28.3
L&T	174.3	21.8
TISCO	149.2	18.6
Bajaj Auto	141.7	17.7
Nestle India	135.0	16.9
Infosys	132.4	16.5
Bank of India	122.2	15.3
Bank of Baroda	118.4	14.8
Ranbaxy Lab	115.9	14.5
Hindalco	100.5	12.6
IDFC	100.0	12.5
Total	**11511.3**	**1438.9**

Note: The dividend as reflected in the annual accounts for the year ended March '02 had been considered. The quantum of dividend is assumed to be constant while calculating the dividend tax.

Source: *The Economic Times dated 01.03.2003.*

Though it was a double hit to the corporates it was only an apparent hit which was evident from the corporate reaction. All the apex bodies of the Indian Industry with the exception of Assochem had welcomed the abolition of dividend tax. C. Parthasarthy Chairman, Karvy Group expressed: We believe that the abolition of dividend tax in the hands of investors is a positive one. The Sensex also gained 6.32 points at the end of the day of Budget presentation whereas previous year this day the Sensex crashed on the introduction of dividend tax by Mr. Sinha as already mentioned.

At the same time corporates felt that they would stand to lose because of the 12.5 per cent dividend withholding tax.

Yes they would lose. Hence many companies planned to avoid payment of dividend distribution tax by coming out with interim dividend announcements before April 1,2003. Some such companies were Shipping Corporation of India, Philips Carbon Black, Assam Petro Chemicals, Gestetner, Gujarat Gas Company and Gujarat Ambuja Exports Limited. While Justifying this attitude of the companies market men said that while the Finance Minister Mr. Jaswant Singh, has freed the small investors of the burden of dividend tax; he has in fact raised the dividend distribution tax payable by the corporates from 10 per cent to 12.5 per cent. A senior stock exchange official reacted that "Due to this increase, several companies wishing to palm off the tax burden to the shareholders have announced plans of offering dividends".

While the Government has made frequent changes in its policy on dividend tax, each time industry has reworked its dividend plans in short notices in order to save on taxes. To quote an instance last year when dividend distribution tax was replaced by dividend tax payable at the hands of the recipients w.e.f. 01-04-2002 by the erstwhile Finance Minister Mr. Yashwant Sinha, there was a mad rush by Indian Companies to pay dividends before fiscal 2001-02 ended in order to save on the taxes in the hands of shareholders. This was because tne largest beneficiaries of tax free dividend for an overwhelming majority of companies were the promoters themselves. Finally the market regulator SEBI had to intervene under instructions from the Finance Ministry and put an end to the dividend pay out issue. Probably the companies like Shipping Corporation of India referred to in the previous paragraph must be those where the promoters are not holding a majority stake. That is why they wanted to pay dividend before fiscal 2002-03 ended so that the tax burden be borne by the shareholders.

Now the other side of the coin-companies whose promoters hold a large shareholding and which proposed to declare dividend before 31-03-2003 had changed their proposal; and decided to declare it after 31-03-2003 so that dividend paid thereafter would be subject to dividend distribution tax at 12.5 per cent payable by the company and not taxable in their hands. To quote a few instances the Board of directors of TVS Motor company has decided to declare and pay dividend on or after 01-04-2003 which was earlier scheduled to be declared during the third week of March 2003. Similarly Sundaram Clayton, another TVS group company had informed the Bombay Stock Exchange that the Directors had decided to declare and pay dividend on or after 01-04-2003 which was earlier slated to ;be paid in the last week of March 2003.The promoters in TVS Motor hold 58.96 per cent on the equity capital of Rs.23.10 crores. The promoters stake in Sundaram Clayton is 80.13 per cent of the equity capital of Rs.18.97 crores. Thus by the reintroduction of dividend distribution tax both retail shareholders and promoters benefit.

Now it is time to decide which is a better method to tax dividends: whether the present dividend distribution tax i.e. tax payable by the companies on the dividend distributed by them which is in vogue from the Financial year 1997-98 except the year 2002-2003 or dividend tax i.e. tax payable by the shareholders on the dividend distributed to them which was the position in the year 2002-03. The immediate and the final answer to the question is dividend distribution tax is a better method, the main reason being it avoids double taxation. When the receipts by a co-parcener from a Hindu undivided family is exempt from tax; when the share of profit of a partner from the firm is e exempt from tax on the same footing the dividend in the hands of shareholders should not be taxed. This has already been suitably illustrated. Another reason which is really pertinent is that in the present day low interest rate regime interest rates payable on Bank Fixed Deposits and Small Savings Schemes have been drastically cut; on Bank Fixed Deposits around 6 to 6.25 per cent is paid and on small savings only 8 per cent is paid. So naturally the investing community looks for liberal dividend payouts from the corporate sector.

If it is taxed (the maximum tax rate being 30 per cent) then the net tax dividend may be lesser than the interest payable on Bank Fixed Deposits and Small Savings Schemes. Hence, the investing community enthusiastically welcomed the reintroduction of dividend distribution tax by Mr. Jaswant Singh.

The Indian corporate sector also respected the sentiments of shareholders and decided to give full advantage of the abolition of dividend tax to the shareholders. 86 corporate heavy weights had given a bonanza of over Rs. 1000 crore by way of additional dividend to their shareholders. The 86 companies form part of the BSE's high profile specified list. Based on their equity capital as on march 31, 2003, these companies would be distributing Rs. 5914 crore as dividend compared to Rs. 4814 crores paid during 2001-02, up Rs.1100 crores or 23%. Almost all the companies had announced substantially higher dividend compared to 2001-02–double or even higher in as many as ten cases. Table II shows the higher dividend payouts both in terms of percentage and in terms of amount by 8 big business houses for the year 2002-03 declared after 31-03-2003.

Table 2: Dividend Payout

Sl.No.	*Name of the company*	*Dividend (%)*	*Pay Out (Rs. crores)*
1.	BPCL	150	450
2.	TISCO	80	295
3.	Infosys Tech	540	179
4.	Bank of Baroda	60	178
5.	Kochi Refineries	100	139
6.	Satyam Computers	150	94
7.	Dabur India	140	40
8.	Dr. Reddy's Lab	100	38

Source: The Economic Times dt. 06-06-2003.

Thus the present system of dividend distribution tax is a better system as it avoids double taxation, shareholder welcome it, corporates respect it and stock markets react in its favour. Hence any Finance Minister must be consistent enough in retaining the dividend distribution tax for favourable long term implication.

Index